SEE HOW
THEY GROW

CONSULTING EDITORS

DR. THOMAS DRAPER
Assistant Professor of Child Development and Family Relations
The University of North Carolina at Greensboro / Greensboro, North Carolina

DR. MARILYN COLEMAN GANONG
Chairperson, Department of Child and Family Development
University of Missouri–Columbia / Columbia, Missouri

VIRGINIA GOODELL
Classroom Teacher and Chairperson, Home Economics Department
Crestwood High School / Mantua, Ohio

SEE HOW THEY GROW

·

Concepts in Child Development & Parenting

·

SECOND EDITION

GLENCOE

Macmillan/McGraw-Hill

Lake Forest, Illinois   Columbus, Ohio   Mission Hills, California   Peoria, Illinois

Glencoe/McGraw-Hill

A Division of The **McGraw·Hill** *Companies*

Copyright © 1987, 1982 by Glencoe/McGraw-Hill. All rights reserved. Except as permitted under the United States Copyright Act, no part of this publication may be reproduced or distributed in any form or by any means, or stored in a database or retrieval system, without prior written permission from the publisher.

Send all inquires to:
Glencoe/McGraw-Hill
3008 W. Willow Knolls Drive
Peoria, IL   61614-1083

ISBN 0-02-668220-6 (Text)

Printed in the United States of America

9 10 11 12 13 14 15   026   02 01 00 99 98

TO THE READER

Imagine two photographs of yourself—one taken when you were a baby and the other taken last week. Of course, it is easy to see how you've grown. And yet, perhaps you can also see some resemblances. In more than just physical appearance, the child you were is part of the teenager you are and the adult you are becoming.

SEE HOW THEY GROW is about the process of child development—how children grow. It is also about the process of parenting—how adults and other caregivers influence and are influenced by the children in their lives. As a teenager, you are close enough to childhood to be able to appreciate all the joys and problems of growing up; you are also close enough to maturity to be able to appreciate all the satisfactions and responsibilities of parenthood.

You already know, and perhaps care for, many children, some in your own family—for example, younger brothers and sisters, nieces and nephews, or cousins—some in your neighborhood—for example, children for whom you baby-sit or for whom you are responsible as a worker in a day-care center, church group, or community program. These experiences will help you understand the developmental processes described in this book, and will help you appreciate the satisfactions of caring for young children. But there is one crucial difference between these relationships and parenting: at the end of your commitment to take care of any of these children, you are free to go on with all the other important parts of your life—school, after-school activities, jobs, shopping, not to mention social life. A parent, however, has a full-time responsibility, and if that role does not always involve full-time care of the child, it does involve finding a competent substitute, which can often be as difficult and frustrating as parenting itself.

It will, we think, be clear throughout the book that we believe firmly in the rewards of parenting and in the special joys children add to a family. It will also, we hope, be clear that we believe that adolescence is a time for personal emotional, intellectual, and social growth—a time for preparing for adult roles, but not necessarily a time for assuming them. SEE HOW THEY GROW is an honest and realistic book about children and parents, not the idealized version of family life often presented in books and television. It has been designed with your needs in mind. In a sense, then, this book is not just about children—it is about you, the decisions you will have to make, and the role you will play in children's lives in the future.

HOW THE BOOK IS ORGANIZED

Traditionally child development has been taught as a series of distinct "ages and stages," that is, clearly separated periods during which children go through more or less the same physical, cognitive, and social and emotional changes. Though these labels are convenient, this approach does not capture the reality of child development, which is a continuous and interrelated process.

SEE HOW THEY GROW looks instead at the whole child. It does distinguish, as you will see, between broad age groupings, and areas of development; however, throughout the book's six units we emphasize the complex links and connections that make up the child's growth as an individual and as a member of a family and a larger society.

By the end of the book, you will have traced the development of a child from conception to adolescence, full circle to the point of making responsible decisions about parenthood.

FEATURES OF THE BOOK

This brief description gives you an idea of how SEE HOW THEY GROW is organized. But there are many additional features that will, we hope, add to your learning and enjoyment.

· Each chapter opens with a one-page story relating the experiences of a parent or caregiver. These *parenting pages* are followed by two questions that are intended to guide you in thinking about the material to come.

· Throughout the book, you will see several different types of special information set apart from the main text in boxes. The "Of Interest" boxes explore characteristics of child care in other countries and cultures. "Based on Fact" presents factual information in the form of charts, graphs, or statistics, to supplement the material in the text. "Self-Probe" boxes offer thought-provoking information about people, events, inventions, and the media. These boxes will, we hope, stimulate your own thinking on some current, and perhaps controversial, issues. "Careers" is a series of boxes that presents diverse profiles of job possibilities that involve working with children and families.

· Important words and terms are printed in **boldface** and are defined in a glossary at the end of the book.

· At the end of each chapter, a "Summary" provides you with an overview of main ideas. Review questions in the "Terms to Know" and "Check Your Understanding" sections will help you determine how well you have mastered the material.

· Finally, a word about the use of "he" and "she" in SEE HOW THEY GROW. Many earlier books in child development described all babies as boys; it would be equally sexist, we believe, to call all babies girls. We have chosen to alternate references to sex, so that in the first section, the baby is referred to as "she" or "her," and in the following section as "he" or "him," and so on throughout the book. Of course, this does not mean that the behaviors or characteristics described apply only to male or female children; it is simply a device that permits recognition of sexual equality while avoiding the repetition of the clumsy phrase "he or she" in each instance.

We hope that you enjoy this book, that you learn from it, and that it will give you information and ideas that will be useful in formulating your own future values and goals. We hope that it will help you clarify your own attitudes about children and about the appropriate stage of life to embark on the important role of parent.

Moreover, we hope that you will tell us what you think about the book. Your comments will be useful in planning future editions of this book. Send your letters to SEE HOW THEY GROW, Glencoe Publishing Co., 17337 Ventura Boulevard, Encino, California 91316.

And now, you are ready to start the book and to SEE HOW THEY GROW.

THE EDITORS

CONTENTS

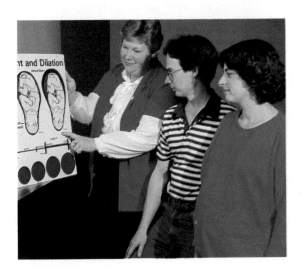

BOXES

Based on Fact: 11, 25, 43, 46–47, 50

Of Interest: 13, 14, 17, 26, 29, 35, 49

BOXES

Based on Fact: 75, 92, 106, 123, 125

Of Interest: 69, 87, 105, 112

Self-Probe: 76, 96, 108

Careers: 73, 78, 110

· UNIT ONE ·

PRENATAL

1
PREPARING FOR PARENTHOOD

Starting a family! What hopes and joys—and worries, too—are expressed in this phrase. Before taking this important step, a couple must weigh many factors: physical, emotional and financial.

2
CONCEPTION AND PREGNANCY

Pregnancy is a time of change and preparation. During these nine months, the mother's body will grow and change as the developing fetus prepares for an independent existence.

3

FROM TWO OF US TO THREE

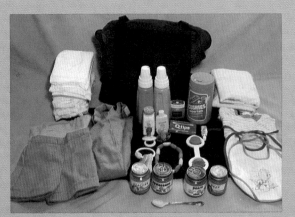

A baby brings many changes to a couple's lives. They need time to get used to the idea that another human being— their child—must be considered in all their future plans.

4

BIRTH!

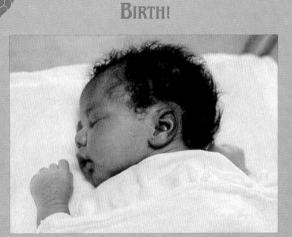

Finally the months of planning and waiting are over. Suddenly all the dreams and hopes come together in one reality: the tiny newborn.

PREPARING FOR PARENTHOOD

"Happy birthday, Shannon! Come here and say hello!"

One-year-old Shannon immediately crawled toward Alan and Brenda, her uncle and aunt. She laughed as Alan scooped her up and handed her to Brenda. Then she planted a kiss on Brenda's cheek, complete with birthday-cake icing.

"Being around Shannon really makes me look forward to having children of our own someday," Alan said the next morning.

"Why not now?" said Brenda. "We always said we'd wait five years before having kids—and it's been almost that long."

"It sure would be great to start a family," Alan agreed. "But do you think we can afford a baby right now? After all, you'd have to quit your job at the photo studio—at least for a while."

"If we put off buying a new car for a few more years, I suppose we could manage," Brenda said thoughtfully. "But our budget would still be tight. And I'm not so sure I want to quit work. It gives me a lot of satisfaction."

"Why couldn't you still work part-time?" Alan suggested. "You could work some evenings while I stayed home with the baby."

"That's a wonderful idea. Of course, we'd have fewer evenings together that way."

"That's true," Alan admitted. "And with so much to do for a baby, we'd have less time to go out with our friends."

"Well, no one ever said being a parent is easy!" Brenda grinned. "And you know, my sister told me once that just seeing Shannon smile was worth more than all that she and Tony had to give up."

"Let's do some more planning—talk to people and read some books," Alan suggested. "Maybe by next year Shannon will have a new cousin to play with!"

·

**What are some other ways—positive and negative—that a new baby
could affect a father's or mother's life?**

·

**Do you think Brenda and Alan are ready to become parents?
Why or why not?**

When a couple are weighing the decision to start a family, they must first examine their life as it is now and then consider what it will be like after a baby is born. They need to be aware of the many ways in which their lives will be changed by a child. And they must decide whether they are willing and able to accept these changes.

THINGS TO THINK ABOUT BEFORE BECOMING A PARENT

What are some of the important things a couple should talk about before making their decision? A good way to start would be to consider their own physical health. Ideally, both husband and wife should have no major health problems. If there is a chronic illness that is likely to continue after the baby is born, the couple should think about how this might affect their ability to care for their child properly. If the man has a serious illness, he may have trouble meeting the new and changing responsibilities that come with fatherhood. If the woman has a serious medical problem, it can have an even greater effect on their plans. She must be sure that her body is healthy enough to carry the baby for the nine months of pregnancy. Even if she is generally healthy, she should have a complete medical checkup and a discussion with her doctor before she and her husband make the final decision to have a baby. The couple will also want to check with the doctor whether any health problems they might have could affect the health of their child.

The age of the wife when she has a baby must also be considered. Women younger than seventeen or older than thirty-five run a greater risk of health problems during their pregnancies than other women.

Other problems related to the couple's ages could also arise. A very young husband or wife might feel tied down by a baby and even resent the infant's demands. If the couple think they are too old, they may not feel up to the night feedings and schedule changes that a baby is sure to bring.

Of course, only the couple themselves can decide whether or not they are emotionally ready to have a child. They must honestly evaluate their personalities and habits to see how much they are willing to change. If they want a baby, they must accept the fact that they will have to settle down and take on the responsibility for an utterly dependent human being. A couple who like to go out dancing every night are not ready to be parents unless they can cheerfully give up this activity for the sake of the baby. Nor are a couple whose marriage is troubled by basic disagreements and conflicts. It is important that a wife and husband establish a loving, stable relationship with each other before they take on the roles of parents. Only when both partners have understood and accepted all the changes parenthood will bring should they decide to have a baby.

Prospective parents should spend plenty of time looking at the ways in which a baby will affect their finances. Will they have enough money to get along after the baby is born? This question is not as simple as it sounds, for having a child means adding expenses to their budget. Some of the costs can be estimated beforehand, but others may be unexpected. They may also have to face the loss of part of their income if either parent stops working.

The best way to approach this problem is to draw up a budget sheet showing the income and estimated expenses they will have after the baby is born. Income should include only the money that is actually going to be earned from that time on. A wife's or husband's income, no matter how large, should not be included as part of the budget if she or he plans to stop working. Only income from permanent full-time and part-time jobs or other sources should be tallied.

Philip and Elizabeth are preparing for the birth of their first child. Although they will be borrowing some items of clothing and furniture from friends, their budget will have to cover many added expenses for the baby.

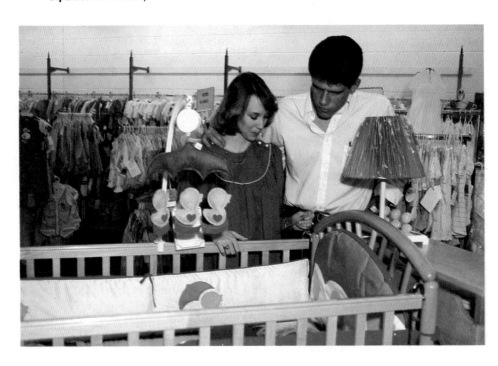

Once this is done, expenses can be added up and measured against the income. A childless couple may have a hard time figuring out exactly how much raising a baby will cost. But they can get a pretty good idea by asking their friends who are already parents, by reading, and by doing some investigating.

Included in the list of expenses must be the fees of the **obstetrician**—the doctor who cares for the woman during pregnancy and birth—and the cost of hospitalization when the mother gives birth. If the couple have health insurance policies, they can figure the exact amount by comparing the maternity coverage under their policies with the expenses for hospitalization and doctor's care. The estimated fees of a **pediatrician**—a doctor who specializes in babies and children—should also be added to this figure, since the new baby will need checkups and perhaps other medical care.

The cost of the various items of furniture, clothing, personal supplies, and feeding equipment for the baby comes next. The couple should make a list of all the things they will need when the baby is born and then price them at stores or ask friends how much they paid. The box on page 11 gives a typical list of items that prospective parents wil need for their baby. They may not have to spend money for all the items, however. Some things, such as clothing, can be "hand-me-downs" from relatives or friends whose babies have outgrown them.

Finally, the couple should consider whether their house or apartment is big enough to accommodate a new member of the family. If they need more room and can afford to move to a bigger space, they must add the cost of increased rent or higher mortgage payments to their budget. They should also include the cost of occasional baby-sitting or daily child care.

After determining these expenses and adding on all their present living costs, the couple can then compare their income with their expenditures to see if they have enough money for a baby. If their income falls short, they may decide to take money from their savings, if they have enough. This can only be a temporary solution, however. Perhaps the couple can increase their income through part-time work, or they can decrease their expenses by cutting out some of the extra luxuries that may be weighing their budget down. Discussing all the problems and possible solutions will help the couple decide whether they can afford to add a new member to the family.

Many working women who want to have a baby take off several months or even a year from their jobs and then go back to work. If her employer is willing, a woman may take a **maternity leave**—a period during which she gives birth and spends some time with her baby before returning to her job. Although the mother has traditionally been the chief caregiver in a family, more and more fathers are sharing this responsibility. A husband may cut down on his working hours to help his wife with the child. In some homes, both parents hold part-time jobs and each stays home with the baby half the day, until the child can attend nursery school at age two or three. Some businesses grant a **paternity leave**—time away from work during which the father can help care for his child. At the end of the leave, he can return to his job, which has been held for him.

If both parents must work during the day, the couple may have to look for suitable childcare for the baby. If possible, this should be arranged even before the baby is born. If the couple's parents, brothers or sisters, or other relatives live nearby, an arrangement might be made with one of them. A professionally trained caregiver could be hired to come to the home and care for the baby, but this can be expensive. Paying a neighbor or friend for this service would probably cost less. The child could also be sent to a day-care center, where a trained staff cares for a⸱ supervises her along with other children

7

Only by weighing all these different factors—physical and emotional readiness for parenthood, economic considerations, and child-care needs—can a couple really know whether they should take a step that will change their way of life permanently.

STARTING A FAMILY: ALTERNATIVES

Most couples who have decided to take this step want to have their own baby. However, this is not the only way to bring a child into a family. A couple who cannot have their own child for medical reasons or who choose not to bring another child into the world can adopt an infant or older child, or they can take a foster child into their home.

Legally, adopting a child means taking the full responsibility for the child until she is fully grown. Adoption binds parents and children together in every legal way. The only difference between adoptive and natural parents is that the adoptive mother did not conceive or bear the child herself. The child takes her adoptive parents' name and is usually not told who her biological parents are—in fact, even the adoptive parents may not know. (In recent years, however, some adopted persons have asserted their right to know who their biological parents were.)

When a couple agree to accept a foster child, the wife and husband are given only partial legal responsibility for his care. Foster children are only temporary visitors; their parents may have had to give them up for a time because of problems such as illness or death in

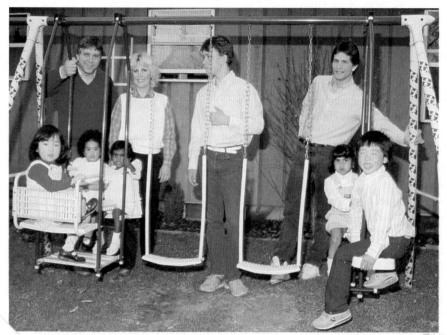

Parents may gain an "instant" large family by adopting children of different ages. Adoptions are permanent. They are the parents' way of saying that they want these children and accept them as their very own.

Part of the fun of pregnancy is planning the area where baby will sleep. Newborns should be kept conveniently close to their parents in a sleeping area or room that is cheerful and well-ventilated.

the family. Most of these parents want to take their children back as soon as they are able to care for them. This can often be painful for foster parents who have grown very attached to a child.

Another way children are brought into a family is when a person marries someone who already has children from a previous marriage. Stepchildren create an "instant family" for the stepparent that can be as rewarding as her or his own natural children.

These alternatives to childbirth are very attractive to people who are concerned about overpopulation. They know that there are millions of children around the world who need homes, and they feel that it would be better to help a child who is already living.

THE BABY'S PHYSICAL NEEDS

Whether children come into a family by adoption, placement in a foster home, the remarriage of a parent, or birth, they all have the same basic physical needs. Infants are totally dependent on their caregivers to provide them with sufficient food and clothing and a comfortable, safe place to sleep. Their caregivers also must give them the opportunity for the exercise they need to stay healthy; take them

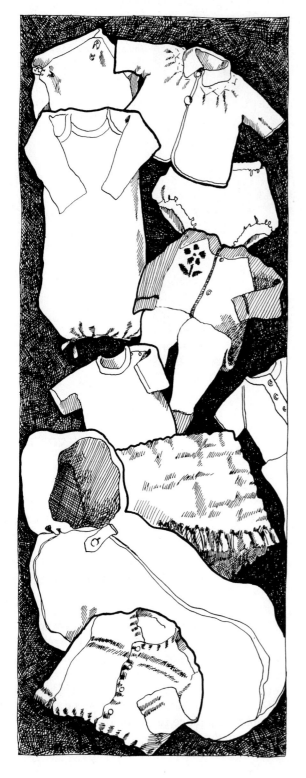

to a pediatrician for regular checkups; and generally make sure they are safe from harm.

Parents-to-be can plan for many of these needs before the baby's birth. They can prepare a room or part of a room for the infant's use and can buy all the things she will need during the first months of life. Such preparation for the child's arrival will take some of the chaos out of the baby's first weeks at home. In addition, it will help prepare the husband and wife for their new roles as father and mother.

The choice of a baby's room will depend upon the dwelling the couple live in. If it has an extra bedroom, that can become the baby's room. If not, a simple room divider can be set up to screen off a space for the baby. Whatever arrangement is chosen, the space should be quiet and clean and should have good ventilation. The space can be decorated to make a bright, cheerful, safe environment for the baby. It may be necessary to repaint the walls with nontoxic paint, because many house paints contain lead, which can poison an infant who manages to pick some off the wall and eat it.

Furniture should be simple and practical. The infant needs a crib to sleep in. The safest cribs have bars set close together so that the infant cannot get her head caught between them. (All cribs sold after December 1973 meet this requirement.) Along with a chest of drawers or other place to store clothing and supplies, it is also useful to have a changing table on which a caregiver can change the baby's diapers or dress her. If there is no room for an extra table, the top of the chest or some other surface can be used. The changing surface should be at a convenient height so that the caregiver can easily tend to the baby without stretching or stooping. A trash can for throwaway diapers or a diaper pail completes the furnishings. The bedding, bath supplies, and feeding equipment needed are listed in the box on page 11.

Planning the baby's personal layette—the

10

Prospective parents can use this guide when planning for the bedding, bath, and feeding supplies their infant will need.

BEDDING

2 rubber or heavy-gauge plastic sheets to tuck under crib mattress

5 or 6 quilted cotton pads to put under baby

4–6 crib-sized sheets or regular flat sheets

2 or 3 crib-sized blankets (material depends on climate)

BATH

1 plastic or rubber bathtub for bathing infant

3–4 towels large enough to wrap baby in

pure soap

cotton balls

rustproof safety pins (if cloth diapers are used)

baby shampoo

FEEDING EQUIPMENT

Women who plan to breast-feed their babies need at least 3 bottles and 6 nipples for occasional bottle feeding of water, juice, and formula.

Women who do not intend to breast-feed will need the following equipment.

9 nursing bottles (8 ounces each)

2 nursing bottles (4 ounces each) for juice and water

12 bottle nipples

1 kettle for sterilizing bottles

1 pair of tongs for lifting bottles out of kettle

1 measuring container for mixing formula

1 nipple jar and cover

Instead of using glass nursing bottles, some women may prefer plastic bottles with disposable bottle liners.

---

clothing she will need—makes many parents-to-be nervous because they don't know exactly how many things their baby should have. The following is a list of typical clothing needs for infants up to six months of age.

4 shirts (sleeve length depends on climate)

4 nightgowns

3 sacks and kimonos (short jackets and long gowns)

2 sweaters

2 pairs of waterproof pants

4 receiving blankets

1 bunting (a zippered bag that covers infant up to shoulder) or 1 coat and cap

4 stretch suits

4–6 dozen cloth diapers or several boxes of disposable diapers

It is generally not necessary to provide more of these items than are shown on the list, since a baby will rapidly outgrow her first items of clothing.

CHOOSING AN OBSTETRICIAN

One of the most important decisions to be made during a woman's pregnancy is the choice of doctor to care for her and deliver the baby. To make the right decision, the couple should first determine the answers to the following questions.

What kind of doctor do we need? Most couples choose a doctor who specializes in **obstetrics**, the area of medicine that deals with pregnancy and birth. Family doctors may also care for mothers-to-be and deliver their babies, especially in small towns and rural areas where specialists are not available. Hospital clinics are another source of good medical care. In addition, nurse-midwives are becoming increasingly popular. (See the "Of Interest" box on page 13.) They often work with doctors in a hospital or in some cases may deliver them on their own in the parents' home. Only women who expect a routine, uncomplicated birth should use a midwife. No matter what kind of health-service professional you choose, you must trust her or his judgment and be able to talk to her or him freely about your questions and problems. Above all, you must respect the physician's skill.

Is the doctor well qualified? If you have a trusted family doctor, you can ask him or her to recommend a good obstetrician. Or you can call up the best hospital in your area and ask for the names of staff members. You will want to know if the doctor you choose has received adequate training in her or his field at an accredited hospital. The American Board of Obstetrics and Gynecology certifies physicians who have such training and who have passed special examinations. You can call a doctor's office to ask if he or she is a "diplomate" in obstetrics and gynecology.

Will the doctor be available if labor begins at an unexpected time? For both parents' peace of mind, it is essential to find out in advance how the doctor handles emergency calls on weekends and at night. Often several doctors form a group practice together, so they can take turns being "on call" for their patients' emergencies during non-office hours. A single practitioner is always on call, unless

Many fathers-to-be enjoy accompanying their wives to the obstetrician's office. They want to know how they can be of help during the pregnancy. The doctor's role is to answer all questions about the pregnancy and birth. He arranges for the expectant mother's monthly visits to his office, and he explains that these visits will occur twice a month in the eighth or ninth month of the pregnancy. He discusses his fees and the hospital costs. His nurse may reserve a hospital bed for the anticipated day of the baby's birth.

Midwifery

When most people think of having a baby, they think of doctors wrapped in white gowns, a sterile delivery room, harsh lights, and instruments and equipment to meet any emergency. Even though doctors deliver most of the babies in North America, they are responsible for only a small number of deliveries throughout the world—less than 20 percent. Who delivers the rest? In countries like England, Germany, Sweden, and the Netherlands, the answer is midwives—health-care professionals who are specially trained to deliver babies. And in Asia, Africa, and Latin America, nonprofessional midwifery is common.

Midwifery is an old practice that is coming back into use in the United States. During colonial times, when men were not permitted to deliver babies because of women's modesty, midwives were almost always used. This practice began to change as people's view of childbirth changed. Many women—especially those in the upper classes—began to believe that childbirth was a "disease" that could only be controlled by instruments, drugs, and surgery. However, as late as 1910, midwives still played an important role in the United States. They delivered half of all the babies in the country.

But the forces of midwifery were weakening. Doctors, pointing to the poor training and wide-spread incompetence of midwives, demanded that the delivery of babies be turned over to them. Supporters of midwives maintained that with proper training, midwives could provide the best care for the greatest number of women.

Few agreed. By 1930, many states had passed laws restricting the practice of midwifery. In that year only 15 percent of all births were delivered by midwives. By the 1970s, this figure plummeted even further, and midwives were taking responsibility for less than 1 percent of U.S. births. Today midwifery has once again become an alternative for many women, but it has a long way to go before it is fully accepted as an alternative to the medical model of childbirth.

The new wave of American midwives is made up of nurses with a master's degree and certification in nurse-midwifery. In most cases, they deliver babies under the supervision of a physician. European midwives work independently. Under the U.S. system, when a birth has no complications, the midwife completes it on her own. But if there is any sign of trouble—a drop in the fetal heart beat, for example—a physician is brought in to take over the birth. To avoid these complications of childbirth, many midwives prefer to deliver only low-risk pregnancies. These are pregnancies that proceed normally and have little chance of complications.

The midwife movement is helping to answer one of the most crucial problems in our society—the problem of what to do about the high cost of medical care. Midwives are less expensive than physicians and in many cases provide a more personal approach to an important moment in a couple's life—the birth of their baby.

Source: James W. Vander Zanden, HUMAN DEVELOPMENT (New York: Alfred A. Knopf, 1978).

After a typical hospital birth, parent and child share a few precious minutes together in the delivery room before they are whisked off to separate places. The mother is taken to her hospital room to rest and recuperate. The newborn is taken to the hospital nursery where he is cared for and soothed by a nurse instead of his mother. The two meet and get to know each other only for a few hours each day during their stay in the hospital.

Some people believe that there is a better way for mother and child to establish a bond of love during the child's first few days of life. Instead of separating the mother and child during the hospital stay, they prefer a shared living arrangement. This arrangement is called rooming-in.

Rooming-in allows the mother to get to know her baby while she is in the hospital. It gives her the opportunity to care for the newborn right from the start. This reduces her anxiety about being able to handle this responsibility when she goes home. In addition, rooming-in gives the father the chance to get to know and feel comfortable with his child.

Rooming-in is not for everyone. A mother who went through a difficult delivery may not have the strength to have her infant with her throughout the day. Many mothers also believe that being separated from their infants for a few days makes no difference at all in their child's development.

Not all hospitals allow mothers to room-in with their newborns. A woman who wants to do so must research the hospitals in her area to find one that offers this arrangement.

there are special arrangements for another doctor to substitute during certain hours. In either case, a doctor is always available in an emergency. When your doctor is not in the office, the receptionist or answering service can take your message and have the doctor get in touch with you.

Will the doctor allow the husband in the delivery room? Find out what a doctor's usual procedure is for handling a normal birth. You may prefer to use a doctor who believes in having the husband present at the delivery. In addition to helping to make the birth easier for their wives, many husbands want to witness the joyful event of their child's birth.

How much will it cost to have the baby? Doctors' fees for obstetrical care vary greatly throughout the United States. They may range from moderate in rural areas to very high in large cities. In addition, the hospital charges its own fee. For most parents, a percentage of these expenses is covered by their health insurance plan. The couple should check their policies to find out exactly how much they will owe after the insurance is paid.

What hospital is the doctor affiliated with? When you choose a doctor, you are at the same time choosing the hospital with which he is associated, or affiliated. The hospital should be reasonably close to your home and have a complete range of facilities and staff to handle any emergency that might arise. Some hospitals offer new mothers the opportunity to "room-in" with their babies. (See the "Of Interest" box on this page.) That is, the baby is allowed to stay in the mother's room rather than the nursery, the section of the maternity ward where all the newborns are kept together. If the mother prefers to room-in, the couple must find out in advance if the hospital allows it. Some do, but many do not. If your doctor's hospital does not meet these criteria and he or she does not practice in any other hospital, you might consider changing doctors.

· SUMMARY ·

- Before starting a family, both the woman and the man should be healthy and emotionally ready for a child.
- A couple should estimate the expenses of a baby to see if their income can meet the costs.
- If both parents plan to work after the baby is born, good child care must be arranged.
- Some couples choose to adopt a baby or care for a foster child. Stepchildren can create an "instant family."
- Infants are totally dependent on others to meet their physical needs: food, clothing, exercise, medical care, and a place to sleep.
- Choosing a doctor or clinic is important for the health of a pregnant woman and her unborn child.

TERMS TO KNOW

maternity leave   paternity leave
obstetrician   pediatrician
obstetrics

1. Many women are cared for by a(n) _____ during pregnancy and birth.
2. Children are often taken to a(n) _____ for checkups and medical care.
3. A father may be granted a(n) _____ to help care for his child.
4. _____ is the area of medicine that deals with pregnancy and birth.
5. A(n) _____ gives a woman time away from her job to give birth and care for her baby.

CHECK YOUR UNDERSTANDING

1. What are three things a couple should consider before becoming parents?
2. How may a couple's health affect their decision to become parents?
3. Name two basic indications that a couple is emotionally ready to have a child.
4. What is the best way for a couple to decide whether or not they can afford to have a child?
5. How might housing be affected by a new family member?
6. Besides giving birth to a baby, what are three other ways of starting a family?
7. Name six basic physical needs for which infants are totally dependent on others.
8. What six questions must be asked to choose an obstetrician wisely?

· 2 ·

CONCEPTION AND PREGNANCY

"Congratulations!" Dr. Marshall said. "You two are going to be parents!"

Hector and Dolores Sanchez looked at each other and grinned. "Before you leave," continued Dr. Marshall, "I'm going to tell you what kind of diet to follow, Mrs. Sanchez. You'll want to be sure to eat the proper food and the right amounts."

"Don't worry, Doctor. I'll see to it she does!" Hector said.

"Good! And don't be afraid to stay active, Mrs. Sanchez. In fact, I want you to get some exercise every day."

"When is the baby due, Doctor?" Dolores asked.

"Well, I calculate the due date to be around June 5. Anything within two weeks of that date would be considered on schedule."

Dolores hesitated a moment. "Doctor, do you think there is any chance that something will go wrong?"

"Every pregnant woman runs some risks. But in your case, the risk is very low," Dr. Marshall explained. "You're in good health. You've told me you don't smoke, drink, or take drugs. And you're too young for us to worry about problems that older women might have."

"What about the possibility of an inherited disorder?" Hector asked. "I've heard about tests you can perform to make sure."

"I'm glad you understand that certain defects can be passed on within a family. But neither of you has a family history of inherited defects. Special tests are necessary for some pregnant women, but you're not one of them, Mrs. Sanchez."

"That's good to know, Doctor," Dolores said with a relieved smile. "I want everything to be perfect for our baby!"

"Just keep on taking good care of yourself, and your chances of having a normal, healthy baby are excellent," said Dr. Marshall. "Now, let me tell you more about what to do and what you can expect during the next nine months. But don't ask me whether to expect a boy or a girl—that's up to you!"

•

If you were an expectant parent, what questions would you ask your doctor?
•
**Did you know there are some disorders a child can inherit from the parents?
Can you name any?**

One of the most wonderful experiences in the world is the sight of a newborn infant—his delicate eyelashes, his perfectly formed hands and feet with their tiny nails. Even doctors who have delivered dozens of babies cannot help marveling each time at the miracle of life. Indeed, it does seem miraculous that so complex a creature could be fashioned out of the single young cell that results from the union of two parent cells. Let's take a closer look at the way this cell develops into a human being during the period of **prenatal** development—the process of growth before birth.

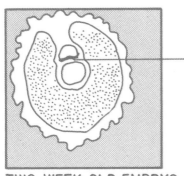

DEVELOPING
BODY
CELLS

TWO WEEK OLD EMBRYO
(MICROSCOPIC IN SIZE)

During the nine months of pregnancy, the small ball of cells shown above develops into a baby—complete with eyelashes and fingernails.

HOW LIFE BEGINS

Prenatal development begins at the moment of conception, or **fertilization,** the union of two sex cells—the mother's **ovum** (egg) and the father's **sperm** (or spermatozoon). It is complete at birth, when the baby is developed enough to survive outside of the protective environment of his mother's body.

For fertilization to take place, **ovulation** must occur. That is, an ovum must be released from one of the **ovaries,** the organs in a woman's body that produce eggs. Ovulation usually takes place once a month, midway in a woman's menstrual cycle, about fourteen days or so before the first day of the next menstrual period. (There are exceptions, however, and it is possible, though rare, for ovulation to occur at almost any time in the cycle.)

From the ovary, the egg passes into one of the two **Fallopian tubes,** which connect the ovaries to the **uterus.** If it is not fertilized by a sperm cell within about twenty-four hours, the egg will die. This means that intercourse must take place either within a day after ovulation, or within forty-eight hours before ovulation, since the sperm can survive only for about two days.

Most of the sperm never even reach the Fallopian tube where the egg is waiting. Out of

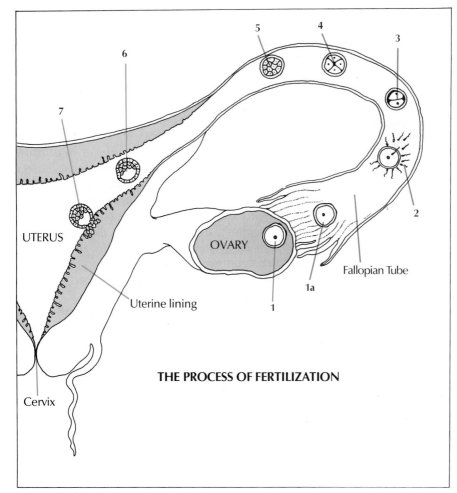

THE PROCESS OF FERTILIZATION

UTERUS

OVARY

Fallopian Tube

Uterine lining

Cervix

On a regular cycle the ovary produces an egg (1) which travels through the Fallopian tube (1a). Fertilization begins when a single sperm cell unites with an egg (2) and forms a cell called the zygote (3). The zygote subdivides into hundreds of new cells by repeated divisions (4). The clump of cells travels down the Fallopian tube toward the uterus (5). The ball of cells becomes hollow in the center (6). Half of these cells develop into a baby. The other half becomes the placenta and umbilical cord. Two weeks after conception the cells forming the baby are firmly planted in the uterine wall and are called the embryo (7).

the hundreds of millions of sperm released by the male during intercourse, most die while still in the **vagina** (the female sex organ). The rest swim through the uterus to the Fallopian tubes. Of the few thousand sperm cells that reach the tube containing the egg, only one can fertilize it. The nucleus of the sperm cell merges with the nucleus of the egg cell, forming a new single cell that is capable of creating new cells by repeated divisions. This new cell—called a **zygote**—divides into two cells; the two cells into four; the four into eight; and so on. By the fifth day after fertilization, the zygote is made up of about 500 cells.

Cell division begins almost immediately after fertilization. Within a few days the zygote begins to travel down the Fallopian tube into the uterus, which will be its home for the rest of the prenatal period. The zygote attaches itself to the wall of the uterus, which is richly supplied with blood vessels. By now the zygote has begun to change from a small mass of cells into a ball of cells with a hollow center. Half of the ball is made up of cells that will develop into a baby. The other half forms the **placenta** and the **umbilical cord**, which make it possible for the baby to absorb food and other substances from the mother's bloodstream, and also for waste materials to pass out. Now the zygote begins to develop rapidly.

18

THE EMBRYO

By about two weeks after conception, the ball of cells that will become a baby is firmly planted in the uterine wall. It is receiving nourishment through the placenta, and it floats in a protective membrane containing a watery substance called the **amniotic fluid.** From now until the end of the eighth week (or second month) after conception, it is called an **embryo.**

Great changes occur during this period as the embroyo begins to develop the specific organs and systems of the body. During the third and fourth week after conception, the central nervous system of the embryo begins to develop, the blood vessels and stomach begin to form, and the beginnings of a heart start to beat. By the end of the fourth week, the embryo has increased in size about 7,000 times! During the fifth week, the brain develops at a rapid pace, and begins to form different structures. Major changes also take place within the heart, and the beginnings of eyes, lungs, arms, and legs begin to emerge. By about the end of the eighth week all the major bodily systems have begun to develop, and the face, arms and legs, and hands and feet are forming, so that the embryo has the appearance of an infant—though it is not much longer than an inch (2.54 centimeters).

This rapid development makes the embryo extremely vulnerable. Certain harmful experiences might affect the embryo's growth at this time—for example, a viral infection, poisons or drugs in the mother's bloodstream, or an accident, such as falling downstairs. Such things can cause birth defects or even the death of the baby before birth.

THE FETUS

By the ninth week after conception, the embryo has undergone many changes. From now on it is called a **fetus.** The fetal period lasts until the baby is born, about thirty weeks later.

The changes that take place in the fetal period are not as dramatic as those of the embryonic period, but they are still very important to the complete development of the infant. The arms and legs grow longer, the nails and eyelids begin to appear, and the external sex organs develop. At four months, the fetus weighs 4 ounces (113.4 grams) and is about 4 to 5 inches long (10.2 to 12.7 centimeters). By about the fifth month, the fetal heartbeat can be heard through a special stethoscope (or even earlier if more sophisticated equipment is used). The mother may begin to feel the movement of the fetus's arms and legs. As early as the sixth month, the fetus gains the capacity to breathe on its own, and during the sixth and seventh months, its body weight increases a great deal. A **premature** baby born between the sixth and ninth month could survive, although many do not. By the end of the ninth month, a normal child born alive has a 99 percent chance of survival.

HOW HEREDITY WORKS

So far we have followed the development of a baby from fertilization up to the end of the prenatal period. Now we shall return to the moment of conception to see how it happens that the baby develops into the particular individual that he is.

Each sex cell—sperm and ovum—has twenty-three **chromosomes** in its nucleus. These are microscopic, threadlike materials that carry the hereditary characteristics of the parents. When the sex cells unite, their chromosomes combine in pairs to give the fertilized egg a complete genetic "package" of forty-six chromosomes. Each chromosome contains thousands of molecules called **genes,** which are believed to be the smallest units of heredity. The chemical structure of each gene

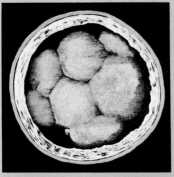

30 hours after conception

84 hours

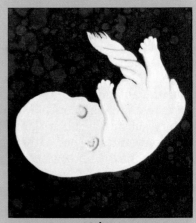

24 days

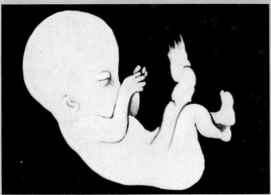

4½ weeks

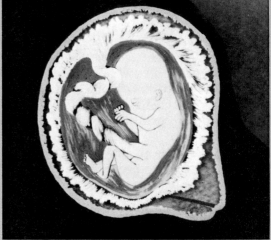

14 weeks

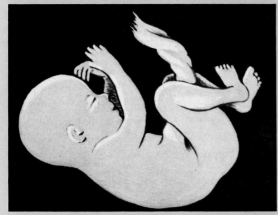

16 weeks

A look at prenatal development
at various stages.

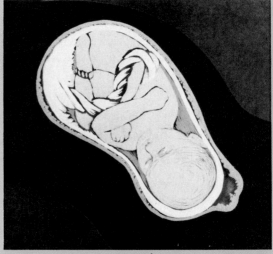

22 weeks

contains the genetic "code" that determines a particular hereditary trait. Some genes carry the specific traits that we share with all other humans: They determine that we will have hands rather than paws, smooth skin rather than fur, two legs rather than four. Other genes make each person a special individual. They give a person red hair instead of brown, for example, or the potential to grow to six feet instead of five.

Of the twenty-three pairs of chromosomes that come together at fertilization, only one pair decides the sex of the baby. These special sex chromosomes are of two different types, called X and Y. The mother's egg always carries an X chromosome, while the father's sperm may carry an X or a Y. If the sperm that unites with the egg carries an X chromosome, the baby will be a girl. If the sperm carries a Y chromosome, the baby will be a boy.

Every individual is a unique combination of traits inherited from the parents. Family members who have inherited some of the same characteristics resemble each other strongly.

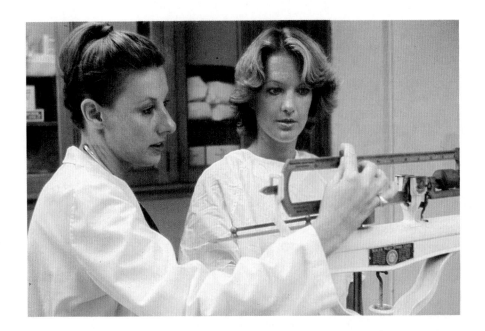

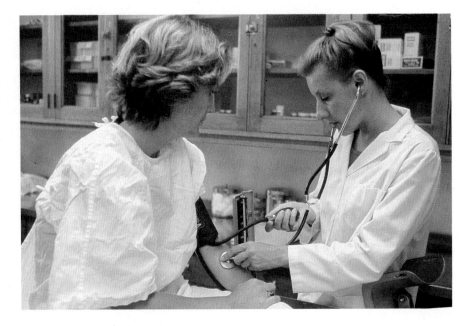

A woman who suspects she is pregnant should visit her doctor as soon as possible for an accurate pregnancy test. Monthly visits to the obstetrician reassure the expectant mother that her baby is developing normally.

Once the genetic package is formed at the moment of conception, nothing can be done to change it. In this sense at least, the individual's fate is sealed.

CHARACTERISTICS OF PREGNANCY

A woman may not suspect she is pregnant until about thirty days after conception. At that time, she will have missed a menstrual period. She may have other physical clues as well.

The pregnant woman may feel sick to her stomach when she awakens in the morning. This common early sign of pregnancy is sometimes called "morning sickness." The nausea usually disappears after breakfast, but sometimes a woman may actually throw up if she so much as smells food. Some women may feel nauseated in late afternoon or early evening. And many women do not experience nausea at all when they become pregnant. In addition, many women have the need to urinate more frequently, and some have a vaginal discharge. Breast changes are another sign of pregnancy. As early as the fourth week after conception, the breasts become enlarged and tender.

Charting the basal body temperature may also help confirm pregnancy. This is the body's temperature when measured first thing in the morning before getting out of bed. Before ovulation the basal temperature is below 98°F (36.7°C). It rises above 98°F after ovulation and stays higher until menstruation, when it drops once more. If a woman has conceived, her temperature will remain high.

The most common test of pregnancy is a laboratory test, administered by a doctor four weeks or more after conception. A sample of the first urine that the woman has passed in the morning is tested for a body chemical present during pregnancy. Within several hours, a diagnosis of pregnancy or non-pregnancy is made. Family planning clinics can also provide accurate pregnancy tests, often for free. Drugstores sell test kits for home use that can be accurate if used properly; but even slight changes can alter the results.

As the pregnancy progresses, the woman experiences other changes. Her abdomen begins to protrude as the uterus expands, and from that point on she gains weight, either early in her pregnancy or toward the end, depending on the individual pregnancy. In

the fifth month, she begins to feel a movement in her uterus that resembles the fluttering of tiny birds' wings. In reality, these are fetal movements called **quickening.** These slight sensations change into unmistakable kicks in the sixth month, when they may actually become visible through a woman's clothing. In addition, the nipples and the circle of skin around them darken.

Even though each woman may have different symptoms, the ones just described are the most common. Among other possible signs of

A feeling of well-being is important during pregnancy. By the fourth month, the expectant mother begins to "show" she is carrying a child.

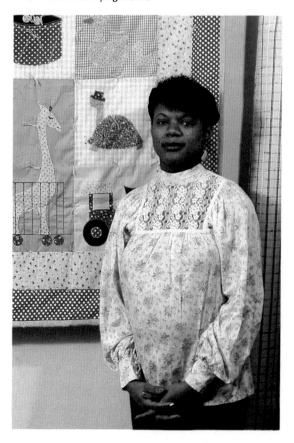

An expectant mother must be sure to eat well-balanced meals that provide extra nutrients for herself and her baby.

Today the situation is dramatically different. Most women realize how important it is to take care of themselves before their babies are born and to take advantage of the information and care available to them. Good prenatal care helps to ensure the good health of both mother and baby.

A woman should see her doctor or obstetrician as soon as she thinks she is pregnant. The doctor will diagnose the pregnancy, take the woman's medical history, tell her about the different aspects of good prenatal care, and set up a series of regular checkups.

One of the most important things the doctor will talk about is how the unborn baby's world is affected by the mother's personal habits, especially what she eats. Most doctors agree that women should gain approximately 20 to 24 pounds during pregnancy to ensure the health of their babies. This does not mean just an increase in calories, but rather a sensible approach to the nutritional needs of her body. An inadequate diet may result in an underweight baby. On the other hand, too much weight can put strain on the woman. Each woman's doctor will advise her about her individual dietary needs during pregnancy.

For good nutrition, a pregnant woman's daily diet should include:

4 or more servings of milk or other dairy products
3 or more servings of meat, fish, poultry, *or* eggs
4 servings of vegetables and fruits, including leafy or green vegetables and citrus fruit
4 servings of cereal products and whole-grain or enriched breads

In addition, the doctor may also warn the woman about the dangers of smoking or using drugs during pregnancy. Recent studies have shown that *tobacco* may cause some serious problems in newborn infants, including premature birth and low birth weight. *Alcohol* is

pregnancy are extreme fatigue, unusual food cravings, indigestion, constipation, increased need for sleep, aches in the joints and muscles (especially backaches and aching feet), varicose veins, changes of mood, and dark patches on the face.

CARE OF THE PREGNANT WOMAN

Centuries ago, women and their babies frequently died during childbirth because of the lack of proper medical and prenatal care.

Here is a sample daily menu that fulfills the nutritional requirements of the pregnant woman. As you can see, it contains food from the four basic food groups.

A Sample Menu for the Pregnant Woman

BREAKFAST

- 1 serving of fresh fruit—1 medium orange, ½ grapefuit, 4 ounces fruit juice, or 8 ounces tomato juice
- 1 serving of whole-grain cereal with milk
- 1 or 2 eggs
- 1 slice of whole-grain or enriched bread

LUNCH

- ¼ pound serving of meat, fish, or poultry
- fresh salad
- 2 slices of whole-grain or enriched bread
- 8 ounces of milk
- ½ cup fruit

AFTERNOON SNACK

- 8 ounces of milk
- fruit

DINNER

- 1 serving of meat, fish, or poultry
- string beans, broccoli, or other green vegetable
- potato
- 1 slice of whole-grain or enriched bread
- salad
- ice cream, pudding, or other milk dessert

BEFORE BED

- 8 ounces of milk or an equivalent amount of cheese

Source: Greta Fein, CHILD DEVELOPMENT (Englewood Cliffs: Prentice Hall, 1978), p. 86

Old superstitions and incorrect notions about pregnancy persist, even in a modern society such as ours. Here we discuss only a few of these popular fallacies.

Is an expectant mother "eating for two"? People used to encourage pregnant women to pile their plates high at mealtime, since it was believed that they had to fill their stomachs for two. That is simply not true. The number of calories a pregnant woman consumes should increase by about 200 a day over the number she took in before becoming pregnant. Even though this is an extra bonus to women who enjoy eating, it is certainly not enough to turn every meal into a feast. The important thing is not just quantity of food but quality—a nourishing, well-balanced diet.

Should a healthy pregnant woman stay in bed to avoid a miscarriage? Only in rare cases, and then only under doctor's orders. Pregnant women should lead normal lives—and that includes doing a moderate amount of exercise if they are able. Of course, they should avoid lifting heavy objects and engaging in sports that may cause accidental injury to the abdomen. In general, women should use their own common sense and listen to what their own bodies tell them about what they are able to do.

Do a pregnant woman's thoughts and emotions affect the fetus? People once believed that a pregnant woman should listen to beautiful music, look at great works of art, and read good books so that her baby would be able to appreciate these things later in life. It was also thought that the woman should avoid ugliness or unpleasant experiences for fear of upsetting the unborn child. In fact, intellectual or educational experiences in themselves can have no direct influence on the fetus, although they may certainly benefit the mother. Yet it is true that the mother's emotional state can affect the fetus in some cases. Extreme anxiety and tension for a long period can produce chemical changes in her body that are stressful to the developing fetus. And, of course, if she is unhappy and feels negatively about her pregnancy, she may fail to take adequate care of herself.

a particularly dangerous drug because it may cause retardation and affect motor development in the infant. *Caffeine,* an ingredient in coffee and cola drinks, may also be dangerous to the fetus if taken in large quantities. *Drugs* such as narcotics (like heroin), as well as certain prescription and nonprescription medications, can cause a variety of complications and birth defects. A pregnant woman should never take any kind of medicine without first checking with her doctor.

A number of other factors may also be harmful to the developing embryo or fetus, and the obstetrician will warn the woman to avoid these at all costs. *Viral infections* may cross the placenta and pass from the mother's bloodstream into the embryo. In most cases, these viruses do not damage the embryo, but German measles, or *rubella,* is an important exception. Rubella has been shown to cause a variety of serious defects including mental retardation, heart malformation, deafness, and eye damage. A *venereal disease,* such as syphilis, can also be transmitted from the vagina to the fetus in the uterus. These infections may result in serious problems such as **stillbirth** (the birth of a dead infant). *Radiation* of various kinds, including X-rays,

Most physicians encourage women to exercise during pregnancy. Exercise helps blood circulation and contributes to the expectant mother's feelings of good health. A daily routine of moderate exercise should be established. Exercise routines are often more enjoyable when performed with the help of others. Involving prospective fathers in these exercise programs may give them feelings of participation in the pregnancy and serve as practice for the childbirth exercises used to make labor easier. Many communities offer exercise programs tailored to the needs of prospective parents.

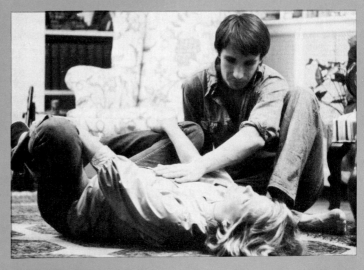

has been linked to serious birth defects. *Accidents* may cause the mother to lose the baby.

Since pregnancy is considered a normal, healthy process, most doctors will not recommend major changes in a woman's general hygiene and personal routine. Rather, they will suggest a commonsense approach that takes into consideration the needs of both the mother and the unborn child. This approach includes moderate exercise and sufficient rest.

How much exercise to take is a personal matter for each woman. It depends on how well she feels and how much exercise she was accustomed to before becoming pregnant. A certain amount of exercise is almost always recommended. It has been shown to help improve blood circulation, increase appetite, and provide more restful sleep. Swimming is particularly good because the added weight of the fetus is held up by the water and does not tire the woman so quickly. Walking is another good choice.

PROBLEM PREGNANCIES

Even though most pregnancies are normal, certain complications may end a pregnancy or cause serious health problems for the infant.

Miscarriage is the expulsion of the incompletely formed fetus from the mother's body, usually before the fifth month of pregnancy. Many miscarriages are caused by abnormalities in the fetus itself, but at the present time most are still unexplained. Those caused by abnormalities are nature's way of discontinuing the development of an unhealthy fetus. Other miscarriages may be caused by serious illness or accidents occurring to the mother.

Premature infants are fully formed babies that weigh under 5½ pounds (2.5 kilograms) at birth. They may also be judged premature by certain measures based on appearance and behavior. Their low birth weight is usually

caused by their failure to remain in the uterus through the complete term of the pregnancy. Premature infants often have serious problems because their organs have not developed enough to support life outside the uterus. They commonly have difficulty breathing and run a greater risk of infection. But with modern technology, including incubators that strictly control the newborn's environment, many premature infants have excellent chances for survival.

The average time of delivery is 266 days (38 weeks) from conception, or 280 days (40 weeks) from the beginning date of the woman's last menstrual period. When a baby is not delivered until well after its expected birth date, it is usually because of a mistake in calculating the due date. Most women who are three or more weeks late begin to worry and feel very uncomfortable, but in most cases, nothing at all is wrong with the fetus. If the obstetrician does suspect problems, she or he can induce labor, which will bring on the birth.

HIGH-RISK PREGNANCIES

Some problems usually cannot be predicted much in advance, but other problems that make a pregnancy a "high risk" can. These include the age, weight, and medical history of the mother, a family history of inherited disorders, Rh incompatibility (see page 29) with the fetus, and a previous history of miscarriage or of underweight or premature babies.

A pregnancy can become a high-risk one if the mother is under seventeen or over thirty-five years old. Mothers under seventeen are more likely to have miscarriages or babies with low birth weight. Women over thirty-five, and especially those over forty, have an increased risk of bearing an infant with **Down's syndrome** (previously called mongolism). For some reason the child has an extra chromosome in each cell of the body.

Bearing a child with a birth defect can be one of the most devastating experiences in a couple's life. They mourn the damage to or death of one child, and they are afraid to have another for fear that the defect will appear again.

Often these fears are well founded. Certain birth defects, like hemophilia or sickle-cell anemia, are hereditary—that is, they are passed down from one generation to the next. If a couple have had one child with a genetic birth defect, the chances are that any future children they may have will also suffer from it.

There is no sure way of avoiding all birth defects, but genetic counseling can help alert parents-to-be of potential danger. Genetic counselors, who are generally physicians or genetic specialists, examine the family history to try to find out if there are any diseases that show up in different generations. They also examine the couple and any living children to try to uncover any clues that a genetic problem may exist.

After all this information is collected, the counselor determines what a couple's chances are of giving birth to an afflicted child. If the odds are high—one in four, for example—the couple may decide against having a child. If they are willing to take the risk, the pregnant woman is advised to undergo amniocentesis to find out if there is a problem even before the child is born.

Genetic counseling cannot prevent birth defects. It can only help parents-to-be understand the likelihood of giving birth to a child with a certain disease and explain the disease to them, so they can make a wise decision about whether to have a baby.

The abnormality results in mental retardation and slow physical development. Down's syndrome is an example of a **genetic defect** —a physical or mental defect that is passed through the genes.

A woman who is severely underweight may not be able to become pregnant in the first place, and if she does, the fetus might be harmed by the mother's malnourished condition. Overweight women have problems with their own health during pregnancy. They often have trouble breathing and may develop blood clots. Both underweight and overweight women have to be carefully watched by a physician throughout the pregnancy.

Women who have serious medical problems, such as heart disease and diabetes, are often advised not to have children. Women with known serious medical problems should consult their doctors before making a decision about becoming pregnant. If they do get pregnant, they should carefully follow the doctor's advice. If a woman has already had a child with a genetic defect, her chances of having another are high.

Among black people, about one in fifty suffers from sickle-cell anemia, an incurable blood disease. If a healthy black couple both carry the sickle-cell trait in their genes, each of their children has a 25 percent chance of having the disease.

A rare but serious problem that can arise in pregnancy is **Rh incompatibility.** The Rh factor is an inherited substance present in the blood of some persons. Those who have this factor are called Rh-positive; those who don't are Rh-negative. The presence or absence of the Rh factor does not affect a person's health in any way. But if an Rh-negative woman and an Rh-positive man have a baby who inherits the Rh-positive trait, there can be tragic consequences. This is because the pregnant woman's body reacts to the Rh factor in the baby's cells just as it would to a foreign substance such as a

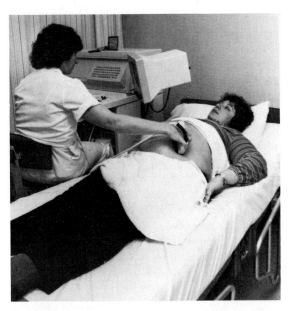

An ultrasound image, or sonogram, can be used to check the development and position of the fetus. Reflected sound waves form an image of the fetus on the monitor. The test can reveal the presence of certain birth defects and, in some cases, the sex of the unborn baby. Unlike amniocentesis, ultrasound does not require taking a physical sample from the uterus.

To give a baby the best possible start in life, a woman's body should be physically mature and healthy. Beyond that beginning, here's a partial list of things to remember:

AVOID
• junk foods, fatty foods
• cigarettes
• alcohol
• drugs
• radiation
• excessive stress

DO
• eat nutritiously
• wear comfortable clothing and sturdy shoes
• go for regular medical checkups
• exercise
• relax!

virus. It does this by producing antibodies—chemical substances that fight against "invading" substances in the body. The mother's antibodies pass through the placenta into the fetus's bloodstream and destroy its red blood cells. This can seriously harm or even kill the fetus.

Usually, in a first pregnancy not enough antibodies develop to harm the infant. But once the mother has been sensitized to Rh-positive cells, the problem may arise in later pregnancies. Fortunately, the problem can be avoided altogether if the mother is given a special vaccine within three days of her first delivery. Of course, this means a couple must be tested *before* they have a child, to find out if there is any danger of Rh disease.

Finally, pregnant women who have had previous miscarriages or have given birth to underweight or premature babies must be carefully watched by their physicians. Medical treatment can often prevent the recurrence of such problems.

Several of these conditions can be detected before the baby is born through a test called **amniocentesis.** By inserting a needle through the mother's abdomen into the uterus and withdrawing a small sample of the amniotic fluid that surrounds the fetus, doctors can detect genetic problems, including Down's syndrome and sickle-cell anemia. They can also use this test to determine the age and sex of the fetus.

Amniocentesis involves some risks of its own to both mother and fetus. Therefore it is not performed unless there is a valid medical reason. Expectant mothers who do not fall into any of the high-risk categories do not need to undergo amniocentesis. They have an excellent chance of delivering a healthy baby —provided they take good care of their own health before and during pregnancy.

- Pregnancy begins when the father's sperm fertilizes the mother's ovum.
- Chromosomes contain genes that determine the baby's physical features.
- The first sign of pregnancy is a missed menstrual period. Various pregnancy tests are available from doctors, clinics, and drugstores.
- During the first nine weeks, the embryo begins to form all major body systems and organs as it grows inside the mother's uterus.
- After the ninth week of pregnancy, the developing baby is called a fetus.
- A pregnant woman should eat a well-balanced diet and avoid drugs, alcohol, and tobacco.
- Some potential risks or problems can be identified early in the pregnancy.

TERMS TO KNOW

amniocentesis
embryo
fertilization
fetus
genetic defects
miscarriage
ovum
premature
prenatal
sperm
uterus
zygote

1. The _____, or male sex cell, and the _____, or female sex cell, unite at the moment of _____ to form a new single cell called a(n) _____.
2. A test called _____ can detect _____ such as Down's syndrome.
3. Illness, accidents, or an abnormality in the _____ may cause a(n) _____.
4. Most _____ infants weigh less than 5½ pounds because they did not remain in the _____ for the full term of the pregnancy.
5. In the second through eighth weeks of _____ development, the _____ begins to develop specific organs and systems of the body.

CHECK YOUR UNDERSTANDING

1. What is a zygote? An embryo? A fetus? To what stage of pregnancy does each correspond?
2. Give three examples of inherited characteristics.
3. How is the sex of a baby determined?
4. What physical signs might cause a woman to suspect she is pregnant?
5. Describe two ways of confirming pregnancy.
6. What personal habits should an expectant mother follow to ensure her health and that of the baby?
7. Why are rubella and venereal diseases dangerous to the developing baby?
8. When is a baby considered premature?
9. Describe six situations in which a pregnancy becomes "high risk."
10. Name and describe two medical tests that can detect problems in the unborn child.

·3·

FROM TWO OF US
TO THREE

Yolanda came into the apartment bursting with excitement. "Charles, just wait till you see the beautiful baby things my sister-in-law gave me today," she told her husband. "And my brother gave me a great idea for decorating the baby's room!"

Charles barely looked up. "That's nice," he said.

Yolanda put her hands on her hips. "Charles, you're not even listening to me!" She stopped when she saw the miserable expression on Charles's face. "What's bothering you?" she asked.

"I'm sorry, honey. I just can't get excited about the baby anymore."

"Why not? You wanted this baby so much!"

"And I still do! But . . ." Charles hesitated. "I'm not even sure I can explain it. I . . . I just don't feel like I'm a part of you or the baby anymore. Whenever we see friends, they make a big deal over how big you've gotten and the way the baby kicks. No one seems to remember that I'm the father and that I'm part of the family, too."

Yolanda walked across the room and sat on the couch next to her husband. "I guess I have been preoccupied with the changes in my body and with getting ready for the baby's arrival. I'm ashamed to admit it, but I didn't notice that you were feeling left out. But from now on things will be different. This baby is a fifty-fifty deal—and I'll let everyone know how I feel!"

Charles smiled and put his arm around Yolanda's shoulders. "You know, it's hard to stay angry at a pregnant woman—especially when she happens to be my wife."

•

**What could Yolanda do to help Charles feel more involved in the pregnancy?
What could Charles himself do?**

•

Why do you think that a prospective father has the emotional need to feel part of the pregnancy along with his wife?

Having a baby means change. There are changes in the way each parent thinks about herself or himself. There are changes in the couple's relationship with each other. And there are changes in the responsibilities they must bear. It is often easier for them to adjust to the physical changes that the wife experiences during pregnancy than it is to cope with the social and emotional changes that can turn their world upside down. Parents-to-be have to learn to make many adjustments.

PREPARING FOR CHANGE

The realization that nothing will ever be the same after the birth of a baby comes earlier to some couples and later to others. With their baby's due date less than two months away, Tom and Kate Saunder had not even begun to consider how different everything would be after the birth. They put off thinking about it until after they went shopping for baby furniture. When the Saunders realized that their carefully planned budget would have to be drastically revised, they also started to think about other ways that having a child would affect their lives. Every couple should plan for such changes when they are planning the pregnancy itself. The place to begin is with an understanding of the changing needs for love, security, and protection that having a baby means.

Having a baby means loving a child of your own. This love is different from that shared by a wife and husband. The infant comes into her parents' lives as a stranger, and is totally dependent.

Having a baby means providing security and protection. Infants cannot feed or clothe themselves, or protect themselves. Parents must accept the responsibility of giving their newborn child constant care. They must adapt their schedule to the baby's needs and give up some—though not all—of their independence and freedom to a life that revolves around a totally dependent human being.

CHANGING PERSONAL ROLES

The arrival of a third member of the family brings about changes in a couple's relationship with each other. Almost all the habits they have established must be reevaluated, and many will have to be adjusted. The first step a couple must take is to get used to their new roles as parents. They may be used to thinking of themselves as marital partners or as persons identified with a particular career or field of interest. Now they must learn to see themselves in the roles of father and mother as well.

While change can bring stress, a change in roles can also bring a couple closer together. Preparing for the baby requires many joint decisions. For example, will one parent be responsible for full-time baby care? Or will they take turns? Or can a relative help out? Different families will make different choices depending on their needs.

Women who do not work outside the home must adjust to the new and ever-present demands a child will make on their time. They will no longer have as much time to devote to themselves, their husbands, and friends, and must reorganize their activities around the needs of the baby.

Women who hold jobs may face even more changes in their personal roles. They must consider the possibility of giving up their work and their salaries—either for a short while or for some years—or of finding and perhaps paying for adequate child care.

A woman may find that even though raising a family is satisfying, she has mixed feelings about leaving her job. She may regret that she can no longer get the particular sense of professional accomplishment and independence that her work brings. She may also find herself

Becoming a parent is an irreversible step. Once the baby is born, permanent changes occur in the parents' lives. Babies need care 24 hours each day. They are unable to do anything for themselves. In addition to showing love and affection, parents must tend to all of baby's physical needs. People react to the responsibilities of parenthood in different ways. Some easily make adjustments in their personal lives. Others may become anxious, depressed, or resentful. All new parents must learn to deal with restrictions on their personal freedom. Parents cannot leave home without arranging for someone to care for baby.

34

In Western society, a mother-to-be often receives more attention in the community than a father-to-be. It is usually not until after the baby is born that the father's role becomes more active. In other cultures, however, fatherhood is viewed in a different way. Among some peoples, the husband of a pregnant woman shares her condition in a symbolic way.

For example, among the Kurtachi of the Solomon Islands (in the Pacific Ocean near New Guinea), fathers-to-be practice a ritual that anthropologists call the couvade. This ritual serves to demonstrate the bond between father and child. When a woman gives birth, it is clear that the baby is hers. But there is no such obvious link between the father and his child. The couvade draws the attention of the community to this relationship. To the Kurtachi, the ritual observed by the father is an important and even a necessary part of the pregnancy and birth.

The couvade begins during the wife's pregnancy. Both husband and wife must restrict their diet, avoiding certain foods. As soon as labor begins, the husband moves away from his wife to live with neighbors. He is forbidden to lift or carry heavy objects, for it is believed that this might injure the child. He also avoids handling pointed objects like knives, for fear of killing the unborn baby. He does not work and spends his days resting.

On the fourth day of this observance, the father may see his wife and child, but he still may not work. It is not until the fifth day after birth, after the couple have bathed themselves in the sea, that he can go back to his normal work and family life.

Although our culture is very different from the Kurtachi's, we, too, are beginning to recognize the important role of the father during pregnancy and birth. More and more fathers are taking an active part in preparing for the birth of their children and participating in the delivery itself.

Source: James W. Vander Zanden, HUMAN DEVELOPMENT (New York: Alfred A. Knopf, 1978).

pinching pennies, particularly if her income had been an important part of the family budget. And she may have difficulty adjusting to the fact that her day, which was once spent with other adults, now revolves around an infant who cannot give her the intellectual and social stimulation she is accustomed to.

Men, too, go through many changes during their wives' pregnancy. Even though a man does not personally experience the pregnancy, he is affected by his wife's moods and physical condition. He may find that she needs a great deal more understanding and emotional support from him than usual. When the baby arrives, the father may have to bear the full economic burden of supporting his family, at least for a time. If he does work full time, he'll be spending more of his free time at home with his family instead of pursuing his own outside interests. He may be helping his wife with household chores when he is not at work, as well as caring for and playing with the baby. But even when the mother has the major share of child care and housework, there need not be any sense of injustice in the different roles of woman and man. If the husband and wife feel that they are equal partners in this new venture, they can share both the rewards and responsibilities of parenthood in a spirit of joy and cooperation.

CHANGING FAMILY HABITS

These various changes affect family life in different ways. One of the most important is the restrictions that a baby's needs place on a couple's freedom. No longer can they make last-minute plans to go out. Their activities must be planned far in advance and must be built around the infant's sleeping and feeding schedules. Once the baby arrives, parents quickly realize that their days of traveling light are over for a long time! Every time they go somewhere with the baby, they must carry a supply of diapers, clothing changes, bottles, and more—and each item must be planned for and prepared in advance.

Having a baby also means cutting back the amount of time a couple can spend with their friends. Especially during the first few months after birth, a baby's needs must come first, and there is less time for social life. In most cases, friends and family realize the demands a new baby makes and try to help the new parents as much as possible.

Couples will also find that many of their interests change once the baby is born, and that they may no longer have as much in common with their friends, especially their childless friends. New friendships often develop at this time, as parents find themselves drawn to other new parents who share the same experiences with them.

An expectant couple must also be prepared to adjust to changes in their everyday routine and in the way they run their household and use their money. Once a baby is born, even the routines that they take for granted, such as eating and sleeping, change. As every parent soon learns, an infant's needs come first—even if it means putting off dinner or getting up in the middle of the night to feed and comfort a crying baby.

Perhaps the biggest change, aside from the arrival of the baby herself, is the new financial responsibilities that come with parenthood. Adjusting to a much tighter budget may be as difficult as adjusting to the baby herself, especially when many of the extras, such as vacations and nights on the town, have to go.

A couple who work together to save some money before their baby's arrival can head off serious financial problems before they occur. And they can continue to avoid problems by carefully planning their daily budget once the baby arrives.

AN EMOTIONALLY HEALTHY PARENT MAKES A DIFFERENCE

Understanding these many role changes will help the parents accept the pregnancy and develop a positive state of mind. This is particularly important for the mother because the way she feels about her unborn child will affect the way she takes care of herself—whether she makes regular visits to the doctor for prenatal checkups, eats a proper diet, and gets adequate rest and exercise.

Even with a positive attitude, many women may find that although they are filled with enthusiasm about their pregnancy one day, they are depressed or worried the next. These mood changes, which may be extreme at times, are because of the hormonal changes that are taking place in a woman's body. They may also result from normal fears many women have about becoming a parent. For example, the inexperienced woman having her first child may worry about whether she will be a "good mother." Or the very active woman who has many interests outside the home may wonder how she will adjust to a totally new schedule of activities.

It is helpful for women to realize that they may also go through an emotional upheaval after the baby is born, in the form of **post partum depression** or "blues." This may occur as early as a few days after the baby is born or several weeks later. It often coincides with the time a mother comes home from the hospital, where she was showered with attention and care, to find herself alone with the major responsibility for the care of her newborn infant

Attachments between parent and child are formed at meal time. A father's help in feeding and caring for his newborn baby strengthens his emotional ties to his new child.

and household. Even though post partum depression is very common, doctors are not exactly sure what causes it. They do know that it is seldom cause for alarm, since it usually clears up in a short time without any treatment.

Women should also expect their husbands to go through mood swings of their own, both before and after the baby is born. Many husbands feel left out during their wives' pregnancy. Their wives, whose bodies are changing in such a dramatic way, get all the attention.

Few seem to remember that the baby will change the father's life as well. Many husbands respond with jealousy and anger; they want people—and especially their wives—to notice them and to recognize that their role as the father is just as important as that of the mother. Once the baby comes home from the hospital, a husband may resent the attention she requires—attention that used to be directed at him. At the same time, he may feel left out of all the activity centered on the infant.

When both wife and husband are aware of these common emotional reactions to the changes that come with parenthood, they can make efforts to help each other with understanding and patience. Both the mother and the father must also adjust to their baby and *learn* to love her, realizing that this love does not always come automatically. Many parents expect to be overwhelmed by feelings of love as soon as they see their baby, and they may be disappointed if this does not happen exactly as they had imagined. The life-long bond between parent and child develops gradually. For the parents it is built on time shared together, and by their realization that the newborn infant is a shared joy and responsibility. With this will come the understanding that some attention is needed by every member of the family.

MOTHER'S MILK OR FORMULA?

One of the most important choices to consider before a child is born is whether the mother will breast-feed or bottle-feed her newborn. It is important to consider breast feeding for two reasons: first, because of the special emotional bond between mother and child that is promoted from the experience of breast feeding, and second, because of the health benefits of mother's milk.

Mothers who breast-feed develop a special closeness with their infants. Women who are mothers for the first time find this especially encouraging, as it gives them a sense of self-confidence. The woman who accepts breast feeding as a natural, positive act can also get a feeling of great satisfaction from nursing her child with her own body. Of course, the infant also gains a feeling of security and warmth from nursing.

The health benefits an infant receives from mother's milk are also important. Mother's milk is easier for babies to digest than cow's milk, and it also gives the infant protection against some infections, since it contains disease-fighting antibodies produced by the mother's body. Breast-fed babies are less likely to develop allergies to different foods as they grow older, and rarely suffer from constipation, as do many bottle-fed infants. Furthermore, breast-fed babies can regulate the amount of milk they drink, and are less likely than bottle-fed babies to be overfed.

Breast feeding is more efficient, convenient, and economical than bottle feeding. Women who breast-feed have their milk ready at all times. They are never faced with sterilizing bottles or mixing and warming a **formula** (prepared milk for infants). Another advantage to the mother is that breast feeding stimulates her body to produce a **hormone**— a natural chemical "messenger"—that helps her uterus return to its normal, nonpregnant condition.

There are some disadvantages to breast feeding. The first few times an infant breast-feeds may be difficult for the mother, who may feel anxious about her ability to feed the infant. She may not know what to expect and may be upset by the initial soreness of her nipples. This anxiety produces tension that can actually interfere with the flow of milk. To avoid this, a new mother should relax before feeding her baby, and when she puts the baby to her breast she must try to adapt to the infant's needs and method of sucking. If a mother's milk dries up or decreases, as occasionally happens, it is usually related to anxiety and fear of failure. At times, illness may also cause a decrease in the milk supply.

Even though breast feeding offers many advantages, women who cannot breast-feed for some reason, or who choose not to, should not feel inadequate for doing so. Each mother must do what she is comfortable with, for her own sake and for that of the infant, who can easily sense anxiety in the mother. Infant formulas are nutritious, and bottle-fed infants can be given just as much love and cuddling as breast-fed infants. Also, bottle feeding has the

All family members need time to prepare for the arrival of a new baby. Newborn babies mean changes in many household routines and more responsibilities for everyone. Young children need special attention before the baby's birth. They are curious about the physical changes in Mommy, and may need some explanations about the birth process. There are many wonderful books available which help prepare children for a new baby's arrival.

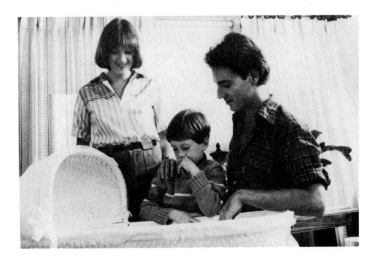

advantage of allowing the mother to leave the infant for more than three or four hours at a time, and it allows the father or another caregiver to enjoy feeding the baby, too.

PREPARING OTHER FAMILY MEMBERS FOR THE NEW ARRIVAL

If there are already children in the family, the parents must prepare them for the birth of a new baby. This should be done in advance of the expected birth date so that the children will have time to get used to the idea of having a brother or sister. (Of course, exactly when parents tell a child depends on the child's age and ability to understand.)

Once children are aware of the forthcoming birth, they should be encouraged to participate in the plans for the baby. They can help to decorate the new baby's room and to choose supplies needed for the new arrival. If a child has to give up his bedroom or bed for the new baby, this should be arranged well ahead of the birth, and the child should be made to feel that he is being asked to move because he is more grown-up now, not because the new baby is more important than he is.

Parents should emphasize that the child who will soon be born is a member of the family and that she is as important to the other children in the family as she is to the parents. One way to make a child feel comfortable about the new arrival is to have him visit other families with infants of their own. This will give the child an opportunity to watch and touch a newborn baby, something he may never have done before.

A crucial time in a child's adjustment is when his mother goes to the hospital for the delivery. Not having his mother at home may make a very young child fear that something has happened to her or that she has abandoned him. To help the child get over these fears, the father must assure him that his mother will be back soon. As soon as it is possible, the child should speak to his mother over the phone and should be in touch with her throughout the hospitalization. Many hospitals now have "family hours" when children can visit their mother.

Grandparents, aunts, uncles, cousins, and other close relatives must also be prepared for the baby's arrival—especially if they are going to help care for the baby after the birth. It is important to set ground rules right at the start. New parents should let their relatives know that they will be happy to receive their advice in caring for the child, but that the final decisions in child care must be their own.

· SUMMARY ·

- Parents-to-be must plan to adapt their daily routines to the baby's needs.
- The arrival of a baby changes a couple's relationship. They have less time to themselves, but more opportunities for sharing and closeness as a family.
- New parents often experience emotional changes such as depression or jealousy.
- The parents' love for their child develops gradually as they care for and get to know the new baby.
- An important decision is whether the baby will be breast-fed or bottle-fed.
- Other children in the family should be prepared for the new baby's arrival.

TERMS TO KNOW

formula
hormone
post partum depression

1. An important decision is whether the baby will be breast-fed or given _____.
2. The emotional upheaval women can go through after a baby is born is called _____.
3. A(n) _____ is a chemical produced by the body.

CHECK YOUR UNDERSTANDING

1. What is the best time to plan for the changes in roles and family habits that a new baby will bring?
2. Summarize the changes in family habits that can be expected when a baby is born.
3. Should parents expect to feel an overwhelming attachment to their baby right away? Why or why not?
4. Why is it important for the mother to consider breast feeding?
5. What are the health benefits an infant receives from mother's milk?
6. List two advantages of bottle feeding.
7. What are some ways a brother or sister can participate in plans for the arrival of a new baby?
8. For a young child, the mother's stay at the hospital for delivery of a new baby is particularly difficult. Why? What would make this easier for the child?

· 4 ·

BIRTH!

Megan Shaw and her husband, Tom, were seated in a large conference room in Central Hospital, along with six other couples. They were all expectant parents who were studying the Lamaze method of natural childbirth.

"Last week you learned several muscle-relaxing techniques," the instructor said to the women. "Today we're going to discuss the Lamaze method of breathing in tempo with the different kinds of contractions you'll experience during labor. You will learn to change your breathing pattern as the contractions change, while your husbands time the contractions and help you concentrate on breathing. When you actually go into labor, this concentrating will help ease the pain of childbirth."

When the class was over, Tom asked his wife, "Do you think all these exercises will really help? I've always heard that labor pains can get pretty bad."

"I'm sure they will help. My friend Irene said she couldn't have made it through labor without them. Anyway," Megan said with a laugh, "we'll find out in about a month's time!"

"Well, at least *you're* confident about it," Tom said. "After all, you're going to be doing all the work."

"Not all of it," Megan reminded him. "I need you to guide my breathing and help with the other techniques we've learned. Even just knowing you'll be there makes me feel more confident."

"That's good to hear," said Tom. "Even though I'm a little nervous about it, I'm glad I'm going to have the chance to see our baby born. And I'm sure that your giving birth without drugs is better for the baby's health."

Megan grinned and squeezed her husband's hand. "With a team like us and Lamaze, how can we go wrong?"

•

How do you think concentrating on a special breathing pattern might help a woman to bear the discomfort of labor?

•

Tom wants to participate in the delivery of his baby. Can you think of any reasons why a husband and wife might decide not to have the father present at the birth?

Approximately 266 days after conception, a baby is born. To each new mother and father, the birth of a child is an awesome experience. Nevertheless, it is an experience repeated by millions of others every year throughout the world. Even though each newborn has an individuality unique to him, the general process of birth is more or less the same for all.

WHAT IS LABOR?

Labor is the natural process by which the baby passes out of the mother's body when he is ready to be born. In a series of involuntary muscular contractions, the baby is moved out of the **uterus** and through the **birth canal**, or **vagina**. The mother can also aid labor by voluntarily pushing, or bearing down, with her abdominal muscles.

In most cases, the baby who is ready for birth has settled head down in the uterus, so that he begins to move head first through the birth canal. The baby's skull is made up of pieces of bone whose parts are not firmly joined together as they will be in adult life, and so the skull molds itself to the shape of the birth canal. As the spherically shaped head comes down the birth canal, it causes the canal to expand, or widen, so that the rest of the baby's body can easily pass through it.

However, not all deliveries are head first. In a small number of cases, the feet and buttocks appear first. This is called breech presentation. If the mother's pelvic bones are not wide enough for the baby to pass through, or in the case of some other problem, the doctor may deliver the baby by an operation called a **Caesarean section** (see page 48).

THE SIGNS OF LABOR

A pregnant woman may experience early signs of labor as soon as two weeks before the actual delivery. She may have occasional painful contractions of the uterus and may feel the baby dropping into position for birth. At about the same time, she may notice a pinkish discharge from the vagina. This discharge is blood-tinged mucus that has been dislodged from the **cervix**—the entranceway between the vagina and the uterus. The rupturing (breaking) of the **amniotic sac**, which contains the fluid in which the **fetus** floats, is usually one of the most dramatic signs that real labor is about to begin (although this does not always happen). About two pints of clear, watery fluid will flow from the vagina soon after contractions begin, although sometimes contractions may occur before the rupture. Starting out slowly and with mild force, the contractions gradually become stronger and more frequent. When they come every fifteen minutes, the doctor should be called to advise about going to the hospital. In most cases, doctors advise women to wait until contractions are five minutes apart before actually entering the hospital.

THE STAGES OF LABOR

The fetus leaves the mother's uterus and is born in a process that usually takes about thirteen hours. However, labor may last as long as thirty hours, or as few as four. (When labor lasts less than three hours, it is called precipitate labor. Short-term labor of this kind may endanger the baby because the birth canal has not had a chance to stretch to the size of the baby's head.) Labor is marked by three distinct stages.

During the first stage of labor, the cervix widens to allow the baby to pass from the uterus into the birth canal. This process, which is called dilation, is complete when the cervix widens to about 4 inches (10 centimeters), or about the width of an adult's hand.

At the early part of this stage, uterine contractions are mild, coming every twenty to

The Newborn's Journey Into the World

1. The head of the baby must first drop into position to make its way through the birth canal.
2. Once the head is in position, the baby's body flexes and begins to move down the birth canal.
3. As the baby moves lower in the canal, his body begins to rotate.
4. It completes the rotation and begins to extend.
5. The body completes the extension as the head emerges through the vagina.
6. Once the head is clear, the baby rotates once more. After the shoulders, the rest of the body slides out.

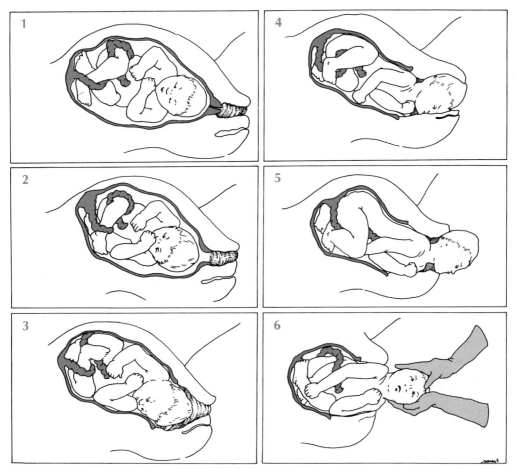

Source: WILLIAMS OBSTETRICS, 16th edition, by Jack A. Pritchard and Paul C. MacDonald (New York: Appleton-Century-Crofts, 1980).

twenty-five minutes and lasting between thirty-five and forty-five seconds. By the time the first stage of labor is over, the contractions are extremely powerful. They come more frequently and last sixty to ninety seconds.

During the second stage of labor, even stronger uterine contractions force the baby out of the uterus and into the birth canal. Contractions come every one to two minutes and last for more than one minute. As the baby descends through the birth canal, the mother pushes down with her abdominal muscles and diaphragm until the baby is born. The greatest effort is over once the head has come out of the opening of the vagina. It takes only a few more contractions for the shoulders to appear, and once this happens the rest of the body slides out. Birth is complete when the doctor has cut the **umbilical cord**, which still connects the baby to the **placenta** still inside the uterus.

The third stage of labor comes after birth. About ten minutes after the infant is born, the mother is instructed to bear down and push once more. When the placenta and other materials—together known as the afterbirth—come out of her body, labor is over.

METHODS OF CHILDBIRTH

Once labor has begun, there are two basic ways of relieving the pain of childbirth. Medication can be given, or "natural" methods for relieving pain can be used.

The methods of childbirth used in most North American hospitals rely on a variety of drugs to lessen or completely eliminate the pain. The mother may be given painkillers or drugs to make her sleepy, such as sedatives, tranquilizers, or antihistamines. When the baby is about ready to be delivered, she may be given a **local anesthetic**, which numbs part of her body without putting her to sleep, or (more rarely) a **general anesthetic**, which makes her unconscious.

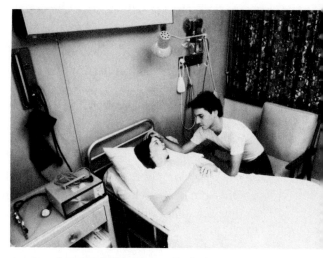

A woman's first child labor is usually the longest. For succeeding children, labor shortens. Labor pain does not intensify until just before birth occurs.

There are different problems with each of these drugs, the most serious being the possible harmful effects on the baby. The drugs the mother is given may be absorbed by the baby through the placenta and affect such vital functions as the baby's intake of oxygen. This may cause the newborn to be sluggish and sleepy. In a recent study of infants whose mothers had been given drugs during delivery, researchers found that the drugs seemed to affect the infants' vision, muscle tension, and maturation. These effects lasted up to three weeks after birth. Some researchers now believe that the effects last for a much longer period. Even local anesthetics, which are considered relatively safe for the fetus, have an unfortunate side effect. They eliminate the mother's natural urge to push the baby out of her body and make it more likely that the doctor will have to use forceps during the delivery (see page 47). All these factors caused the American Academy of Pediatrics to recommend officially "that the least possible medication during childbirth is probably the best."

In "natural" methods of childbirth, the woman is fully conscious and has been prepared physically and psychologically for labor and delivery. These methods deal with the pain of labor in a different way. Instead of relying on medical aids for childbirth, they emphasize psychological preparation of the parents-to-be, as well as physical exercises and mental concentration for the woman. Both the husband and wife attend a series of classes that teach them the techniques of natural childbirth. The best known of these techniques are those developed by Dr. Grantly Dick-Read, who introduced the concept of natural childbirth in England in the early 1930s, and those of Dr. Fernand Lamaze, who introduced his method in France in 1951.

Dr. Dick-Read believed that the fear of childbirth caused women's muscles to tense and fight against the natural forces of labor. This muscle tension caused pain. Dr. Dick-Read sought to eliminate fear by educating women and helping them to feel more at ease about the natural process of childbirth. He also taught that certain relaxation exercises could help reduce the pain of labor.

The Lamaze method teaches parents how to relax during childbirth. In formal classes given in most communities, parents learn a series of breathing exercises which are used at different stages of labor.

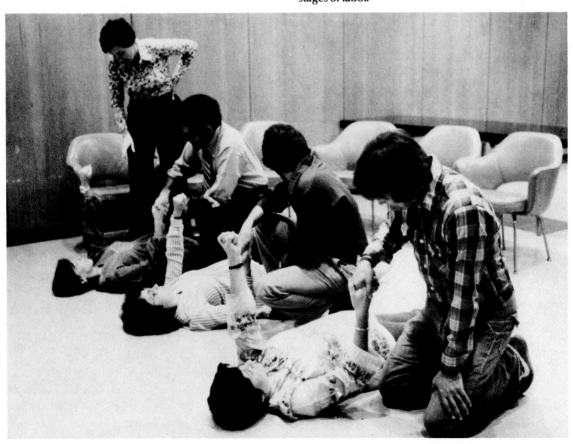

This chart summarizes the three stages of labor. It describes the strength, duration, and time between the contractions, the progress of the birth, how the mother feels during each stage, techniques used to ease the pain, and what the coach—who is often the father—can do to help. As you can see, the first stage of labor differs from the remaining two in that it is divided into three separate parts.

THE STAGES OF LABOR

Stages	Contractions	Progress of birth	Mother's mood
STAGE I			
Early labor	Come 20–25 minutes apart and last 35–45 seconds. Are mild in intensity.	Cervix dilates to 2–3 centimeters.	Thrilled that labor has finally begun but unsure of what lies ahead.
Accelerated (early active)	Come 2½–5 minutes apart and last 45–60 seconds. Pain has become more severe.	Cervix dilates 2–8 cms. Baby's head moves down birth canal.	At beginning of stage, deals well with contractions. Toward end, begins to feel tired. Doubts ability to hold out.
Transition (late active)	Come 60–90 seconds apart and last 60–90 seconds. Force of contraction is extremely powerful, causing extreme pain.	Cervix dilates 8–10 cms.	Exhausted, upset, and withdrawn. Feels like giving up. Experiences back pressure, trembling limbs, and urge to push down.
STAGE II			
Expulsion	Come 1–2 minutes apart and last more than 1 minute. Contractions are strong.	Baby moves through birth canal and is born.	Renewed energy to continue. Now works with contractions and feels she is making progress.
STAGE III			
Placental	Mild	Placenta is expelled from mother's body.	Ecstatic and relieved. May want to hold baby right away.

Source: Patricia Hassid, TEXTBOOK FOR CHILDBIRTH EDUCATORS (Hagerstown, MD: Harper & Row, 1978), p. 92-93

Techniques used	Coach's role
Mother should avoid exerting herself.	Keep the mother relaxed. Help her avoid beginning her childbirth techniques too early. Prepare her for trip to hospital.
Breathing in a rhythmic way.	Time contractions and count off seconds. Encourage mother to follow childbirth technique. Help make her more comfortable with ice chips, back rub, and so on.
Puff-blow rhythm during contractions. Mother blows out for urge to push. Between contractions, mother follows relaxation and rhythmic breathing techniques.	Keep encouraging the mother, reminding her that she is almost at the end of the first stage of labor. Pace the rhythm of her breathing, support her lower back, give her comfort.
Pushing.	Encourage her pushing activity. Remind her to follow proper pushing techniques. Support her shoulders and legs, if necessary.
	Repeat doctor's instructions to stop pushing when head is being delivered.
Push for delivery of placenta.	Share joy at the birth of the baby. Hold the newborn.

In the Lamaze approach, which is now the most widely used method of natural childbirth, women learn to breathe in a certain pattern while they are experiencing the labor contractions. When a woman concentrates on her breathing in this way, her attention shifts away from the sensations of pain, so she does not experience them as intensely. Women learn correct information about childbirth, so they won't be frightened by superstitions or other wrong ideas they may have. They are also taught muscle-relaxing exercises, which they practice every day before the delivery. In essence, the Lamaze technique does for a pregnant woman what a good training program does for an athlete. It prepares her physically and psychologically for the experience she will go through and gives her enough information to actively help her body through the natural process.

In both the Lamaze and Dick-Read methods, fathers play an important role in the preparation and delivery. They help their wives prepare for labor, and learn ways to make them more comfortable during the process. Fathers are encouraged to help their wives during the actual labor and to be present during the delivery.

OTHER TYPES OF DELIVERY

In both the standard and natural childbirth techniques we have described, the baby is expelled through the birth canal without any outside help. Although that approach is preferable, it is sometimes necessary for the doctor to provide help.

In delivery by **forceps**, the baby is helped out of the mother's body by the use of a metal instrument that resembles a large pair of tongs. The doctor uses the forceps to help turn the head into the proper position for birth and to aid mothers whose natural tendency to push has been blocked by anesthesia. Forceps are

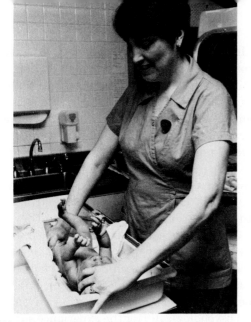

With the umbilical cord cut, the newborn is now physically separate from the mother. Shortly after birth, a nurse cleans the baby, fastens an identification bracelet on his wrist, and takes an impression of his tiny footprint.

BIRTH AT LAST!

When the baby has been delivered, the doctor holds him up by the ankles to help clear his breathing passages of mucus. If the newborn has trouble breathing, the doctor may gently slap his back to get respiration started. The umbilical cord is then clamped a few inches from the abdomen and cut. (The remaining cord will dry and drop off by itself.) At this moment, the mother and infant are for the first time completely separate human beings.

While the mother is waiting for the placenta to be delivered, the baby is "cleaned up" by the nursing staff. They remove the cheesy white material that protected the baby's skin while

Opening her eyes on a new world—how does the newborn feel? No one is quite sure, but the "Of Interest" box on page 49 offers one doctor's theory.

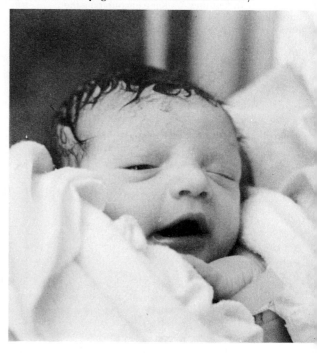

also used to speed up the delivery when the mother or child is in some kind of distress.

Sometimes the baby cannot be expelled through the vagina and must be delivered by a **Caesarean section**—an operation by which the baby is taken out of the uterus through the abdomen. Caesarean sections are used in between 10 and 20 percent of all deliveries. This method of delivery may be chosen for any of several reasons. As mentioned earlier, there may not be enough room for the baby to pass through the birth canal. Other reasons include abnormal position of the baby in the uterus, inadequate contractions of the uterus, and certain complications of late pregnancy. Because it involves surgery, a Caesarean section always requires either general or local anesthesia.

48

The moment of birth is a joyful occasion for the parents of a newborn. But is birth a joyful experience for the baby? In his book *Birth Without Violence*, Dr. Frederick Leboyer of France describes the traditional methods of hospital delivery as a painful assault on the newborn child. Here is what Dr. Leboyer says about the moment of birth:

The infant is crazed with pain. And for a simple reason: suddenly nothing is supporting his back.

And it is in this paroxysm of confusion, of despair and distress, that someone seizes the baby by a foot and suspends it over the void.

The spinal column has been strained, bent, pushed, and twisted to the limit of its endurance—and now it is robbed of all support.

And the head, so supremely involved in the passage outward—now it also is dangling, twisting.

And this at the very moment when, in order to calm this vast terror, this panic, what is essential is a coming together with the mother, a reuniting.

If our deliberate intention was to teach the child that it had fallen into an indifferent world, a world of ignorance, cruelty, and folly, what better course of action could we have chosen.

Dr. Leboyer believes that this jarring experience of birth can be psychologically damaging to the newborn and that a more soothing transition to the outside world is needed. In Leboyer's idealized setting, there are no harsh lights or loud, frightening noises to upset the newborn during his first seconds of life. When the birth is complete, the newborn is gently laid on his mother's stomach and tenderly massaged for about four or five minutes. The umbilical cord is cut only after the infant has been soothed by the warmth of his mother's body. Then the baby receives a gentle, warm-water bath that reminds him of his peaceful, secure home in the uterus. While many doctors would not agree that birth is as upsetting for the child as Dr. Leboyer believes, his ideas have made people aware of the infant's need for and response to gentleness and love from the first moment of his birth.

Source: Frederick Leboyer, BIRTH WITHOUT VIOLENCE (New York: Alfred A. Knopf, 1975), p. 28

he was in the uterus. They also put a drop of silver nitrate solution into each of the baby's eyes, to protect him from any chance of infection due to gonorrhea, a veneral disease. The baby is also examined for defects (see the box on page 50).

When the proud parents look at their newborn infant, they will find a tiny human being with characteristics all his own. The proportions of his body parts are different from what they will be later on. His head is one-fourth the size of his entire body and may be oddly shaped at first. His body is spindly, and his arms are longer than his legs. The genitals of both male and female infants seem large in relation to the rest of the body. The infant's skin is wrinkled and discolored. Prominent veins appear all over the body, the hands and feet may be peeling, and the fingers and toes are often bluish and cold from poor circulation.

The newborn has fat cheeks, a short flat nose, and a receding chin. He may have dark hair on his head and body, or be bald. The two **fontanels,** or soft spots, in the baby's skull helped it to squeeze through the birth canal. The baby's eyes are a smoky, dull color—they change to their true color later on—and seem

About a minute after delivery, the newborn's physical condition is tested by means of a system developed by Dr. Virginia Apgar. A trained assistant observes the infant and rates him on a scale of 0 to 2 on five items: pulse, respiration, muscle tone, reflex irritability, and skin color. A perfect Apgar score is a 10, but scores of 7 to 9 are considered normal. If a score is between 4 and 6, the infant's chances of survival are only fair. If it is 3 or below, the newborn requires immediate attention if he is to survive.

In addition, the Brazelton Behavioral Assessment Scale is used to measure the neurological responses and behavior of the newborn. Over a period of twenty to thirty minutes, the newborn is given about thirty different tests. These tests are scored according to nine different ratings. The tester checks the infant's general body tone, alertness, and motor skills. She or he also notes the infant's different responses to such stimuli as a bell, a pin prick, and a rattle; touches the baby in such a way as to test reflex responses; and checks the infant's ability to orient himself toward different stimuli.

Interestingly, infants who are born addicted to drugs (because their mothers took a drug such as heroin during the pregnancy) respond poorly on the Brazelton test compared with nonaddicted infants. They have inferior motor responses and they are more irritable and less alert than other newborns. This may be due to the drug withdrawal that these infants experience after birth.

large in proportion to the rest of his face. They are fringed with a full set of eyelashes. His teeth have not yet appeared.

All the brain cells the infant will ever have are present at birth, but they are not yet fully developed. Other body structures, such as the bones and muscles, must develop as well, and the newborn's breathing is slightly irregular. In addition, parents who look for tears when their newborn cries will not find any. But they can expect some other fully developed responses. The newborn is capable of yawning, grasping, sneezing, blinking, and winking.

TAKING THE NEWBORN HOME

The moment of birth can be one of the most exhilarating experiences in a parent's life. If the mother is awake during the delivery, she is relieved that the ordeal of labor is finally over and that the new baby will soon be in her arms. If the father has been present at the delivery, he, too, can share this joy.

After a few days in the hospital, both mother and child come home. It is a momentous event, for it means that a new member has joined the family. Now the new family life that the parents have planned for becomes a reality. If they have planned well, the newborn is welcomed into a secure atmosphere in which his physical and emotional needs will be met with love and understanding. As the parents care for him, the knowledge that they are committed to and responsible for another human being—their own child—can help them accept the burden of work and responsibility that comes with parenthood.

- Labor is the physical process by which a baby is born.
- During the first stage of labor, the cervix widens so the baby can pass from the uterus.
- Muscle contractions move the baby along the birth canal in the second stage.
- Birth is complete when the baby emerges and the umbilical cord is cut.
- In the final stage of labor, the afterbirth is pushed from the mother's body.
- To relieve pain during labor, medications may be given to the mother or "natural" methods may be used.
- The father plays an important role in natural childbirth.
- Following birth, the baby is cleaned and tested for possible defects.

TERMS TO KNOW

birth canal
Caesarean section
cervix
forceps
fontanels
general anesthetic
labor
local anesthetic
placenta
umbilical cord
uterus
vagina

1. The _____ are soft spots in a baby's skull.
2. During the process of _____, the _____ widens to allow the baby to move out of the _____ and through the birth canal, or _____.
3. The doctor is more likely to use _____ during the delivery if the mother's natural desire to push has been blocked by a(n) _____.
4. Until it is cut, the _____ connects the baby to the _____, its source of nourishment before birth.
5. If the baby is delivered through the abdomen in a(n) _____, the mother may be given a(n) _____ to make her unconscious.

CHECK YOUR UNDERSTANDING

1. What are some early signs of labor? When might they occur?
2. What are some signs that labor is actually beginning?
3. Briefly describe each of the three stages of labor.
4. What are two types of anesthetic that may be used during delivery? How do they affect the mother and the child?
5. What is natural childbirth?
6. Describe the Dick-Read method of childbirth.
7. How does the Lamaze approach to birth help the mother experience less pain?
8. Why might a Caesarean section be performed?
9. Why is silver nitrate solution put into a newborn infant's eyes?
10. Name five items measured by the Apgar rating system. Why is it important to test the newborn in this way?

· UNIT TWO ·

INFANT
(BIRTH TO AGE 1)

5
PHYSICAL DEVELOPMENT

6
COGNITIVE DEVELOPMENT

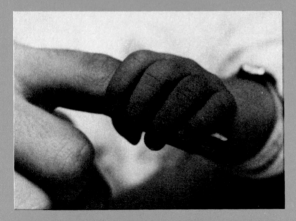

Growth in the first year is more rapid than in any other period of life. Each achievement—learning to hold the head erect, turn over, sit up, crawl, perhaps stand—marks another milestone toward independence.

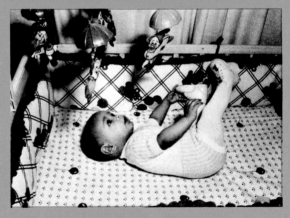

The baby not only grows larger and stronger, but learns more about the world. Seeing, touching, hearing, tasting, and smelling are the beginnings of an infant's education.

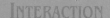

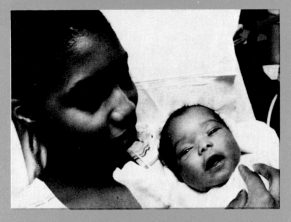

More than any other object, a baby is attracted
by the human face. Through these first twelve
months, the infant forms ever stronger
attachments to other people.

The first year is a period of adjustment for
parents. In learning to take care of the
baby's physical, intellectual, and
emotional needs, they create a
new family unit.

·5·

PHYSICAL DEVELOPMENT
OF THE INFANT

Five-year-old Trevor watched as his baby brother Andy kicked and squirmed in his crib. "Mom," Trevor asked finally, "when will Andy start to get bigger?"

Mrs. Graham joined Trevor by the side of the crib. "You'd be surprised how much bigger he is already. Andy weighs almost twice as much now as when he was born!"

"But that's not what I mean, Mom," Trevor said in frustration. "When will he grow up enough so I can play with him? All he does is eat and sleep and lie around all the time."

Mrs. Graham smiled. "It seems that way, doesn't it? But Andy is really very busy, even when he's sleeping. Just about everything he does helps him to develop."

"What does 'develop' mean?" Trevor asked.

"It means that as he grows, Andy is able to do more and more things. He couldn't even hold his head up at first, remember?"

"Not until he got stronger," Trevor said.

"That's right. Just by eating and sleeping and moving around, Andy keeps getting stronger every day. And the more his body grows and develops, the more he can do."

"But how long will it take?"

"Well, it won't happen all at once. He has to develop little by little. Would you like to help him?"

"Can I teach him how to throw a ball?" Trevor asked.

"You sure can! But let's start by showing Andy this squeeze toy. See how he tries to reach for it?"

"His arms are going every which way!"

"They are, aren't they? But soon Andy will be able to make them go where he wants them to. Next he'll be able to make his hands and fingers work better. Then you can show him how to throw a big ball."

Trevor held the squeeze toy near his baby brother again. "Come on, Andy. I'll help you get ready to play baseball!"

•

How would you have explained Andy's development to Trevor?

•

How are Andy's abilities related to his growth?

Often, when relatives and friends hear the news of a baby's birth, one of the first questions they ask the parents is "Who does the baby look like?" The answer is not as easy as one might expect. The baby's resemblance to other family members may not be noticeable at first. The infant whose blue eyes and black hair make him look "just like his father" when he is born could turn out later to have his mother's brown eyes and hair.

After imagining throughout the nine months of pregnancy what the baby will look like, the parents may be disappointed with the way he really looks. With his wrinkled appearance, the newborn may remind them more of a little old man than a baby boy. And with his nose flattened during the birth process, he may look as if he just stepped out of a boxing ring! At birth, precious though he is, the baby is nothing like the adorable image in his parents' mind.

But all this will change. In a few months the infant's appearance will change and he will probably be just as his parents hoped, or perhaps he will be even more beautiful. Change is the most striking thing about infancy—the period from birth to one year. In no other period of his life will the baby grow so rapidly, learn so much so fast, and form such strong bonds to other human beings.

THE NEWBORN'S SENSES

If someone asked you to think of two words to describe a newborn baby, you might choose the adjectives "tiny" and "helpless." "Tiny" would be a pretty good choice. Most newborns are between 20 and 22 inches long (50.8 and 55.8 centimeters) and weigh between 7 and 8 pounds (3.2 and 3.6 kilograms). Many are even smaller. But a newborn is not "helpless" in every sense of the word. It is true that he is totally dependent on others for all his needs, but right from birth he is sensitive and responsive, able to discover for himself what he needs and to signal those needs to the people who take care of him.

The newborn's abilities are impressive. He is sensitive to tastes, smells, and touch. He can hear and see. He can feel pain. He has been born with all the senses, although they are not yet as highly developed as an adult's.

A baby can tell the difference between a sweet flavor and a bitter one; as early as two or three days of age, he will reject the bitter one and accept the sweet.

A baby can also tell the difference between two smells when both are presented at the same time. He can also tell when an odor is unpleasant. Dr. Lewis P. Lipsett of Brown University has shown that at two to three days old a baby will cry and turn his head away when he smells something that adults consider strong and unpleasant, such as household ammonia.

Babies are particularly sensitive to touch. They respond quickly to a light touch on the skin and will stop crying when gently rubbed or held closely. They can feel pain in the first few days of life, though girls are more sensitive to pain than boys.

A baby responds to loud noises while he is still in his mother's **uterus,** and he can hear at birth. He may blink, jerk his body, or respond in some other way to a loud noise. Babies seem to prefer some sounds over others—music, soft rhythmic drumming, human voices. They respond more readily to high-pitched sounds than to low-pitched ones, and to longer-lasting tones than to short, abrupt ones. They also respond to the cries of other babies. In a nursery, when one infant starts crying, he is likely to be joined by a chorus of others!

Newborns can also see. If a brightly colored object is held at about a distance of 8 to 12 inches (20.3 to 30.5 centimeters) in front of a newborn, he will become alert and try to focus his eyes on it. But objects that are held further

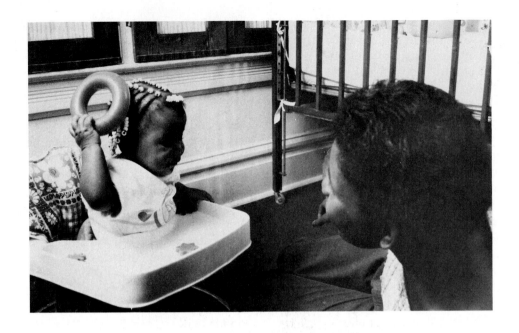

Babies are active beings. Although they depend on others to tend to their physical needs, they are able to see, hear, taste, smell, and touch. Since babies learn through their senses, caregivers should make sure that babies' environments are stimulating.

away are beyond his visual range and probably look hazy and vague to him. The newborn who finds an object within his range will stare intently at it. If it moves from side to side, he will soon be able to follow it with his eyes. A little later he will be able to follow it if it moves up and down very slowly. A newborn is sensitive to extremely bright lights and will shut his eyes and keep them closed until the light is put out or turned away from him.

At birth a newborn can distinguish some patterns and shapes. He prefers patterns to solid colors and likes stripes and angles better than circles. By the age of three weeks, however, he would rather look at a human face than at any geometric pattern. Scientists who have tested baby's reactions to shapes feel that the baby responds more to the pattern of the human face (the arrangement of eyes, nose, and mouth) than to its outline, size, or color, which seem to change as the face moves closer or farther away. But why does the baby show this decided preference for the human face? No one knows for sure, but humans seem to have an inborn tendency to view the face of others of their kind as the most rewarding source of help and gratification. Identifying and focusing attention on another human being is the beginning of **attachment**. It is a very important part of the baby's process of establishing strong relationships with other people.

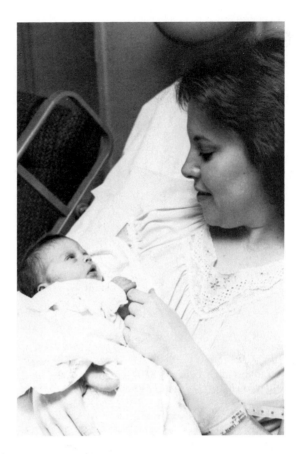

You can observe the grasping reflex when you stroke the palm of a baby's hand. He'll hold on tight. The rooting reflex occurs when the baby searches for something to suck because you've touched his cheek.

THE NEWBORN'S REFLEXES

Another reason that newborns are not entirely "helpless" is that they have highly developed **reflexes,** or automatic reactions to certain kinds of stimulation. The baby does not control these actions but performs them involuntarily. Shortly after birth, he can breathe, suck, swallow, sneeze, hiccup, yawn, vomit, and eliminate wastes from his body. Although the purposes of some of the baby's reflexes are not yet thoroughly understood, some of them are related to the instinct for survival. They help

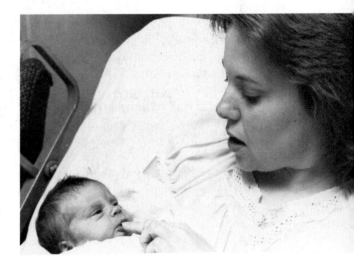

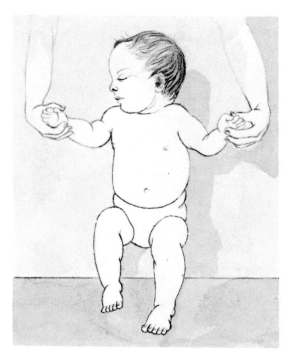

You almost might believe a baby is ready to walk when you notice her stepping reflex.

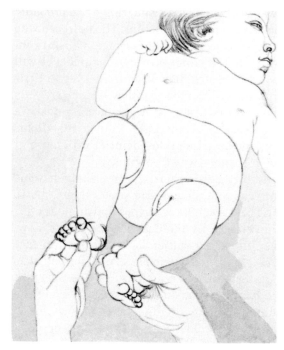

To see the Babinski reflex, touch the soles of a baby's feet. Her toes will fan upward and outward.

him protect himself against harmful experiences and encourage positive ones.

One of the most important reflexes in a newborn baby is the **rooting reflex.** Rooting is the baby's way of searching for something to suck on, and it is strongly related to the sucking reflex. If you touch a baby's cheek, the palm of his hand, or the inside of his mouth, he will turn his head in the direction of the touch. His mouth will open, his arm will flex, and his hand will come up to his mouth. He may suck on his hand for several minutes. Babies root and suck even when they are not hungry. This reflex disappears around the age of nine months.

The **Moro reflex** is a kind of self-protective device. It later develops into the **startle reflex.** If a baby hears a loud noise or sees a bright light, or if his position is suddenly changed, he will "startle," arch his back, and

throw his head back. At the same time he will fling his arms and legs out and then bring them back toward his body, as if he were protecting himself against falling. A light but steady pressure on his body will calm his startled crying.

The **grasp reflex** can be observed when you stroke the inside of the sole of the baby's foot near the toes or the palm of his hand. He will grasp your finger with his toes or fingers and hang on tight. The grasp reflex lasts until about the age of two or three months.

The opposite reflex is called the **Babinski reflex.** Here the baby's toes will fan upward and outward if you touch the outside of the sole of his foot. This, too, disappears, at about eight or nine months.

Babies show several other reflexes that are involuntary during infancy but come back later when they are ready to creep, crawl, and

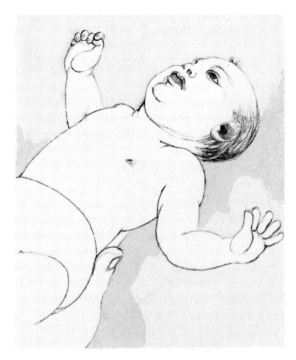

The Moro reflex causes baby to startle. He will arch his back and throw back his head.

Firm pressure on a baby's back will help calm him after a Moro reflex.

walk. A newborn will "walk" across a bed if you hold him in a standing position and stroke the soles of his feet. He will move his arms and legs as if swimming if you hold him on a water surface and support him at the chest. He will make crawling motions if placed on a bed. It is important to realize that at this age the baby is doing these things automatically, not deliberately.

The most recent research on infancy has revealed much about the infant's capacity to respond to his world. Understanding of the neonate (newborn) has changed; we now know that the baby is far more aware of his environment, and earlier influenced by his response to it, than was previously believed.

This new view of the infant as a complex individual is helpful to parents and others who care for infants. The caregiver who knows how to interpret the infant's behavior and understands his sensitivity to the people and things around him is better able to meet the baby's needs with love and tenderness.

BABY GETS BIGGER AND STRONGER

The most obvious change in the baby's first year is that he gets bigger and bigger. By the age of four or five months most babies weigh twice as much as they did at birth, and by the age of one year their weight has tripled. Saul, for instance, weighed 7 pounds (3.2 kilograms) at birth, 14 pounds (6.3 kilograms) at five months, and 21 pounds (9.5 kilograms) at one year. Typically a baby who is 20 inches at birth (50.8 centimeters) will be about one and a half times longer, or 30 inches (76.2 centimeters), at one year. Height is generally doubled by the age of four years. These are averages only; individual babies grow at different rates. If a baby continues to grow at a steady rate, there is no reason to worry. But there is cause for concern if a baby doesn't seem to be growing much at all or if he becomes overweight or obese. Healthy babies often look chubby, but the very fat baby is developing a weight problem that may plague him throughout his life. Some doctors believe that an obese baby is not as healthy as a thinner one and that if the child remains heavy, he will have to watch his diet constantly as an adult.

While the baby is growing larger, his bones and teeth are also developing. A baby's bones have more cartilage (a flexible kind of connective tissue) and less mineral density (hardness) compared with the bones of adults. The baby's joints are more flexible, too, and the ligaments (tissues that connect bones) are not as securely attached. These developing bones are easily injured, either by pressure or pulling, or by infection or **malnutrition** (poor nourishment). No one need be afraid to pick up a baby for fear of hurting him, but a baby is delicate and needs careful handling.

A baby's teeth are formed while he is still a fetus. He is born with all his baby teeth inside his gums. They begin to erupt, or show through, at about six months of age. Usually the first teeth are the "front teeth" (the incisors in the center of the baby's gums on top or bottom).

HOW THE INFANT DEVELOPS

Although each baby is an individual and grows at his own rate, certain general patterns of development apply to all infants. Martin is able to sit up without support at six months, José at seven months, and Diana at eight months; but all three babies first are helped to sit with support.

This pattern of development as well as others is affected by many factors:

- Status at birth: Was he a healthy full-term baby or a premature newborn with a low birth weight?
- General health: Has he been well and thriving, or has he suffered from illness, infections, or other problems?
- General disposition: Is he active and easily stimulated, or is he calm and placid?
- Attitudes of parents or other caregivers: Do they encourage him when he first tries to sit or stand? Or are they too busy with other children or family problems to pay much attention?

Keeping in mind that "normal" development includes a wide range of individual variations, let us now look at the well-established patterns babies follow.

First, babies develop from head to foot. This is the way the **fetus** developed, too, and the same pattern continues after birth. The baby's head is more highly developed at birth than his arms and legs. His body remains top-heavy for many months, and the lower part of his body will not develop enough to enable him to sit or stand until the second half of the first year. Somewhere at the end of the first year, or at the beginning of the second, he will have developed enough control over his leg muscles so that he can take his first cautious steps.

Second, babies develop from the center of their bodies outward. A baby can control his trunk (body) before he can control his shoulders, his shoulders before his arms, and his arms before his hands. **Gross motor skills** (those related to the large muscles of the body) develop before **fine motor skills** (those related to the small muscles of hands and fingers). Another distinction is important to keep in mind: that between the development of **locomotion** (the ability to move from place to place) and the development of **manipulation**

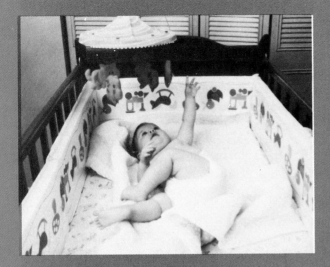

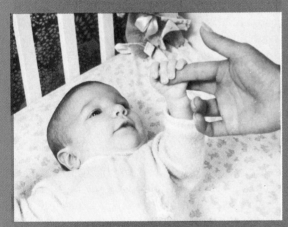

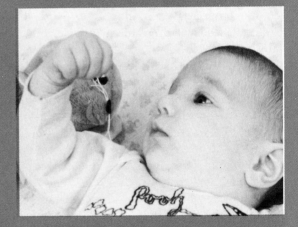

A baby's environment affects the development of his motor skills. Before babies can move around by themselves, brightly colored toys within their grasp assist manipulation development. These objects should be clean and free from small pieces baby could break off and swallow. They should provide different textures for baby to feel and make pleasant sounds when touched. As baby begins to move by himself, appealing objects should be placed on clean floors or rugs to encourage locomotion. Babies should not be confined to playpens for long periods during this stage of their development.

(the ability to use hands and fingers to grasp and hold objects).

Third, the baby progresses from simple to complex activities. In learning to grasp objects, for example, he uses his whole hand for grasping before he can use his fingers. The newborn's range of possibilities is limited to relatively few simple activities. Of all of them, he seems to prefer sleeping the most. Some newborns sleep about twenty hours a day. Peter H. Wolff, a neurophysiologist (a scientist who studies the nervous system) at Massachusetts Institute of Technology, observed month-old babies and discovered that they sleep at least twelve to fourteen hours a day. When awake, they spend more time crying than in other activities, and they alternate between periods of drowsiness and periods of alertness.

Gradually the baby sleeps less and spends more of his waking time actively responding to the objects, and particularly the people, around him. He learns more complex skills, like holding a rattle, pushing food into his mouth or away from it, or throwing toys out of his crib and then crying for someone to give them back.

Of course, as the baby's skills become more complex, his needs become more complex as well. An unhappy newborn can usually be comforted with cuddling, food, or a change of diapers; but a ten-month-old who has wedged himself between two pieces of furniture and cannot figure out how to free himself is going to need more help.

LEROY: A "TYPICAL" INFANT

Keeping in mind that each baby is a unique human being whose development ought not to be measured against another baby's, let's look at how Leroy, a "typical" infant, developed from birth to the age of one year.

At *birth*, Leroy was a healthy baby who showed all the normal newborn reflexes. By the time he was *one month old,* he could lift his head briefly when lying on a bed, and he could roll part of the way from his side to his back. When his head was unsupported, it was floppy and unsteady. He kept his fists clenched or slightly open most of the time, and he could grasp someone's finger or a rattle placed in his hand, but he would let go quickly. He still slept most of the day and—to his parents' relief—most of the night as well.

By the time he was *three months old,* Leroy could hold his head erect more or less continuously and had begun to lift his chest off the bed. In his bath and crib, he kicked his feet vigorously and waved his arms about aimlessly. He could hold onto objects for much longer than he was able to one month earlier. He even began to try to reach for objects within his view, but he couldn't grasp them.

Within the next few months, Leroy began to show much more progress. His permanent black hair started to grow in. He was also developing control over his trunk and shoulders. By the age of *six months,* when his father or mother held him in a sitting position, his back was firm. He could hold his head erect continuously, and he could roll from one side right over to the other. He had discovered his toes and found them interesting playthings. He could sit with some support—for example, with pillows behind him in his carriage. This upright position gave him a better view of the world, which he inspected carefully when his grandparents took him to the park. He could hold a rattle with both hands.

By the age of *nine months*, Leroy was well on his way toward greater independence. He could sit without support and could roll over from front to back and all the way back again. He could crawl comfortably, pushing and pulling himself along with a distinctive waddle. He could even turn around while crawling. He could pull himself up from a crawling to a standing position, but he did not know how to get down again. He would then cry for help, and someone would usually come to his rescue.

He had also learned much better control over his hands and could grasp a small object with his thumb and forefinger. He had discovered that when he held a pan in each hand and brought them together, they made a loud and interesting noise. And, to his parents' distress, he had discovered the electric outlets in the wall, and wanted to poke at them with his fingers. A set of blocks attracted his attention for a while. At first he just picked them up and looked at them, but he was soon able to put one on top of the other to build the world's smallest tower.

At *twelve months,* his first birthday, Leroy was now not just an infant but a little boy. He was not really walking yet, but he could climb up and down stairs, holding on to the banister for security. His crawling speed had increased dramatically, and it often seemed to his parents that he could walk if he wanted to but that he preferred crawling. He opened his birthday presents, with a little help. He was able to take the covers off the boxes and remove the toys, and put the toys back in again. Some of the gifts puzzled him, but he laughed with delight when he found that moving a certain toy back and forth on the rug made a clacking noise.

Throughout his first year, Leroy had developed not just *motor skills* (the ability to move, to handle objects, and control his body) but also *learning skills* and *social skills.* Although these development patterns will be discussed in more detail later, it is important to note now that physical growth and development are just part of the total picture of the infant's progress.

FAILURE TO THRIVE

Just as it is important not to measure one baby's development rate against another's, nor to push the baby to progress faster than he is able to do on his own, it is important to recognize signs that a baby may *not* be progressing normally. Doctors, nurses, and other health-care professionals are trained to recognize such signs, but frequently the best observers of the baby's development are the people who care for him daily. These people should mention any troubling indications of a baby's lack of progress to the doctor or nurse who checks on the baby's health and growth from month to month.

The most obvious sign that something may be wrong is a baby's failure to gain weight and grow. This problem is called a "failure to thrive," and it may be caused by poor nutrition, an infection, defects in the baby's metabolism (the process of converting food to energy), or some other medical problem. Sometimes a baby may fail to thrive for psychological reasons, perhaps because he lacks a warm relationship with his mother or other caregiver. For some reason the proper atmosphere to encourage growth has not been established. In these cases the parents must seek professional help.

Another danger signal is a pattern of development very much different from the one we described for Leroy. Susan, for example, was a listless and inactive newborn; her reflexes were weak, and by the age of three months she could still only hold her head up with a great deal of effort. Ronnie, at nine months, could not sit even with support; and Toni could sit alone only at the age of one year. These babies were so far from the norm of development that their families had to consult experienced medical specialists.

There are many possible causes for such problems: genetic defects, mental retardation, physical handicaps, disturbed family life, or lack of warm, loving care. Many of these situations can be remedied; others cannot be changed but can be recognized. In cooperation with the baby's family, professionals can help arrange new ways of coping with the problem.

It is very important to recognize the infant who is truly "different" and in need of special attention, so that whatever help is available can be given as early as possible.

FEEDING THE BABY

As babies grow and flourish during their first year, their needs change. One of the most important aspects of caring for an infant is feeding. Feeding the baby properly is, of course, essential to his growth and well-being. But it is also essential to his social development—that is, to his growing awareness that other human beings provide warmth, nourishment, and love.

This is one reason breast feeding is favored over bottle feeding by many families and doctors. The breast-fed baby is held and cuddled by his mother and both derive a sense of closeness and pleasure from the experience. Of course, bottle-fed babies can be treated just as lovingly, but in breast feeding it is a natural part of the process. Bottles should never be "propped." An infant should always be held while feeding.

Mothers who nurse must continue to eat a full, nutritionally sound diet, for they are supplying their baby's nutritional needs as well as their own. During the time a mother is nursing, she should include in her daily diet at least a quart of milk; four servings of fruits and vegetables; three or more servings of meat, poultry, fish, beans or eggs; four servings of cereal and grains; and some butter or margarine. She should avoid alcohol and tobacco. Maintaining a proper diet will eventually help her lose the extra weight she gained during pregnancy, because her body burns up calories when it produces milk.

While mother's milk is an excellent food for an infant, today's formulas are nearly the same in nutritional value. However, a little experimentation may be necessary to find just the right mix for a particular baby. Parents who choose bottle feeding should follow the exact instructions for preparing the formula. Vitamin supplements should be given only if the doctor advises it.

Many mothers choose an in-between method. They breast-feed their babies for the first few months but also feed them with a bottle once in a while. this gives them a rest and allows other family members to share in feeding the baby. Babies who are introduced to a bottle in this way find it easier to leave the breast than those who are breast-fed exclusively.

More important than where the milk comes from is the caregiver's feeling of self-confidence while feeding the baby. She or he will convey this feeling to the infant, and he in turn will be more relaxed during feedings and benefit more from the experience.

Not so long ago, babies were fed on a strict schedule. A mother would wait anxiously for the appointed hour to feed her baby, who was often screaming in rage and hunger by that time. Doctors used to advise this rigid schedule because they felt that allowing the baby to determine his own schedule would "spoil" him and give him indigestion.

Now mothers are advised to be flexible in feeding schedules, and it is much easier on both baby and mother. Each baby has its own inner time clock that tells him when he is hungry; furthermore, that time clock may vary from day to day.

A flexible schedule is often called "demand feeding" or "self-regulated feeding." It means that in general the mother follows the baby's cues in determining feeding times. However, the mother can still exercise some control over the timing. For instance, when Mrs. Chan has an appointment to take her baby, Jenny, to the doctor at three o'clock and that is the time the baby usually wakes for feeding, she may wake Jenny at two and feed her before the trip.

By the age of six or seven weeks, most babies

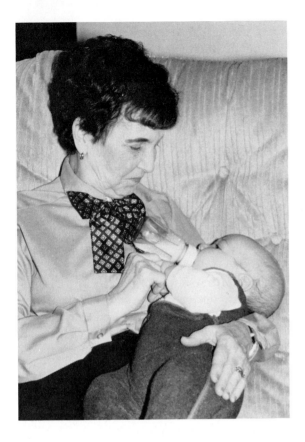

Having family members share in feeding baby helps build good family relationships and teaches them the responsibilities involved in caring for babies.

settle down to a schedule of six feedings a day. As they get older, they gradually eat more at each feeding and can wait for longer periods to be fed. The late-night feeding (2 A.M.) is the one that most parents want to give up first, and they can encourage this by postponing the feeding that usually takes place at around 10 P.M. to 11 P.M. or midnight. The baby will then sleep through a longer part of the night, and gradually will no longer need that feeding. By the time the baby is six or seven months old, he may be on a three- or four-meal schedule.

Most doctors agree that flexible scheduling should not make the baby an absolute dictator. Parents should exercise some control, within limits, over when the baby is fed. They should not overfeed the baby, and if he de-mands constant feeding, they should try to figure out if there is some other explanation besides hunger.

Weaning the baby from breast to bottle is done at different ages in different cultures. In many societies babies are breast-fed until the age of two or three. North American mothers generally try to wean their babies at about the age of six months, although some choose to breast-feed for a year or longer. Weaning from bottle to cup is also generally begun during the second half of the first year. Some mothers prefer to wean directly from the breast to the cup, without using the bottle at all. This is done whenever the infant is ready —perhaps at fourteen to eighteen months.

The baby himself will give some clues when he is ready to be weaned from the bottle. He will start to play with his bottle or other foods at the end of his feeding. He may try to hold his bottle himself. He may be more easily distracted at mealtime. He may be able to eat in his highchair by himself and does not need to be held. He shows an interest in learning to drink from a cup when it is offered to him.

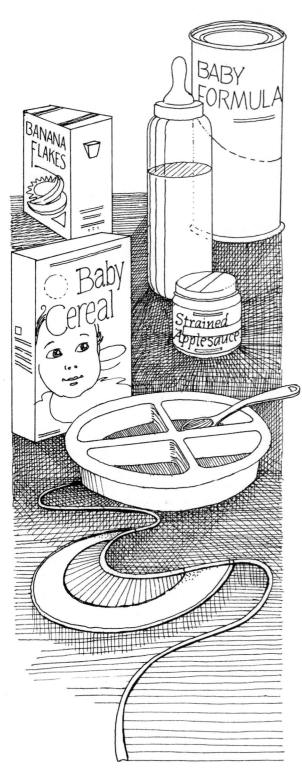

Baby's first solid foods are cereals and strained fruits and vegetables. Unbreakable utensils should be used so that the baby can be encouraged to feed himself.

Many mothers find another development important in starting to wean their babies: the eruption of the first teeth, which may make breast feeding painful to the mother.

At whatever age the baby is weaned, the process should be gradual. It might take a few months or so to wean a baby completely, but in this way there will be no sudden, upsetting changes in the baby's daily routine. One way to begin is to offer the baby juice from a cup, and to encourage him to handle his spoon. Once weaning is begun, it should be continued. An on-again, off-again process will only take longer and frustrate both infant and mother.

Solid foods can be added to the baby's diet within the first few months, although some parents and doctors prefer to wait until about six months. Usually the first food to be offered is cereal mixed with milk. Other foods that are easily digested are mashed bananas, applesauce, and mashed potatoes. Pediatricians may recommend different solid foods for different babies, and parents should follow the doctor's advice. Generally, though, doctors suggest adding only one new food at a time, so that any allergies or digestive problems can be easily identified.

Either prepared baby foods or homemade baby foods can be used. Doctors warn against adding too much sugar or salt to homemade baby foods. The person who prepares the food may not like the taste of unsalted or unsweetened foods, but the baby doesn't notice the difference, and the unnecessary ingredients may promote bad eating habits later on.

When the baby is six months old or so, he can be given "finger" foods—fruit, crumbled cooked meat, hard-cooked egg, cheese, cooked vegetables, crackers, bits of soft toast—anything he can pick up and put into his mouth —even if most of it gets into his hair and on his

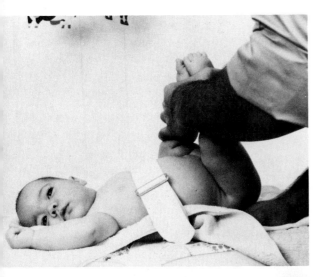

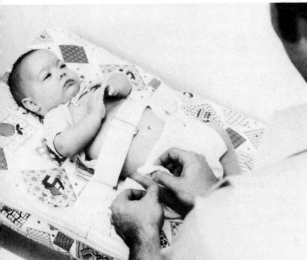

Frequent diaper changes help prevent diaper rash and infection. Soiled diapers are removed. The baby is washed with wet cotton and dried with a soft cloth. Excess baby powder should be avoided.

face. Babies can also eat some of their foods with a spoon. This may also be messy, but it is a valuable learning experience for them. Most children do not really feed themselves completely until they are two or three years old, but these important steps toward independence are taken in the first year.

ELIMINATION

Newborn babies may have several bowel movements each day; for the first few days the **stools** will be greenish-black and sticky. The consistency and color of the stool, and how often the baby moves his bowels, depend on whether he is breast-fed or bottle-fed. A baby may have several bowel movements a day, or only one every two or three days. Parents quickly become familiar with their baby's pattern of elimination, and they are usually the best judges of when something seems to be wrong. They should report significant changes to the doctor.

Wet diapers need not be always changed immediately, but it is best to change a baby's diaper as soon as possible after a bowel movement. With approximately eight to ten changes a day, a lot of diapers are needed.

There are three main ways of keeping an infant in fresh diapers: (1) using cloth diapers that are washed at home, (2) using a diaper service, which delivers fresh diapers and picks up used ones to be washed, and (3) using disposable diapers. The least expensive method is washing cloth diapers at home, but it takes a lot of time and effort. Diaper services cost more and may not be available in every area, but they are more convenient, and the diapers are sterilized so that diaper rash is less likely to occur than with home-laundered diapers. Using disposable diapers generally costs about the same as using a diaper service. They are also convenient, but they may cause diaper rash. Unlike cloth diapers, they are not biodegradable; that is, they are a source of pollution in the environment. Each family must choose the method that serves its needs best. One choice might be to combine diaper service with home laundering, and to use disposable diapers when traveling.

Toilet training in the first year is nearly always a waste of time. Overeager parents may "catch" a baby in time to put him on a potty chair for a bowel movement, but the baby is too young to learn from the experience. Trying to toilet-train the young baby can be frustrating to him and useless as well.

BATHING THE BABY

Until the baby's naval and, in the case of many male infants, the circumcision heal, which usually takes about two or three weeks, he should be given only sponge baths, not placed directly in a tub. It is important to assemble all the materials beforehand: a small plastic oval tub placed on a table or counter; a diaper or small towel to keep the baby partly covered; a cake of mild soap; a washcloth and towel; clean baby clothes; and an apron for the person giving the bath. *A baby should never be left unattended,* for he can fall off a table if left alone for a few seconds.

The room temperature should be 75° to 80°F (23.8° to 26.6°C) and the water temperature 98°F (36.6°C). If you don't have a bath thermometer, test the water with your elbow. It should feel warm, but not hot.

When everything is ready, take off the baby's clothes and partially cover him with a towel or diaper. Babies often object to baths, not because they don't like water but because they are upset by drafts or changes in temperature. Keep his body covered except for the area being washed. Start by washing the face and work down, supporting his body firmly with your other hand. Then pat him dry gently. Twice a week, wash the baby's scalp with a mild shampoo and rinse it carefully.

When the baby is ready for a tub bath, you must still remember to hold him firmly and to stay with him the whole time. Only two or three inches of water should be placed in the tub. He can be bathed with a sponge outside the tub and rinsed in it. Pat, rather than rub, the baby dry because his skin is sensitive.

As soon as babies get used to this new routine, they start to like it. They often kick

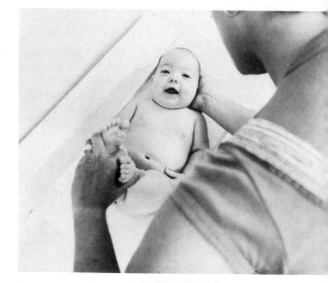

Babies react differently to baths. Some coo, while others protest loudly. Learning to hold baby properly takes practice, but makes bath time easier.

vigorously and wave their arms about, so the bath time becomes an exercise period, too.

After the bath, mineral oil or baby lotion can be put on the baby's skin, especially if it's dry. (However, some babies may have an allergic reaction to oils or lotions.) Baby powder is also helpful, since a baby's skin is easily chafed.

68

The practice of wrapping an infant tightly in long bands of cloth, called swaddling clothes, is an ancient custom. Swaddling is mentioned in the Bible, in European poems of the Middle Ages, and in plays by Shakespeare (1564–1616). It is still practiced in some cultures today. One variation, common among Native American tribes such as the Sioux Indians, is to wrap the baby tightly and attach him to a cradleboard, which his mother carries on her back. Swaddling keeps the infant warm, protects him from scratching himself, and allows his mother to go about her work in the home or field without worrying about his safety.

Some scientists who study the cultures of the world have wondered if swaddling affects a baby's personality, since it restricts his movement for much of his first year. Geoffrey Gorer, an anthropologist, has suggested that swaddling influenced the national character of the Russian people, as the practice was common among the Russian peasants (and to some extent other classes as well) up to this century. According to his theory, the Russian custom tended to encourage two contrasting personality traits. The periods of being tightly bound taught the baby to accept his "fate" and to obey authority. But at times when the swaddling clothes were changed and he had freedom of movement, the baby learned to give in to a free, impulsive, emotional mood. Gorer sees both these character traits expressed in the masterpieces of Russian literature.

Some people have criticized Gorer's theory on the grounds that it gives too much importance to just one element of child rearing. Others claim that there is not even such a thing as "national character" at all. Whether or not it is true, Gorer's idea does raise interesting questions about the influence of child-rearing practices on later psychological development.

Source: Erik Erikson, CHILDHOOD AND SOCIETY, second edition (New York: W.W. Norton & Company, Inc., 1963), p. 388-392

CLOTHING

Styles in baby clothes have changed to reflect the more casual, relaxed life style North Americans favor today. No longer is a baby dressed up in fancy, frilly outfits; he is dressed for warmth, protection, and comfort. Of course, parents and grandparents still love to dress the baby up for a special family event. But most of the time babies wear clothes designed for easy wear, easy care, and easy changing.

Young babies grow very quickly, and for the first few months all they need are diapers, gowns, undershirts, stretch suits, and, in cool weather, sweaters, hats, and blankets for outings. A blanket sleeping suit can be used on cold nights. When the baby starts to crawl on the floor, he needs sturdier clothing—cotton or corduroy overalls, T-shirts (with snaps or wide openings for the head), and stretch suits.

A baby's clothing should always fit loosely, especially around the arms or legs. When in doubt, buy clothing one size too large. The baby will grow into the outfit very quickly.

Until the baby starts walking, he needs no shoes or socks. Many stretch suits and overalls are made with feet.

Babies should not be dressed too heavily or too lightly. If a baby perspires freely, it may mean that he is wearing too many layers of clothing. If he loses color from his face, he is probably cold and needs more clothing.

SLEEPING

Newborns sleep most of the time—from fourteen to twenty hours a day. Some babies need

Babies sleep most comfortably in a quiet environment. They require a light cover, but no pillow. Sleeping patterns vary for infants, but most sleep from 14 to 20 hours each day. Constant sleeplessness may be a symptom of illness.

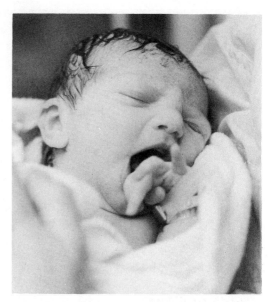

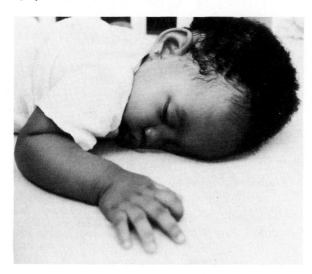

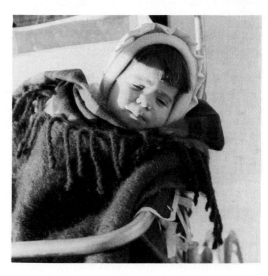

less sleep right from birth; others need more. Most babies prefer to sleep on their stomachs. This position prevents the baby from choking if he should spit up. Many tiny babies seem more comfortable when stretched crosswise at one end of their crib or bassinet, with their heads tucked up against the crib bumper. This contact seems to give them a feeling of security.

Babies should be kept warm but not overheated while they sleep. They do not need heavy blankets; a light cover or sleeping bag will do if the room is kept at a comfortable temperature (65° to 70°F or 18.3° to 21.1°C).

A fussy baby who seems tired but can't get to sleep can be comforted by rocking, cuddling, and soft music. Lullabies are an age-old remedy, and for a good reason: They do soothe babies. A doctor may prescribe medication to help a baby sleep if he has a specific medical problem. But most sleeping problems are tem-

70

porary, and he may develop a dependence on medication. In any case, no medication should ever be given without a doctor's advice.

As the baby grows older, he sleeps less; and by the time he is five months old or so, he is taking two or three naps a day and probably sleeping through the night. A difficult period for both baby and parents may occur at the end of the first year, when the baby is too old for both a morning and an afternoon nap but too young for just a morning nap. He will often grow fretful in the late afternoon, and be too tired to eat supper. One way to avoid this is to delay the morning nap until right after lunch; the baby will then be refreshed for most of the afternoon and will probably fall asleep right after an early supper.

Sleep habits vary in babies just as they do in adults. Some babies fall asleep instantly and sleep soundly for long periods. Others take brief naps and are easily awakened. There is not much that parents can do to change one type of sleeper to another; they can only try to adjust to the baby's own timetable.

Babies who are getting enough sleep show good weight gain, have good color, and look bright and alert. An infant who is not getting enough sleep will be listless and fatigued and will lack interest in toys or food. These symptoms should be discussed with a doctor or other health-care professional. Sleeplessness may be a sign of illness.

ALERTNESS AND WELL-BEING

A healthy, well-nourished, well-rested baby eagerly responds to all kinds of stimulation. In fact, if there were no stimulation in his world, his general health would suffer and he would become inactive and droopy. A baby can receive stimulation by playing by himself, with other persons, and with toys.

An infant responds most to persons talking to him, singing to him, and holding him. Peo-ple are his favorite "playthings." But of course a baby cannot be tended constantly, and must learn to amuse himself. He will discover that toys and other objects are also fun to look at, touch, listen to, and eventually hold.

For the first three months or so the best toys for a baby are things he can look at. Mobiles are brightly colored hanging toys with dangling objects that move in a breeze. A mobile can be hung over a crib about a foot from the baby's eye level. Some mobiles make sounds as they move. Another object for a baby to look at is a small fish tank placed near the crib. He can also look at posters pasted on the ceiling or wall. During this period, he will discover his hands, and will examine them carefully as if they were just another toy.

A baby likes to listen to sounds as well. Music boxes, records, wind chimes, bells, and loud-ticking clocks will all interest him—at least for a time.

As soon as a baby can hold on to a toy, he likes soft rubber balls, rubber rattles, stuffed animals, and other toys that are easy to grasp. Parents should be careful not to give the baby anything with sharp edges or parts that may come loose and be swallowed.

Babies from three to six months old can usually handle objects and like to examine things with different textures—furry, smooth, bumpy. Some teething toys—small rubber or plastic tubes—offer babies a chance to look, touch, and also suck. At about six months babies also become fascinated with their toes.

"Cradle gyms" give the baby a chance to exercise his arms and legs by pulling on rings and bars. Other types of crib toys have knobs to pull, buttons to press, and handles to turn. Each time the baby pulls, presses, or turns, the toy makes a different sound.

Babies also like to look at themselves, and there are several toy mirrors especially made for this purpose. Never give a baby a regular glass mirror, which might break.

In the second half of the first year, when the

Babies are attracted to both toys and everyday objects in the home. While exploration should be encouraged, those items which are toxic, breakable, or have small pieces or sharp edges should be put out of reach.

baby starts to sit and crawl, he likes to play with pull toys, soft animals, nesting toys, blocks, balls, squeeze toys, and many others.

Not all of the baby's playthings need to be bought. Many common objects around the house are fun for a baby—pots and pans, clothespins, wooden spoons. However, parents must be very careful not to let the baby play with anything that he might swallow or that might cut or otherwise harm him.

Toys are fun, but most important in developing a baby's alertness is the kind of play that involves him with another person. Games like "peek-a-boo," "bye-bye," "This little piggy went to market," and imitating sounds are traditional ways of playing with babies. They keep the baby amused and help teach him an important lesson for his social development. Through this kind of play he learns that relating to other human beings is a rewarding source of enjoyment.

Pediatric Nurse

Joyce Campbell, R.N., had completed her talk on nursing as a career for a group of high school students. "Are there any questions?" she asked.

"Why did you decide to be a nurse?"

Joyce laughed. "I guess I'm just the old cliché come true. I always wanted to be a nurse, ever since I was a little girl. I liked helping people even then—and now I take care of sick babies."

"Don't you think women should aspire to be doctors, instead of nurses?"

Joyce was emphatic in her reply. "Nursing is a very demanding profession in its own right. Of course, women who want to be doctors should have every opportunity, but it should also be recognized that nurses play a very important role in patient care. Often men choose to be nurses, too."

Joyce is a pediatric nurse and works in the children's ward of a large teaching hospital. She is part of a health-care team consisting of doctors, nurses, technicians, and social workers. She takes care of the children's medical needs as ordered by the doctor. She makes sure that the children take their medications, changes the dressings on surgical patients, checks temperatures and pulses, records all significant information, and generally makes the patients comfortable.

Pediatric nurses can also work in other settings: in a doctor's private office, in hospital neonatal intensive care units where they care for sick newborns, in schools, and in child-care institutions. Public health nurses usually work in clinics and spend a great deal of time with children.

Graduation from high school is the first step in becoming a nurse. After that, there are three possible routes: a two-year nursing program in a community college leads to an associate degree; a diploma program offered by a hospital school of nursing usually takes three years and includes much practical experience; and a four- or five-year baccalaureate program leads to a bachelor's degree. To become a Registered Nurse (R.N.), it is necessary to pass a state licensing exam. Graduates of all three types of programs take the same exam.

Nurses can specialize, and go on for advanced degrees, including masters' degrees and doctorates. Those who wish to pursue careers in administration or research usually obtain these degrees.

Several new professional opportunities for nurses have opened up in the past ten years. Nurse-practitioners are nurses in private practice. They make house calls, see patients in the office, and refer patients to a doctor when necessary. Nurse-midwives deliver babies either in the hospital or in the home. They need special training and clinical experience to be certified in most states.

Nursing is a rigorous profession, and it requires excellent health, physical stamina, and a sense of dedication. Hours are often long, and although working conditions vary, they may be poor. A children's ward, however, is often the most pleasant place in a hospital, since the staff usually works hard to make it a cheerful and bright place for their young patients. Salaries vary, and are usually good for nurses with special training, such as pediatric or neonatal intensive care nurses.

Nursing offers many personal rewards: the chance to learn and perform technical medical procedures competently; the opportunity to share information and expertise with colleagues; and above all, the sense of satisfaction of knowing that you are helping sick children and their parents.

WHEN BABY IS SICK

Most babies are well most of the time. An important part of keeping a baby healthy is taking him for regular checkups to a pediatrician, family doctor, nurse, or clinic. "Well-baby checkups" help give the doctor some guidelines about how each baby is progressing, so that any problems can be detected early. The doctor will keep medical records, but the parents should also keep their own record of the baby's weight and height at each checkup, the **immunizations** he receives, and any other information that might be important later on.

One important reason for taking the baby for regular checkups is to make sure that he receives his immunizations on time. Immunizations prevent diseases that commonly affect children. Some immunizations are given by injection; others are given orally (by mouth).

Fortunately, today no child need suffer from diseases like diphtheria, whooping cough, and poliomyelitis (polio), which used to kill or cripple children. However, because these diseases are now so rare, parents sometimes do not realize the importance of immunizing the baby against them. Unless the baby is immunized, he is just as vulnerable to one of these diseases as children were a hundred years ago, as recent epidemics of polio and measles have shown.

The doctor's advice on immunization should be followed for each baby. Sometimes the usual schedule of immunizations is altered to fit the individual needs of a baby. The "Based on Fact" box on page 75 shows a typical schedule.

Pediatricians guide parents in caring for their babies. Infants should have monthly checkups to ensure good health and proper development.

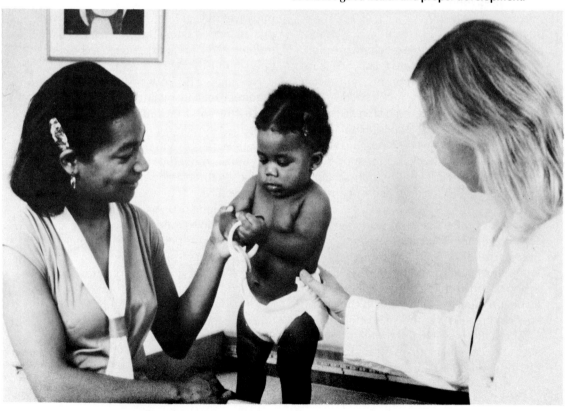

IMMUNIZATION SCHEDULE

Baby's Age	Type of Immunization	Disease It Prevents
2 months	DPT (a three-in-one shot)	diphtheria, tetanus, pertussis (whooping cough)
	oral polio vaccine (given by mouth)	poliomyelitis (infantile paralysis)
4 months	DPT oral polio vaccine	
6 months	DPT	
12 months	tuberculin test	tuberculosis (Test does not prevent disease, but indicates if child has it.)
15 months	live measles vaccine rubella vaccine mumps vaccine	"red" measles German measles mumps

Note: Smallpox vaccination is no longer recommended.

Schedule recommended by the American Academy of Pediatrics.

But babies sometimes get sick despite everyone's best efforts. Babies cannot explain where they hurt or exactly how they feel, so parents must be alert to other signals that a baby can give.

Perhaps the most obvious clue is that the baby is not behaving normally. He may be cranky, listless, or irritable. He may fall asleep at unexpected times or be difficult to wake. He may refuse to eat, or he may sleep restlessly. His crying may sound different from his usual cry of hunger, discomfort, or anger.

Other signs of illness are more direct. The baby may vomit or have **diarrhea**. His stools may be bloody, show mucus, or be discolored. His skin may be pale and clammy. He may have a runny nose, a cough, or heavy breathing. He may have a skin rash.

Fever is an important symptom. It usually means that there is an infection somewhere in the body. The baby's temperature should be taken with a rectal thermometer. A temperature of 101°F (38.3°C) usually means that the baby is ill and should be kept quiet and watched for further symptoms.

A baby with a fever should be given plenty of fluids (water or juices) because he can easily become dehydrated (lose body fluids). The same is true of a baby who has diarrhea. Some of the serious complications of illness in infants result not from the infection itself, but from the harmful results of symptoms like fever or diarrhea.

It is best to report all symptoms of illness to the doctor. Minor illnesses can develop into serious ones if left untreated. Sometimes the

Each year in the United States, between 7,500 and 10,000 apparently healthy babies die suddenly, usually after being put to bed for a nap or for the night. They do not cry out, gasp, or show any other sign of distress. No one has been able to find an explanation for this tragic occurrence, and so it has been named the Sudden Infant Death Syndrome (SIDS). It is sometimes called "crib death" or, in Great Britain and other Commonwealth countries, "cot death."

Researchers are working hard to try to find the cause or causes of SIDS. They have a few clues: SIDS strikes babies from one week to one year old, but most of the victims are between two and four months of age. SIDS deaths are more common in the winter. Many of the babies had mild colds or runny noses a few days before the attack. Boys seem to be more at risk than girls. Although SIDS strikes all races and economic groups, the incidence is higher among poor people. SIDS also is higher among premature babies and babies born to women who smoke heavily.

Many possible causes have been considered and rejected: a mysterious virus infection, allergy to cow's milk, vitamin deficiencies, immature kidneys. One common explanation—that the babies smothered because their parents carelessly placed pillows or blankets in the crib—has also been ruled out.

There are probably several causes of SIDS. It is known that a small number of these deaths result from a rare form of poisoning called botulism. One source is contaminated honey, so honey should not be fed to children under a year old.

The most widely accepted theory at present is that SIDS babies have poorly developed breathing mechanisms. All babies have sleep apnea (short periods during sleep when they stop breathing for a few seconds), but for some reasons SIDS babies stop breathing for longer periods—20 seconds or more—and unless they are roused and started breathing again, they will die.

Some babies who are revived after a "near-miss" episode are then monitored at home with electronic equipment. This equipment signals the parent when the baby has stopped breathing for too long.

One of the most difficult problems connected with SIDS is helping parents to overcome their sense of guilt. Uninformed relatives and friends often add to the parents' grief by their thoughtless remarks.

Think about how you would feel if a baby in your family died from SIDS. Suggest some appropriate ways for family and friends to comfort the parents. Also consider the positive and negative ways in which attaching a baby to an electronic apnea monitor while he sleeps would affect the parents.

---

doctor will suggest watching the baby to see how the illness progresses; other times the parents will be asked to bring the baby to the office for an examination. If medication is prescribed, it is important to follow the directions exactly and give the prescribed dose for as long as indicated. Sometimes parents stop medications when the baby starts to feel better, and the illness returns. Unless the doctor orders it, never give leftover medicine prescribed for one illness if the baby gets sick again at a later date.

One fairly common problem in young infants is **colic**. Colic is not a disease; the term is used to describe any continued, vigorous crying whose cause is difficult to identify. As many as 80 percent of small babies may be affected to some degree. Usually colic begins about the second or third week after birth and disappears by itself by the third month.

Colicky babies are not sick; they generally are well nourished and healthy. For some reason they have periods of uncontrollable crying or screaming that may occur regularly at the same time every day or irregularly. At other times the baby is perfectly content.

Beyond the usual checking to see that the baby is dry, fed, and otherwise comfortable, you can do little for a colicky baby except to try to soothe him by doing whatever seems to work—rocking, cuddling, patting. Parents frequently get very upset with a colicky baby, and their frustration makes the baby even more irritable. Patience and calm are the only effective means of getting through this trying period.

Another common problem—one that probably affects every baby at some time—is diaper rash. Here the best treatment is prevention. Change the diapers frequently, and make sure the skin is kept clean and dry. A protective powder or ointment may be helpful. If the baby has diaper rash, do not use plastic pants, and remove the plastic covering from disposable diapers. In warm weather leave the baby without diapers altogether. Fresh air and sunlight will help heal the inflamed areas. Severe cases should be brought to the attention of a doctor.

PREVENTING ACCIDENTS

In our society today, illness is not the chief threat to the well-being of infants: They are more in danger from accidents. Not all risks can be removed from the baby's life; parents who try to bring up their baby in a totally risk-free environment are creating an artificially "safe" atmosphere that does not give the child a chance to learn how to protect himself.

However, no baby should be exposed to certain risks. Babies should never be left alone in a house, an apartment, or a locked car, even for a few minutes. They should never be left unattended on a table or bed where they might fall off. They should never be left close to a hot stove or radiator. Pets and toddlers should not be allowed to play with the baby unless an adult is on hand to supervise.

For young babies, choking and suffocation are the main threats. A plastic bag (especially the kind that comes from dry-cleaners) should never be left in a baby's crib or carriage, since he may put it over his face and suffocate. Avoid using clothing that ties around the neck. Babies should not be tied in their crib or placed where they can reach a Venetian blind cord or the like and get entangled in it. Babies can also choke on their food, especially pieces of meat that are too large for them to handle.

The National Safety Council recommends that toys should be "washable, large enough not to fit in a mouth, ear or nose, but light enough not to cause injury if the child drops the toy on himself. The toy should be made of nonbrittle material (never glass). The eyes of a teddy bear or cloth stuffed animal should be sewn on—not attached with pins. Embroidered eyes are safest."

Once the baby is crawling, the entire home must be child-proofed. This means removing heavy objects from tables that might fall on the baby or shatter if he knocks them over. It means covering up electric outlets with safety caps and anchoring lamps and other furniture that might be tipped over by a creeping baby.

It is particularly important to remove all poisonous materials from a baby's reach. This includes medicines (aspirin is a very common cause of death in babies), cleaning products, gardening supplies, lead-based paints, and all other products that are not meant to be eaten. The baby's natural inclination is to taste anything new he discovers, and even small amounts of these substances can be dangerous.

Falls are also a major cause of injuries in children. There is no way to prevent all falls, but care should be taken to keep windows

Pediatrician

- Josette Brown works in a well-baby clinic in a section of a large city.
- Charlotte Sorenson has a private practice in a suburb of the same city.
- Tony Marino does research on babies with digestive problems and teaches at a medical school.
- Raul Silva works in a genetic counseling center, giving advice to families whose children were born with birth defects.

All these people are pediatricians—that is, doctors who have been specially trained to care for babies and children.

Many pediatricians spend most of their time following the development of normal, healthy children. Others concentrate on special areas of pediatric medicine: kidney diseases, heart disorders, neonatology (care of sick newborns), allergies, child psychiatry, to name just a few.

The first steps to becoming a pediatrician are college and, after graduation, medical school. Applicants must have high academic and personal achievements. An aptitude for science and mathematics helps, too. Many medical schools, however, look for well-rounded individuals who have done well in whatever field they chose to study in college. To offset the high cost of medical education, there are many loan and scholarship programs for qualified students.

After four years of medical school a graduate works one year as an intern, that is, an assistant in a hospital. This intensive period of practice is followed by two or three years as a resident (a staff member of a hospital). Doctors who have already decided on pediatrics as a specialty can begin their advanced training as interns and continue it as residents. At the end of the residency, those who want to be certified by the board of experts in their specialty must take a comprehensive examination.

More women go into pediatrics than into any other specialty. Part of the reason may be that this specialty has traditionally been more open to women than others, such as surgery. However, women also choose this specialty because they feel that they can bring special insights to the problems of mothers and children.

Although pediatricians must complete a long, demanding term of education, the field offers definite rewards. One is financial success. Pediatricians, like other medical specialists, may earn large incomes, particularly if they set up a private practice in a wealthy area. However, many other opportunities exist to work in different settings and still earn above-average incomes. Some pediatricians combine private practice with clinic work or research; others teach, work with parents' groups, lecture, or write. Pediatrics offers the chance to be involved with all those who are concerned with children, as well as the children themselves.

A less obvious reward is the satisfaction of healing sick children and of watching healthy ones grow to adolescence. But the pediatricians must also be prepared for failure; many childhood diseases are still incurable and many children die from accidents. In these cases the pediatrician must counsel the family through its grief—and must overcome her or his own sorrow at the loss of a patient. A career as a pediatrician demands not only hard work and dedication, but also maturity and compassion.

Infants should always be placed in a car seat when traveling by auto. Simply holding the baby does not provide protection should there be an accident. Be sure the car seat is appropriate for the age and size of the baby.

closed or barred, to block off stairs with a gate until the baby is old enough to climb up and down safely, and to keep a harness strap on an active baby in a carriage. A baby's high-chair should be sturdy and have a broad space between the legs so that it will not tip over.

Despite all precautions, babies will have some accidents. Most of them will be minor and result in scrapes and bruises and tears, but no serious injury. Still, every home should be prepared for a more serious emergency. The medicine cabinet should contain first-aid materials—an antiseptic (such as hydrogen peroxide), petroleum jelly, sterilized gauze pads, plastic bandage strips, and so on. It should also contain two items for poison treatment—syrup of ipecac and powdered activated charcoal (both available in drugstores). These should be given only on a doctor's advice, but it's a good idea to have them on hand if the need arises and the doctor suggests one or the other remedy.

A good book of first-aid treatments is a valuable reference. The phone numbers of the doctor, fire department, police department, and nearest poison control center should be taped to the phone.

If an emergency arises, it is most important to act quickly and to stay calm. If you have read beforehand what to do in cases of burns, bleeding, falls, broken bones, or choking, you will not be as likely to panic. Call for help as soon as possible and continue treating the baby appropriately until help arrives. (You can find more information about safety and first aid on pages 361-365.)

DISABILITIES

While most babies are normal and healthy, some babies have special problems. Katie, for example, was born with a dislocated hip and had to be placed in a body cast until she was

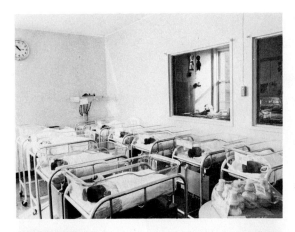

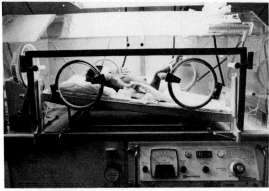

Newborns await going home in a hospital nursery.
A specially trained medical staff and modern
equipment ensure infants' proper care. Incubators
are used to treat babies who have medical problems.

poor nutrition during pregnancy, or smoked or drank heavily. These babies often have many problems at birth, primarily with breathing. They are often treated in **neonatal intensive care units,** sections of hospitals that have highly trained staff and special equipment for treatment. Many of these tiny babies who would have died only a few years ago can now be saved; however, they sometimes suffer from the treatment itself and may have development difficulties later on. Others seem to thrive once they pass the danger point. Because these techniques of **neonatology** (the branch of medicine that treats the health problems of newborns) are so new, very little is known about the long-term effects. In most neonatal intensive care units, every effort is made to give the baby normal nurturing, involving the parents if possible, so that he is not deprived of the normal experiences of a newborn.

Genetic defects, environmental causes, and exposure of the **embryo** to toxic (poisonous) substances are some of the many possible causes of mental retardation, another problem that can occur in infants. While many of these mental deficiencies cannot be cured, it is becoming clear that these children need and respond to stimulation of all kinds just as normal children do. Their development may be quite a bit slower than the average, but they can usually progress much more than was previously believed.

There are many sources of help for parents whose babies have special needs. There are professionals, of course—doctors, nurses, and therapists—but there are also many self-help groups. These are organizations made up of parents or families of children who have the same problem. Such a group works with the professionals in obtaining the best medical care. Its members share their experiences and give each other emotional support. The group also helps families to recognize the children's problems and to appreciate their accomplishments.

four months old. Maria seemed perfectly normal to her parents until it was discovered that she did not respond to loud noises and was partially deaf. Antonio was born blind. Each of these babies can be helped to lead a normal, happy life, but the handicap puts extra strains on them and on their family.

One increasingly common problem is the treatment of low-birth-weight babies. Sometimes these babies are premature (born early); other times they are full-term babies that are born with very low birth weights, sometimes because their mothers are very young, had very

· SUMMARY ·

- Newborn babies can taste, smell, see, hear, and feel pain. They have natural reflexes such as sucking, swallowing, sneezing, and yawning.
- Height and weight increase rapidly in the first year.
- Babies follow a well-established pattern of development. Gross motor skills develop before fine motor skills.
- A baby's failure to grow and gain weight may be due to poor nutrition, a medical problem, or a psychological problem.
- Babies need frequent feedings and diaper changes and a lot of sleep.
- A healthy, alert infant responds to being held, talked to, and sung to.
- Health care for babies includes checkups and immunizations.
- Accidents can be avoided if parents are alert to potential dangers.
- Resources are available to help families cope with disabilities.

TERMS TO KNOW

Babinski reflex
colic
fine motor skills
grasp reflex
gross motor skills
immunizations
Moro reflex
rooting reflex
stools
weaning

1. The _____ is the baby's way of searching for something to suck on.
2. Babies with _____ cry continuously even though they are not sick.
3. _____ is changing a baby's food supply.
4. You can observe the _____ by stroking the palm of a baby's hand.
5. A baby develops _____, which are related to large muscles, before _____.
6. The _____ is the infant's reaction to a loud noise or bright light.
7. A newborn baby's _____ will be greenish-black and sticky.
8. Infants should be given _____ to prevent common diseases.
9. Babies demonstrate the _____ by fanning their toes.

CHECK YOUR UNDERSTANDING

1. What are reflexes? Give three examples of those the infant shows shortly after birth.
2. What factors affect the child's pattern of development?
3. List three patterns of development in infants.
4. What is "failure to thrive"? What are some possible causes?
5. Describe the difference between feeding on a strict schedule and feeding on a flexible schedule.
6. What are two recommendations given by doctors for introducing solid food to a baby's diet?
7. List three ways of keeping a supply of fresh diapers.
8. Why is it important for a baby to play with people as well as toys?
9. Give five examples of clues indicating that an infant may be ill.
10. What are some sources of help for parents whose children have special needs?

·6·

COGNITIVE DEVELOPMENT
OF THE INFANT

"I'm bored," Melba Johnson announced to her husband, Cliff. "Our baby is not due for two whole months, and I've got everything ready that I can think of—clothes, diapers, crib, carriage, everything."

"What about toys?" Cliff asked. "From the books on child care I've been reading, I've found out that even newborn babies can learn a lot from toys. Let's go over to the toy store and see what they've got for infants."

"I've got an even better idea!" said Melba. "Let's make some toys ourselves. A project like that would help pass the time more quickly."

Cliff and Melba looked through their books on baby care, and decided that a mobile would be the best first toy for their soon-to-be-born baby. Its brightly colored moving shapes would attract the baby's attention, give the baby something to focus on, and help the baby recognize shapes and patterns—all important first steps in learning.

Melba and Cliff looked around their apartment for objects that they could use for the mobile. They found some bright red and yellow plastic jar covers, a small blue plastic bottle from a cosmetic sample, and a set of shiny metal measuring spoons.

Together they assembled the mobile with wire and a wooden bracket. They arranged the objects so that the mobile would look just as interesting from underneath—the baby's view—as it would from the side—the parents' view. Then they attached it to the crib and watched as the objects moved slowly in the breeze.

"Now all we need is the baby!" Melba said.

•

How does a mobile help a baby to learn?

•

What other kinds of learning toys might a couple make for their baby?

The newborn baby has a remarkable range of sensory abilities, as we have discovered. She can hear, see, taste, smell, and feel. These senses give her the capacity for **perception**—for receiving immediate information about the world around her.

Our knowledge and understanding of the world first comes through our senses. But these perceptions are received by the newborn in a confused and disorganized way. In order to understand what her senses are "telling" her, the baby must go through a learning process.

This learning process is directly tied to the process of physical growth. As the baby's brain and body develop, she can gain greater control over her senses. The perceptions of the newborn are abstract and general; as she grows and learns, she makes them more specific. Here is an example. All newborn babies share the general ability to make sounds. Whether a baby is born in Kenya or in Canada, her first cries and other noises sound very much the same. At this age a baby can make a wide variety of sounds, though they may not resemble the sounds of her parents' language. But as the baby learns to recognize the differences between sounds and to mimic specific sounds, she imitates the speech patterns of her family and community. Once she has begun developing skill in a specific language, she can no longer easily produce sounds that are very different from the sounds of her own language. For example, an English-speaking child or adult usually finds it hard to imitate certain sounds used in French or Spanish. But a young infant from any country can easily make these sounds.

Similarly, a baby first responds to the sight of her mother's face or some other familiar face. By the time she is nine or ten months old, she is firmly attached to a particular person, and it is not easy to substitute another.

PIAGET'S THEORY: THE SENSORIMOTOR PERIOD

The work of a Swiss psychologist named Jean Piaget (born 1896) has been an important influence on current practices in child rearing and education in many countries. His famous theory describes how children's intellectual, or **cognitive**, skills develop from infancy to adulthood.

Piaget's theory holds that all children pass through certain clearly defined periods in their intellectual growth. The first is called the **sensorimotor period** and it lasts from birth to one and a half or two years. Piaget divided this period of development into six stages.

In Stage I (birth to 1 month) the baby is **egocentric**, or aware only of herself. She does not realize that she is a distinct person, separate from her mother and father, her bottle, and the rest of the world. Her body movements are gross and uncoordinated and characterized by **neonatal** reflexes.

In Stage II (1 to 4 months) the baby forms new response patterns through a combination of her earlier reflexive actions. For example, her fist finds its way to her mouth through a coordination of arm moving and sucking.

In Stage III (4 to 8 months) the baby continues to form new response patterns and repeats them intentionally. She may shake a rattle, and when it makes a noise, she will shake it again.

In Stage IV (8 to 12 months) this coordination of movements and perceptions becomes more complex. Now the baby begins to understand that her actions lead to specific results. When she sees an object she wants, she may push aside obstacles to reach it, or she may try to get it by pushing her parent's hand toward it.

If someone hides a toy, however, the baby acts as though it no longer exists. This is because she has not yet developed what Piaget has called **object permanence.** That is, she does not know that an object continues to exist after it has passed out of her sight. As the baby progresses through this stage, she will learn to follow with her eyes an object that disappears from view, looking for a ball that rolls under a couch or for a bottle that someone takes away. By the end of this stage, games such as "peek-a-boo" delight the baby, because she is learning that objects exist apart from her perception of them—a very important developmental step.

In Stage V (12 to 18 months) these familiar behavior patterns are varied in different ways as the baby experiments. In Stage VI (18 months to 1½ or 2 years), the child starts to experiment mentally as well as physically. These last two stages will be discussed further in the next unit.

Piaget's theories have been criticized by some people who say that he sets the boundaries of his stages too rigidly. Nevertheless, Piaget's work revolutionized our understanding of the child's development. It called attention to the intellectual development of the infant—an area of study that was previously unexplored—and it showed that this development unfolds in an orderly way, just as physical growth does. It pointed out the importance of developmental steps that were previously taken for granted.

Still, Piaget's theory is only a broad outline of the child's pattern of development, and individual babies may vary widely from that pattern. Much depends on the baby's personality, her environment, and her genetic heritage, and on other influences we still know little about. Some babies (like some older children) learn best through hearing, others through seeing. Some have to touch something to really know what it is all about. Babies, as has been demonstrated, are alike in many ways, but each baby is also unique.

LEARNING ABOUT THE WORLD

When we think about babies learning to do something, we usually think of specific abilities. "Tommy learned to roll over today," the baby-sitter tells his mother. "Dawn learned to drink from a cup when she was six months old," her father remembers. But these specific abilities are part of a larger pattern. The baby is learning about the world and her place in it. Without this growing sense of reality, learning would be purposeless and haphazard.

One thing the infant learns, as Jean Piaget points out, is that objects are permanent. To a newborn there are no lasting realities: Objects and people come in and out of view. If her grandfather leaves the room, it appears that the baby thinks he has disappeared forever. Gradually, the infant learns to understand the concept of permanence.

The baby also learns to understand concepts of space and time. Through experience with touching and handling objects, she gradually learns that objects have shapes and edges, and that small boxes fit into larger ones. Similarly, she learns that small boxes can be taken out of larger ones. She also learns, through crawling and walking, how she fits into the larger spaces of rooms and houses. In her crib or playpen she feels big; on the floor she is dwarfed by the furniture and the open space.

Time is an even more abstract concept, and babies in their first year develop only the most elementary notions of it. For the young baby there is only one time—the present. However, she does begin to get a sense of "before" and "after" by doing certain things in sequence. She cries, is picked up, and is fed. She will not develop a more complicated sense of time—a sense of the past and the future—until she is older.

Causality—the idea that certain actions cause certain results—is another complex notion. The groundwork for an understanding of

At six months babies begin to recognize their caregivers. Parents learn to interpret their child's non-verbal signals and respond to their needs. As babies develop, they learn to talk by imitating others. It is important to speak naturally with infants and not use baby talk. Babies enjoy musical sounds and rhymes which are not too loud. By the time infants are nine or ten months old, they may not be willing to communicate with strangers.

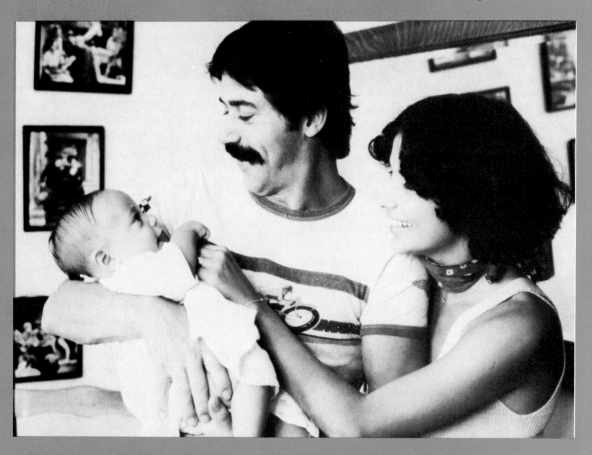

this idea is laid in the infant's first year. Babies are not really able to grasp the relationship between many of their actions and the results, but they do learn that *some* things they do produce results. Gradually Roberto learns that it is pulling the ring on the cradle gym, and *not* kicking his legs, that starts the music. Babies develop this sense of causality through trial and error, and it is still only weakly developed at the end of the first year.

MEMORY

The use of memory—remembering people, objects, and events—is very important to the learning process. The first thing that the baby learns to remember is the face of the person who spends the most time caring for her. Six-month-old Laura recognizes her mother's face when she appears; three months earlier she did not seem to know if it had been her mother or another person who picked her up when she cried.

Two types of memory tasks are *recognition*, or the ability to recognize something that one has seen before, and *recall*, or the ability to remember where something has been placed or other such pieces of information. Babies develop recognition before recall, but between the ages of eight and twelve months they do learn to remember, for example, where to look for a toy that has fallen out of the crib. At least, they remember it for a short time.

These memory feats may seem very simple. And so they are, but they are very important. In learning, just as in walking and talking, the child learns step by step. Without these basic skills and concepts, the child cannot go on to more complex behavior.

LEARNING TO TALK

On her first birthday Elaine had a vocabulary of three words: "mama," "da," and "'bye." That may not sound like a very great accomplishment, but it is. At birth Elaine could only cry; by the age of one she had mastered some of the basic steps of language.

Communicating with others is one of the most important skills a human being acquires. There are many ways to communicate: through touch, through gestures, through written symbols, through art, through music, through sign language. But by far the most significant is the power of speech.

Before a baby learns to talk, she practices many ways of communicating **nonverbally,** that is, without words. Crying, of course, is the earliest means of communication. During the first month the baby's crying is **undifferentiated**. That is, it is mostly a reflex reaction to the environment. Whether the baby is hungry, cold, wet, or in pain, her cries for help sound pretty much the same. Parents and others must figure out what need the baby is signaling. Is it time for a feeding? Is she uncomfortable? Does her diaper need changing?

Generally, crying is considered a sign of some discomfort, but it may be that some crying gives other information to us. Interpreting a baby's crying is one area that adults are still learning about. Perhaps the baby is telling us more than we think, but we do not know how to translate the cries. For example, Howard L. Golub of the Massachusetts Institute of Technology has developed a computer-based model of the newborn's cry using the cries of fifty-five normal babies. Matching this standardized model against the cries of babies with abnormalities, it may be possible to diagnose physical problems in newborns much more precisely than is now possible.

After the baby's first month, her crying becomes **differentiated**. Now she seems to cry in different patterns when she is hungry, uncomfortable, or angry. Her cries vary in pitch, intensity, and pattern. Although she is not consciously trying to produce these different types of crying, they soon become recognizable to her

A North American baby's first word is often "mama." So is a Chinese baby's, and an East African baby's too. In fact, all over the world, "mama" is one of the the first words that infants babble, long before they actually learn to speak the language of their country. How is it that babies born into totally different language groups use the same word for "mother"?

"Mama" is typical of the sounds that a baby playfully experiments with toward the end of the first year. Before that, the baby made only indistinct sounds that didn't sound anything like words. According to one theory, when the baby begins to repeat syllables like "ma-ma," "na-na," and "ba-ba," the parents are pleased at this sign of progress and imagine that these sounds are the baby's first words. It may in fact be the adults who originally assigned the meaning of "mother" to the sound "mama." Mothers, by responding to the sound with smiles and attention, teach their babies what it means. Similarly, a nursery word like "nana" comes to be associated with grandmother or nurse, and "dada" or "papa"—or "baba" in some parts of the world—comes to mean "father." (Of course there are variations. For example, in Hindi, the chief language of India, "mama" means "uncle.")

In the words that adults use for "mother" in various languages, we also find similarities, chiefly in the use of the sound *m*. Here are a few examples of how different peoples say "mother":

German: *Mutter*
Spanish and Italian: *madre*
Polish: *matka*
Swahili: *mama*
Hebrew: *ima*
Chinese: *mu-ch'in*
French: *mère*
Swedish: *moder*
Hindi: *mata*

Children, of course, usually continue to use the word "mama," or something like it, when they call their mothers. In English, a child may say "mommy," "mom," "mummy," "mum," "maw," or "ma." And a father may be called "daddy," "dad," "papa," "pop," "paw," or "pa."

parents. They can tell a cry of hunger from a cry of pain and respond appropriately.

Right from the beginning we see that communication involves two processes: sending messages and interpreting them. For the most part the baby only sends messages; it is the family's task to interpret them. But the baby is also receiving a message in turn: that communicating her needs brings a response.

The next stage in learning to talk is *cooing*, the name we generally give to a variety of simple sounds made by babies six weeks to three months old. These throaty gurgles and squeals are produced by chance movements of the vocal cords, which by this age have matured sufficiently to permit the baby to make simple sounds. The first sounds are generally vowel-like sounds like the *e* sound in the word "red" or the *u* in "run." One of the first few consonants the baby utters is *h*, which is associated with gasping and crying.

By the age of three or four months, the baby has begun to produce more consonant sounds, such as *m, n, p, b, d,* and *t,* and her vowel sounds are more distinct. At six months she enters the *babbling* stage. She repeats a variety of sounds as she lies contentedly in her crib or carriage. She may babble "ma-ma-ma-ma" or "da-da-da" or "boo-boo-boo," sometimes very loud and clear. It's not known if there is any purpose to these babblings, however; the baby seems to do it just for the fun of it. It probably

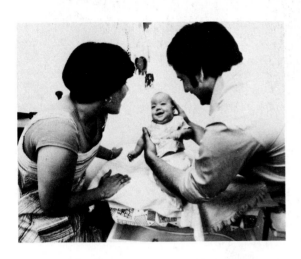

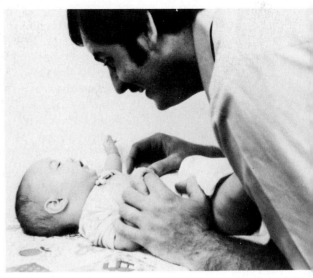

feels good to her mouth and sounds good to her ears. Deaf children often start to babble, but soon stop, probably because they cannot hear themselves and thus are not stimulated by the sound of their own voices.

Somewhere in the second half of the first year, a baby will begin to imitate sounds that she hears, often apparently quite by accident. She will listen attentively to some sound and then begin to babble; her babbling is an imperfect imitation of the sound she has heard.

Later, perhaps at the age of nine or ten months, she will consciously imitate the sounds made by others. She may understand only a few words—her own name, "bye-bye," and perhaps a few others—but she takes increasing delight in imitating speech through babbling.

Real language generally begins at about the age of one year. The baby will learn to associate words like "dada" and "mama" with specific persons. (See the "Of Interest" box on page 87.) She will also obey simple commands like "Clap hands." If she is crawling, she will stop when her name is called and come to the per-

Babies enjoy imitating the sound they hear. They lie in their cribs seemingly taking delight in babbling. "Ma-ma-ma" and "da-da-da" can often be heard at this stage. It is unknown whether these sounds refer to the parents. Children who speak languages with other words for mother and father also make these sounds in infancy.

son who calls her. She still babbles but now has added a few real words to her vocabulary. Her simple words may stand for more complex ideas. She may point to the door and say "'Bye." She may mean "I want to go outside," or "Mommy went out." She may cry and say "Ba," which may mean "I am hungry and want my bottle," or "I threw my ball out of the playpen and now it's gone." She may become frustrated when her simple words are not understood in different circumstances. It takes patience and some experimenting to find out just what she is trying to communicate. Of course, the process of learning to speak goes hand in hand with the process of learning to understand a language. This development of this understanding follows a pattern, just as learning to speak does.

According to the psychologists Eleanor Kaplan and George Kaplan, there are five stages in this process: (1) *Newborns* respond to sounds, and can tell which direction they are coming from. They can also distinguish between different sounds, depending on frequency, intensity, duration, and tempo. (2) At about *two weeks* of age, infants start to tell the difference between voices and other sounds. Voices are now more effective in calming a crying baby and in encouraging her to make contented cooing sounds. (3) At the *end of the second month*, babies start to tell the difference between the emotions expressed by different tones of voice. They smile and coo when a voice is friendly, and cry or withdraw when it is harsh. They can also tell the difference between a voice they have heard before and a stranger's. (4) At about *five or six months* of age, babies become conscious of intonation—the pattern of sounds that make up sentences. They can tell the difference between questions, exclamations, and statements, even if they do not understand the individual words in the sentences. (5) Toward the *end of the first year*, babies can distinguish among the various individual sounds of their language. They can

tell the difference between pairs of words that have the same final sound but a different beginning sound (like "cat" and "hat").

DIFFERING PATTERNS

At one year Eddie has learned to listen to people speaking to him, he has learned how to make different sounds, and he has learned to connect meanings with words. He has started to build a vocabulary. His next step will be to increase his vocabulary and to put the words he knows together in sentences.

As in all areas of child development, babies learn to talk at different rates. Joan, a lively, friendly baby, was speaking a few short but complete sentences before she was a year old. More reserved and shy, Joshua seemed to prefer to listen rather than talk himself. Yet both Joan and Joshua are normal, intelligent babies.

Besides personality differences, the child's environment influences the rate at which she learns to speak. Babies whose parents talk to them frequently seem to join in the conversations at an early age, whereas babies who are handled in silence and whose parents do not seem to find much pleasure in talking to them learn to speak more slowly. Of course, this doesn't mean it's a good idea to constantly bombard a baby with sounds. A baby needs to have some time to herself, to experiment with making her own sounds.

Slowness in learning to speak is not by itself a sign of abnormal intelligence. Many normal children do not talk much until they are two or three years old. But if a child seems slow in other ways as well, the doctor will probably recommend some testing.

There are certain ways to encourage a baby to learn to talk. Speak to her clearly and slowly and in a soothing tone. Humming, singing, and talking to the baby during routine events such as feeding, bathing, or changing diapers all give the baby a sense of being loved as well as cared for physically. Name objects as you give them to the baby. Short, repetitious, rhythmic verses and songs delight babies. Games with action as well as words ("This little piggy went to market" and "pat-a-cake") amuse them a great deal as well. Year-old babies enjoy looking at simple picture books while someone points out the objects and names them. They particularly like pictures of animals and small children. Of course, all these activities must be geared to the child's age and development. It makes no sense to try to read to a three-month-old, but at that age, the baby will surely respond to lullabies and gentle talk.

HOW BABIES LEARN

It is easier to see the pattern in *what* babies learn than to explain *how* they are doing it. Acquiring a simple new skill, whether it is sitting up or grasping an object or imitating a sound, involves very complex relationships between the baby's brain and her body.

The brain is the key organ in cognitive development. Along with the spinal cord, it is part of the *central nervous system*, which is the complex network throughout the body that permits messages to be "sent" and "received" between the brain and the nerves in various parts of the body.

The brain is made up of three parts: the

Every section of the brain has a particular function in the learning process. Babies receive input from their five senses (hearing, smell, taste, sight, and touch). This input is catalogued by the brain and stored in its proper place.

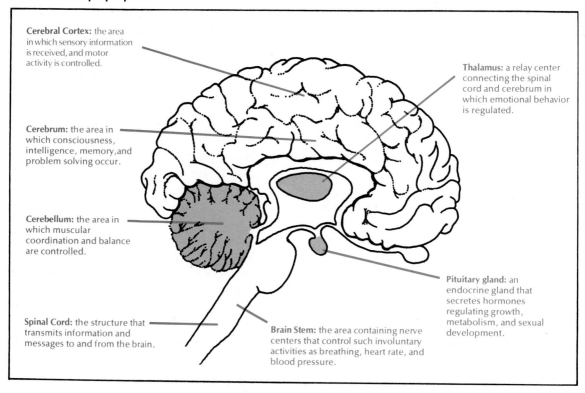

Cerebral Cortex: the area in which sensory information is received, and motor activity is controlled.

Thalamus: a relay center connecting the spinal cord and cerebrum in which emotional behavior is regulated.

Cerebrum: the area in which consciousness, intelligence, memory, and problem solving occur.

Cerebellum: the area in which muscular coordination and balance are controlled.

Pituitary gland: an endocrine gland that secretes hormones regulating growth, metabolism, and sexual development.

Spinal Cord: the structure that transmits information and messages to and from the brain.

Brain Stem: the area containing nerve centers that control such involuntary activities as breathing, heart rate, and blood pressure.

hindbrain (including the cerebellum and the brainstem), the midbrain, and the forebrain (including the cerebrum). Every area of the brain is associated with a particular function, although no one area is completely responsible for any single function. The cerebellum coordinates muscular movements and, along with the midbrain, monitors posture. The brainstem governs involuntary actions such as breathing. The cerebrum, occupying the topmost portion of the skull, is the largest section of the brain. It is divided into two hemispheres—left and right. The left half controls the right side of the body, and the right half controls the left side. The upper surface of the cerebrum—the cerebral cortex—contains most of the master controls of the body. The cortex grows more slowly than other parts of the brain. However, it is quite well developed by the time a baby is two years old.

Some general learning theories can be applied to babies. One is **classical conditioning** (or associative learning). The best-known example of this kind of learning is the experiment with dogs made by Ivan Pavlov, a Russian scientist, in the late 1890s. Before he fed the dogs, he rang a bell. The dogs salivated when they saw and smelled the food. After repeating this procedure several times, Pavlov rang the bell but did not offer any food. Yet the dogs had learned to connect the ringing of the bell with feeding, and they salivated at the sound of the bell alone.

Of course, human beings are not dogs, and there is some debate about whether they can be "conditioned" like animals. But it is clear that babies do learn to associate certain activities with certain sounds, smells, or sights A hungry baby sitting in her highchair has learned to associate the sight of the can opener with food, so she starts to get excited when she sees it taken out of the kitchen drawer.

Another kind of learning is called **operant conditioning**. B. F. Skinner, a psychologist, has become famous for his experiments with pigeons and rats. According to Skinner, when animals (and people) are rewarded for certain actions, they will continue to perform them. He used a series of experiments with pigeons to prove his case. Pigeons were rewarded with food when they pecked at a green bar in a specially constructed box, and they were punished by a mild electric shock when they pecked on a red bar. It did not take long for them to tell the colors apart and to avoid the red bars.

Here again, human beings cannot be compared to pigeons. But babies, just like everyone else, generally want to get pleasure out of their activities. They will continue to do things (like smiling, cooing, and crying) that bring rewards (like a parent's loving response) or the expected results. The reward, however, must be a meaningful one.

Reinforcement has been shown to be more effective in some cases if it is intermittent (that is, if the reward is given after *some* trials) rather than if it is continuous (given after every trial).

Still another type of learning is **imitative**. Watching other people and trying to do what they do is an important way babies learn. First, babies imitate familiar acts, such as waving or clapping. Then they try to copy a part of a new activity, because the whole is too complicated. A baby may, for example, imitate the sound made by two blocks banging together instead of the motions made in a whole series of block-building exercises. Later the baby tries to imitate the effect without going through all the steps. For example, one researcher spun a top while a year-old baby watched. The infant could not duplicate his skill, but she got the toy to move by turning it with both hands. Finally, in the second year, the baby is able to imitate familiar and unfamiliar sounds and gestures rather accurately.

No single theory explains how infants learn. Learning is a complex process that involves all these types of responses and others.

Here are some selected items from infant intelligence tests to give an idea of what kinds of behaviors can be measured.

CATTELL

Key age: 6 months

Secures cube on sight. (When child is sitting in upright position before a table, a one-inch cube is placed within easy reach.)

Lifts cup. (A straight-sided aluminum cup is placed upside down within easy reach of child as he is sitting at the table.)

Fingers his reflection in mirror. (While child is in sitting position, a framed mirror is held before him so that he can see his own reflection but not anyone else's.)

Key age: 12 months

Beats two spoons together. (Tester takes two spoons, one in each hand, and beats them gently together while child watches. Then they are presented to child, one in each hand.)

Places cube in cup. (Aluminum cup and one-inch cube are placed before child and he is asked to put "block" in cup. If no response, placing cube in cup is demonstrated and request repeated.)

Marks with pencil. (Paper and pencil are placed before child and she is asked to write. If no response, writing is demonstrated and request repeated. Credit if child makes any marks on paper.)

Rattles spoon in cup. (Aluminum cup is placed before child and spoon is moved back and forth in it, hitting edges; then spoon is placed beside cup with handle toward child.)

Has speaking vocabulary of two words. ("Ma-ma" and "da-da" are not credited.)

Hits doll. (Rubber doll with whistle is put face up on table before child and tester hits it gently with open hands several times. Credit if child makes a definite attempt to hit doll.)

GESELL

Key age: 28 weeks

Lifts head.
Sits erect momentarily.
Holds two cubes more than momentarily.
Retains bell.
Vocalizes **m-m-m** and polysyllabic vowel sounds.
Takes solid food well.
Brings feet to mouth.
Pats mirror image.

Key age: 52 weeks

Walks with one hand held by someone.
Tries to build tower of cubes, fairly.
Dangles ring by string.
Tries to insert pellet into bottle.
Uses two words besides "mama" and "dada."
Gives toy on request.
Cooperates in dressing.

BAYLEY

5.8 months
Explorative paper play. (Present a piece of paper to child so he may grasp edge of it.)

5.8 months
Accepts second cube. (When child is holding one cube, place a second within easy reach.)

5.9 months
Vocalizes pleasure.

5.9 months
Vocalizes displeasure.

6.0 months
Reaches persistently. (Place cube just far enough away from child so he cannot reach it. Credit if he reaches persistently.)

11.5 months
Inhibits on command. (Say "No, no," when child puts an object in mouth or on some other pretext. Credit if he inhibits.)

11.6 months
Strikes doll. (Place small rubber whistle doll on table. Hit it smartly to produce whistle, encourage child to do the same. Credit if he imitates the hitting motion.)

11.7 months
Imitates words. (Tester says several words, like "mama," "dada," "baby." Credit attempts to imitate.)

12.1 months
Imitates rattling of spoon in cup with stirring motion. (Credit if child succeeds in making a noise in cup by a similar motion with spoon.)

Source: Kessen, Haith, Salapatek, "Infancy" from CARMICHAEL'S MANUAL OF PSYCHOLOGY, volume one, third edition, edited by P.H. Mussen (New York: Wiley, 1970).

MEASURING INFANT INTELLIGENCE

In most situations there is no need to measure a baby's intelligence. It is enough to know that the baby is growing, learning, and developing normally. Parents and others who are very anxious about whether a child will grow up to be "smart" are placing too much emphasis on only one of many aspects of an infant's development.

Still, there are some situations in which it is useful to be able to judge a baby's intelligence—for example, when there is a suspicion that a child may be mentally retarded or when parents who have one retarded child want reassurance that their second child is developing normally.

Intelligence is very difficult to measure, particularly in babies. Intelligence is the ability to learn and to use knowledge, or to understand concepts and relationships. As we have seen, those skills are just beginning to develop in babies. They cannot talk, and language is the primary tool by which a tester evaluates intelligence. One can observe babies' behavior, but their behavior is rather limited. Still another problem is that babies have no motivation to participate in the tests. The baby does not know or care she is being tested. Why should she make a tower out of blocks—even though she is capable of doing it—unless she wants to?

Keeping all these limitations in mind, here are the three most popular tests used to determine infant intelligence:

The **Gesell Developmental Schedules** are standardized observations that measure four major areas of development. They cover an age range from four weeks to six years. The observations emphasize *motor behavior* (holding the head up, sitting, creeping, and so on), *adaptive behavior* (eye-hand coordination, problem-solving ability, such as being able to put a round peg in a round hole), *language behavior* (understanding others, babbling, facial expressions, gestures), and *personal-social behavior* (feeding herself, responding to others, and so on).

The **Cattell Infant Intelligence Scale** covers the ages from two to thirty months and is an adaptation of standard adult intelligence tests. It largely tests perception (paying attention to voices or bells) and motor abilities. The **Bayley Scales** cover the ages from birth to thirty months and also mainly adapt items from adult tests. The "Based on Fact" box on page 92 shows some of the items on these three tests.

Whatever value infant intelligence tests have in indicating a child's developmental progress, they are not much help in predicting later achievements in school. They can tell in very general terms which children are so deficient in developmental skills that they are likely to have problems. For the great majority of babies who are not deficient, there is no way of telling which ones will be superior or inferior in intelligence.

INFLUENCES ON INTELLIGENCE

Many factors are involved in how a baby learns. Some believe that the main influence on a baby is probably the genetic "blueprint" inherited from her parents. But later on, other influences seem to be more important, and the genetic influence can be overridden, depending on what happens to the baby.

For instance, malnutrition can have a devastating effect on a baby's learning abilities. Infants who are severely malnourished suffer brain damage that apparently cannot be reversed.

By themselves social and economic class are not related to intelligence. Babies born to poor, middle-class, and rich families show the normal ranges of intelligence. It is likely, however, that the difficulties of coping with unemployment, poor health, stress, discrimination, and instability faced by poor families do have an effect on some babies. It is not that a baby suffers because she has fewer toys or other material goods than do babies born to richer families. But those who care for her may be unable to find time or energy to spend with the baby in productive ways. Adults whose every ounce of energy is devoted to earning a living or dealing with other kinds of stress are often unable to do more than take care of a baby's physical needs, and frequently lack the knowledge of what the infant needs beyond the physical. One of the problems our society faces today is finding ways to give financial and educational support to families with many economic and social problems so that they can raise children with strong enough learning skills to improve the family's economic status.

Psychologists and others concerned with child development have long debated about whether "nature" (genetics) or "nurture" (environment) is more important in determining a child's future. There is no easy answer, but it seems clear that both are important. A child is born with a certain inherent genetic potential that cannot be changed. But what happens to her later in life depends as much on family life, schooling, and other influences as on her genes.

Furthermore, children can change, often dramatically, when their environments change. Although there is no doubt that very early experiences are critical in a child's development, there is no reason to give up on a child whose infancy has been deprived in some way. Studies of Korean war orphans adopted by American families have shown that despite their early deprivations, they adjusted well to a more stable environment, and when they reached school age they showed intelligence and achievement comparable to those of other children.

A GOOD LEARNING ENVIRONMENT

Fortunately, most North American babies born today are not subject to the most extreme forms of deprivation common in much of the rest of the world: starvation, severe illness, and extraordinary poverty. Most parents do want to provide their babies with a good environment to grow physically and intellectually. They often ask, "What can we do to help our baby learn?"

The answer is that there are many things to do and most of them come naturally. Taking care of the baby's physical needs, making sure she is properly fed and clothed, keeping her healthy—these are the first steps, for a baby needs a strong body and an alert mind in order to be able to learn. Taking care of the baby's emotional needs as well is important—holding her when she cries, comforting her when she is frustrated or angry, laughing and smiling and talking with her.

Beyond these basic steps, parents can make sure that the infant's environment—whether at home, with a baby-sitter, or at a day-care center—is stimulating and interesting and appropriate for the baby's developmental level. We have already discussed some of the toys and types of play that are appropriate for babies of different ages. Some research suggests that it is not the number of toys that an infant has that counts, but the variety. A few toys that are right for the baby's age and developmental level can be sufficient. It is easy to tell when toys are right, because if they are not, the baby will not play with them. However, parents and other adults must be alert to a baby's changing skills. New toys can be offered at intervals until the infant shows by her interest that they are right.

Toys should be chosen to provide opportunities for babies to do many different kinds

Learning environment is important in developing babies' cognitive abilities. Infants need stimulating objects which appeal to them. They enjoy mobiles, rattles, and soft items in interesting and colorful shapes. Toys need not be store-bought. Egg cartons, plastic containers, and paper towel tubes are some of the "found" objects which often attract babies. In addition to a good learning environment, babies need to interact with their caregivers. Infants learn through observation and imitation. Their optimal development depends on their being loved, comforted, and reassured.

B. F. Skinner, the psychologist who developed many of the principles of operant conditioning we have described, devised an ingenious "baby-tender" for his daughter Deborah when she was born in 1944. Skinner built a crib-sized living space with sound-absorbing walls and a large picture window. Air entered through filters at the bottom and was warmed and moistened. Then it circulated upward, through and around the edges of a tightly stretched canvas mattress. Over the canvas passed a strip of sheeting 10 yards long, which could be changed for a clean section by cranking.

When she was born, Deborah was placed in the baby-tender. She wore only a diaper and was completely free to move about. The air was always warm, moist, and filtered. Loud noises were muffled, and a curtain over the window shielded her from bright lights. Skinner made special toys for her to grasp and rigged a music box so that she could play a tune.

Deborah seemed to thrive in this protected atmosphere, Skinner writes in his autobiography, *The Shaping of a Behaviorist*. She slept well, developed strong muscles, was resistant to colds and other infections, and seemed content. She was taken out of the baby-tender for feeding and for changing her diaper, and after the age of six months she spent about one and a half hours a day in a playpen or chair.

Skinner tried to market the baby-tender under the name "Heir Conditioner," but it was unsuccessful. There were manufacturing difficulties and some bad publicity when a magazine article called the device a "baby box," which seemed to suggest that Skinner was experimenting on his daughter just as he did with pigeons in the so-called "Skinner box."

The baby-tender idea never caught on, although some people even today have similar custom-made baby-tenders. Why do you think most people resisted the idea? What do you think are the advantages and disadvantages of the device? How might an infant feel about spending most of her time in a baby-tender instead of being in close physical contact with her parents?

Source: B.F. Skinner, THE SHAPING OF A BEHAVIORIST (New York: Alfred A. Knopf, 1979).

of things—build, cuddle, throw, roll, put together, take apart, string, and sort. They should provide different kinds of stimulation—touch, sound, and sight.

As important as it is to provide the baby with many kinds of stimulation, it is just as important not to overstimulate. Sometimes parents are so eager to give a baby the proper learning environment that they offer her too many toys, too much talk, too many new experiences. Faced with that bombardment of perceptions, the baby is likely to tune out most of them. A more relaxed atmosphere is best. The baby is the best guide; watch her, listen to her, and gradually introduce new toys and experiences that will encourage her to learn.

Consistency is also important. Learning is part of a baby's everyday existence, but it is not an activity that can be precisely scheduled. There should be time in every day for quiet play, for talking, for singing, and for other learning activities, but these activities should be flexible. "Learning activities" should not be saved up for a special day; they should fit into the baby's normal routine.

Further, babies need encouragement. They should not be held back when they are ready to learn. Sometimes busy parents, perhaps already overburdened with caring for other children, try to restrict a child's interest in creeping and standing, because it imposes still more demands on them. But if babies are stifled in

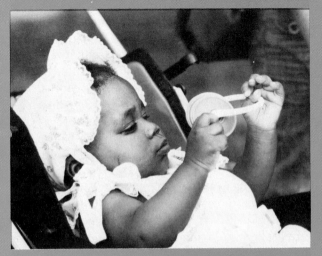

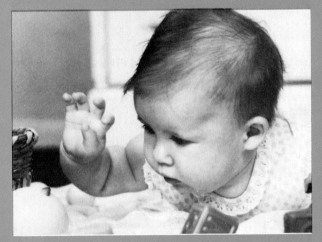

Babies need time to themselves to explore their environment. They enjoy objects which can be patted, pulled, hit, looked at, or simply touched. Parents must supervise these activities, but should try not to interfere with them unless the baby is in danger.

one area, such as motor development, they are likely to be stifled in others, such as cognitive development. Older children can be enlisted to watch the baby or to do other chores so that the mother or father can watch the baby. Of course, the baby's desires cannot always be the guide; sometimes she must be restrained, even if it is frustrating to her. But in general the baby's growing interest in exploring should be encouraged.

One of the best ways to promote an infant's intellectual development is to provide appropriate, supervised activities in an emotional atmosphere of loving acceptance and encouragement.

FIVE BABIES AND WHAT THEY HAVE LEARNED

Let us now take a look at five babies at different ages and see what they have learned. Although we concentrate on their mental achievements, it must be remembered that their physical development, as described in the last section, has proceeded in stages along with their intellectual growth.

Cheryl is one month old. She is a rather passive baby and does not cry a great deal. She responds to her mother's voice, though, and has begun to make small throaty sounds. She is alert about one hour out of every ten. She can coordinate her eyes in following light or an object sideways and up and down. She prefers patterns to colors, brightness, or size. Cheryl expects to be fed at four-hour intervals and cries when she needs to be changed. Her eyes follow a toy if it is moved from her side toward the center of her body. She gets excited when she sees a person or a toy, but sees them only if they stay in her line of vision.

Jon is three months old. An active baby, he has quite a vocabulary of sounds—cooing, gurgling, chortling, squeaking, and more. He listens to voices and smiles in response. He can be attentive up to three-quarters of an hour at a time. He can follow an object from side to side for at least ten seconds when it is moved slowly in front of his face. He can distinguish near and far objects in space, and becomes bored with repeated sounds or images. If an object is dangled in front of him, he will swipe at it with a closed fist or reach with two hands for it. Jon can hold an object in his hand voluntarily. He has begun to show memory, and he waits for an expected reward like a feeding. He has begun to recognize and differentiate family members, and he quickly calms down if he sees a human face. His own hands and feet interest him greatly, and he likes to explore his face, eyes, and mouth with his hand. When he hears a sound, he searches with his eyes to find the source. He responds to most kinds of stimulation with his whole body.

Six-month-old Steven is already an energetic baby. His vocal range includes babbling, which he varies by tone, volume, pitch, and speed. His vocabulary includes mostly vowels, but he has begun to use a few consonants (m, n, l, s, sh, and b). He expresses pleasure and displeasure with his voice, by grunts, growls, or gurgles. When he is really excited, he squeals with delight. He can turn and twist in all directions. Music appeals to him, and he stops cooing to listen. He can stay alert for two hours at a time, and he is awake nearly half of the time now. He reaches persistently for anything that comes in his range, usually, but not always, looking at the object. He likes to turn his toys upside down and look at them from a different perspective. He inspects objects at length, and when he drops something, he will reach to grasp and pick it up. He can transfer objects from one hand to the other. He can hold one block in his hand and reach for another. He has begun to understand the relationship between his hands and the objects they are handling.

Self-feeding may be messy, but it's a learning experience for baby. It's also a sign of baby's growing independence from her caregivers.

At nine months of age, Alison already has a vocabulary of two words: "mama" and "dada." What is more, she knows that these words refer to specific people. Her intonation patterns of speech have become more distinct, and her parents can tell whether she is happy or sad by the sound of her voice. She can imitate coughs, tongue clicks, and hisses. She understands and responds to a few words besides her name, the most important of which is "no-no." If she is asked to do a simple thing, like "wave bye-bye," she can understand and respond. She has begun to recognize that objects have dimensions, and she approaches a small object with her finger and thumb, and a large object with both hands. She likes to put her fingers in the holes of her pegboard. Her memory has improved, and she can remember a game like "peek-a-boo" that was played the day before. She can anticipate the return of a person who leaves the room, and uncovers a toy she has seen hidden. Alison can pick up and manipulate two objects, one with each hand. She can hit or push two objects like blocks against each other. She may drop one of two blocks to pick up a third, or she may put one in her mouth to pick up a third. She has begun to be aware of vertical space and is afraid of heights. She has also shown the first traces of persistence, refusing to allow herself to be distracted when she wants to get out of her playpen.

Peter, twelve months old, has a vocabulary of eight words; besides, he can make words that imitate the sounds of animals ("bow-wow"). He babbles short "sentences" that are not really English but sound like real sentences in some private language of his own. He has learned that objects are detached and are separate things that can be related in time and space and absorbed into his play. He likes to look at objects from different directions, rotate them, turn them upside down, stack them, knock them over, and put them into containers and take them out. He can search for a hidden object even if he has not seen where it was hidden but only knows where it was last seen. He may even look for it in more than one place. He remembers events for longer and longer times. He can imitate actions more precisely and deliberately. Peter uses his right hand more often than his left to reach things, and he can use one hand to hold objects and the other to explore them. He has become an active experimenter, using trial and error to discover new ways to do things and solve problems, such as untangling two toys. Peter recognizes different people, and strongly expresses his likes and dislikes. After he is shown how, he can build a tower of two or three blocks. He can group a few objects by color or shape. He may think out a series of actions before he tries them, like putting all his toys into a box and then dumping them all out.

Of course, each baby follows a slightly different timetable, but these five "typical" examples show just how remarkable the infant's capacity to learn really is.

· SUMMARY ·

- Infants learn mainly through using their senses and through their physical movements.
- The infant is just beginning to understand concepts such as time, permanence, and causality.
- Infants learn to communicate in stages—crying, cooing, babbling, and talking. They also start to understand a few spoken words.
- Several theories of learning can be applied to infants: classical conditioning, operant conditioning, and imitative learning.
- A baby's intelligence is influenced by genetics and environment.
- The best learning environment for a baby is stimulating, interesting, and suited to the individual child's developmental level. Consistency and encouragement help a baby learn.

TERMS TO KNOW

causality
cognitive
differentiated
egocentric
imitative

nonverbally
object permanence
perception
reinforcement
sensorimotor period

1. A baby has developed _____ when she realizes that objects exist apart from her _____ of them.
2. _____ learning, such as copying the action of waving, is an important part of the baby's _____ development.
3. In Stage I of the _____, the baby is _____, or aware only of herself.
4. At about one month of age, a baby's crying becomes _____, helping her to communicate her needs _____.
5. Infants gradually develop the idea of _____ by learning that some of their actions produce results.
6. Operant conditioning is a type of learning that involves receiving rewards, or _____.

CHECK YOUR UNDERSTANDING

1. What four concepts about the world and her place in it does an infant learn?
2. What is an example of a recognition task that an infant might master? A recall task? Which type of memory task will a baby master first?
3. What is the difference between undifferentiated and differentiated crying?
4. Briefly describe the stages of the infant's speech development, from crying to the use of real language.
5. What factors influence the rate at which a child learns to speak?
6. How does operant conditioning relate to a baby's learning?
7. What is imitative learning?
8. Name the three most popular tests used to determine infant intelligence.
9. What are three basic ways parents can help their baby learn?

· 7 ·

SOCIAL/EMOTIONAL DEVELOPMENT
OF THE INFANT

Betsy Owen could not believe what was happening. Gary, her friendly, outgoing baby, had suddenly begun to scream and cling to her sweater just when she was about to go out for a lunch date.

The baby-sitter, Willie, was perplexed, too. "Babies usually like me," he said. "I can't imagine what I did to upset him. He took one look at me and started to scream."

Betsy wondered what was wrong. She knew Gary wasn't sick, since he had just had a checkup the other day. Maybe he had become too attached to her. In two months' time, Betsy was planning to go back to work, since Gary would be a year old by then. Now she began to wonder if that would be possible.

Despite her worries, Betsy decided to leave Gary with Willie as planned. She went to meet her friend Carmen for lunch, and over their meal she told Carmen about Gary's tantrum. "Do you think I've spoiled him by spending so much time with him?" she asked anxiously.

"Oh, no," said Carmen with a laugh. "It's perfectly normal for a baby Gary's age to cry when you leave. You should have heard how my Carlos used to howl when he was Gary's age, even when I left him with his grandmother. Of course, my little one is just two months old—she couldn't care less who I leave her with."

"But is he going to be so miserable every time I go out?" Betsy wanted to know.

"I'm afraid so, at least for a while," said Carmen.

Betsy returned home early just to reassure herself. Gary was playing happily on the floor with Willie, but as soon as he saw his mother, he chortled with glee and crawled to her as fast as he could move.

●

What are some things that a baby-sitter could do to comfort an infant who is crying because his mother went out?

●

How might a mother like Betsy make separation easier for herself and her baby in the future?

In every culture, the birth of a baby is a special event. It marks not only the creation of a unique human being, but also the arrival of a new member of the family and of the larger community as well. In a small community, such as a tribal village, all the people participate in celebrating a birth. In a larger community, many friends and relatives will congratulate the parents and join with them in rejoicing over the newborn. From birth, a baby is already part of a group, whether large or small. Although the newborn is not yet truly a social creature, the first relationships he has with the members of his group will affect his social and emotional development. Of course, these relationships work both ways, and the baby also influences the behavior, responses, and attitudes of the people around him.

During infancy, the child gradually gains a clearer sense of himself and forms attachments to other people, at the same time that his physical abilities and cognitive skills are developing. There is, in fact, a strong relationship among all three areas of development. All the physical and cognitive factors we have discussed so far also help to shape the infant's emotional development and determine how he becomes a special individual with a personality all his own.

THEORIES OF PERSONALITY DEVELOPMENT

Many people have tried to explain why adults grow up to be so different from each other. Frequently they have singled out early childhood experiences as an important influence. In Western society two influential theories about early childhood development are those of Sigmund Freud (1856–1939) and Erik Erikson (born 1902).

Freud, the Austrian doctor who founded psychoanalysis, believed that all humans pass through certain phases in the course of their development from birth to adulthood. In the first phase—during infancy—the primary interest is in pleasure that can be obtained through the mouth, primarily by nursing or eating but also by sucking on things such as a pacifier or the thumb.

Whereas Freud stressed biological needs and instinctive desires, Erik Erikson, an American psychoanalyst, believes that cultural and social influences are most important in personality development. He describes a series of eight "crises" in life that influence ego, or personality development. The first crisis—**basic trust** versus basic mistrust—occurs in infancy. Erikson believes that the creation of basic trust—through consistent attention to the infant's needs—lays the foundation for later emotional growth. The trusting baby is content because he feels that his world is a safe place, and he is able to develop a secure sense of his own value as a person. The baby who has been mistreated or neglected feels frightened and insecure and is likely to have emotional or behavioral problems later on.

While the theories of Freud and Erikson are not the last word on personality development, they have strongly changed the way that adults think about and care for infants.

INFLUENCES ON PERSONALITY DEVELOPMENT

These broad theories tell us a great deal about infants, but they do not explain why no two babies—just as no two adults—have exactly the same personalities. We might be able to think of possible explanations, but there is no way to prove that certain personality traits are linked to specific influences. "Glen has his father's temper," says Aunt Margo. "Francine is so independent because she is an only child," her father explains. Actually, each child's personality is the product of many intertwined sets of influences. Some are genetic and some environmental; some are strong and some weak; some are relatively fixed and others changeable.

One of the stronger influences is the baby's temperament, or basic disposition. Babies seem to be born with a certain set of characteristics that influence their behavior. Right from birth Catherine was restless, jumpy, extremely sensitive to stimulation of all kinds, easily distracted, and irregular in her patterns of eating, sleeping, and elimination. Her younger brother Paul, on the other hand, was agreeable to change, regular in his habits, more easily soothed, and relaxed. There is not much parents can do to change this inborn behavior pattern. Babies do change, however, as they mature. But it is hopeless to try to turn a very active baby into a quiet and passive one.

The parents' personalities come into this picture, too. Parents who are themselves active and energetic appreciate a baby who is like themselves; they may be disappointed if he is not. On the other hand, parents who like to take things more slowly may feel overwhelmed by a very active baby who is constantly in motion and seems always to need their attention. The process of adjusting to each other's temperament is not always smooth. Even very young babies are sensitive to the feelings of others. A baby can sense his parents' anxiety, exhaustion, or ill health through the way they handle him. This in turn affects his own development.

The cultural heritage of a baby's family also contributes to his personality development. People of different religions, nationalities, and ethnic groups have different beliefs about raising children. They will teach their children the particular values and customs of their own cultural group, and their expectations of how children should behave will influence the child from a very young age. These cultural differences are especially noticeable in the United States, whose people have a wide variety of backgrounds.

Another influence on personality is the baby's sex. There is much disagreement about which sex differences are inborn and which ones are learned, but most people believe that the biological differences between males and females do have some influence on personality. Also important, however, is the way parents treat babies of different sexes. Studies have shown that in general they look at and talk more to girls and encourage more physical activity and independence in boys. Many parents today feel that it is better to treat children as individuals rather than as "little men" or "little women." Nevertheless, cultural traditions which hold that boy babies and girl babies should be treated differently are still a strong influence on parents.

The baby's birth order in the family is still another influence. A first child is likely to be given more attention as a baby than are later arrivals to the family. He is likely to become more independent, more sociable, and more competitive simply because he is the first. Parents treat their first child differently; in some ways they are more involved with him, but at the same time, they are more anxious and less sure of themselves.

Much also depends on the type of family the baby is born into. In North American society, the **nuclear family** (consisting of the mother, the father, and their children) used to be the most usual environment for bringing up babies. Today many other family situations exist. Parents may be separated, divorced, or widowed, so that only one parent brings up the baby. Or a baby may be part of an **extended family,** where other adult relatives such as grandparents, uncles, and aunts may help care for children. Many mothers of young children work, and their babies are cared for by relatives, by baby-sitters, or at day-care centers. Each of these distinct situations will have an effect on the emotional life of the baby. But we cannot say whether any one of these arrangements in itself is better or worse for the baby

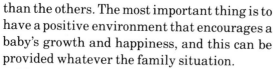
Many different people make up a baby's world.
Baby's attachment to others will be affected by
how frequently she interacts with them.

than the others. The most important thing is to
have a positive environment that encourages a
baby's growth and happiness, and this can be
provided whatever the family situation.

Most research on child development has fo-
cused on the mother as the primary caregiver.
As more babies are raised in nontraditional
family settings, questions about the role of
other people in the baby's personality development will become even more important.

Fortunately, most babies are adaptable.
They can adjust to different situations and different adults with reasonably good results.
Most important is that those who take care of
the baby should be aware of his very strong
needs to form attachments to them.

ATTACHMENTS TO OTHERS

At first the baby experiences only himself.
This does not mean that he is not aware of his
parents or of other people; he is indeed keenly
aware of them. But to him they seem to be extensions of himself instead of separate people.
It is as if the arms that cradle him, the hands
that touch him, are somehow parts of his own
body.

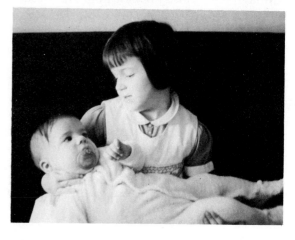

Most North American childrearing practices are based on the idea that the child will be brought up by his biological family—his own mother and father—or, in some cases, by other relatives. In Israel a very different practice has emerged—that of communal childrearing. Pioneers in a young country born of social and military upheaval, Israel's citizens have set about consciously trying to create a new society. Women have been needed as workers as well as mothers, and child-rearing practices are geared to free them from full-time parental responsibility. These goals are most clearly seen on the kibbutz (pronounced kib-BOOTS), a relatively small settlement mainly devoted to agriculture, but usually with some industry as well. About 4 percent of Israelis live on kibbutzim. Each community is a single economic, social, and political unit. All property belongs to the community, and in turn the community provides what its members need. The kibbutz is, in effect, one big family and one big work place.

How are children raised in this special setting? Usually from the fourth day after birth, kibbutz babies live in a special children's house with other babies their own age. They are raised as a group, and are in the charge of a kibbutz member who is assigned the job of caregiver.

The baby's mother nurses her at the children's house until she is six months old, when she is weaned. Her father visits her at the children's house, and later in the first year she makes visits to her parents' home.

The kibbutz caregiver, not the parents, tends to the children's basic needs. The role of the peer group—the child's age-mates, with whom she spends most of her time—is more important in this system than in ours. Her peers provide her with companionship, stimulation, and a sense of security. A child frequently is more upset when one of her age-mates leaves the room than at the departure of her parents or caregiver.

When infants can crawl, they are placed in large playpens, where they play alone for hours at a time. They must resolve their own conflicts because no one will intervene to settle a struggle over a toy or similar problem. Instead of becoming "bullies" or withdrawing, the babies learn to accommodate to each other's needs and to help each other. A very strong sense of group identity and cooperation is formed through these experiences.

Bruno Bettelheim, a psychiatrist who has worked with children, studied the child-rearing practices on an Israeli kibbutz. In his book *The Children of the Dream,* he says that the kibbutz system is well suited to the kibbutz society and fulfills its goals—creating an egalitarian society. All members of the kibbutz are guaranteed health care, housing, food, and education. In return the kibbutz controls most aspects of the members' lives. However, living on a kibbutz is voluntary in Israel; those people who find the life too stifling or controlled can leave. Those who choose to stay appear to feel that their sacrifices of personal goals are well worth the rewards they share in building a special kind of community.

Source: Bruno Bettelheim, CHILDREN OF THE DREAM (New York: MacMillan, 1969).

However, even at an early age he is forming **attachments,** or bonds, to other human beings. Many researchers now believe that important bonds between mother and child are formed within the first few hours after birth.

That is one reason more and more hospitals are allowing mothers to room-in with their babies after birth instead of whisking the newborns away to the nursery ward.

Some intriguing clues about the process of

This chart is based on the work of Mary D. Ainsworth, a psychologist who has studied attachment behavior in African babies. She showed that babies demonstrate their growing attachment to their mothers through certain behaviors occurring in a certain sequence. Although the ages at which babies exhibit these behaviors may vary, the behaviors themselves and the order in which they appear seem universal.

ATTACHMENT BEHAVIORS

1. DIFFERENTIAL CRYING: Baby cries when held by someone else, but stops when picked up by mother.

2. DIFFERENTIAL SMILING: Baby smiles more readily at mother.

3. DIFFERENTIAL VOCALIZATION: Baby babbles and coos more to mother.

4. VISUAL-MOTOR ORIENTATION: Baby keeps looking at mother, even when apart from her.

5. CRYING WHEN MOTHER LEAVES THE ROOM.

6. FOLLOWING: Baby creeps or walks after mother when she leaves the room.

7. SCRAMBLING: Baby climbs over mother more often than over others, exploring her by playing with her face, hair, and clothes.

8. BURYING FACE IN MOTHER'S LAP: The babies studied did this only to their mothers.

9. EXPLORATION FROM MOTHER AS A SECURE BASE: Baby leaves her side but returns from time to time; this contrasts with the distress the baby shows when the mother herself gets up and goes away.

10. CLINGING: Baby clings when afraid of stranger, when ill, or when mother returns after an absence.

11. LIFTING ARMS IN GREETING: Baby does this when mother returns after an absence.

12. CLAPPING HANDS IN GREETING.

13. APPROACH THROUGH LOCOMOTION: Baby creeps or walks to mother as soon as possible after she returns from an absence.

Source: Mary Ainsworth, "Patterns of Attachment Behavior Shown by the Infant in Interaction with his Mother," volume 10 (Detroit: The Merrill-Palmer Quarterly of Behavior and Development, 1964), p. 51-58

bonding have been found in animal studies. Harry Harlow and Margaret Harlow, psychologists at the University of Wisconsin, studied infant-mother relationships among rhesus monkeys. They found that infant monkeys taken away from their mothers and raised in isolation showed severe emotional distress. When they were taken out of isolation and placed with other monkeys, the infants' behavior was abnormal and they avoided contact with the others. The Harlows also experimented to see what would happen when infant monkeys were taken from their mothers and raised in cages with surrogate, or substitute, mothers. Each baby monkey was given two such "mothers"—both were cylindrical forms made of wire mesh, but one was covered with terry cloth, while the other was bare. Bottles to feed the infants were connected to both "mothers." The Harlows found that the baby monkeys much preferred clinging to the cloth figure than to the wire figure, even when they were getting milk only from the wire "mother." The infants even recognized the cloth "mother" after a year's separation. The study concluded that it was not just feeding that created a lasting bond, but the provision of close bodily contact. However, even the babies

raised by the cloth "mother" did not grow up normally. They missed some of the vital **interaction** that only their real mothers could have provided.

The study of bonding in human infants and their mothers is currently of great concern to researchers. They are interested in how these bonds form, what encourages them, and, just as important, what discourages them. Much less attention has been paid to other bonding pairs—father and infant, for example—but these bonds may also turn out to be highly sig-

The Harlow experiments with monkeys are world famous. These psychologists studied the interactions between monkeys and surrogate, or substitute, mothers. In one set of experiments, when a frightening mechanical toy was placed in cages with the wire-mesh mother, the monkeys huddled in a corner or raced about frantically. In the cages with terry-cloth mothers, the monkeys clung to the surrogates for comfort. To create lasting relationships between infants and their mothers, close bodily contact also is very important.

The stereotypical picture of a new father shows him at first as a helpless bystander pacing the floor of the hospital waiting room while his wife gives birth, and then as a proud but still helpless bystander handing out cigars to his friends and colleagues. Margaret Mead, the well-known anthropologist, once said that in our culture fathers are a biological necessity but a social accident.

The father-infant bond is no doubt more important than anyone has realized. But very little research has been done to determine in what ways fathers develop an attachment to a baby, how his experience differs from the mother's, and how it affects the baby.

One study, conducted by Ross D. Parke, examined the interactions of a small group of fathers and their infants, aged two to four days old, in a nursery in Madison, Wisconsin. These fathers had attended childbirth education classes and had been present at both labor and delivery. Dr. Parke found that when both parents were with the newborn, the father played a more active role than the mother. He held the baby nearly twice as much as the mother, talked more to the baby, and touched the baby slightly more than the mother. However, the mother smiled at the baby significantly more than the father. Furthermore, when the father was present, the mother tended to smile even more at the baby and take a generally more active role in touching and handling him.

Dr. Parke repeated his study again in a larger group of parents in a Cincinnati hospital. Here the fathers had not taken a course in childbirth education. Again he found similar results; the only difference was that these fathers also tended to take responsibility for feeding.

In studies conducted at Boston Children's Hospital Medical Center under the direction of Dr. T. Berry Brazelton, a pediatrician, fathers of young infants related just as much to their babies as the mothers, but in different ways. Fathers tend to play games with babies right away, making faces and sounds to entertain them. Mothers tend to be gentler and more soothing.

Think about the ways in which you have seen fathers relate to their children. Are they usually excluded from child-care by the women in the family?

Or do they choose not to participate for lack of interest or time? What do you think the father's role should be in infant care?

Do you think that there are differences between the way a father and a mother feel about their baby? Are there differences in the way the baby feels toward the mother and father?

nificant for babies. (See the "Self-Probe" box on this page.)

While we do not know exactly how bonding occurs, we do know that it does happen in normal infants. At the age of one month, many babies smile back at a face or voice. They make eye-to-eye contact. The sight of a human face will often calm a crying baby. By the age of two months, the baby smiles at people other than his mother, such as his father, grandparents, sisters and brothers, and baby-sitter. A three-month-old baby smiles spontaneously and immediately. Of course, adults respond to this and smile back. The baby's behavior is thus rewarded, or reinforced. By this age as well the baby knows several people and may even have some preferences about who holds or feeds him. By the age of five or six months, a baby can distinguish between a familiar person and a stranger. And what is more, he knows whether he likes the person or not. By this time he also has learned to distinguish between himself and his mother in a mirror. He will pat his mirror image and smile at himself.

This growing sense of self and others also brings some distress to the baby. While as a tiny baby he reacted in almost the same way to all people, by the age of eight or ten months he may be afraid of people he does not know. He may even cry when approached by a friendly, smiling stranger. By this age he knows his mother, and does not want her to leave him, even with another familiar person. Babies who are raised in an environment with few adults seem to fear strangers more than those who have much contact with many different people. Fear of strangers, or **stranger anxiety,** seems to be particularly intense in babies who have formed very close attachments to their caregivers. Although the baby's emotional distress may upset his parents, particularly if the "stranger" is a close friend or a visiting relative, they should understand that it is actually a sign of his cognitive development. As we saw earlier, the newborn responds to the pattern of features on a human face, but he does not yet make a distinction between one face and another. The infant who shows stranger anxiety has now learned to identify the particular face of the person he is most attached to, and he is disturbed when he sees faces that look different from it. As cognitive development proceeds, he will gradually learn to accept the sight of other friendly people outside his immediate family.

COMFORT AND DISTRESS

Babies communicate a significant emotional state—distress—through crying. It is, as we have seen, their main method of communication. How the baby cries and how the parent responds are important in determining how deep the attachment between them will become. Parents soon learn to interpret the cries—as a sign of hunger, pain, or boredom, for example—and so they can respond appropriately. Or at least they try to. However, even if their efforts to comfort the baby—feeding, changing, holding him—are successful, that may not be proof that they have understood the meaning of the cry. It may be simply that the comforting gestures satisfy and reassure the baby.

Many mothers who breast-feed assume that a crying baby is hungry. But one study showed that when mothers gave up breast feeding because they felt their babies were hungry and cried too much, the babies cried just as much when they were switched to a bottle.

Peter Wolff, a psychologist, has studied the patterns of babies' cries and has identified several types: (1) the *basic rhythmical cry,* which is often called the hungry cry, although it may not be associated with hunger; (2) the *mad* or *angry cry,* in which the baby forces excess air through his vocal cords; (3) the *pain cry,* distinguished by a sudden onset of loud crying and then a long cry, followed by a long period of holding the breath; and (4) the *cry of frustration,* which starts from silence, like the pain cry, but does not involve extended holding of the breath. In this type of crying, the first two or three cries are long and drawn out.

According to Wolff, there are several reasons babies cry in the first week of life: hunger, cold temperature, pain, and disruption of sleep. Apparently being wet or having soiled diapers does not make such young babies cry. Wolff found that babies who were undiapered stopped crying just as often as those whose diapers were changed.

In the second week, another reason for crying occurs—when a feeding is interrupted. By the third week, when the baby is in a fussy mood, a variety of stimulations such as a human voice or "pat-a-cake" motions may cause him to cry. When he is relaxed and content, these same activities make him smile. Similarly by the fourth week, a fussy baby will

Child Photographer

Appointments, May 12

9:00 A.M.— Photo sitting with Melanie, 2 years old. Parents want both black-and-white and color shots to send to grandparents.

10:00 A.M.— Appointment with Reynolds family to select photos from proofs.

10:30 A.M.— Meet Sam Dayton at *Herald* office to plan photo spread on day camp.

11:30 A.M.— Photo sitting with Lazar children (Susan, 12; Victor, 8; Jim, 5): individual and group photos.

12:30 P.M.— Lunch meeting with high school photography students to plan photo contest.

Phyllis Brady has a busy morning ahead—and that's just half the day. The life of a photographer is often hectic and pressured, but it is also exciting and varied. Phyllis is a free-lance photographer. That is, she does work for many different people and gets paid by the job—unlike salaried photographers who work on the staffs of companies, magazines, or newspapers. She has her own studio and darkroom, where she develops and prints her photos.

Phyllis's speciality is photographing children. She has a way with children, and they seem to relax quickly in her studio. She never tries to "pose" them in formal arrangements. Her photographs have a natural, unposed look.

Photographers usually build up a business slowly on the basis of personal references. They have to be able to show a portfolio of their work to prospective customers.

Photographers develop their craft and individual styles over years; however, academic credentials are not as important as demonstrated talent. One can take photography courses in high school, at adult education programs at community or four-year colleges, or in workshops run by photographers or clubs. Art and design courses are also desirable.

Photographic equipment, darkrooms, and studios represent a considerable investment of money; however, these can be acquired gradually. Many photographers start out as assistants to already established professionals; other jobs are available in commercial darkrooms or in large photographic studios.

In addition to their commercial work, many photographers take pictures for exhibitions of their own work, or for use in magazines or newspapers or books.

The first requirement for success in this field is talent; then hard work, perseverance, and attention to detail enter the picture. The job is best suited for those who can organize a busy schedule efficiently and still manage to pursue their creative interests. Photographing children takes special skills. To capture the child's personality and mood in a form that can be cherished for years is a challenge and a joy.

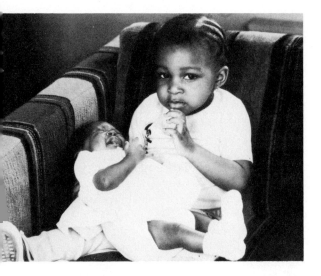

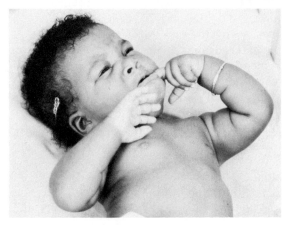

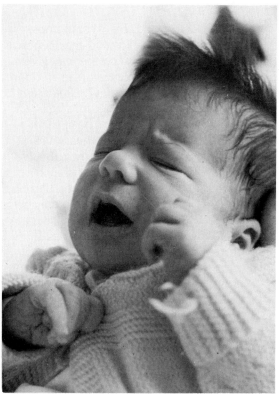

Babies cry for many reasons. They are hungry, tired, bored, in need of help, ill, or want comforting. Parents learn to distinguish the different cries and ascertain the problem. Experts believe that children should be comforted whenever they cry to build a sense of trust between the child and his caregivers.

cry when he is tickled. Some babies cry when they are first introduced to cereal. For reasons unknown, they rarely cry when given fruit.

Between the ages of one to two months, the baby will cry when he is left alone or when a familiar toy animal is removed. These reactions get even stronger by the age of two or three months, and now when his caregiver leaves or when a toy is taken away, the crying may be accompanied by thumb-sucking.

What can be done to comfort a crying baby? If the cry is really caused by hunger, and some cries surely are, he can be fed. If it is caused by being too cold, he can be dressed more warmly.

If he is in pain—because of an open diaper pin, say—that can be fixed. But these are the easy-to-understand cries of distress. The most troubling signals the baby gives are those that seem to be general fussiness, irritability, frustration, and boredom. Here the answer is that whatever works to soothe the baby is the right response. The traditional methods—rocking, cradling, singing, patting, cuddling, humming, swaddling him with blankets or clothing—all work for some babies at some times. In general, rhythmic movement and soothing sounds seem most effective in calming babies.

A rather dramatic example of the calming

What should you do when a baby cries? This question arises time and again among parents, baby-sitters, and other caregivers. Sometimes a baby is picked up and tended to immediately; other times he is left to "cry it out"; sometimes, because he is left alone in his crib or playpen, he cries for a while before someone even hears him.

In many cultures, particularly in the less developed parts of the world, no such question arises. When a baby cries, there is an immediate response. The baby may be carried on his mother's back for most of the time, and he is breast-fed as soon as he shows signs of fretting. Child care is not just the responsibility of the mother, but of many people in the community, particularly young girls under the age of ten. The baby is handled constantly by many people, and his discomforts are eased as quickly as possible. Among the mountain-dwelling Arapesh, a tribe of the Pacific island of New Guinea, there is a saying, "A child's crying is a tragedy to be avoided at any cost."

These patterns of child rearing are typical of hunter-gatherer societies, such as certain African tribes who wander from place to place, hunting animals and gathering wild plants for food instead of living in settled agricultural or industrial communities. Some anthropologists have argued that since this type of existence is similar to the way the first human societies lived, it sheds some light on what is "natural" human behavior. They point out that modern child-rearing practices in the Western world are very different from this "natural" model. Independence, self-reliance, and the parents' busy schedules are emphasized in our culture, while the hunter-gatherer societies are more child-centered. This is seen especially in the way such peoples approach the problem of relieving a baby's distress.

There are, however, some arguments on the other side. We are not really sure, for example, that present-day hunter-gatherer peoples really live the same way that early humans did thousands of years ago. Besides, even if they are similar to our ancestors, their customs do not necessarily meet the needs of society today. Parents who live in a modern industrialized society cannot adopt cultural patterns of a totally different type of society. For example, if an American child were raised to be totally dependent on a small group, he would have difficulty leaving that group when he became an adult.

These examples do show, however, that our child-rearing practices are determined not only by parents' individual preferences and the baby's needs, but also by the culture in which we live.

Adapted by permission. Judy Dunn, "Distress and Comfort," in the series THE DEVELOPING CHILD, edited by Jerome Bruner, Michael Cole, and Barbara Lloyd (Cambridge: Harvard University Press, 1977), p. 87-93

effect of sound on a newborn baby was demonstrated by Lee Salk, a child psychologist. Among newborns in one nursery, he placed a machine that made a sound imitating the human heartbeat. Another group of babies were kept in a separate nursery without the heartbeat machine. The babies who heard the "heartbeat" gained more weight and cried less than the babies in the ordinary nursery. Salk concluded that the newborns who heard the rhythmical sound were more relaxed and less anxious than the other babies.

Perhaps more important than the particular method chosen to soothe the baby is just the fact of responding itself. Even though the seemingly inconsolable baby continues to cry, he should not be abandoned. Even what appears to be an ineffective response reassures

Tenderness and patience are needed to comfort a crying infant. Persistent crying may be a signal that something is physically wrong with the baby.

the baby that someone cares. It reinforces his budding sense of trust.

Many parents are wary of responding too quickly or too often to a baby's cries, for fear that they will "spoil" him. Not all experts agree on this subject, but many believe that it is not possible to "spoil" a young baby and that it is much better to try to soothe him than to ignore him. The baby is not consciously trying

to monopolize his parents' time, although it may seem that way to them; he is simply expressing his needs in the only way he can. Of course, there is a difference between a crying three-month-old and an older baby. When a baby is ten months or a year old, he has learned that he can attract his parents' attention by crying. By that time there are certain occasions when it is not wise to give him everything he wants simply because he cries. If, for example, Ken cries because his mother takes away his older sister's marbles when Ken starts to put them in his mouth, that is no reason to let him keep them. Or if Juanita cries because she is put to bed and wants to watch television with her older brothers instead, she should not be allowed to stay up just to stop her tears. But for young babies the best response to crying is prompt and loving attention.

Babies who are brought up in institutions and who are deprived of interaction with their mothers or a mother-substitute suffer deeply from the loss of a human partner who responds to their cries. The effects of such a loss are sometimes devastating, as some studies have pointed out, although there are also other factors in an institutional environment that may affect an infant's behavior. Babies who are physically well tended, but whose cries are not answered, soon become listless and withdrawn. Their physical health and their mental growth also suffer.

Babies need many things, as we have already seen, but most of all they need love. They feel loved when they are able to be in touch with other people—through bodily contact, through sounds, through voices—and in this way they develop a sense of trust.

PROMOTING INDEPENDENCE

The baby learns to trust others little by little. Learning to trust himself—to gain the confidence he needs to move toward independence—is a more subtle achievement. Yet it is just as important for healthy emotional development and, eventually, for a positive sense of his own worth.

Of course, no human being is truly independent. We are all tied to others through bonds of love, obligation, and our common humanity. Society could not function without an understanding of our mutual dependence. In Western society, independence and individuality are highly valued, and so we train our children to become independent as early as possible. This is not true throughout the world, however. The Japanese, for example, stress the bonds of interdependence and mutual obligations. Children in each society are raised somewhat differently.

Certainly an infant in his first year is largely dependent. But there are signs that this young individual is learning how to do things for himself, to express his own personality, and to recognize the limits of his own powers.

To encourage independence in a baby, parents can do various things. The baby makes many of his first attempts to assert himself at feeding time. Here parents must learn to trust the baby's sense of what is right for him. As long as the baby eats a balanced diet, approved by his pediatrician, there is no need to try to force him to eat more than he wants to, or to eat foods that he does not like. If he loves peas and wants them at every dinner, let him have them. Or if he makes a face and spits out prunes, try pears. However, his tastes may change later, and it is worth offering him prunes again in a few months to see if he will now accept them.

The baby's efforts to feed himself should be encouraged, even if it means that the feeding takes longer and results in drips and spills. The baby can only learn if he is allowed to try for himself. Using a spoon, however awkwardly, and his fingers will give him a sense of mastery over an important activity of life.

Similarly, a baby can learn to help dress himself as early as nine months of age. He can be asked to hold out his arms and legs when being dressed. Dressing himself completely comes much later, but his early experiences will make that time much easier.

Playtime is another source of growing independence. A baby who sits up, crawls, and rolls over should be praised for his achievements. He should be allowed to struggle a little, too— to reach a ball that has rolled across the playpen—because that will strengthen his sense that he can control his own body. His caregivers can invent little games—putting a ribbon around his foot and letting him remove it—that let the baby show off what he can do.

All these attempts to encourage independence should be geared to the baby's developmental period. A baby given a task that is too complicated for him will only become frustrated and angry.

Independence comes from a sense of security and from opportunities for freedom. It cannot be forced. Furthermore, babies often choose when and how they want to be independent. When Jamie is busily playing on the floor, he may crawl on his own into the next room and play there all alone. But he may wail in misery if his mother goes out of the room and leaves him alone.

Like many emotions, a sense of independence is a changing mood. One day little Ann is confident, happy, assertive; on the next she clings to her father and whines when he puts her down. Independence comes slowly, and sometimes unevenly. The infant who is given a basic sense of security will eventually take charge of many aspects of his own life.

AN INFANT'S EMOTIONS

Emotions are not easy to study or analyze. Not only are they quick to change, but they are also difficult to describe. Think of how poets have struggled over the ages to tell us about "love," and how many different kinds of "anger" there are.

Since adult emotions are so difficult to define, what can be said about infants' emotions? Certainly they have feelings and are sensitive to even the slightest changes in environment and in the moods of their caregivers. As we have seen, they can communicate different emotional states through crying and body movements. But we are not really sure when they develop complete emotions in the adult sense.

A newborn seems to have only two simple emotional states—unhappiness and happiness, or perhaps dissatisfaction and satisfaction. Many of the baby's responses that look like expressions of emotion are actually reflexes, such as the **Moro reflex.** As the baby matures, his emotions become differentiated; that is, they develop into more clearly recognizable different feelings of frustration, rage, affection, and so on.

Fear is one emotion that babies seem to develop at a relatively early age. As they become more aware of their environment and of the size and shape of objects, they begin to realize that they are small and vulnerable. They may be frightened by a loud noise, an abrupt change in temperature, or a sudden movement. They may fear people who speak loudly or pick them up roughly.

Fear of heights is common, and seems to be related to baby's growing sense of space. Other anxieties, such as fear of the dark, may develop in the second year, when the child has broadened his experiences and improved his imagination.

The infant's fears are normal. A baby has a sense of his need to protect himself, and anything strange and forceful is likely to appear threatening to him, even if it is not. Frightened babies should always be reassured and comforted, no matter how unrealistic the fear.

Babies can also be angry. An infant's anger is just another form of self-protection. At first it is a way of expressing the urgency of his needs.

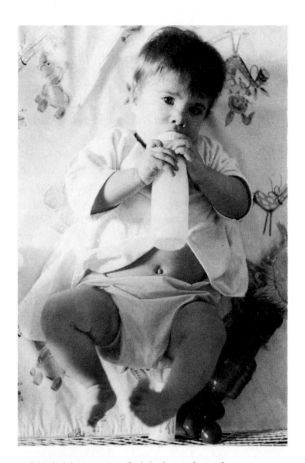

Babies begin to assert their independence by attempting to feed or undress themselves. In infancy this independence is not consistent.

The most common reason for an outburst of rage is a delay in being fed. The baby is angry when he has to wait for food, and he shows it by crying, screaming, waving his arms and legs, and tensing his body.

Later he will show similar responses when his movements are restricted. As Selma Fraiberg puts it in her book *The Magic Years,* "The desire to look, to touch, to handle is as urgent for the baby as hunger and as necessary for his intellectual growth as the books we will give him later on. Too many restrictions on mobility create irritability, temper outbursts and conflicts between the baby and family."

Until a baby is a year old, his outbursts of anger are spontaneous. He is simply reacting to the stresses he feels in the only way he knows. Parents are often troubled by these outbursts. They may become angry themselves, but this only adds to the baby's rage. If they are overanxious and try to stop his outburst by giving him something, they are teaching him that this behavior is a good way to get what he wants. At times the angry baby may actually have a real need—such as food—and this need must be met. But at other times the best reaction is simply to be calm and patient, to comfort without giving in to unreasonable demands. Babies cannot be allowed to hurt themselves or to have everything they want, but their feelings must always be acknowledged with understanding.

Perhaps, as Wolff's study of babies' crying suggests, babies do experience more varied types of emotion than we realize. We can tell, however, when a three-month-old is happy and when a six-month-old is mad. We know that babies form very early and strong attachments to others, that they derive pleasure from their contacts with these favored people. But it is not clear exactly when complex emotions like love develop.

PATTERNS OF SOCIAL AND EMOTIONAL DEVELOPMENT

Remembering all the individual differences that affect a baby's emotional and social development—genetic inheritance, inborn temperament, environment, health, parents' attitudes and habits—let us review the development of some "typical" babies to see what kinds of progress they make in their first year.

Most of the time Joel, one month old, is impassive. Although he cries quite a lot, much of the time his crying cannot be attributed to a specific need. He smiles at his parents when they smile at him, and he makes eye contact with them. He likes to be held and cuddles into the person holding him. He even seems to recognize his mother's voice when she speaks to him.

Babies don't hide their emotions. It's apparent when they are angry. Temper tantrums are not usually a problem unless they occur too frequently.

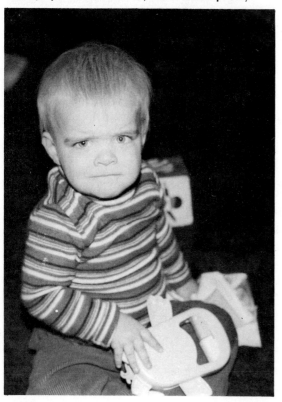

At three months, Cicely is quite involved with her parents and also with her grandmother, who takes care of her several days a week. She has begun to chortle and squeal, sometimes when people appear, but other times just for her own amusement. She has begun to realize that her hands are extensions of herself and takes delight in examining them. She smiles spontaneously and turns her head to look at someone who speaks to her.

Six-month-old Maria knows her name and smiles when she hears it. She likes to look at herself in a mirror and touches her image with what seems to be affection. She likes children, too, and smiles and reaches out to touch her older brother and sisters when they play with her. Maria is beginning to be afraid of strangers, but she is surrounded by many people much of the time, and so it hardly presents a problem. Nicholas, at nine months, is clearly very attached to his mother. She can hardly leave the room without his crying and reaching for her. When she is around, though, he is a very cheerful and even a sociable baby. He likes to perform his small repertory of tricks—playing "pat-a-cake" and "peek-a-boo"—and then wait in anticipation for the approval he expects. He tries to imitate what his parents do when they play with him. Other children interest him, but he will not let them touch his toys.

At twelve months, Michael is quite sophisticated emotionally and socially. He has discovered that he is a person in his own right and is quite proud of that fact. However, his growing sense of independence is still very weak, and he needs frequent reassurances that his parents are around to help him out of trouble. He likes other people, and has developed preferences for certain toys. Along with his growing skills, Michael is learning to assert himself, often to his parents' dismay. He sometimes refuses to eat a food that he has always loved; naptime has become a battle; and he will not give up a toy or other object when asked. But despite these negative periods, Michael is a happy, cheerful child. He has a strong sense of himself and of others, and he has brought joy to his whole family.

PROBLEMS IN EMOTIONAL DEVELOPMENT

Sometimes even very happy babies develop habits that concern their parents very much. They suspect that the baby is showing signs of an emotional problem. One such habit is *head banging,* which is common among babies six months to a year old. Some babies bang their heads rhythmically and forcefully against the sides of the crib. Another variation is rhythmic head rolling. Still other babies get on their hands and knees and jounce against their heels in a steady rhythm.

Parents are particularly concerned because they feel head banging will hurt the baby and that it is a sign of abnormal intelligence. In fact, this distressing habit does not seem to harm babies at all. It is probably a way of releasing tension, since babies seem to bang their heads more before going to sleep than at any other time. Some precautions can be taken by caring parents. They can pad the sides of the crib so that the baby will not bruise his head. They can play some soothing, rhythmic music that might satisfy the baby's needs. Cuddling him or giving him a warm bath before bedtime may also be helpful. Scolding or trying to restrain him will not help and may even make him more tense.

Another very common behavior that worries parents is *thumb-sucking*. A normal reflex behavior, thumb-sucking takes place even in the uterus. Most babies suck their thumbs (or fingers) at a very early age. Parents worry that this behavior will cause protruding teeth and that it is a sign that the baby is deprived emotionally. Dentists generally frown on thumb-sucking past the age of four or five, and some orthodontists advise discouraging the habit in the early years as well. Professional opinion, however, is divided on this question. Most babies who suck their thumb outgrow this habit naturally, and unless they are not developing normally in other ways, it is not a cause for concern.

Similarly, many babies develop an extreme fondness for a particular object—a toy, a blanket, even a special piece of cloth. Such *security objects* are usually soft reminders of the bodily contact that soothed all cares when the baby was smaller. He usually needs them only at naptime or in new circumstances. It is perfectly normal for these attachments to develop, and despite parents' fears, babies eventually give up the treasures.

Another habit that is of concern is *pica,* that is, eating substances like paint, plaster, dirt, or cloth. It is not very common, but it occurs frequently enough to worry parents. This habit is not well understood by doctors. One possible cause may be a diet deficiency or the body's inability to make use of certain food substances. Another cause may be an emotional disturbance. Pica should be discouraged because children may eat very poisonous substances, such as chips of paint that contain lead. If babies continually eat something that shouldn't be eaten, particularly if they favor just one substance, the doctor should be consulted.

Young babies with severe emotional problems generally show many signs of distress— lagging physical growth and mental development. They cannot express their needs in speech, but they express their despair with their bodies. More often than not, they become withdrawn, passive, inactive, and unresponsive. These symptoms are part of the "failure to thrive," which we have already discussed. They have often been observed among babies in institutions who have not been given stimulation and individual attention. The symptoms can also occur in a seemingly well-cared-for baby whose mother (or other caregiver) for some reason has not formed an emotional attachment to the baby.

In these cases both the mother and the baby need help. The mother may be unsure of her new role; she may not have wanted the baby in the first place; she may be distracted by personal health or marital problems and unable to devote the proper attention to the baby. Or perhaps she has a personality that is altogether different from the baby's and she is having difficulty adjusting her ways to fit the baby's needs. Professional counseling can often make a big difference in helping her to cope with the baby, and in helping the baby thrive.

One special group of children—autistic children—do not develop normal emotional or social relationships. They do not develop a clear sense of self or of others. They retreat into a world of their own. Very little is known about the causes of **autism.** Unlike failure to thrive, it does not seem to be related to the parents' behavior toward the child. Much can be done in training these children to live with their families and to take care of themselves, but unfortunately there is as yet no cure.

Such extreme cases are rare, and for most babies, emotional development is normal. Sometimes there are setbacks—for instance, there may be a separation or death in the family. Babies react to severe emotional stress within the family. Recognizing that such events can affect the baby's emotional development is very important. Steps can then be taken to lessen the impact on his growing sense of personal attachments. Providing a loving substitute parent, and trying to ensure a stable environment at home—no matter what the crisis—can make these periods less traumatic for the baby.

· SUMMARY ·

- Personality is influenced by temperament, parents' personalities, culture, sex, birth order, and type of family.
- A baby soon forms attachments, or bonds, to other human beings—especially to the mother or other principal caregiver.
- Babies are often fearful of strangers. Gradually they learn to accept new people.
- Responding to an infant's crying reinforces his sense of trust.
- Babies should be encouraged to learn to do things themselves when ready.
- As babies mature, they develop emotions such as fear and anger.
- Behaviors such as head banging and thumb sucking are generally no cause for concern. Other unusual behavior may signal an emotional problem.

TERMS TO KNOW

attachments
autism
basic trust
bonding

extended family
interaction
nuclear family
stranger anxiety

1. A(n) _____ includes relatives such as grandparents, aunts, and uncles.
2. According to Erikson, _____ is established through consistent attention to an infant's needs.
3. Children affected by _____ do not develop normal emotional or social relationships.
4. _____ is a fear that seems particularly intense in babies who have formed very close _____ to caregivers.
5. The _____ consisting of a mother, a father, and their children is not as common as it once was.
6. Babies need _____, or meaningful activity between themselves and a caregiver, to grow up normally.
7. _____ is the process of forming attachments to other people.

CHECK YOUR UNDERSTANDING

1. According to Erik Erikson, what happens if an infant is not able to develop basic trust?
2. List six influences on personality development.
3. What is meant by the statement, "At first the baby experiences only himself"?
4. How does a growing sense of self and others bring distress to the baby?
5. List four patterns of babies' cries identified by Peter Wolff.
6. How can a crying baby be comforted? Why is it important to respond to a crying baby?
7. What can be done to encourage independence in a baby?
8. Why do babies develop fear?
9. Name two situations that commonly cause a baby to be angry.
10. What signs of distress are shown by infants with severe emotional problems?

·8·
INTERACTION
WITH THE INFANT

Sarah was settled in her crib at last. Her parents, Jim and Karen, sat down in the living room to relax. "I can't believe Sarah is three months old already," said Jim.

"I can't either," Karen said. "But that reminds me of something we need to talk about. I'll be going back to my job in January, and we should work out some arrangements for Sarah."

"I've been thinking about that," said Jim. "My boss said it would be all right if I worked the Saturday shift at the plant and took Mondays off. That way I'll be home one day when you're at the office."

"Good," Karen said. "It should be fun having Sarah to yourself for a whole day—although it involves some work, too."

"I already know about that," Jim smiled. "Anyway, that just leaves four days a week. Do you think we could get a sitter?"

"Well, that nice Mrs. Ballantine we've had before might be willing to come in every day," Karen said. "I'll ask her about it next week."

"She seems like such a warm person," Jim said. "But if she's not available, there are a couple of day-care centers in town that we could look at."

"We'll have to think it over carefully before we decide," Karen said. "And we should also think about our evenings. Let's try to plan meals ahead so we both have more free time before dinner to play with Sarah."

"Okay. And after dinner, one of us can bathe her while the other does the cleanup," Jim suggested.

"That sounds good," said Karen. "Even with both of us working, we'll get to spend some time with Sarah every day."

Jim nodded. "With the months going by so fast, she'll be grown up before we know it. We don't want to miss a single day of it!"

•

Do you think it is important for both parents to participate in child-care planning when the mother goes back to work?

•

What other ways can working parents arrange to spend time with the baby?

Many factors influence the infant's physical well-being, cognitive development, and social/emotional growth, as we have seen. Among these important factors are the early experiences the infant has in interacting with the people around her. The most influential people in an infant's world are usually members of her immediate family—primarily the mother and, increasingly in today's families, the father. She also comes into contact with other significant persons, such as her grandparents, aunts and uncles, brothers and sisters, and baby-sitters or other caregivers who are not members of the family. It is important that these people understand and respond to the baby's physical and psychological needs and interact with her in ways that will help her to learn and grow.

The role of the baby's caregivers is to provide safety and security, stimulation that promotes development, and an atmosphere of love and understanding. Of course, every family has personal problems now and then, but if there are very serious problems, it may become difficult for the parents to provide the kinds of interaction the baby needs. For example, the baby's mother may become ill and require hospitalization; other family members may be too distracted by the crisis to devote sufficient time to the baby. Or an insecure marriage may collapse after the birth of the baby, bringing emotional distress to both parents and affecting their relationship with the baby.

Problems of the larger society can affect the family, too, and whatever affects the family also affects the baby. For example, widespread unemployment, shortages of natural resources, and inflation put a strain on individual families as well as the nation as a whole. Babies born today are entering a rapidly changing world, and the adults who raise them must provide a safe and secure environment in the midst of uncertainty.

FULFILLING PSYCHOLOGICAL NEEDS

An infant has many psychological needs—for love and understanding, physical affection, acceptance, and security. The basic responsibility of parents is to ensure the dependent infant's safety and well-being. They must protect her from danger—for example, they must never leave her alone in the house or on a bed or changing table, or in the care of irresponsible people. She must be properly fed and cleaned, and given prompt medical attention when she is ill. All these basic things are obviously necessary for the baby's health, but it is also important to understand that physical well-being is the first step in an infant's psychological development. The simple acts of feeding, changing, bathing, and holding a baby not only fulfill a baby's primary physical needs but also give her a sense of emotional security.

Of course, much depends on the manner in which these routine acts are performed. If she is handled roughly or in a mechanical, indifferent manner, she will not develop a strong sense of security. If her needs are taken care of only after long bouts of crying, she may begin to get the idea that it is not worth the struggle to get attention, and lapse into a state of lethargy.

Most important is the general atmosphere around the baby; it should be reasonably stable, calm, and relaxed. Parents cannot always avoid emotional upsets in their own lives, but they can make efforts not to take out frustrations on the sensitive baby. Tending to the baby ought not to be just a chore for the caregiver, but also a source of pleasure.

Another way that caregivers can promote psychological well-being is by understanding the baby's stage of development and not expecting more than she is capable of ac-

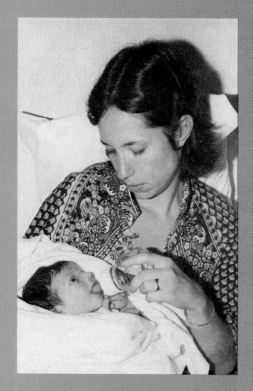

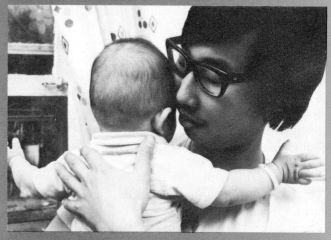

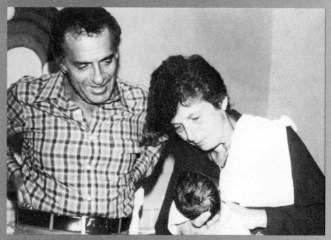

Fulfilling a baby's psychological needs is an important part of child care. Parents and other caregivers must handle baby with love and understanding to develop the baby's feelings of acceptance and security. Parents should have similar philosophies in dealing with baby and the same expectations for the baby's behavior. Babies should be treated consistently by all of their caregivers. Infants need to understand what behavior is acceptable to their families and what limits have been set for them. In this way babies learn their family roles and become socialized.

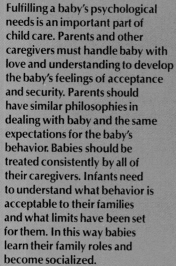

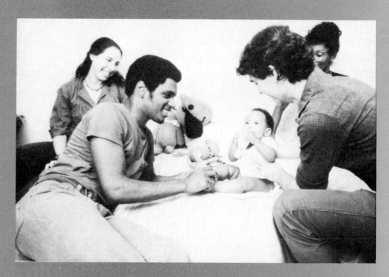

complishing at that time. All too often, especially with their first child, parents want to push their baby too far, too fast. They may be overeager to see the baby take her first steps or utter her first words. Especially if there are young cousins or other small babies in the household, the children may sense that they are being pitted against one another in a competition for adult approval. It is sometimes hard to draw the line between encouraging a baby's development and pushing her, but one clue is the baby's own responses. If she resists and seems frustrated or angered by adults' attempts to get her to do something, she is not yet ready for the activity. As we have seen, all babies follow the same developmental sequences, but each individual baby sets her own pace. Allowing the baby to take her time, but being alert to changing abilities and interests, will make the atmosphere more comfortable and in the long run will stimulate the baby's personal growth.

It is important, too, to begin to develop habits of **consistency** in taking care of the baby. Although in the first year there are many changes in schedule and behavior patterns, caregivers can begin and continue some practices that will help the baby later on. Feeding is one important area; once the baby starts to feed herself, she should continue to do so, even if it is sometimes faster and more convenient for an adult to feed her. It is confusing to a baby to be given conflicting messages—don't, for example, encourage her to feed herself sometimes but not allow her to feed herself at other times. A sense of regularity and consistency also gives her a sense of security. She begins to learn what the boundaries of her world are, and where she should not venture.

PROMOTING LEARNING

Parents are more conscious today than ever before about the value of early learning experi-

CHECKLIST FOR INFANTS' TOYS

1. SUITABILITY
   Does it suit the baby's developmental age?

2. SAFETY
   Is the toy made so that it cannot be broken or taken apart and the parts swallowed?
   Can it be put into the mouth safely?
   Is it free of poisonous substances?
   Is it free of sharp edges?

3. FLEXIBILITY
   Can the toy be used in many ways to encourage the baby's imagination?

4. DURABILITY
   Will the toy last?
   Is it worth the money?

5. ATTRACTIVENESS
   Is it designed to appeal to babies?
   Is it brightly colored?
   Is it simple in shape?
   Is it easy to handle?

ences for the baby. Keeping in mind the child's developmental level, they can offer her toys and activities that best meet her learning needs. As a general guide, in the first three months the baby is most attracted to things she can watch and listen to—mobiles, colorful posters, hanging disks, ticking clocks, music boxes, and so on. From four to six months, as hand-eye coordination develops, she likes things she can grasp and manipulate—rattles, squeeze toys, stuffed animals. From seven to nine months, she will enjoy toys that she can pound, bang, throw, and shake—blocks, balls, rattles. From ten to twelve months, the now actively creeping baby likes to follow objects in her path, such as balls and pull toys. The "Based on Fact" box on this page contains a

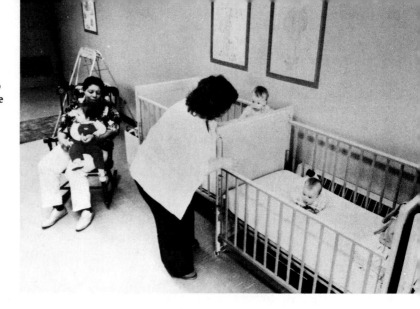

The availability of a good infant day care facility with a competent and understanding staff can be a boon to working parents. Selecting a day care center is an important decision that should not be made hastily.

checklist for some other factors to consider in providing play materials.

Fortunately, there are many interesting and well-designed toys on the market today produced by manufacturers with a knowledge of child development. And it is possible to make toys at home that suit the baby's needs. Finally, many ordinary household objects can be turned into toys by a clever baby and inventive parents.

Of course, much learning takes place without any toys at all. The human interaction that is so important to the baby's psychological development is also crucial to her mental development. Think of language: One of the baby's most important steps in her first year is mastering the beginning stages of language, and this takes place almost exclusively by the interchange of human voices.

Here, too, a relaxed, warm relationship is important. Babies want to learn—it comes naturally to them. Parents must be careful to encourage this spontaneous attitude and not to place too much emphasis on accomplishing a particular skill at a particular time.

SUPERVISION

A baby needs constant supervision in her first year. That does not mean that caregivers should anxiously hover over her every minute of the day, but simply that all her activities must be under the care of a responsible person. Of course, she can be left to sleep in her crib or to play in her playpen, as long as someone is nearby.

Working parents should choose baby-sitters and daytime caregivers who understand the baby's emotional as well as physical needs. The need for constant supervision drains parents' energy, and it is helpful to have someone else on hand occasionally to share their responsibilities. Seeing new faces is also good for the baby, even though she may protest. She should get used to the idea that there are many friendly and helpful persons in the world besides the one person to whom she is most attached.

One alternative to having a relative or a baby-sitter care for the baby is **infant day care.** Most day-care centers accept only toddlers, but more are beginning to take infants as well. In considering day care for an infant, parents should check a center's facilities to see that they are light, clean, and attractive. There should be ample play materials for babies. Most important is the staff. They should be relaxed and sensitive people, who do not get upset by the infants' demands and

Battered Babies

Every year at least a million American children are beaten, starved, burned, or otherwise maltreated by their parents. An estimated 2,000 die of their injuries. Less than a third of these cases come to the attention of child-care agencies. Many of those abused are babies under a year old, and they have been called "battered babies."

What causes parents to harm their own children? For each tragic case, there is a different set of circumstances. Most of them, however, revolve around a parent's inability to cope with the stresses of life and particularly of parenthood. Beset by many problems—economic, social, or personal —the parents resent the demands that the baby makes and lose control over their anger. Many times they do not intend to hurt the baby, only to "make him stop crying," "teach him not to throw food," or "not to wet his pants."

The abusive or neglecting parent may be the mother or the father, rich or poor, married or single. Religion is not a factor, nor is age. Perhaps the only link among the many cases is that a large number of abusive parents were themselves mistreated as children. They have not learned appropriate ways of dealing with frustration in their lives, and they repeat the same destructive behavior with their own children. They frequently have unrealistic expectations of what a baby will do for their lives and are angry when the baby does not make them happy. Immature and insecure, they often look to their baby for the very love that they, as parents, should be giving.

There are many problems in trying to help these babies and their parents. First, many cases are not reported because other people are reluctant to interfere or because they have no proof that the baby is being abused. Second, taking the baby out of the home can only be a temporary solution, since the problem may continue when the child is returned. Third, the parents must be helped to understand and control their behavior, and this requires the kind of support and counseling that is frequently not available or is not accepted by the parents. One successful method seems to be a self-help group of parents with similar problems who share their experiences and try to help each other to prevent further abuse.

Consider how you would feel if you suspected that a baby was being abused by her parents.

What do you think you would do about it?

What kinds of actions by outsiders would be helpful in such a case, and what kinds would not?

who interact with the infants frequently and with understanding. They should respond to the infants without delay and speak in a pleasant tone of voice. They should not be assigned to care for too many infants at one time; a ratio of one adult to every three infants is recommended. Parents can visit infant day-care centers at various times of the day to see the normal routine in action. A center that discourages parents from just "dropping in" is probably not a good choice.

GUIDANCE AND DISCIPLINE

Discipline is a learning process for the child, not just the pressure to follow rules and regulations for the convenience of adults. The goal of disciplining a child is to help her learn what is acceptable or appropriate behavior and what is not, so that she will choose the acceptable behavior on her own. Discipline can only be effective if it is geared to the child's age and development and if it makes sense in a particular situation. Discipline should not be equated with punishment, and it should not be an outlet for a parent's own anger or frustration.

Children need limits — and what is more, they want them. Children who grow up without any boundaries placed on their behavior have a frightening sense that they are all-powerful. They may keep trying out new, unacceptable behaviors in an effort to make someone tell them to stop.

What is appropriate discipline in the baby's first year? Infants are not yet conscious of what is "good" or "bad" behavior. They cry for many reasons, but not to irritate their parents. They put the wrong things in their mouths because they are curious, not because they are "naughty." Before babies become aware of the consequences of their actions, formal discipline is of little use.

It is the parents who must discipline themselves to react reasonably and appropriately to dangerous or troublesome behavior. Parents should not put up with everything a baby does, but they themselves must intervene to stop inappropriate behavior, not expect the baby to stop herself.

Parents can anticipate problems and try to avoid them. Removing tempting but forbidden objects from the baby's reach is a much more sensible way of avoiding broken vases or tipped tables than a spanking. Taking the baby out of the playpen when she starts to fret is more likely to put her in an agreeable mood than an angry scolding. If she continues to crawl into her brother's room and tears up his books, make sure his door is closed at all times. Another technique is to divert the baby's attention. When you must take a forbidden object away from her, give her an appropriate toy in exchange.

Certainly limits must be set on a baby's behavior, for her own safety and for the comfort and convenience of others as well. But these restrictions should always be made without anger and punishment. Consistency is important here, too. When a baby throws a toy on the floor and her father laughs, she expects the same reaction next time. If, instead, he becomes angry the next time, she will be confused. Discipline can be an expression of love, but the child's interest and point of view must always be considered. The long process of learning to control one's own behavior begins in the first year, when parents gently and sensibly set appropriate limits.

SENSITIVITY TO BABY'S NEEDS

If one word could be used to express the attitude that enables parents to give a baby the best chance for development—to provide the right blend of discipline and freedom, stimulation and soothing—that word might be "sensitivity." Mary Ainsworth, a psychologist, has given a good description of what it takes to be a sensitive parent. (Her description uses the term "mother," but holds true for any other relationship.) Dr. Ainsworth says: "The sensitive mother is able to see things from her baby's point of view. She is tuned-in to receive her baby's signals; she interprets them correctly, and she responds to them promptly and appropriately. Although she nearly always gives the baby what he seems to want, when she does not she is tactful in acknowledging his communication and in offering an acceptable alternative. The sensitive mother, by definition, cannot be rejecting, interfering, or ignoring."

Certainly no one person can be totally sensitive to a baby's needs at all times. But these ideals, if kept in mind all during the baby's first year, can help her to be steady and secure as she enters the toddler stage, with all its triumphs and troubles.

· SUMMARY ·

- An infant needs love, understanding, acceptance, and security.
- Loving attention to a baby's physical needs gives the baby a feeling of security.
- Parents should understand the stages of a baby's development and not expect more than the baby can do.
- Babies want to learn. They learn from toys, situations, and being with people.
- Infant day care is an alternative for working parents.
- The goal of discipline is to help the child learn what is acceptable and what is not.
- Parental sensitivity gives the baby the best chance of development.

TERMS TO KNOW

consistency
discipline
infant day care

1. An alternative type of supervision for babies of working parents is ＿＿.
2. ＿＿＿, or always following the same course of action, gives the baby a sense of security.
3. ＿＿ helps a child learn what is acceptable behavior and what is not.

CHECK YOUR UNDERSTANDING

1. What is the role of the baby's caregivers?
2. Give three examples of ways that parents can promote psychological well-being in infants.
3. What types of toys would best meet the learning needs of a two-month-old?
4. List five major factors to consider when choosing a toy for an infant.
5. What should parents look for in an infant day care center?
6. What is the goal of disciplining a child?
7. Give two techniques for stopping an infant's inappropriate behavior.

· UNIT THREE ·

TODDLER
(AGES 1–2)

9
PHYSICAL DEVELOPMENT

10
COGNITIVE DEVELOPMENT

A toddler's first steps mark the beginning of the transition from babyhood to childhood. Between the first and third birthdays the toddler shows great improvement at not only walking, but many other physical skills.

Learning to talk is another milestone. The toddler is also learning to think, to solve problems, and to remember past events. Imagination is growing, too, and may overwhelm the toddler at times.

11
SOCIAL/EMOTIONAL DEVELOPMENT

12
INTERACTION

Toddlers are delightful, energetic, and loving. They can also be tense, easily frustrated, willful, and destructive. These ups and downs are all part of the path to greater independence.

Although the toddler years are sometimes rocky, they bring special joys to parents. Patience, love, and understanding can reassure the toddler who is wavering between wanting to stay a baby and wanting to be grown-up.

· 9 ·

PHYSICAL DEVELOPMENT
OF THE TODDLER

Melissa arrived at her regular Friday night baby-sitting job just as Mrs. Boyd was setting dinner on the table for her two-year-old twins. "I'm glad you're here early," said Mrs. Boyd. "Could you help Joel and Todd with their meals while I finish getting ready?"

"Sure, Mrs. Boyd," said Melissa. "It will be a good chance to see the twins' physical skills. I'm going to report to my child development class on what a typical two-year-old is like."

Mrs. Boyd smiled. "As soon as you find out, tell me!"

Before the evening was over, Melissa understood what Mrs. Boyd meant. Although both of the boys could feed themselves with a spoon, Joel was much messier than Todd. On the other hand, Joel could peel his banana by himself, while Todd insisted that Melissa do it for him.

The more Melissa observed the twins, the more differences she found. Joel was better at catching and throwing a ball, but Todd could climb stairs without holding Melissa's hand. When Melissa brought out some crayons, Todd immediately began scribbling circles on the pages of a coloring book. Joel ignored the crayons as he marched around the room, banging two wooden blocks together.

"I don't understand how they can be so different," Melissa told her class on Monday. "And I certainly don't know which one is the typical two-year-old!"

"Let me ask a question," said Mrs. Harper, Melissa's teacher. "Each of you in this room has your own special interests and abilities. Which one of you is a typical teenager?"

"We all are, in a way," Melissa said after a moment.

"That's basically true. You're all different, yet you all have some things in common. It's just the same with toddlers. They may not pick up exactly the same skills at the same age. But overall, most follow a similar pattern of development."

"I can think of one thing the twins have in common right now," said Melissa. "They're both full of energy!"

•

What other similarities can you identify between Joel's and Todd's physical development?

•

Do you think it is possible to describe "typical" abilities for an age group? Why or why not?

Toddlerhood marks a turning point in a child's development. As the baby gradually emerges from infancy and enters the **toddler** stage—the years between one and three—she begins to acquire new skills and discovers the excitement of doing things on her own. In physical development, the toddler literally takes her first steps toward an important accomplishment—walking. She begins to feed herself and drink out of a cup—although not without some spills. And by the end of this stage, she will have abandoned diapers for the most part and learned to use the toilet. Although still a baby in many ways, the child is starting to move toward greater independence in the toddler years.

PHYSICAL GROWTH

The toddler's physical growth is not as dramatic as the infant's. She grows and gains weight at a slower rate. By the age of two, toddlers weigh about 28 pounds (12.7 kilograms) on the average and are about 33 to 35 inches tall (83.8 to 88.9 centimeters). The proportions of the child's body begin to change, and this contributes to the ability to walk. Before an infant begins to creep, the proportion of her legs to her trunk remains about the same. When she is held up in a standing position, her legs are so short that she seems scarcely higher off the ground than when she is sitting down. But when she begins to crawl, at about seven

Although a toddler's bones are still somewhat soft, his legs lengthen at this age, enabling him to learn how to walk.

or eight months, the legs start to grow longer in relation to the trunk. Rapid lengthening of the legs continues while the toddler is gaining skill in locomotion.

The toddler's brain is continuing to grow rapidly, and this makes her head, like the infant's, seem large in proportion to the body. Her bones are starting to get harder, but they are still relatively soft. At this age, poor nutrition or disease may interfere with the proper hardening of the bones.

The baby teeth continue to emerge during the toddler years, and by about three years old most children will have their full set of twenty. (Not until age six will the first of the thirty-two permanent teeth erupt.)

MOTOR DEVELOPMENT

The greatest physical growth for a toddler is in the muscles. As the nervous system develops, the child is able to make more complex movements with the fine muscles of the hands and fingers. Using a spoon, blowing the nose (while an adult holds the tissue), and turning the pages of a book one at a time—all are skills requiring the use of the fine muscles.

The child who has discovered that she can open and close a jar by turning the lid will often repeat this movement over and over again with never-ending delight. Other great joys include trying to pull shoelaces open, undoing buttons and buckles, and working zippers. An older child or adult who plays with a toddler may find that he has to curb this eager activity if he wants to keep his shoes, shirt, pants, and wristwatch on!

The large muscles of the child's arms and legs grow stronger with activity, and she can control them better. Perhaps the most exciting achievement in gross motor development for the child is walking. And once she is steady on her feet, she also begins to run, jump, skip, and climb up and down stairs. The more she moves—and the toddler is constantly on the move—the better coordination and balance she achieves.

Motor development in early childhood follows a definite pattern. Each child must learn certain motor skills before she can go on to master others. A good example of this developmental process is learning to walk.

WALKING

Most children can stand up without support at about one year of age. Between about thirteen and fifteen months, they start walking without help, though they are not very steady and often tumble over. The awkward "toddling" gait of the beginning walker is what gives this period of childhood its name. By the age of two and a half, a child is usually able to walk quite well. How did this momentous achievement come about?

Learning to walk means learning a series of skills. The first of these skills are learned in infancy. An infant leans forward from a sitting position and then begins to crawl around on hands and knees. Later she can pull herself up and stand, supporting herself by holding on to a chair or the edge of her crib. She may even try taking a few steps, still holding on. The child will learn to stand alone, and then she will try walking while holding on to an adult's hand. Finally she will walk unassisted.

The toddler's senses are also developed through movement. She learns to coordinate her eyes with her body movements to see where she is going as she walks. She feels the ground with her feet as she toddles forward. As she balances herself in motion, she gains an awareness of her entire body in space. Putting one foot in front of the other seems simple, but it is a complicated skill that requires the coordination of the nerves, muscles, and senses.

The age at which an individual child begins to walk depends on the physical factors of

Motor Development of the Toddler

This chart shows the sequence in which children learn specific motor skills. The ages are average; not all children will perform each skill at the indicated age.

FIFTEEN MONTHS

Gross
Creeps up stairs.
Walks sideways and backward.
Can toss a ball.
Climbs on low chairs and tables.

Fine
Picks up small objects with thumb and forefinger.
Can open small box.

TWO YEARS

Gross
Jumps in place.
Can walk up and down stairs.
Pushes self in toys on wheels.

Fine
Builds a small tower of five or six blocks.
Draws circles.
Strings beads.
Holds a cup.
Eats with a spoon.

velopment as good nutrition and the satisfaction of other bodily needs.

FEEDING AND NUTRITION

Toddlers, like everyone else, need a balanced diet that includes items from the basic food groups: (1) milk-cheese group, (2) meat, poultry, fish and beans, (3) fruits and vegetables, and (4) breads and cereals. At about two years old, a child begins to show specific tastes in foods and can be allowed to have the kinds of foods she likes as long as she eats a variety of foods that provide the nutrients she needs.

Meals should look attractive and colorful and be served in small amounts. Toddlers can be given simple foods like those fed to the year-old baby. Since the jaw is not yet fully developed, toddlers are not yet able to chew very

Providing toddlers with a variety of finger foods helps them learn to feed themselves. Good finger foods for toddlers include carrot and celery sticks, scrambled eggs, pieces of melon and banana, cheese chunks, cooked green beans, and crackers.

tough or fibrous foods, such as steak, nor can they digest them thoroughly.

Most young children do not like strong flavors or spicy foods. Their tastebuds are delicate and are more widely distributed than an adult's, located not only on the tongue but also in the throat and on the insides of the cheeks.

Since taste is influenced by past experience, children should not be fed too many unnaturally sweet or salty foods. If they come to expect food to taste this way, they may reject many nutritious foods that are not so highly seasoned. Fruits are a nutritious source of natural sweetness, and many other foods contain enough natural salt for the child's needs, so there is no reason to add a lot of table salt.

Soft drinks, rich cakes, jams, candy, and other sugary foods can spoil a child's appetite. They also add calories without providing much of the essential nutrients needed for growth and health. Sugar is to be avoided also because it is a direct cause of tooth decay. Of course, occasional treats such as a slice of birthday cake or a special holiday sweet can be given, but very sugary or starchy foods are not healthful as part of a steady diet.

If a child is given snacks between meals, they should consist of healthful foods, not non-nutritious "junk foods" that may lead to poor eating habits later in life. No snacks should be offered to a toddler right before a meal. Nor should snacks be used as a reward for the child, especially sweets or other nonnutritious snacks. The child may begin to associate these foods with praise, approval, and love. This might lead to overeating and obesity later on if the child (or adult) turns to "comforting" but highly caloric foods when she is feeling anxious or depressed.

At the toddler stage, children are eager to feed themselves. Finger foods such as hard-boiled eggs and carrot sticks are easy to handle and great fun for them. Such foods fulfill the child's desire to examine her food, yet do not create a mess for caregivers to clean up. With other foods, spills and dribbles are inevitable. Small children who are just learning to manipulate table utensils and drink from a cup cannot be expected to be neat. They are too young to be taught good table manners.

Many toddlers become very fussy at mealtime and even refuse to eat. Children around the age of two are notorious for their habit of screaming "No!" to almost everything (even to things they really want).

When Isaac was a year old, he used to smile and chuckle as he tasted each morsel of food, and he finished everything his parents gave him. Then, one day, when he was two and a half, he didn't want to eat his lunch at all. His mother immediately thought the child was sick. She put her hand on his forehead to see if he had a fever, but his skin was cool. After trying a few more times to persuade him to eat, she gave up and let him down from his highchair to play. Isaac dashed out of the kitchen and began to bang on a toy drum and sing at the top of his voice. He certainly did not seem ill at all.

It is not a problem if a toddler misses a meal or eats only a few bites. Children should not be forced to eat or made to feel that they must "clean their plates" in order to win their parents' affection. The fact is that toddlers need much less to go on than might be expected, because their growth has slowed down since infancy. Also, toddlers' interest in food often decreases because they are so occupied with the many new things they are doing. At times they are simply too busy learning about the world to care about stopping for lunch.

TOILET-TRAINING

Learning to use the toilet is another great achievement of toddlerhood. Successful toilet-training depends on the physical and emotional development of the individual child. Most children can be toilet-trained at about two and a half years old. By this age they are

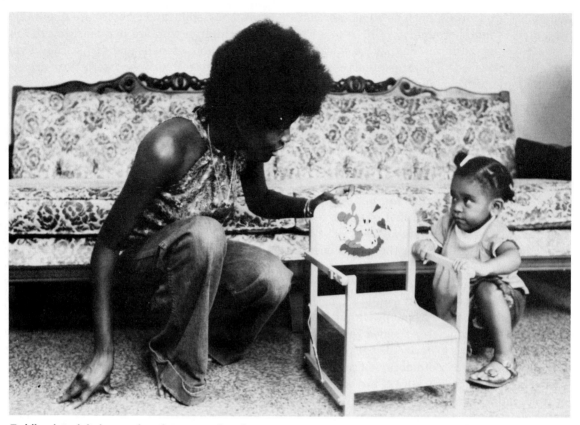

Toddlers let adults know when they are ready to be toilet-trained. They may express interest in their portable toilets or in the toilet habits of others.

usually able to control the **sphincters**—the muscles that enable them to restrain elimination—and wait until they can get to the toilet. They must also be able to know ahead of time that they need to use the toilet, and they must be able to get to the bathroom themselves or signal to an adult that they need to be taken there. Unless the child has control of her muscles and can anticipate her need, she is not ready to be trained, no matter what her age.

Usually a toddler first becomes aware of elimination *after* it has already occurred, and she may tell her caregiver what she has done. Gradually she will learn to be aware that she is moving her bowels or urinating *while* she is doing it. Finally, she will learn to recognize

that she is about to eliminate and can make her needs known *beforehand*. At this point, efforts to toilet-train the child will probably be the most successful. When children are ready, they are also willing, for they are eager to acquire a skill that their parents want them to have. Children also feel proud of their ability to control their bodily functions, just as they took pride in learning to walk and mastering other physical activities.

The child herself may show that she is ready to learn by expressing an interest in the toilet habits of adults and older children in the family. She is interested because she knows that using the toilet is a sign of being grown-up. At this point, the parents can explain the process to the child and suggest that she might like to try it sometime. If the child resists, it is too soon, and the parents should continue to wait.

If she responds to the suggestion, she can be held over the toilet or, even better, put on a special potty chair that is scaled to the toddler's size. The child can be given time to get used to seeing the potty around, perhaps for a few days or even weeks. Then, at the times of day when she usually has a bowel movement, a parent can remove her diaper and bring her to the chair. When the child uses the potty successfully, a few words of praise will help to encourage her. However, if praise is overdone, the toddler may become resistant merely as a show of independence, especially if she senses that this training is extremely important to her parents.

A child should never be punished for not "performing." If she is at all anxious, uninterested, or resistant, the training should be stopped for a while and begun again later. Children should never be given laxatives or enemas to force them to "produce" on command, since this can be psychologically harmful. Parents and caregivers should also not try to encourage use of the potty by indicating to the child that her soiled diapers or clothes are "dirty" or "disgusting." Making the child feel ashamed or anxious about her natural bodily functions will not help and is only upsetting to her.

Most children master toilet-training quite easily if allowed to do so at their own rate. Bowel training is usually achieved first, then bladder control. At first, boys as well as girls will sit down to urinate.

It may not be until about the age of three that the child achieves nighttime control. Thus, a toddler who uses the potty during the day will still need diapers at bedtime or naptime until she achieves full control.

Even children who are trained will have accidents. A child should never be scolded for failing. If she fails often, the training should be postponed for a time. Children are learning so many new things at this age that they may well fall behind in one area.

A child who has already been fairly well trained may suddenly become stubborn and refuse to use the potty for a while, reverting to her old babyish ways. Or she may balk at toilet-training as a means of exercising power over her parents. She has learned that she can refuse to obey their wishes. If such a power struggle exists, the parents would be wise to deal with it before they attempt toilet-training. Above all, training should be carried out in a relaxed way, without pressure and with an understanding of the child's physical, emotional, and mental stage of development.

CLOTHING

Since toddlerhood is a time of energetic physical activity, the child feels most comfortable when she can move freely. The toddler's clothing should be loose-fitting, and the fabric should be flexible enough to move with the child and durable enough to outlast rough play. Toddlers like to go barefoot, and it is good for

Toddlers may undress themselves at any time of day. It is a form of play which gives them a feeling of independence.

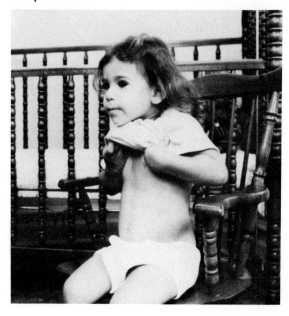

Children's Fashion Designer

SKIRTS AND TOPS FOR
BACK-TO-SCHOOL!

Girls will love these outfits in bright Fall colors—peppy plaids and snappy solids to mix and match. Sizes 7–14. At fine stores everywhere.

Sam Bolognese looked at this ad with satisfaction. He had designed these fall outfits—the first assignment he had handled on his own since joining the company. And seeing the finished products modeled in the full-color ad, he knew that his designs would sell. Better still, the young girls who wore his designs would feel comfortable and look good.

Like all fashion designs, Sam's creations had started with a sketch. Then patterns were made—drawn to size on paper and then cut out of muslin. The muslin pieces were sewn together and fitted on a model. After modifications were made, a sample garment was made in the fabrics he had chosen. These samples eventually reached production and were chosen by department store and specialty store buyers for their back-to-school promotions.

Designers of children's clothes must understand how children's bodies develop at different ages. They must also have an extensive knowledge of fabrics and their durability and laundering features. They must know how to create clothing that

children can put on easily by themselves or that parents can help them with, if they are too young to dress themselves. The final product must be not just economical and sturdy; it must also appeal to parents and to children as well.

A fashion designer must be a creative, imaginative, skilled person. He or she must be able to work quickly and understand clothing construction thoroughly. Courses in sewing, art, design, textiles, and merchandising are helpful. Graduation from a fashion design school is often a key to a job in the industry. Many fashion designers start as assistants or as beginners in the workroom, cutting and sewing garments.

Salaries are potentially very high in the fashion industry, but competition is very keen. There may be a great deal of pressure to complete designs, and workrooms are often crowded and noisy. This industry, however, is always exciting and challenging, and those who love fashion thrive on the hectic atmosphere.

Although a designer of children's clothes works only some of the time directly with children, their needs must be uppermost. Perhaps the greatest reward of the job is seeing a happy child playing in a comfortable and attractive outfit that one has designed and brought to the market.

them to do so. Walking without shoes helps strengthen their arches, which are usually rather flat. When they must wear shoes, they should wear socks also; otherwise the shoes may give them blisters.

Children of this age often have definite tastes in clothing, just as they do in foods. They

can be allowed to choose, within reason, what they would like to wear. If a caregiver asks a child whether she would like to wear her blue sweater or her yellow jacket, for example, she will also have the chance to learn the difference between colors.

Toddlers like bright colors and clothes

with designs of animals or cartoon characters, rick-rack, and colorful trim. They also enjoy feeling the different textures of their clothing—rough knits, smooth cottons, soft flannels. They particularly delight in outfits that they can zip or snap themselves. At first, toddlers need help in dressing. For example, they cannot yet tell the difference between the front and back of their clothes. Young children can undress themselves more easily. By the age of three most children can both dress and undress without much assistance.

BATHING AND HYGIENE

Toddlers still need to be bathed by a caregiver and supervised at all times while they are in the tub. However, a toddler is beginning to take more interest in bathing and will want to participate by handling the soap and washcloth. Although young children often protest having their hair shampooed, they generally take pleasure in their baths—especially when they have a few toys to play with. Pouring water from one container to another is a favorite bath-time activity. The toddler also enjoys toy frogs or other animals that can be wound up and made to move through the water. Children who are learning to talk like to name all the objects in and around the tub.

Children may be introduced to the art of cleaning their teeth as early as two years of age. They do not see it as a boring necessity of life, but rather as a grown-up activity that they are eager to imitate. Unlike the older child who has to be reminded to brush her teeth, the toddler may even demand to do so. She considers it a necessary part of the routine that she has come to expect after meals.

Toddlers may not be very efficient in brushing their teeth at first. The child is likely to chew on the brush and to miss the sink when rinsing out. But gradually she will get better at it, and it is good to establish this habit early in life, since brushing is very important in the proper care of the teeth. At this age the child need not use toothpaste. She can start out just brushing with water.

SLEEP AND REST

The toddler is so busy discovering her world that she will often keep on going until she is totally exhausted. Parents and caregivers

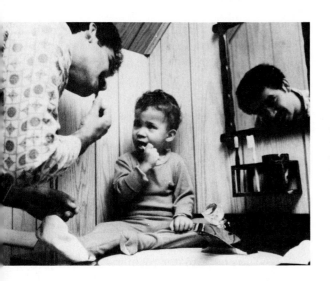

Toddlers learn good hygiene through imitation of adults and through play. Baths are desired when there are lots of water toys in the tub.

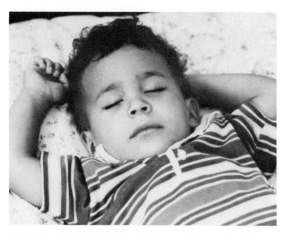
Toddlers often exhaust themselves in play and may stop for a nap in the middle of an activity.

must step in to see that the child gets the rest she needs.

Children of this age are afraid of separation from their parents, and this fear often emerges at bedtime. This is why many toddlers refuse to go to bed even if they are tired. Sometimes a child turns bedtime into a test of her power over adults. In order to make sure a toddler gets enough rest, she should have an adequate daytime nap and a long, restful sleep at night.

Naps may be adapted to the needs of the parents. For example, a working parent would like to spend more time with his or her child in the evening. In this case, the child can be given a long nap in the afternoon so that she doesn't have to go to bed quite so early at night.

A set routine at bedtime helps to ease the transition into sleep. Reading a story, giving good-night kisses, singing, and other gentle activities soothe the child and prepare her to sleep.

Toddlers may insist on taking a favorite doll or other toy to bed with them. Some toddlers go to bed with an entire zoo of stuffed animals.

This is the age, too, when a child can set up a going-to-bed ritual in which the same series of actions is repeated exactly. Each step of the ritual—from brushing the teeth to the precise placement of each stuffed animal on the bed—must be followed. The child may even insist on repeating some of the steps if she feels she is being rushed or "cheated."

If bedtimes and naps are scheduled at regular hours, the child will expect them. She will get into the habit of resting at a particular time. A child can be allowed to stay up for special occasions, but this should not become routine. When a child outgrows naps, a period of quiet play may be substituted.

A DAY IN THE LIFE OF AN ACTIVE TODDLER

Two-year-old Faye is in almost constant motion. At 6:45 in the morning she calls out "Mama!" to signal that she is awake and ready to start her day. When her mother offers her a choice of two or three outfits to wear, Faye picks a bright red sweatshirt and proudly pushes her hands into the sleeves. Faye's mother helps her put on her pants and shoes.

Once dressed, Faye races to the kitchen for breakfast. After drinking her orange juice out of a small glass, she dawdles over her cereal. She stirs it, puts a few spoonfuls into her mouth, spills a little, and decides not to eat the rest.

After breakfast, when her mother suggests that she sit on the potty chair, Faye refuses with a loud "No!" She runs to her room instead and takes her favorite picture book, sits down on the floor with her feet straight out in front of her, and "reads" to herself.

Next Faye happily builds a tower with four or five blocks and then, with equal satisfaction, knocks it down. When her mother gives her a piece of paper and large crayons, Faye makes circular and up-and-down marks—and a few of them wind up on the linoleum floor instead of the paper. She brings the drawing to her mother and asks, "What is it?"

Faye runs back to her room and carries out

Faye is a typical toddler. She is loving, playful, and curious. Her day is filled with activity. She keeps her caregivers busy with her constant demands. They need energy and patience to tend to her needs and protect her from harm. Some refer to this stage of development as the "terrible twos" because these children constantly test the limits that have been established for them. Caregivers need to be firm but nonthreatening during this stage.

her little chair. Then she goes back again to get Oopie, her doll. She drags out a box of wooden beads and gleefully dumps them on the floor.

Finally it is lunchtime. After playing with her food a bit, Faye eats half a peanut butter sandwich on whole-grain bread, a few carrot sticks, and a small banana. She has no trouble finishing her milk. Faye's mother has to coax her into her room for a nap. The child can be heard singing and talking to herself until she falls asleep.

In the afternoon, Faye's uncle comes to take her to the park. Faye slowly makes her way down the apartment house stairs one step at a time, holding firmly on to the rail. When they get to the playground, Faye sees a kiddie car that some other child has abandoned for the moment. She pushes herself around in the car, naming aloud the various objects she sees as she goes along. Finally a little boy comes up to her and indignantly demands the return of his car. Faye lets him take it and runs off to climb up the slide.

After they return home, Faye has her dinner with the rest of the family. Her father bathes her, diapers her for the night, and helps her into her pajamas. At about seven o'clock she climbs into her crib, and her father tells her the story of "Chicken Little." Faye demands to hear the story several times, but finally allows herself to be tucked in—along with Oopie and several stuffed animals—and kissed good-night.

HEALTH CARE

The best way to combat illness is to prevent it. This means that a child should have regular medical checkups—twice a year for the toddler. Between twelve and fifteen months, children should be receiving certain inoculations against disease. (See the "Based on Fact" box on page 75.)

Diphtheria, measles, mumps, polio, rubella, whooping cough—these are the major childhood diseases for which vaccines are readily available. Many people have become rather casual about vaccinations in recent years. In North America, for example, polio vaccinations dropped off from 84 to 60 percent during one ten-year period. The results of such neglect can be tragic, for an unvaccinated child may get polio and be severely crippled.

Visits to the doctor can be frightening to small children. Parents can help by explaining to the child beforehand what will happen in the doctor's office. If the parents tell the child that the examination will not hurt, however, they may be putting the idea of pain into her head and making her more worried. It is best not to mention pain at all. If the examination does cause a little discomfort, the parent can soothe and reassure the child without making too big a fuss about it.

A small child will feel more secure if she sits on a parent's lap during an examination. Some pediatricians prepare a child by "examining" the parent first. For example, the doctor might use a stethoscope on the father or mother and then use it on the child.

A serious illness or a special examination that calls for a stay in the hospital is especially upsetting to toddler. To calm her fears, parents can explain as much about her illness as she is able to understand. They can describe what it will be like to stay in the hospital and help her understand that the people there are going to help her get better. If possible, they should take the child to visit the hospital before her stay. A child of toddler age is very much afraid of separation from her parents, so they should try to stay with her as much as possible when she is in the hospital.

ACCIDENTS

The active toddler has no awareness of the sharp corners she may run into, the dangers of

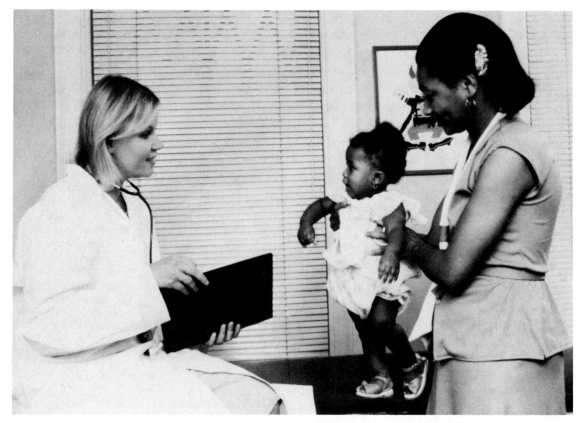

A toddler should visit her pediatrician twice each year for general medical checkups and all necessary inoculations.

taking a taste of household cleaning fluid, or the way a hot toaster can singe her fingers. As soon as a baby begins to creep, the parents must begin to childproof their home. It is important that the toddler be able to move about freely without constantly being told not to touch things. The only way to avoid the need for such nagging and keep the child out of harm is to put dangerous or breakable objects out of the child's reach.

Although toddlers are accident-prone, it is wise not to be overprotective. Small children will inevitably fall and bump their heads many times as they learn to walk and during their play. If someone keeps telling a child,

"Don't do that, you'll fall," he or she may protect the child, but may also be holding back her development. Children must learn to pick themselves up and start over again. Parents and caregivers should take the necessary safety precautions and then let the child go.

Statistics tell us that for children one to four years of age, most accidents involve a motor vehicle. The next most common accidents are falls and burns. Small children can also accidentally drown or be poisoned at this age.

Toddlers should not be carried on a bicycle or motorcycle without specially designed and approved safety equipment. A toddler should never be allowed to run out into the street or

Outdoor play equipment is responsible for thousands of toddler accidents each year. Safe play areas have soft surfaces, such as sand or turf, to break falls. Good equipment has no sharp edges or protruding metal parts. Well-designed play areas for toddlers contain a variety of items which stimulate creative, but safe, play. Toddlers enjoy climbing, swinging, crawling into and through things, water play, and building. Adults must be nearby to supervise toddlers at all times.

into a driveway. In a car, a small child should never sit in the front seat. She should be held in the lap or kept secure with a special device in the back seat. Make sure the child is far away when other motorized machinery, such as a lawn mower, is in use.

A fall from a high place could be serious. At home, gates can be installed at the bottom and top of steep stairs. A child who is playing on a slide, a seesaw, monkey bars, or other climbing equipment should always be supervised.

Never leave a child alone in the kitchen, especially when food is being cooked. When a small child is in the kitchen with a caregiver who is cooking, all the pot handles should be pointing toward the back of the stove.

Keep toddlers away from burning light bulbs, matches, and electrical appliances. Put tape over electrical outlets or use a plug cover if the outlet is at toddler level. The child might stick a bobby pin or other object into the outlet and get a bad shock.

It is important never to leave a toddler alone during bath time. A small child could drown or electrocute herself by playing in the tub with an electrical appliance such as a hairdryer. She might also burn herself by turning on water that is too hot. Never leave a child with water running in the tub even for a few moments. A child can drown in as little as an inch of water.

Keep all cleaning materials and other chemical products on a high shelf, where a curious toddler cannot reach them. If they must be kept on the child's level, keep them locked up. All medicine should also be in a high cabinet or locked away and should be sealed with childproof caps. Make sure house and garden plants are not poisonous. A list of poisonous plants can be obtained from the U.S. Department of Agriculture. Have the phone number of a poison control center handy just in case the toddler does manage to swallow a harmful substance.

· SUMMARY ·

- Toddlers continue to grow rapidly, but not as fast as a newborn.
- The fine muscles of the hands and fingers are developing.
- Walking is the most dramatic achievement in gross motor development.
- Active play is important to the child's physical development.
- Toddlers need a balanced diet of simple, easily digested foods.
- Most toddlers begin to master toilet-training if allowed to do so at their own rate.
- Toddlers can start participating in dressing and bathing themselves.
- The toddler needs a daytime nap as well as a long, restful sleep at night.
- Regular medical checkups and vaccinations can help prevent common illnesses.
- Childproofing the home helps avoid accidents.

TERMS TO KNOW

maturation
sphincters
toddler

1. The _____ period is a turning point in a child's development.
2. The muscles that enable a toddler to restrain elimination are the _____.
3. The _____, or full development, of the muscles and nerves is necessary before a child can learn to walk.

CHECK YOUR UNDERSTANDING

1. List six factors that help determine the age at which a child learns to walk.
2. Why is play important to a child's overall development?
3. What types of playthings are unsafe or inappropriate for a toddler?
4. Give four reasons why a child may lag behind in physical or motor development.
5. Why should caregivers avoid giving toddlers unnaturally sweet foods?
6. What three requirements must be met before a child is ready for toilet-training?
7. By what age are most children able to dress and undress with little help?
8. Why is it important to have a regular schedule and routine for bedtime and naps?
9. How often should a toddler have a medical checkup?
10. Name three types of accidents that could happen if a toddler is left alone during bath time.

·10·

COGNITIVE DEVELOPMENT
OF THE TODDLER

Kim Lee and her mother were preparing lunch. While Kim ladled some soup into a large bowl, Mrs. Lee carried dishes of rice, fish, and vegetables to the table, where her little son David was waiting in his high chair.

"Mama lunch!" the little boy exclaimed.

"Yes, David, Mama is bringing you your lunch," she said.

Kim came in with the soup and sat down. Her mother handed her a bowl and said, "Please put some food in David's bowl."

"Baby like rice?" Kim asked as she handed David his bowl.

"Rice!" repeated David with a grin.

"Kim," said Mrs. Lee, "please don't speak to your brother in baby talk. It's very good that you're giving him lots of chances to imitate your speech. But if you speak to him like that, how will he learn the way to talk correctly?"

"I thought maybe he wouldn't understand grown-up talk," Kim said. "Sometimes I can't understand what he's saying."

"Then just try to guess and repeat to him in a complete sentence what you think he means. Then you can reply to what he said."

Kim began to eat but kept her eyes on David as he carefully guided a small spoonful of fish into his mouth.

"Hey, you're really learning fast," Kim told him. "Pretty soon you'll be able to eat with chopsticks, too, like Mom and me."

"Eat chop-tick," said David, pointing to Kim.

"That's right, I'm eating with chopsticks," Kim said as her mother smiled.

•

What other situations, besides mealtime, could provide good speaking practice for David?

•

Why is it important to speak to a toddler in complete sentences?

The toddler's experience of life is quite different from the infant's. As we have seen, the infant is the center of his own little world. His major concerns are with the satisfaction of his needs and with efforts to control his own bodily movements. But the toddler is gradually learning that he is part of a larger world, and he wants to know more and more about the objects around him. This is the age of experimentation. Once a child has begun to walk, he sets out on a series of adventures in which he acquires new cognitive as well as physical skills. The toddler is just beginning to understand and learn how to control the world he lives in.

THE FINAL STAGES OF THE SENSORIMOTOR PERIOD

The child moving from infancy to toddlerhood is still in the phase of cognitive development that Piaget calls the **sensorimotor period.** In this period the child is learning largely by means of his bodily movements and his senses. In *Stage V* of this period, roughly ages twelve to eighteen months, the child is still concerned with things he can perceive through seeing, hearing, tasting, touching, and smelling; but now his understanding of these things is growing stronger. For example, the child is discovering that objects can behave in different

Toddlers learn through their five senses. A trip through the grocery store provides lots to look at and touch. Children should be allowed to explore, but they must be closely watched.

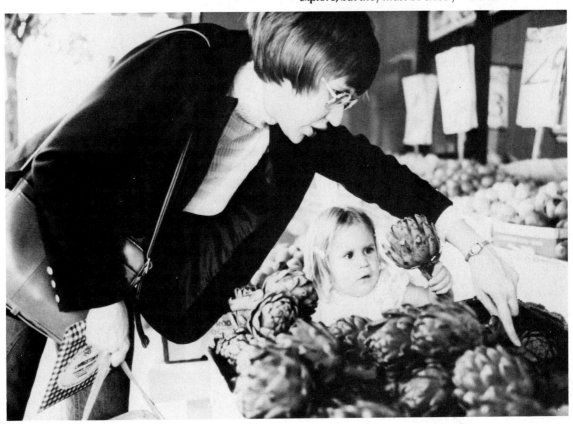

Toy Designer

Sandy Hirsch watched attentively, notebook in hand, as a group of two-year-olds played with sets of triangular nesting blocks. Sandy noticed which colors they preferred, which blocks they had difficulty fitting into the next larger size, and which ones seemed too small to handle easily. All of this information was important to Sandy, a toy designer for a company that specializes in educational toys. Before any new toy is marketed, the designer needs to be sure that it is suitable for the children for whom it is designed. The test subjects were busily involved with the toys, Sandy noted with relief, and seemed on the whole to approve the new design.

Children's toys range from simple to elaborate, from inexpensive to costly, and from time-tested to brand-new. Toy companies compete vigorously for their share of the growing market for toys. They look to toy designers to come up with new ideas—or new variations on traditional ideas—to attract the buyer's attention.

The toy designer plays an important part in developing new products. He or she must be a skilled craftsperson, able to work easily with all kinds of materials to develop models of possible new toys. Imagination is also important. A good knowledge of toy construction, production, and marketing, as well as of federal safety regulations, is also vital.

Most of these skills develop through practical on-the-job experience. Toy designers frequently start as assistants or on the production or business ends of the business. Some toy designers work independently and sell their designs to manufacturers.

It is important for toy designers to thoroughly understand children's interests, needs, and stages of development in order to create appropriate toys.

The job is frequently fast-paced and high-pressured, especially when the holiday line is under development. But the rewards are ample, both in income (highly successful toy designers are well paid) and other benefits. Although designing toys is a business, it is also a creative endeavor—and one that contributes greatly to children's learning and enjoyment.

ways, depending on what he does to them. He tries out new and varied ways of handling things to see what will happen. Piaget called this **directed groping**. As an example, Piaget described how his little son Laurent, sitting in his highchair, broke off pieces of bread and dropped them to the floor to see where they would land.

Another development of this stage is that a child learns new means to achieve a desired end. Through trial and error, he learns how to pull a toy toward himself by using the string attached to it or by moving it with a stick. He discovers that by tilting a toy, he can get it through the bars of his playpen. The child's behavior is thus becoming more directed toward achieving a particular goal—a sure sign of increasing intelligence.

In the final sensorimotor stage, *Stage VI*, somewhere between the ages of eighteen months and two years, the child starts to experiment mentally as well as physically. That is, he thinks about *how* he will go about achieving a goal and figures it out without having to go through trial-and-error "groping."

Joey, for instance, wants to get his toy truck, which his mother has placed on a table. He knows that he can reach the table by climbing up on the chair next to it. He starts to climb, holding his teddy bear in one arm. Suddenly Joey realizes that holding the teddy bear is making it hard for him to climb; he needs both hands to pull himself up onto the chair. He thinks for a moment and then puts the teddy bear down before climbing up to reach his truck. Joey has mentally invented a solution to his problem.

The toddler at this stage cannot think logically, but he is beginning to think in terms of symbolic concepts. He has some notion of time and is able to understand the difference between yesterday and today, and the meaning of soon, before, and after. He can learn simple relationships such as big and small.

Around the age of two, most children begin to develop the capacity for symbolic thought. This is shown in simple imaginative play. When a toddler pretends that a stuffed animal is a baby, he is engaging in symbolic thought. Language is another important symbolic activity in which the toddler is beginning to gain skill.

THE BEGINNING OF THE PREOPERATIONAL PERIOD

Between the ages of two and three, the toddler enters a new period of development which Piaget calls the **preoperational period**. In

The toddler years are an exciting time for parents as they watch their child learn about the world at a very rapid pace.

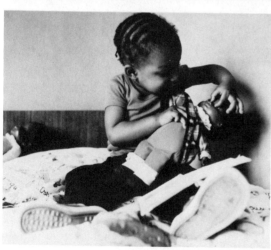

Children try out various roles through play. They may pretend to be a doctor for a while, or a parent, or even an animal tamer. During exploratory play they attempt to make discoveries, while in passive play they listen to or watch others.

general, its early stage is characterized by the use of **symbolic representation** as seen in the child's greater capacity for imitation, make-believe, memory, and language. The toddler is also learning to classify objects, though at first his classifications may be very general ones. For example, he may identify a wide variety of four-legged animals as "doggies" and different kinds of wheeled vehicles as "cars." The preoperational period continues until about age seven and will be further discussed later on.

Although two-year-olds do have some understanding of cause and effect, it is not well developed. For example, they may link together two unrelated events simply because they happen at the same time. Sarah's birthday happened to be on the Fourth of July, but it was several years before she realized that fireworks were not part of her own birthday party!

156

Between the ages of one and three, a child is still very far from developing a conscience—an inner sense of right and wrong that guides behavior. The toddler understands that there are certain things she must not do, but does not understand *why* these activities are wrong or undesirable.

The toddler cannot yet reason about her actions, nor does she have enough language skills to grasp explanations or talk about her wishes instead of acting on them. By the time children are speaking more fluently, their ability to understand explanations will also have improved. In the meantime, the rules of behavior must be patiently reinforced by frequent reminders—not to touch certain things, for example, or to hit people—and praise when the child does what is right.

The word "no" is the easiest way to communicate to toddlers that they must control their impulses and moods. But while the child hears "no" dozens of times a day—and frequently uses the word herself when she doesn't want to cooperate—she is not yet able to say no to herself.

For example, a child who has been repeatedly told not to touch some delicate dried flowers has to go through a struggle each time she feels the urge to play with them. Often she will repeat the prohibition aloud to herself: "Mustn't touch." At other times she will give in to her urge, and it seems to her caregivers that she is just being stubborn. Actually, these failures at control are a normal part of the learning process by which the child eventually acquires her own sense of right and wrong.

Of course, breaking a few flowers is not much of a "crime" from the adult point of view. But the toddler's mind does not distinguish between breaking something and a more serious act, such as hitting a baby brother. To her, both are simply urges that she feels compelled to carry out. Since she cannot express her jealousy of the baby in words, she seeks to do so in action. It is often easier for a toddler to deal with such conflicts if some substitute action is suggested—such as hitting a punching bag or a doll.

How does the level of cognitive development influence a child's ability to understand moral rules?

Toddlers may not accept what they see if it runs counter to their own wishes. A toddler may see a car coming and yet run into the street after a ball unless someone stops him. His reasoning seems to be that the car cannot hit him because he wishes to get his ball. He doesn't yet understand that the world is independent of his wishes and that he cannot control it magically.

THE IMPORTANCE OF PLAY

Though playing helps children to develop physically, various kinds of play are also vital to the child's cognitive development.

One of these kinds is **exploratory play**, in which the child discovers how things work. The curious toddler likes to examine and handle many different objects. He takes a new toy and squeezes it, smells it, shakes it, puts part of it in his mouth, pounds on it, and so on. He discovers that a musical toy makes a pleasant sound when he pulls a string or presses a button.

Much exploratory play appears aimless or meaningless to those who don't understand that the child is trying out new skills and seeking knowledge about the things around him. Adults and older children are used to the idea of starting a project with a specific goal in mind and then carrying it through. The toddler is more interested in an activity itself than with a specific outcome of his efforts, so he doesn't always feel the need to complete a task. His attention span is fairly short, too, and he is easily distracted from one activity to another.

Sometimes small children also seem destructive to adults because they frequently break their toys and other objects. But even in breaking an object, the child is learning about it. As long as the things he plays with are not harmful when broken, or too valuable to be destroyed, there's no harm in his taking things apart and trying to piece them back together. If he breaks a favorite toy and then cries unhappily when he cannot make it work again, that is a lesson, too.

Objects that can be taken apart and put back together—such as construction toys with parts that snap together—offer more satisfaction as well as instruction. When toddlers match pegs to holes and fit smaller objects, such as boxes, into larger ones, they are learning concepts such as **spatial relationships,** shape, and relative size. Rita, at twenty-five months, can recognize some alphabet shapes and is able to match plastic letters to corresponding indented forms on a board. However, she is not yet able to figure out how to get each letter securely in its place; she tries to force the *M* into its form, not realizing that she has it upside down. She will eventually master this activity through trial and error.

When a child observes or listens to others, he is engaging in **passive play.** The toddler can sit quite contentedly and watch older children at play. Later he may try to imitate their actions. A toddler also learns from listening to a story or having a book read out loud. These stories teach him new words and also communicate ideas and values to him.

LEARNING TO TALK

While children are expanding their range of experience and knowledge of the world, they are also making progress in the learning of language—a dramatic and uniquely human accomplishment. Like walking, learning to talk is a turning point in the child's overall development. Talking is of course an important part of communicating with others. It enables the child to express his needs, desires, thoughts, and emotions with greater precision. Language also helps the child to reason and think about his experiences in a new way.

No matter what language they learn, children seem to go through predictable stages in acquiring language—just as they learned to walk by stages. General milestones of development are listed in the "Based on Fact" box on page 159. The age ranges given are broad, since not all children progress at the same rate. As the box shows, learning language is not just a matter of speaking; it also involves understanding the speech of others. Children can comprehend much of spoken language before they are able to speak coherently themselves.

We have seen that the infant's babbling consists of a wide variety of sounds, some of which are completely unlike the sounds of the language he hears spoken by his family. Gradually he begins to imitate more of the familiar sounds of his own family's speech.

The baby's first wordlike sounds are often two-syllable repetitions like "mama" and "bye-bye." He does not use these sounds meaningfully at first, but soon the responses of his caregivers teach him that these sounds have meaning. For example, a mother will smile and speak encouragingly when she hears her baby say "mama," and he soon learns to call her with this word. At the age of one, many children use a vocabulary of three or four words, mixed in with their own **jargon** of incomprehensible sounds.

LANGUAGE DEVELOPMENT OF THE TODDLER

12 MONTHS OLD

Understanding: Can follow simple instructions ("Come here").
Recognizes familiar names and words, including own name.

Speaking: Uses 3–4 words such as "mama," "dada," "cup."
Uses baby jargon.
Imitates some sounds made by others.

12–18 MONTHS OLD

Understanding: Can follow slightly more complex commands ("Give Grandpa the ball").
Can point to pictures of familiar objects and to parts of own body when they are named.

Speaking: Uses 10–20 words.
Uses single words as a sentence ("Cup" can mean "I want my milk," "Where is my cup?" etc.).
Still uses jargon.
Has difficulty pronouncing some consonants (may say "yunch" instead of "lunch").

1½–3 YEARS OLD

Understanding: Continues to understand one-step commands; cannot follow instructions consisting of several steps.
Identifies more and more common objects as they are named.
Understands relative size (big and small).

Speaking: Knows more than 200 words by age 2; about 500 by age 3.
Creates 2-word sentences expressing action ("Baby cry") or possession ("Mommy shoe"); then begins to use 3-word sentences, showing sense of word order.
Starts to use past tense and plurals.
Refers to self by name at first ("Dina go park"); then learns to use pronoun ("I").
Asks the names of objects.
May stutter as a normal part of acquiring language fluency.

Through imitation, the child adds to his store of single words. However, he may not always use these words to label things correctly. Piaget noted that his daughter, at age thirteen months, used the word "bow-wow" for many different things, including horses, cars, and people. It was not until three months later that she used the term exclusively for dogs.

By the age of one and a half years, most children are still using a great deal of baby jargon. Many have their own private vocabulary of sounds whose meanings can sometimes be guessed. Twenty-month-old Patrick used to point and ask "Bee-goo?" whenever he wanted something. His grandmother figured out that the child was probably imitating the word "bigger," because she had often told him that he could play with certain objects "when you're bigger."

In the next step of language development, the toddler uses a single word as a complete sentence. For example, "Dada!" might mean "Here comes Daddy," "Daddy, come here," "Where is Daddy?" or perhaps, if the child is pointing to a pair of shoes, "These are Daddy's shoes." The tone of voice and the circumstances in which the one-word sentence is uttered usually provide a clue to the meaning.

At the same time, the child can usually identify objects, or pictures of objects, that another person names, even if the child cannot say the words himself. For instance, Sonya can point to her eyes, nose, and mouth when asked. She can also follow simple instructions, such as "Get the ball," but she cannot follow commands that consist of more than one process.

Next the child begins to combine two or three words to form a simple sentence: "Nana go bye-bye," "See nice kitty," "Get down." These sentences often show that the child has developed an elementary sense of word order—for example, he puts the verb before the object, as is customary in English. However, he may not do this consistently. Two-year-old Bruce is as likely to say "Lunch eat" as he is to say "Eat lunch."

By age two, most children are using quite a few of these short sentences. For a while they will refer to themselves by their names— "Dina go park"—before they learn to use the pronoun "I." By age three, a child may be very talkative indeed, constantly asking questions ("What's that?") and describing aloud whatever he happens to be doing. Children may

Toddlers learn to talk through imitation and repetition. By interacting with others during everyday activities, toddlers become familiar with the names of the common objects in their environment.

Speech defects are among the most common handicaps in children. Most of us are able to get a fairly good grasp on the use of language by the time we're four or five, and by the time we're seven or so we're using language as freely as adults. Many children, though, aren't that lucky. They lisp, stammer, stutter, repeat themselves, or just seem incapable of putting together a normal sentence.

Speech defects occur frequently because they may be due to any one or more of a variety of physical and emotional problems—or some combination of them.

Probably the most common physical cause of speech impairment in children is deafness or some other hearing difficulty. Children with good hearing learn how to speak by listening to and imitating others. That accounts not only for our common agreement on how words should be pronounced but also for regional accents that allow for differences in pronunciation. Naturally, children who can't hear what others are saying—or who, because of some hearing problem, hear something different from what a person with good hearing hears—can't imitate. They must be taught to speak by special methods involving mimicry of mouth movements and sensitivity to the different vibrations made by different sounds.

On the other hand, there are children whose hearing is excellent but who have poor vision or an imperfect sense of touch. If such children have difficulty, for example, distinguishing the shape of a person from that of a tree—or feeling the difference between a piece of sandpaper and the polished surface of a mirror—they may have difficulty learning the words that identify the different qualities (roughness, smoothness) or objects (person, tree) and

mix them up when trying to speak. Oddly enough, they may also have difficulty in keeping track of time, because so much of our sense of time depends upon our seeing or feeling the change in things.

Another important physical cause of speech defect or impairment may be brain damage or mental retardation—that is, the failure of the brain to develop normally—as happens, for example, in children with Down's Syndrome.

Then there is a long list of obvious physical causes that can usually be dealt with by corrective surgery. These causes might include a cleft palate, badly positioned (or missing) teeth, a harelip, tongue "tie," or a badly receding or projecting jaw.

It is always important to remember, of course, that speech impairments are not always caused by physical problems. Emotional difficulties may be at the source of the impairment, as is often true in stuttering or stammering, for example. To complicate the matter even more, speech difficulties that were originally caused by physical problems may make children so self-conscious and put them at such a disadvantage in school and social relationships that emotional problems arise as well.

Early detection of speech defects or deficiencies in the child is crucial if proper diagnosis is to be made in time to develop an effective course of therapy. In North America, detection is usually left to the child's teacher or pediatrician. In Europe, however, a growing practice has been to set up diagnostic and remedial speech clinics for children suffering from some speech impairment and to provide special classes for them wherever they may be helpful.

hold conversations with their dolls, or simply chatter to themselves. On the other hand, many three-year-olds are still not very talkative. As in other areas of growth, some children start earlier and some later.

Speech development is a long process, requiring both physical and cognitive skill. It takes a while before children can pronounce words properly and form complex sentences that correctly follow the rules of grammar. Many children stutter when they first start using words; they need time and practice to get the words out. Small children often speak quite loudly, too, as they have not yet learned to control their voices. Although a child's noisy chatter may sometimes be annoying to adults, it is important to allow and encourage a child to practice speaking. Later he will learn to lower his voice when necessary.

HOW IS LANGUAGE ACQUIRED?

Encouragement and stimulation are an important aid to children's language development. Yet children do not have to be taught to speak; the normal child seems to acquire language skills on his own. How can this remarkable achievement be explained?

Perhaps the simplest theory of language acquisition states that learning takes place by **observational learning** and **reinforcement.** The child learns by imitating adult speech, and what he learns is reinforced when the adults respond to his efforts. This view is related to B. F. Skinner's theory of **operant conditioning,** in which behavior is reinforced by rewards (in this case, the approval expressed by the parents when the child utters a recognizable word).

It is clear that imitation plays an important part in learning to talk. But this theory fails to explain why children frequently do not repeat phrases exactly as they have been spoken. Even though little Elias hears his older brother say "Where is that book?" the toddler continues to say "That book where?" Eventually Elias responds to his brother's attempts to correct him, but for a long time he sticks to his own version of the question. Another problem with the imitation theory is that children are often heard to create sentences of their own which they have never heard spoken and could not have copied.

According to a second theory, we humans are born with a built-in or *innate* capacity for language learning. In effect, we are preprogrammed—like computers—for language development. Since this development proceeds by definite stages, a child's skill at building sentences depends on the particular stage he is in at the moment. This would explain why Elias kept saying "That book where?" even when his brother corrected him.

Still another theory puts the emphasis on children's *needs* and their relationship with their environment. As they need to express themselves, they learn language accordingly. They begin with the names of things they want or need. Then they go on to use verb forms like "gone" or "all gone" and phrases like "more milk."

The point could also be made that language is an open-ended skill. A great many combinations of words are possible, once a person has mastered the rules of grammar and acquired a sufficient vocabulary. A creative speaker can easily put together sentences he has never heard spoken before.

Especially in the early stages of language learning, children are very aware of rules, but they are not always aware of exceptions to the rules. When Nancy was asked where she had gone, she answered: "I goed to the park." Nancy is aware that -*ed* is used to form the past tense of a verb. She hasn't yet learned the exceptions, the verbs with irregular past tenses such as "went." With time, experience—and a supportive, stimulating environment—children gradually master the basic rules of grammar and other language skills.

· SUMMARY ·

- Toddlers are still learning through their body movements and senses.
- Through trial and error, toddlers learn new ways to get desired results. Next they start to experiment mentally as well as physically.
- Toddlers have greater capacity for imitation, make-believe, memory, and language.
- Exploratory play teaches a child how things work. Passive play involves watching or listening to others.
- Learning to talk proceeds gradually by definite stages. Some children start earlier, some later.
- The child learns language mainly by imitating. His language skills improve with adult encouragement and reinforcement.

TERMS TO KNOW

directed groping
jargon
observational learning
passive play

preoperational period
reinforcement
spatial relationships
symbolic representation

1. Imitation, make-believe, memory, and language are examples of _____.
2. In Piaget's theory, the _____ begins at about age two or three.
3. A one-year-old may use a few real words mixed with his own _____.
4. Fitting small boxes into larger ones helps toddlers learn about _____.
5. Dropping bread from a high chair is an example of what Piaget called _____.
6. Learning to speak may be a combination of _____, or hearing adults speak, and _____, or being rewarded.
7. A toddler who watches other children play is engaging in _____.

CHECK YOUR UNDERSTANDING

1. At what age is a child likely to engage in directed groping? What does this activity teach the toddler?
2. How is a toddler's method of solving a problem different at 18 to 24 months than it was at 12 to 18 months?
3. Does a child in the early preoperational period understand cause and effect? Explain.
4. Describe how exploratory play can help a toddler's cognitive development, even though the activity may seem aimless to an adult.
5. What can a toddler learn from having a story read to him?
6. Name two aspects of learning language. Which does a toddler become skilled at sooner?
7. What are three theories of language acquisition?

·11·
SOCIAL/EMOTIONAL DEVELOPMENT
OF THE TODDLER

The company picnic was in full swing when Joe and his daughter Peggy arrived.

"Let's see what's going on, Peggy," Joe said. "Look, here are some boys and girls just about the same age as you." He pointed to a nearby group of five or six toddlers. They were chasing after a runaway soccer ball with excited shrieks.

"Wouldn't you like to play with them?" Joe coaxed. "I'm sure they'd let you."

Peggy stood silently with one finger in her mouth, holding on to Joe's pant leg with her other hand. "Don't want to," she said finally.

"Why not?" asked Joe.

Peggy shrugged. "Can I sit with you?"

"I'll tell you what," Joe said. "Why don't you sit here by yourself and watch them for awhile. I'll be right here." He stepped back a few feet while Peggy settled herself on the grass.

Joe's friend Francisco came up to join him. "The kids are sure having a ball."

"I just wish Peggy would be more sociable," Joe answered. "Your Marisa always joins right in, but not Peggy. And they're about the same age—almost three."

"Well, Marisa's used to people," Francisco explained. "She has a grandpa who lives with us, an aunt, and five brothers and sisters."

"That's a point," Joe said. "Peggy's an only child. She's really only used to me and her sitter."

"I'm sure she'll be playing right along with the others in a few minutes," Francisco said. "She just needs to check things out first. And she's probably learning a lot just by watching."

"Still, I wish she had more opportunities to play with other children. Then maybe she wouldn't be so shy."

"Why don't you bring her over to our place next weekend?" Francisco offered. "The more the merrier!"

•

Why didn't Peggy play with the other children at the picnic?

•

In what ways could a big family help the social development of a toddler?

Physically and cognitively, the toddler is making great strides along the road to greater independence. She is experimenting with new activities and discovering that she can do many things by herself. She is also exploring the powers of her mind and becoming capable of more complex thought.

At the same time, the toddler is going through an important transition in her social and personal growth. She is developing a strong sense of herself as an individual. She also has a growing awareness of herself as a member of a group—the family. On the one hand, she is eager to express her emerging personality, to exercise her new-found powers, and to assert her independence. On the other hand, she is still a baby in many ways, dependent on her family. Through her relationships with family members, the toddler is learning to cooperate and get along with other people. In other words, she is encountering society and finding her place in it.

THE FAMILY

Although the toddler is becoming aware of the larger world that lies beyond the home, her social life is mainly centered in the family. Through interaction with family members, the child learns how to function as a member of society. This learning process is called **socialization.**

A child is being socialized when she learns to greet people when they arrive and to say good-bye when they leave; when she is scolded for poking her aunt in the eye; when she learns to expect certain events, such as meals, at certain times of the day. These and other lessons teach children what kinds of behavior are expected of them. Often the expectations vary, depending on the particular culture a child is born into. In our society, a toddler gradually learns to eat properly, with a fork or spoon in-stead of the fingers. But in India, eating with the fingers is the proper way. However, even an Indian toddler learns that she should not just plunge her hand into a plate of food; she must be taught to use her fingers in an acceptable, neat manner when she eats.

Some aspects of socialization take place through direct teaching—as when parents explain to their unself-conscious toddler that people should not undress in public. Other kinds of behavior are not taught formally, but the child learns them by imitating the actions of family members or by observing how they respond to her own actions. Approval means a great deal to toddlers, and they quickly discover which actions please their parents and which are unacceptable.

Of course, family life teaches a child more than just rules of behavior. The family is an extremely important influence on the child's overall development. The early experiences in the home lay the foundation for all the toddler's later experiences—how she perceives, understands, and responds emotionally to events in her life. In fact, the influence of the family is so strong that it becomes very hard to determine which aspects of a child's personality were shaped by family relationships and which were part of her genetic inheritance. And even though experiences in later life may change some of the personality traits formed in childhood, the effects of these early influences can never be completely erased.

Not all families are alike, so naturally children from different kinds of families will have different experiences. Some families are large and close-knit. Their children become accustomed to having warm relationships with many people besides their parents—**siblings,** grandparents, uncles and aunts, and other relatives. They will not have to depend entirely on their parents for all their needs, since others will take care of them, too. In a family with many children, older ones will often be put in charge of watching over the little ones.

Families provide the physical necessities of life. But beyond food, clothing, and shelter, children have the need for security, love, and understanding which the family also fulfills. For much of a child's early life, the family continues to be the major source of emotional support and knowledge of social customs and standards.

Should adopted children be told they're adopted? Adoption authorities today all agree the answer is definitely yes. This brings the matter out into the open—truthfully—and lets everyone deal with it as an accepted fact of family life. To hide the fact of adoption, as used to be done, or to ignore it until the child learns of it by accident, is asking for trouble. It makes adoption seem like a bad thing when, in fact, it's a very happy occasion for everyone concerned.

When an adopted child begins to ask questions, it should be made clear that it was not his "fault" that he was given up for adoption and that his first parents probably had to give him up because of circumstances over which they had no control. It's most likely the parent or parents were unable physically, financially, or emotionally to provide a good home.

With older children, if the subject comes up, the difference between biological parents and adoptive parents can be explained in detail. With a younger child it's not necessary and would probably just be confusing.

On the other hand, it's not a good idea to keep reminding a child that he is adopted. It could make him feel uncomfortable, as if he were an outsider in the family. And trying to make adoption sound good by telling the child he was adopted because he's someone "special" can give him an inflated view of himself and possibly cause resentment among his sisters and brothers.

Do you think older adopted children should be told who their natural parents were, if they ask? Why or why not?

In contrast to the **extended family** is the smaller, relatively isolated family made up of parents and children—the **nuclear family**—or perhaps just one parent and one or more children. In these smaller families, the toddler's early relationships will largely be with just a few people. Her perception of social and personal roles—including sex-role identity—will at first be based on her interaction with these few. She will depend more on her parents, for without the help of relatives, they will have to see to all the needs of the child themselves.

Families also vary in their life style and their approach to child rearing. Depending on the cultural, religious, or ethnic background of the family, the child will learn particular values, beliefs, customs, and behaviors. Social

class and income level also affect the toddler's experiences. Children of educated professionals who earn high salaries will be used to one way of life; children of poor, unskilled laborers will be used to another. Life styles vary in other ways, too. Living in a small country village is very different from living in a big city, for instance.

Perhaps most important are the personalities of the individual parents, how they get along with each other, and their general outlook on life. Toddlers acquire much of their own sense of identity by modeling the behavior and actions of their parents. In a very poor home, for instance, the family may be warm and supportive, and the child learns the value of cooperation and sharing. Or the parents might be bitter and resentful, and the child

Identical twins—born from a single egg fertilized by a single sperm—not only look alike, but may even share the same mannerisms, the same habits, and the same likes and dislikes. These similarities are not necessarily due to a common upbringing. Studies of adopted twins who were raised apart have revealed amazing similarities. In some cases, twins who grew up separately even ended up marrying people with the same names.

But even though identical twins are alike in many ways, they are still individuals and can have different rates of development. As toddlers, one twin may crawl and walk earlier; or one may start talking sooner.

This is also true of fraternal twins—nonidentical twins born from two eggs fertilized simultaneously. Unlike identical twins, who are always of the same sex, fraternal twins may be of the same sex or different. Since girls generally develop more rapidly than boys, a female twin will often be ahead of her brother in some ways.

These differences can have an affect on children's social/emotional development. The normal rivalry between siblings can be very intense between twins, especially if they feel they are competing with each other for their parents' praise or attention.

It has long been considered a "cute" custom to dress twins alike and even give them similar names (like Eddie and Freddie). And since it's so convenient to have them keep each other company, they may be expected always to play together instead of meeting other children.

Many child psychologists now feel that these practices are unwise. Instead, parents should encourage a positive sense of uniqueness in each twin. This may be especially important during toddlerhood, when the child is just starting to gain a clear sense of individuality.

grows up with a painful sense of being deprived. Much depends on the environment created by the family members.

Of course, no parent is perfect, nor is there any such thing as an "ideal" parent. After all, parents are unique individuals just as babies and children are, and each has his or her strengths and weaknesses. But if the parents are basically content together and give their child loving care and emotional support, then the inevitable conflicts and strains of daily life will not interfere with the toddler's development. Learning to handle conflicts and unpleasant emotions is an important part of the socialization process.

An atmosphere of affection and security is vital to the toddler's healthy emotional development. As Erikson has pointed out, it enables children to develop **basic trust** in themselves and others, and helps them to gain a sense of **autonomy,** or independence. In Erikson's theory of development, autonomy plays an important role in toddlerhood.

AUTONOMY

The toddler learns and expresses autonomy in a number of ways. In learning to walk, for example, the child must let go of her parent's hand—an expression of trust—and take steps by herself. This is one move from dependence to independence. A stronger display of independence comes when the toddler no longer stays near her parent and decides to walk farther away. She delights not only in the joy of physical movement but also in the emotional satisfaction that comes with this sign of self-sufficiency.

Many household items are safety hazards for children. As toddlers become more independent they explore objects they formerly ignored. Caregivers must take safety precautions by placing dangerous items out of reach. Special latches are available which make it difficult for toddlers to get into drawers and closets. Covers for electrical outlets are also sold. Kiddie gates are not usually effective for keeping children of this age out of unsafe areas, because most toddlers have the ability to open hooks or push the gates over.

Similarly, the toddler takes great pride in learning to control her bowel and bladder functions. She recognizes that using the toilet is a sign of being more grown-up. The feeling of being able to control her own body in this way is rewarding.

However, although toddlers are happy about this important achievement, they also feel a little resentful of their parents' demands concerning toilet use. The toddler enjoys her budding sense of power—the ability to choose to do a thing or not to do it. Sometimes she refuses to eliminate when placed on the potty or toilet, just as a way of asserting her autonomy. Later on, she may forget to go to the potty when she needs to, and soils her clothing. The child then feels ashamed of her failure; her self-control

was not as great as she had imagined. She feels doubt about her abilities. This example illustrates one of the stages in Erikson's theory of psychological development. He calls it the crisis of autonomy versus shame and doubt, and it is typical of children in the second year of life.

THE EMOTIONAL LIFE OF THE TODDLER

The toddler is self-centered and believes that the world revolves around her. She demands immediate fulfillment of her desires and is furious when she cannot get what she wants. Eager to try out her new-found powers, she

Toddlers vary in their ability to amuse themselves. Some children can play alone contently for some time. Others need constant interaction with other people.

Although young children are largely self-centered, a recent government-sponsored study shows that they are capable of comforting others from as early as one year of age.

Marian Radke Yarrow, chief of the Laboratory of Developmental Psychology at the National Institute of Mental Health, studied children between ten months and two and a half years. In the study, young mothers were trained to be aware of their children's cries, startles, and facial expressions. Whenever someone around the baby showed emotion, the mother described the child's reactions into a tape recorder. For example, one mother reported that her fifteen-month-old son saw that she was very tired. He patted her gently and offered her his bottle.

At around eighteen months of age the children started "trying on emotions." They would imitate a wince or cry when a parent cried. Yarrow feels that this imitation suggests the capacity for an empathetic sharing in the feelings of others. She also believes that at this point children either become more sympathetic or have a reaction of relief: "I'm glad it's not me." Yarrow stresses that this may be the crucial point in a child's moral development. The parent's behavior instructs the child to go one way or the other.

These findings seem to give support to psychologist Martin Hoffman's theories about moral development. Hoffman thinks that there is no basis for the common assumption that all ethical behavior is rooted in selfish motives. Instead, he believes that concern for the welfare of others is based on a natural feeling of distress in response to someone else's suffering.

crows with triumph when she succeeds in fitting together a puzzle, and cries with frustration when she cannot reach a toy on a high shelf. The toddler is bursting with imagination, dreams, and fears. Sometimes she feels ready to tackle the world—and then suddenly becomes shy and frightened, as if she has just realized that she is not so ready after all.

Feelings and moods are intense for the toddler—and changeable. Ned is inconsolable because he can't find his favorite blanket. But he stops in mid-scream when it is produced, and rushes to claim it with an expression of rapture. Like all toddlers, he expresses his feelings openly and exuberantly.

Toddlers can exert some measure of control over their feelings. They can wait if they are hungry. They can be comforted when frightened. And fortunately for caregivers, they can be easily distracted. Bernette protests angrily when she has to be put into diapers for the night. But she instantly giggles with pleasure when she is handed an amusing clown doll.

NEGATIVITY AND TANTRUMS

The child who is trying out her autonomy can be very stubborn and willful at times. It is because of this trait that people sometimes call toddlerhood "the terrible twos." Two-year-old Esther seems to be always hungry, yet when her mother tells her that it's time for lunch, she shouts "No! No!" Then, when her mother takes the food away from the table, Esther begins to scream in rage: "Want yunch!" When the food is brought back, she sits down and calmly begins to eat.

At times, such behavior certainly does seem "terrible" to Esther's mother. But she reminds

A toddler's emotions are intense. Shouts of glee or piercing screams are common at this age and occur at the most unexpected moments. Caregivers must be patient with their child. They can change unwanted behavior by distracting the toddler with a favorite toy or activity.

herself that this is simply evidence of her daughter's emotional growth. Esther is showing that she knows she is an individual and can make her own decisions. In this situation, Esther's decision was not really appropriate—after all, she really was hungry for lunch. Gradually, as she gains a more secure sense of self, the kinds of decisions she makes and the way she expresses them will change.

Almost all toddlers have occasional temper tantrums—when they are tired, frustrated, impatient, jealous, or angry. Often, like grownups, they're not really sure what is bothering them; they just know that they are very upset.

Mr. Calder took his son Emil with him to the supermarket. Seeing a brightly colored cereal package, Emil pointed and told his father that he wanted it. Mr. Calder did not want Emil to eat that brand of cereal, since it contained a lot of sugar, so he explained that the cereal was not on their shopping list and they were not going to buy it. To his dismay, Emil threw himself down on the floor, kicked his feet, waved his arms, and screamed at the top of his lungs. Such tantrums can best be understood as a combination of the child's need to assert himself and his inability to express his emotions in a socially acceptable way.

AGGRESSION AND POSSESSIVENESS

Caregivers often find it necessary to restrain a toddler from striking others or throwing things at them. Such aggressive behavior is another way that toddlers sometimes express their need for independence and their developing sense of self. The toddler wants her own way, and she wants it now! She also has a keen sense of possession and may resent it when another child intrudes upon her territory or tries to take something that belongs to her.

Jimmy, for example, was playing in the sandbox with several toys. Another child came over and reached out curiously for a little red

Sharing is hard for toddlers. They are very possessive with their toys. They won't allow others to use them even if they are occupied with other items. Children at this age may pull, push, bite, or kick to hold on to their belongings. Parents have different philosophies about interfering in these struggles. Some believe children should "fight it out" unless someone is getting hurt. Others feel the children should be separated by adults.

bucket that Jimmy was not using at the moment. Immediately Jimmy snatched his possession out of her reach and gave her an angry shove. "Mine!" he shouted. Jimmy's father came over and tried to persuade the little boy to share his toys, but Jimmy refused indignantly. Yet ten minutes later, Jimmy himself tried to take another child's doll. This time he found himself on the receiving end of a hearty spank.

Children at this age have little sense of the give-and-take of social life. For them, it's apt to be all take-and-grab! Although toddlers enjoy having other children around, they don't really play *with* other children; they play *next to* them. This is called **parallel play.** Three toddlers might all be playing with blocks, for example, but each will build her own tower. They are not yet ready for social skills such as sharing and taking turns.

Not all toddlers are aggressive all of the time. Sometimes they go to the other extreme. When Leila is pushed or hit by another child, she rarely protests, preferring to run to her mother for comfort. Her shyness and clinging seem to be an expression of her uncertainty about growing up. For the moment, she finds it more comfortable to retreat into more babyish behavior. Leila wants to be independent just like other toddlers, but she also wants to make sure that she is still allowed to act like a baby when the going gets rough.

SIBLING RIVALRY

A toddler who is a first child often feels resentful when a new baby comes into the family. From the child's point of view, her new sister or brother is a rival. Smaller and more helpless, the baby seems to claim everyone's attention, making the toddler feel left out. However, children find it easier to overcome the feelings of jealousy and competition that come with **sibling rivalry** if they are given a sense of being responsibly involved in caring for the new-

born. They will also feel satisfied when they are reminded of the privileges of being a "big" boy or girl. Toddlers can do grown-up things that the baby can't, and recognizing this is heartening to the child who is beginning to enjoy her autonomy.

FEARS AND IMAGINATION

The toddler who has achieved a sense of basic trust will tend to be less fearful of sudden noises and strange objects or people. As she is exposed to new situations and people, the strange will become the familiar. For instance, the child may get to know her neighbors' house as well as her own, and begin to make friends with their dog. By degrees toddlers practice coping with the new, and they begin to welcome novel experiences. They start to learn which things to fear as well as which things not to fear. A healthy sense of caution—about playing near traffic, for example—is as important as the feeling of confidence.

Toddlers indulge a great deal in fantasy. They have not yet learned to distinguish the imaginary from the real. Objects, creatures, and situations from the child's daydreams and nightmares can haunt her. She may fear the dark, for instance, and make quite a fuss about going to bed. A night light may reassure her. However, anxiety at bedtime may also be related to the child's fear of separation from her parents.

The toddler's parents are still the brightest stars in her universe, and she may express her worries about losing them in other ways as well. Toddlers often protest strongly when a parent leaves them with someone else. As we have noted, however, they are easily comforted and distracted from their worries. If their anxiety is severe, they will need extra attention. Sometimes children's fears are based on reality—as when a parent really does leave, because of death or divorce. Like people of all

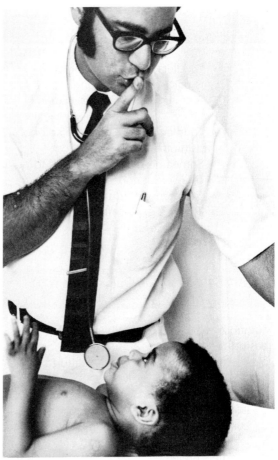

Children need special handling when they're afraid. Their fears must be acknowledged. They may need to be held closely or verbally reassured. Toddlers cope with fears through role-playing and fantasy. They practice new situations until they are familiar or nonthreatening.

ages, children often need help in adjusting to a painful loss.

Imagination is not only a source of worries, of course. Imaginative play is fun and gives children a chance to experiment with social and personal roles. Playtime is a way for a small child to feel big. She can make her own rules and decisions. She can try out grown-up activities, as when she pretends to use the telephone or walks around in her father's shoes. She can also overcome her fears by imagining things to be the way she wants them: She can slay a dragon, or heal a sick doll.

Many children in late toddlerhood invent an imaginative playmate; or they may simply pretend that their dolls or stuffed animals are real live playmates. Henry, during the time he was being toilet-trained, often played at putting a toy monkey on the toilet, occasionally scolding it when it "refused" to sit there. In this way Henry explored some of his own feelings about this new activity in his life. As they approach preschool age, children become even more imaginative in their play, which helps them to explore further their personalities and experiment with social roles.

· SUMMARY ·

- Toddlers learn from their family what kinds of behavior are expected of them. This is part of socialization.
- A child's personality is shaped by family relationships as well as by genetic inheritance.
- Toddlers learn and show autonomy in such ways as walking alone, talking, and using the toilet.
- Sometimes a toddler refuses to perform a newly learned skill. This, too, is a way of asserting independence.
- Children at this age play next to, not with, other children.
- Toddlers express feelings openly and exuberantly. They are imaginative and sometimes fearful.

TERMS TO KNOW

autonomy   sibling rivalry
basic trust   siblings
parallel play   socialization

1. The number of ____, or brothers and sisters, in a family influences social development.
2. Letting go of a parent's hand when learning to walk is an example of ____.
3. Toddlers prefer ____ rather than playing with other children.
4. ____ is the process of learning how to function as a member of society.
5. Children develop ____ in themselves and others when they are raised in an atmosphere of affection and security.
6. A new baby in the family often results in jealousy and competition, or ____.

CHECK YOUR UNDERSTANDING

1. Why does socialization depend on culture?
2. What are three ways in which a child learns expected behavior from family members?
3. Give two examples of major achievements in toddlerhood that are expressions of autonomy.
4. Why do people sometimes call toddlerhood the "terrible twos"?
5. When are temper tantrums most likely to take place in toddlers?
6. What does a toddler's aggressive behavior express?
7. What can be done to ease a toddler's feelings of jealousy and competition at the arrival of a new baby?
8. Why does a toddler's imagination often lead to fears?
9. What are some positive aspects of imagination?

·12·
INTERACTION
WITH THE TODDLER

"Where would you like to go on our vacation this year?" Marc asked his wife, Amanda. "I was thinking we might visit the Romanos in Boston. They've got a big apartment, and they're crazy about Sam."

"I'd love to see them," said Amanda. "But since Sam is coming with us, I think we should plan a trip that a two-year-old would enjoy. Sam's never been out of the city, so Boston wouldn't be anything special for him."

"That's true," Marc said. "We should take him someplace he's never been before. It'll be a totally new experience, so he'll learn more about the world, and have fun too. How about going to the shore?"

"That would be terrific. All three of us could do with some fresh air and exercise. And there are plenty of built-in toys at the beach for Sam. All that sand!" Amanda said. "He'll love hunting for sea shells, too."

"He can discover what the ocean is really like," Marc added. "You know how he loves that book about the sailboat."

"He'll be able to smell wildflowers and touch soft moss and look at bugs. Watching ants in the park has become one of Sam's favorite activities lately," Amanda said with a laugh.

"Then we'll definitely go to the shore," said Marc. "A week by the sea will be a wonderful experience for Sam—and a nice change for us."

•

Amanda and Marc decided to plan a vacation that would be fun for their two-year-old son. Besides being fun for Sam, how will the vacation they planned help fulfill his special needs as a toddler?

•

Suppose Sam's parents couldn't afford to go away for a vacation. How might they plan vacation-time activities in the city that would meet Sam's needs and be fun for them too?

With each new stage in a child's development, parents and other caregivers meet with a fresh set of challenges and rewards. Reading about the physical, cognitive and social/emotional development of toddlers can give you some idea of these rewards and challenges. Yet until you actually take care of a toddler—as a baby-sitter, day-care worker, or parent—it is hard to understand all that the job involves and what a caregiver's feelings are likely to be.

Toddlers are sweet and lovable—but also stubborn and willful at times. Meeting their various and sometimes conflicting needs can be exhausting. There is no magic formula guaranteed to prevent conflicts with a toddler. At times even the most patient parents blow their tops. No caregiver is perfect. Those who take on the awesome task of rearing or working with toddlers must be prepared to give much of themselves, certainly. But they must also know when to draw the line—both for their own peace of mind and for the child's benefit.

UNDERSTANDING THE TODDLER'S CONFLICTING NEEDS

At times, people of all ages have desires or needs that conflict with each other. In the toddler, this is especially evident in the way a child wavers between seeking to be independent and clinging to babyhood.

Typically, children at this age want to be grown-up, but at the same time they are fearful and unsure of themselves. One day a child will shout, "Me do!"—and the next day will demand, "You do it." This is true for activities ranging from getting dressed or climbing into a stroller to digging a hole in the sandbox.

When Elisa and her father leave the house Saturday morning on their way to the supermarket, the little girl insists on going down the front steps by herself. She refuses to hold her father's hand. Once safely down, she proudly scampers back up and repeats the procedure. But when father and child return from the store, Elisa refuses to climb the stairs. She cries for her daddy, who is now loaded down with groceries, to carry her up.

Elisa isn't deliberately trying to make life difficult for her father. For one thing, she is tired. And for almost an hour, she has been obeying his request that she "be a big girl" and not cause trouble in the store. Now she wants reassurance that she doesn't have to be grown-up all the time.

Elisa's parents have discussed her tendency to return to "babyish" behavior from time to time. They have noticed that she often does this soon after learning a new skill or behaving very maturely for a while, as well as when she is tired. They have wisely decided to baby her (within reason) when she asks for it. They understand that this is Elisa's way of making sure that in growing up, she does not have to give up any privileges until she is ready.

On this occasion, her father puts down his bundles and carries his "big girl" up the steps. He sets her down at the top with a smile and a shrug that says he's not fooled by her pretended helplessness.

Toddlers must be allowed—even encouraged at times—to strike out on their own and to do for themselves whatever they can or want to try. Yet in permitting them to become more independent, caregivers must be careful not to push them out of babyhood too fast. They are still very young.

All children this age need to know that they can slip back briefly into being babied whenever they have doubts or fears about being grown-up. Otherwise, they are likely to lose interest in daring to try new things—and they must dare, if they are to learn and grow.

ALLOWING INDEPENDENCE

Whenever we learn a new skill, it usually takes some time to get it right. For instance, not many people are very good at riding a bicycle the first few times they try. The same is true of toddlers, who are just starting to acquire many of the skills that their elders take for granted—such as dressing themselves.

Caregivers must be patient with a toddler who is attempting to manage on his own. He needs encouragement and praise for trying. To criticize him for slowness or clumsiness would only be discouraging and hurtful. Imagine how you would feel if your teachers or parents ridiculed you for not being able to balance yourself the first time you ever got on a bike.

Of course, it can be nerve-racking to wait for a two-year-old who insists on zippering his own jacket and putting on his own boots, especially if you're in a hurry to get somewhere. At times you do have to step in and complete the job quickly to avoid being late for an appointment. At such times you might say, "I know you can do this yourself, but we have to hurry, so I'll help." As long as this happens only rarely, the child will not feel discouraged.

However, if it occurs frequently, he may give up trying to master the task and expect somebody else to do this—and perhaps other things—for him.

Most children are not dressing themselves very skillfully until about age three. But caregivers can give a child a good start if they give him a chance. Last-minute rushes to get somewhere on time with a toddler are less difficult when caregivers give the child enough advance warning to get ready and offer brief, clear instructions in a friendly but firm way.

A child may need at least fifteen minutes to get into his clothes and about that much more time to get into coat, mittens, hat, and other outer wear. It's best to introduce these operations one at a time. First, lay out his clothes and explain, for example: "We're going to visit Aunt Harriet soon. Here are your clothes to put on." Then, after he is dressed, lay out his wraps and give similar instructions. Long, complicated explanations confuse or overwhelm most toddlers. They also resent con-

By age 2, cups have replaced bottles for many toddlers. Training cups with spouts are available, but many feel that these are unnecessary. Children should use utensils which are not too large and which fit comfortably in their hands. Cups should be filled with small amounts of liquid until the children become skilled in holding their own utensils. Frequent spills can be expected at the beginning, and caregivers must show patience.

stant reminders to hurry up. When nagged, they generally tune out or rebel loudly.

When changing from one outfit to another, the toddler will usually have little difficulty taking off the clothes he is wearing. He may need more or less assistance in putting clothes on, depending on the outfit. Nearly all toddlers require some help with getting completely dressed. Children usually need to have their shoelaces tied for them until they are four or five years old. They also may need help with buttoning buttons for almost that long. However, they can usually manage zippers.

Not only are toddlers initially very slow at handling new tasks, their beginning efforts leave much to be desired. T-shirts are likely to go on backwards, and food winds up in the child's hair. It's wise to overlook minor shortcomings. There's no reason why Benny can't play around the house with his shirt on backwards. Any visitor who comments on this can be informed that the boy is being encouraged to be more responsible for his own care.

Corrections should be made without making a child ashamed or hurting his pride. Nina went to the potty on her own at the age of twenty-nine months, but although she sat down, she didn't pull down her pants! Her aunt, who was with her at the time, praised Nina for her efforts, but added a reminder: "Good! I'm proud of you for sitting on the potty by yourself. But next time, don't forget to pull your pants down first."

Both boys and girls should be given the same kind of encouragement to be independent—and the same kind of reassurance and comforting that every small child needs. Studies have shown that parents and other caregivers tend, without realizing it, to encourage boys to become more independent than girls—even at this early age. Girls receive more warnings to slow down, be careful, or "Don't do that—you might hurt yourself." When toddlers do fall or bump themselves— as they do almost every day—boys are more

often encouraged to take this in stride. They are more likely to receive a few comforting words from a distance, while girls are usually picked up and rocked or patted.

This kind of discrimination may explain why girls and boys generally seem to have different personality traits. Adults, in effect, teach small children what is and is not appropriate for their sex. Another example of this is clinging behavior, which is much more apt to be accepted in girls than boys. Some parents may even actively encourage it in girls because they believe it is "feminine." If a little girl snuggles up closer to her parent upon being led into a room full of strangers, she is likely to be touched reassuringly by her parent and smiled at by the other adults present. The same behavior in a little boy tends to be simply ignored, as if the adults feel that the kindest response is to pretend not to notice his clinging. In subtle ways like this, caregivers, along with society at large, encourage little girls to be overly dependent and passive, and discourage little boys from being openly affectionate and showing their real feelings.

REASSURING THE CHILD

Toddlers' conflicting feelings about being independent lead to a good deal of babyish, clinging behavior. Such behavior is also caused by their growing awareness of the real dangers of the world. Also, their **negativism** —their tendency to say "No!" to whatever is offered or asked of them—worries them. The toddler knows that his parents sometimes disapprove when he refuses to do what they want. He's afraid that they might be so disapproving that he will lose their love and protection. At times he will assert his will and try to get his own way anyhow. But at other times he will cling to his parents and act helpless. This is his way of asking for reassurance.

All toddlers behave this way at times. There

Children cling to adults for love and reassurance. Too much clinging is a sign of an emotional disturbance which should be investigated.

doubt he will give up such babyish behavior gradually, as he is ready. But what if a child seems to stop maturing altogether, makes no progress over a period of several months in managing on his own in any way, and loses interest in trying? In that case, the child may have a problem that needs special attention.

Too much clinging is a sign that a child, for one reason or another, has more than the usual amount of fear of losing love and protection. This may be due to disturbing experiences, such as hospitalization or separations from one or both parents. Or it may come about because of too many changes in child-care arrangements—as when the parent who is the major caregiver takes a job, and the child is tended to by a series of strangers. However, even when there is no special situation to cause anxiety, some children just seem more fearful of being abandoned than others.

A clinger needs special reassurance that he is securely loved and in no danger of being abandoned, even briefly. Caregivers must make independence seem less frightening to him by not rejecting him when he demands to be babied. At the same time, they should give him other opportunities to gain confidence and act more grown-up. In this way, he will gradually give up the clinging behavior on his own. Trying to force toddlers to give up clinging—by teasing them for "acting like such babies," punishing them, or threatening to walk out on them—will only make matters worse.

Toby's mother was upset that he lagged behind other children his age in doing things for himself and being willing to part with her. She was dismayed at his furious crying whenever she left him at a day-care center. His clinging to her when she took him to the playground especially worried her. She talked it over with the head of the day-care center, who suggested that she stop pressing the boy to "leave her side" and concentrate instead on helping him do things for himself while she stayed close by.

Following instructions, she began sitting

is no cause for concern if in general a toddler continues to become increasingly independent and grown-up—despite frequently demanding to be cuddled, or insisting that adults do for him things that he is able to do himself, or objecting to letting his parents out of sight. No

near Toby after laying out his clothes and saying, "Let's see you try to put these on." She praised any progress he made at this (or any other task), and took over pleasantly when her help was needed.

When she took Toby to the playground, she sat with him at the edge of the sandbox and looked at a favorite picture book with him. Since he talked very well for his age, their conversations usually drew other toddlers to them and eventually Toby would usually follow some child into the sandbox.

After several months of this, Toby was doing as much for himself as other children his age and joined readily in playground activities. He still usually protested being left at the center, but cried only briefly after his mother left, and was becoming attached to one of the day-care aides.

Toby's excessive clinging and fear of separation did not result from his being deprived of a parent's loving care. He had never been away from his mother for more than a few hours at a time since his birth, and she adored him. But she was raising him on her own, and he hadn't had a chance to form attachments to other adults. She was the only person he looked to for love and protection. Also, she continued to do everything for him long after she should have begun encouraging him to manage on his own. When she finally realized that he was not as independent as other children his age, she tried to push him "out of the nest" too abruptly. He responded by becoming more helpless and anxious. When she changed her approach, Toby gradually became more secure and independent.

CALMING THE TODDLER'S FEARS

The toddler is developing a lively imagination, a sign of healthy cognitive and emotional growth. Imagination enables a child to work out creative solutions to new challenges. It is also an important part of play, when a child imitates grown-up roles, acts out fantasies, or expresses feelings.

However, a lively imagination leads not only to creative thoughts, but also, at times, to fearful ones. Small children may be afraid of many things, some of them realistic (a speeding car) and some of them not (a monster under the bed).

As with clinging, caregivers should never ridicule or punish a toddler for being fearful, no matter how foolish they think his fears are. He needs comfort and understanding above all. When there are no rational grounds for his fear, a sympathetic explanation may help. Janice can be reassured that though the fire engine does make a frightening noise, this is just to warn cars to move over and let the engine hurry by to its important job of putting out a fire. Reading a story about fire engines or making a trip to a fire station might give her further reassurance, as well as be fun.

However, it is not always possible to "explain away" irrational fears. Pierre may continue to be afraid of flushing the toilet, despite a patient explanation of what happens and repeated assurances that "it won't hurt you."

When explanations do not help, it's best to stop talking about the child's fears and wait for time to cure them. Repeatedly urging a toddler to "pat the nice doggy" or "come and see for yourself there's no dragon in the closet" is more likely to increase a fear than to relieve it.

Some fears common at this age are realistic and serve to protect a toddler. Fear of a large body of water is an example. In helping a toddler overcome his uneasiness about letting us lead him a little way into an ocean, lake, or pool, caregivers should make it clear that he must *never* enter the water alone. And, of course, he must be watched to make sure he doesn't.

Fear of large or strange dogs also makes sense. A friendly large dog can knock a toddler over without meaning to. Some dogs do bite.

Children should be taught never to pet a strange animal without first asking permission.

Fear of strangers may also make sense at times. We want children to be friendly, but not *too* trusting of people they do not know. It's unwise to encourage a toddler to talk or play with a stranger who approaches him. The caregiver should allow the child to "make friends" with adult strangers only in safe, familiar surroundings, such as a house of worship or a community center.

MAKING BEDTIME EASIER

Fear of the dark, resistance to going to bed, and occasional nightmares or "bad dreams" are typical at this age, and for several years to come. Nighttime fears are almost as hard on parents as on the child, since they have to cope with comforting the child and persuading him to stay in his own bed. When a toddler wakes up frightened at night, he does need comforting—stroking or holding, plus reassurance that there is nothing to be afraid of. But feeding or playing with him is unwise, as he may learn to expect this—and may wake up to get it.

Also, parents should avoid taking the child into bed with them. There's no harm in doing this on rare occasions—when traveling, for example. But once a child has the idea that he can accomplish this if he puts up enough of a fight, it is extremely difficult to break him of the habit.

A night light calms fears in some cases, but not all. Letting the toddler share a room with a brother or sister may also help. The children comfort each other and do not bother their parents. Some parents have relieved a child's nighttime fears by permitting the family dog or cat to sleep by his bed.

Often, however, parents just have to put up patiently with being awakened occasionally by a frightened child. If this becomes too constant—happens nearly every night over a period of several months—and the child also has many other fears, it would be wise to look for professional counseling.

RECOGNIZING SIGNS OF STRESS

Part of growing up is learning to handle the usual (and sometimes unusual) tensions of everyday life. Most of us have our own habits or techniques of dealing with stress. For example, suppose you were worried about an exam coming up, or angry about a fight you had with your best friend. You might find yourself nervously chewing gum or even chewing on a pencil. Or you might decide to go out jogging or kick a football around to let out some of the tension.

Small children also get tense and emotionally upset at times, and they have characteristic ways of expressing it. A child may acquire such a habit that is undesirable, either physically or socially. Caregivers must not only help to reduce the child's worries or help him to adjust to a difficult situation, but also guide him in expressing his feelings in a healthier way.

Sucking the thumb or fingers is the most common way in which toddlers seek relief from emotional tension. It is seldom helpful to try to break this habit by putting bad-tasting substances on a child's finger or giving him a pacifier instead.

Sucking the thumb will not affect the child's "bite" or the position of his permanent teeth unless he keeps it up regularly past the age of four. It's all right to discourage him from doing it by telling him that he is old enough now to stop and you want to help him do so.

Gentle reminders and offering to play a game with him or just handing him a toy when you see him sucking his thumb may be helpful. It's also wise to consider whether he is under too much stress from day to day. Is he being expected to behave in too grown-up a fashion?

Children show anger in many ways. Making a funny face expresses a strong feeling openly and helps relieve tension.

Scolded too often or harshly? Annoyed or treated badly by a sibling? Though caregivers can't entirely eliminate such stresses in the child's life, they can reduce the overall load.

Other habits the child may form to relieve tension are nail biting, hair twisting or pulling, and lip biting. These need to be dealt with in the same general way as thumb sucking. If they are not abandoned in childhood, they may persist into adolescence and adulthood. If a child is taught to handle tension more maturely, he tends to outgrow these habits.

One important way to help children deal with tension maturely—and help themselves avoid it—is to permit them to express their strong feelings openly and not bottle them up. While destructive behavior must be discouraged, caregivers should acknowledge a child's

right to feel angry. When Camilla tries to strike her father in a fit of rage, he might say to her, "I understand why you're mad. I won't let you hit me, but you may stamp your foot if you like." Or he could suggest that she pound on her wooden pegboard.

Stuttering is often thought to be caused by tension. Many toddlers repeat words and syllables in a way that some people mistake for stuttering. It really isn't. Parents should just ignore this. Calling a child's attention to it may make him self-conscious and interfere with his speech development. Most speech therapists do not think a child's repetitions can be considered true stuttering before the age of four, or later.

All toddlers go through periods when they are unusually difficult or seem especially tense. Generally, patient, loving caregivers can manage to help them overcome their difficulties in time. But occasionally professional help with this may be needed. The crucial question to ask when we are concerned about a child's "problems" is whether he keeps on growing more mature, on the whole, despite his difficulties. If he does, a wait-and-see attitude makes sense. But if he does not progress in any way for several months and some of his behavior becomes decidedly more babyish, then professional counseling should be sought. A doctor or a well-baby clinic can refer parents to a source of help that they can afford.

Sometimes a child continues to progress fairly well, but his negativism, or waking at night, or something else is making life so difficult for his parents or other caregivers that it would be wise to get help with the problem. Sometimes, too, it is wise to secure professional advice *before* a situation creates problems. For example, if a child will have to undergo prolonged or repeated hospitalization or separation from his parents, if one of his parents is very ill, if they are about to divorce, professional counseling can help those closest to the child reduce its stressful effects on him.

All toddlers are destructive sometimes. They often harm possessions and hurt pets, other children, and themselves without really meaning to. Once in a while, when very angry, they intentionally hurt others or themselves. But if they frequently and deliberately do so, parents may need professional guidance with helping their child handle his aggression.

A healthy toddler is energetic and active. However, if a child has trouble sleeping and spends a great many of his waking hours running around wildly and seemingly with no purpose in mind, this should be discussed with a doctor. The child may just need more opportunity to work off steam—on a tricycle, jungle gym, or swing, for example. Or the doctor may suggest that his parents take him to a specialist for further examinations to determine why he has so much difficulty settling down. Some children are said to be **hyperactive** (overactive), a condition that may be caused by slight brain damage that does not affect the intelligence, or by emotional or environmental factors. However, it's not easy for the ordinary person to tell whether a child is truly hyperactive and needs treatment, or is just exceptionally enthusiastic.

Some children never "make trouble," of course. Each child grows in his own way. Some are quieter and more good-humored than others. Very bright children may be "passive observers" who learn as much from watching and listening as from "doing." But if a toddler is extremely passive and undemanding, and never "acts up," he may need more encouragement and opportunities to express his feelings and assert his personality.

PROVIDING OPPORTUNITIES FOR PLAY

The importance of active physical play to toddlers' overall development has been emphasized. Ideally this should occur outdoors, when the weather permits. Caregivers often find it hard to do all their household chores and also take the child outside to play for an hour or so in the morning and afternoon. Sometimes it is best for everybody concerned to let housework slide in order to fit in a quick trip to the park or playground. Toddlers are likely to become extremely restless and demanding if cooped up inside over a long period of time. A change of scene and strenuous play calms the child down and makes it easier for his caregivers to keep their cool.

An imaginative caregiver can think of many ways to encourage safe, active play indoors. Space can be cleared on a carpet or rug for turning somersaults—forward and backward. A low hassock or sturdy footstool can be used to climb on and jump from. (This is best done barefooted.) A simple balance board can be made just by placing a long piece of two-by-four lumber on the floor. The toddler can walk its length on the four-inch side—an exercise that helps develop eye-foot coordination. After as little as fifteen minutes of active play, a child is often ready for quieter activities.

Children become restless indoors. A trip to the playground is fun and provides toddlers with fresh air and exercise.

MAKING LEARNING FUN

In providing toddlers with the stimulating environment needed for development of all kinds, a caregiver must consider each child's individual interests and level of development. For example, very simple puzzles and form boards are fun for toddlers and wonderful tools for learning. But if we offer a two-year-old one that is too hard for him, he may acquire a distaste for all such play. It's best to introduce him to this (and any other new) activity by playing beside him the first time and helping out—when he has trouble matching a shape to its corresponding form on the board, for instance. If he loses interest and it seems that the puzzle is too hard for him, it can be put away and offered again a few months later.

Once a child has developed an interest in puzzles, he can be allowed, with guidance, to select his own. Some children like animal puzzles; others prefer human figures. Toddlers have color preferences, too. Respecting a child's personal taste whenever possible increases his self-esteem and his decision-making ability.

Many household items can be used to foster the skills that puzzles teach. A set of plastic measuring cups of various sizes that nest inside each other makes a fine toy for learning about relative size and shape. A toddler can learn to line the cups up in order of size, as well as nest them.

Toddlers can be taught to identify certain shapes—a circle, diamond, triangle, square, rectangle—with cookie cutters and baking pans. Sixteen-year-old Al made cookies with his nephew, Duane, and cut them out in different shapes. Then, when offering a cookie, he asked Duane which shape he wanted and let him find it himself. Duane learned to say "rectangle" because he thought these were the biggest cookies. He also made the exciting discovery that he could make a rectangular cookie into a square one by taking a well-aimed bite.

Tossing clothespins into a cooking pot is an interesting game and helps develop both fine- and gross-muscle coordination. As the child becomes increasingly skillful at getting all the clothespins in, a container with a smaller opening can be used.

Throwing beanbags onto a square of cloth or cardboard develops the same skills. Caregivers can turn this into a game that teaches toddlers to name and match colors by sewing together four or six squares of fabric of different colors and making beanbags to match the various squares. At first the goal can be to get the red bag on the red square, and so on. In time this can be changed to tossing any bag on any square the child names. Eventually numbers can be stitched onto the bags and squares to teach number recognition.

Many stores sell toys designed to help children learn to lace and tie shoelaces, button buttons, and zip up zippers. The simplest ones consist of a cloth-covered board mounted with the equipment needed to lace, tie, button, and zip. After looking at such toys in a store, parents should be able to create their own version—at a fraction of the cost of buying one. Numerous other entertaining and educational toys can be made at home.

This is not meant to suggest that toddlers require a steady input of deliberate "stimulation" from their caregivers. Just giving them ample opportunity to explore their surroundings is stimulating in itself. Too much outside stimulation, or the wrong kind, has much the same effect on a child as too little. He gives up trying to make sense of what is going on around him and tunes his environment out. This can be seen in the blank look on the face of a toddler who has been sitting in front of the television set all morning. Or the child who, toward the end of a birthday party, curls up in a chair with thumb in mouth.

As long as a child seems happily occupied in his own way, a caregiver need not suggest another activity just for the sake of offering

One of the important cognitive tasks of toddlerhood is learning to understand the concepts of shape, size, and spatial relationships—such as the distance between objects and the relative position of objects in space. Learning to identify different shapes is an early step toward reading, since eventually the child will have to be able to recognize the different shapes of the alphabet.

Infants can see forms, but it takes time before they can tell the difference between forms of different shapes. The first lesson babies learn about form comes when they realize that objects exist apart from themselves.

Both babies and toddlers depend largely on the sense of touch to learn about form and spatial concepts. For example, a baby learns about distance by reaching out for an object, and about size and shape by feeling the object. Gradually the child learns to rely more on the sense of sight to identify shape and size. However, many spatial concepts are not really grasped until the preschool years. For instance, a toddler cannot judge the size of an object that is far away, since things seem to be smaller when seen from a distance.

Understanding the toddler's levels of development can help a caregiver to provide activities that are designed to teach a child the concepts of shape and size when he or she is ready to learn.

A useful game that can be made easily at home is a form board. Simple geometric shapes are cut out of corrugated cardboard, and the child is asked to fit the shapes into the corresponding holes. The easiest shapes for a toddler to identify are, first, a circle, then a square, and then a triangle. The caregiver should show the child how each shape fits into its hole, then remove the shapes and let the child try. Help can be given until the child is able to do it alone.

Simple puzzles can also be bought in a toystore, but be sure that each puzzle piece represents a whole, recognizable figure (such as a house or a ball). A jigsaw puzzle made up of pieces that are fragments of a larger picture will be too hard for a toddler.

The child who is ready can move on to matching objects by shape. Circles, squares, and triangles can be cut out of colored paper, so that all the circles are green, all the squares red, and all the triangles are yellow. The child is then asked to put the matching shapes together. Color is a good cue for the toddler, since classifying by color is usually easier than classifying by shape.

Toddlers may not fully understand the idea of "biggest," "middle size," and "smallest" until about the age of three. But they can start practicing with a few simple games. To start, the caregiver can stand with the child in front of a mirror and ask, "Who is biggest? Who is smallest?" Then the child can go on to sort bigger and smaller paper shapes, or bigger and smaller buttons.

Toddlers also enjoy playing with empty cardboard boxes, plastic containers, and cans (without sharp edges), and these, too, can promote awareness of relative size. Through trial and error, the child learns that the smaller containers fit into the larger ones. More elaborate stacking and nesting toys can be made or bought when the child seems ready for them.

something more "stimulating." Some of the most important learning takes place when the toddler appears to be playing aimlessly—placing assorted objects on top of each other, trying to push a stool between the legs of a chair, staring out a window up at the sky, examining a beam of light or a shadow on the floor. Parents and others should step in with suggestions only when the child becomes frustrated, destructive, overly excited, or obviously bored and at loose ends.

GUIDING LANGUAGE DEVELOPMENT

One of the easiest and best ways you can help a toddler increase his vocabulary and skill with language is to describe activities that are taking place—for instance, when the child goes with you on a shopping trip or while he is watching you do household chores. Name each object that goes into the shopping cart, or is moved for cleaning and dusting. Explain that you are going to vacuum *under* this chair, or dust *over* this doorway, or put an empty container *into* the garbage pail. Illustrating words such as "under," "over," and "into" with a concrete action helps a child grasp their meaning.

It's not necessary always to use simple words and short sentences when speaking to a toddler. This is essential when giving him instructions. At many other times, however, talk to him as you would to anybody else. This gives him a sense of the richness and flow of language. When he needs someone to simplify a comment, question, or explanation, he will show it by a puzzled look or a question.

It's best not to interrupt a toddler to correct his grammar and pronunciation. This frustrates him and can turn him against talking to you. When he has finished speaking, you can correct his mistakes simply by repeating properly what he has just said. Sheila will

gradually give up saying "I dood it" and "I getted it" just from hearing someone repeat after her: "Oh, you did it" or "You got it."

Reading to a child not only increases his vocabulary and his skill with using language; it also fosters an interest in books and readies him to read on his own. Experienced nursery school teachers rarely read a story "straight through" to children. They stop their reading now and then to ask questions about the pictures or about what is happening in the story and to allow the children time to comment. This is a good practice for any caregiver to follow. It promotes learning of many kinds, along with language skills.

FIRST LESSONS IN COOPERATIVE PLAY

It will be several years before the toddler finally masters the art of sharing, cooperating, waiting his turn, and expressing anger verbally, instead of hitting. Meanwhile, restraining him as necessary and reminding him gently that "we don't grab" and "we don't hit" is the best way to help him become civilized. Punishing him physically may just add to his aggressive feelings and make it more difficult for him to control them. Besides, it contradicts the lesson that he is supposed to be learning. If you hit a toddler while telling him that "we don't hit," he will be totally confused.

When a toddler ignores these reminders not to hit, a caregiver can just remove him from the scene of his misdeeds. Jason's baby-sitter, after stopping the little boy several times from hitting and throwing sand in the sandbox, finally warned him that "if you do that again, I will have to take you out of the sandbox."

Jason failed to heed the warning. His sitter picked him up matter-of-factly and carried him, crying and struggling, to the playground swings and put him in one designed for

Cooperative play increases as toddlers develop. Instead of grabbing for toys, they begin communicating to get what they want. Before children learn to share, they must understand which possessions are really theirs.

toddlers. As she gently pushed the swing, she talked to him in a friendly tone about the dangers of throwing sand and how people feel if you hit them. After a while he stopped crying, smiled, and pointed to the sandbox. "Will you be a good boy and play nicely if I let you go back in the sandbox?" his sitter asked. When Jason nodded his head, she led him back. For the remainder of their stay, he behaved admirably, turning to look at her from time to time and ask, "Me dood boy?"

With sympathetic handling like this, toddlers gradually begin to ask for what they want instead of grabbing, and to say "Stop dat" or "Go 'way," instead of hitting. Praising them when they do "play nicely" is a highly effective way to help them progress in this area. They want the approval of their caregivers and are pleased with themselves when they earn it.

A toddler should not be forced to share his possessions against his will. When Dorothy resisted her father's efforts to talk her into giving Tammy a turn on her tricycle, he realized that it was best to accept her refusal. He also apologized to Tammy and her mother, saying, "I'm sorry, but Dorothy just isn't able to share her tricycle yet."

Before a child becomes able to share, he must first learn that his possessions really are his—permanently, not just temporarily. To toddlers, ownership often seems to be a matter of who has possession of an object at the moment. This is not surprising when we consider that a toddler's plate, "his cup," or "his chair" may be his only for the duration of a meal. If caregivers constantly force him to let other children play with "his" toys, he may think that they belong to him for only as long as he hangs onto them.

To help toddlers learn that their possessions really are theirs, parents can provide each child with a place of his own to store his clothes and toys. This can be a small chest for clothes, plus a few hooks for hanging jackets or coats, and some shelves for toys. It may also help to put a label with the child's name on his toys and clothes.

Finally, remember that all of us have treasured possessions that we prefer not to share with anyone else. A toddler's inability ever to share certain favorite toys should be respected. Caregivers might suggest that these toys which the child cannot share be put away out of sight when other children come to play.

DEALING WITH SIBLING RIVALRY

Learning to share love takes even more time than learning to share toys. This is why brothers and sisters may get into explosive quarrels and fights long after they are able to get along well with children outside the family. Two-year-old Denis is not just struggling with his older sister Simone for possession of a ball—or whatever object they both want at the moment. He and she are also competing for parental love and approval.

A certain amount of sibling rivalry is unavoidable—and healthy. It indicates that the children are permitted to show emotions such as anger and jealousy, as well as loving ones. In the long run, this helps them learn to handle their negative feelings toward each other (and everybody else they love) and get along more smoothly.

Of course, parents have to do all they can to see that each child has her or his fair share of affection, praise, and privileges. This is especially necessary after the birth of a new baby, when an older child is apt to feel that the newcomer is getting the bigger share of everything.

The parents of Denis and Simone made a special effort for many months after Denis's birth to show their daughter how much they loved her. They arranged for her to go on special outings alone with one or the other of them, set her bedtime a little later, and in

many other ways stressed that as the older child she had privileges which balanced the attention the younger child received. They did an excellent job of helping Simone understand that treatment can be "fair" even when it is not "exactly the same."

But Denis was no longer a baby. He often played with Simone and, inevitably, had begun to compete with her. At first when the children clashed, their parents took Simone's word that "*he* started it" or "*he* cheated." They sided with her in judging the children's disputes. Then it became apparent that the conflicts were often due to Simone's bossing her brother around or teasing him too much. The parents decided to stop blaming one child or the other. They would say firmly, "We don't care who started it. If you two can't play together happily, then we are going to separate you, and you will just have to play alone." This approach brought marked improvement.

Despite the troubles Simone and Denis had at times, they were very attached to each other—as is true of most siblings. After a time of playing apart—either alone or with children outside the family—they got along much better together.

Sometimes, when one child is clearly in the wrong, parents do have to see that the wrong is righted. However, it's best to avoid this as often as possible, the way Simone and Denis's parents did. Most of the time both children are at least partially to blame. Even if one child actually is blameless at the moment, he or she knows that this is not always true and can accept a caregiver's decision to remain neutral.

Caregivers must supervise disputes closely enough to be able to prevent one child from injuring another. But this does not mean that they should constantly step in at the first sign of conflict. Raised voices do not necessarily mean that children cannot work out an argument on their own. The yelling just means that caregivers should keep an eye on the proceedings. True, a caregiver might have a brilliant suggestion, such as that the children take turns throwing the beanbags. But how much better it is if they can arrive at this solution without outside help.

PLAYMATES

Playing with other children is clearly important to toddlers' development and happiness. Though they more often play *alongside* each other (**parallel play**) than *with* each other, such play is fun and helps them learn many skills, cognitive and social. Certain skills, such as "pumping" a swing, are almost always learned from watching another child. If you try to explain to a child how to swing himself, your efforts are usually useless. But when he watches another child about his own age do it, it stimulates him to try—and shows him how.

Toddlers who are not in some form of group care—a neighborhood play group or a day-care center—can benefit from regular trips to a familiar playground where they have made friends. Toddlers who get to know each other at a playground will run delightedly to greet each other when they meet—evidence that friendships do matter even at this early age.

Formal play groups for toddlers generally meet about two hours a day from three to five days a week. Churches, synagogues, Y's, and similar organizations often run such groups. Many parents set up their own informal groups with friends or playground acquaintances. These groups, composed of no more than four toddlers per caregiver, meet at specified hours in participating parents' homes. The parents take turns supervising the children in their homes and, in good weather, for a play period outdoors.

Yet, no matter how much these little ones enjoy being with other children their age and become attached to familiar caregivers, parents are still loved best. The toddler needs to spend some unhurried time alone with one or both parents each day. His family is still the center of his world.

GUIDANCE AND DISCIPLINE

Almost everything we do with toddlers involves discipline in one way or another. This word does not refer just to correcting or punishing a child when he "breaks the rules." In its best sense, it means providing him with the kinds of rules and guidance that keep punishments and corrections to a minimum. Its ultimate goal is to enable the child gradually to learn to discipline himself.

In many of the descriptions of interactions that we have discussed so far, we have seen toddlers being helped to behave suitably enough with a minimum of punishing and correcting. We will now look at the principles involved in making and enforcing rules to produce these happy results.

The most basic purpose that rules serve is to protect toddlers from seriously harming themselves or others. This is essential for more than the obvious reasons. Our efforts to ensure a child's safety tell him how much we love him. This, in turn, helps him value himself—that is, develop healthy self-esteem. Protecting him from harming others helps him learn to value all life and prevents him from committing acts he will later regret.

Firm, clearly stated rules against running into the street, hitting, turning on stove burners, playing with electrical appliances, and other dangerous activities are essential. These rules may vary somewhat from family to family, because of differences in living conditions and between toddlers. However, certain prohibitions are almost universal.

Yet no set of rules can adequately protect a toddler from injuring himself and others. He is unaware of many potential dangers, and caregivers cannot possibly foresee and make rules against them all. Nor can they count on

"Spare the rod and spoil the child" expresses how most people felt about spanking years ago. Parents didn't give it much thought, but when a child misbehaved they simply spanked. Now parents are often confused about whether to use spanking as a means of discipline. Below are some of the pros and cons of spanking.

IN FAVOR OF SPANKING

· Spanking usually makes the child behave at that moment.
· It gets rid of the parent's anger. It would be more hurtful to the child if the parent continued to feel irritated and disapproving of the child for a long time. The anger might be expressed in constant nagging or trying to make him feel guilty.
· It gets the message across quickly in dangerous situations, such as when a small child runs into the street. Of course, if spanking is used, it should occur immediately so that the child will be sure to associate the spanking with his misdeed.
· It is useful when the child is young and doesn't yet understand complicated explanations.
· It often seems the most appropriate reaction in certain situations, particularly when the child is defiant.
· The punishment is over quickly; enforcing longer punishments may be difficult for the parent.
· If the child is warned ahead of time that he will be spanked if certain behavior occurs, then the child makes the decision; if the parent doesn't really hurt the child and the child knows the parent loves him, then spanking can be useful in disciplining.

AGAINST SPANKING

· Children tend to imitate their parents; if their parents hit them, they may hit their peers.
· Spanking teaches undesirable ways of dealing with frustration.
· It is an insult to the child's dignity, and parents may also lose dignity and feel guilty, as well.
· Use of power in this way by parents may make the child even more rebellious.
· The child may be misbehaving to get attention, and he will even accept spanking to get attention. If this is so, parents should examine the child's needs instead of punishing him.
· The child may be misbehaving in order to get spanked to relieve unconscious guilt feelings.
· When the child really has done something to feel guilty about, the spanking may relieve the guilt too easily and clear the slate so he thinks he can misbehave again.
· It doesn't always prevent further misbehavior.
· The child might start liking to be spanked because making up afterward is so pleasurable.
· Spanking is often not associated with the misdeed. Anger at parents becomes more dominant and pain is associated more with the parent than with the misdeed.
· Spanking as a means of discipline will not keep the child from misbehaving when the parent is not around.

In *Baby and Child Care*, Dr. Benjamin Spock writes that the test of punishment is whether it achieves what you want to achieve without making the child excessively angry or causing him to behave worse than before. Each child has to be treated individually; a punishment that is just right for one child may be too strong for a more sensitive child.

Were you spanked as a child? How did you feel about it? Would you spank your child?

Discipline should be friendly, but firm. Young children must understand the boundaries which have been set for them. Their caregivers must act consistently with the rules they have established. Screaming at children too often and constantly threatening them to behave may cause timidity or rebelliousness. Frequent slaps or spankings teach children that hitting is an acceptable reaction to anger.

toddlers always to obey the rules that are set. So caregivers must be constantly on the alert to protect the toddler.

DRAWING THE LINE SENSIBLY

Protecting the toddler does not mean hovering over him and constantly warning him against possible dangers. In fact, too much hovering and too frequent warnings are likely to make a toddler overly timid or fearful—or else turn him into a rebellious daredevil.

When Janice starts to climb into a rocking chair, her sitter does not rush to steady the chair for her. He just watches and waits. She may be able to figure out how to manage this challenge on her own. If she can, she will have learned a great deal about balancing her own body and a rocking object. It would be a pity to deprive her of this experience unnecessarily.

Minor falls and scrapes, bumps and bruises, are common occurrences in a healthy toddler's life. Caregivers cannot expect to prevent them all—nor should they try. Toddlers learn from such experiences what they can and cannot do and how to manage better next time.

OTHER NECESSARY RULES

High on the list of other necessary rules are those designed to keep toddlers from destroying property. They need to learn to respect other people's possessions—and their own. Though it's best to store treasured breakable objects out of their reach, parents have a right to expect their children not to wreck the furniture or the family's personal belongings.

It's also important to lay down certain bedtime rules. Firmness about the bedtime hour makes it easier for toddlers to accept going to bed and settle down for the night. This can save parents a lot of grief. It's also wise to make it a general rule that the child sleep in his own bed, though, as mentioned earlier, parents should feel free to make occasional exceptions to this rule under certain conditions.

The only rules about mealtime that are appropriate at this age are that a child come to meals when asked and not deliberately throw food around. Toddlers are messy eaters and often picky ones, too. Caregivers must accept a good deal of spilling and toying with food—and not insist that the child "clean his plate" or remain in his seat until others have finished eating. They can encourage him to use his spoon to eat with, but it's best not to nag.

Every household will have some more rules that serve to make daily life manageable and reinforce the family's values. Some families say grace before meals. If toddlers have their meals with the family, they can be expected to be silent during grace. Some families place a higher value on neatness and order than others. This will be reflected in rules about putting toys away, hanging up coats, and numerous other matters. Obviously, failure to obey rules in this general category should not be taken seriously as infractions of rules in the earlier categories. A gentle reminder or correction is enough. However, as long as there are not too many such rules and the two-year-old has adequate freedom to explore and "play messily" at times, each family should feel free to follow its own life style. Children can thrive whether their family is strict or permissive—as long as their basic needs are adequately and lovingly met.

ENFORCING RULES

Caregivers should not make rules that they do not seriously intend to enforce. They should not, for instance, tell Sam that he is never to ride his tricycle in the house, unless they plan to enforce this rule regularly. Otherwise, the child is uncertain about when we really mean business. He may get the idea that any rule can be broken if he pushes hard enough.

However, important as it is to be consistent, all of us occasionally make exceptions to some rules—and that's all right within reason. It's okay to let Sylvia skip naptime "just this once" to be with her grandparents while they are visiting. If exceptions are not too frequent, the child understands very well that they are, indeed, exceptions.

How do you enforce rules when a toddler pro-

tests? The negativism so common at this age can sometimes be overcome with humor. A child who has been saying no to everything can be asked, "Would you like some ice cream after lunch?" (provided you are prepared to give him some). After automatically saying no, he is apt to grin sheepishly and become more cooperative.

At times, however, you may have to pick a toddler up and carry him off to wash his hands, put on his outer wear, come to the table for a meal, or whatever you want him to do. This insults his dignity, but if you are friendly as well as firm, he usually becomes more cheerful in a few minutes.

Tantrums are usually best ignored. Caregivers can just let the child lie on the floor and cry it out. When he stops, they can comfort him and go about their business as if nothing unusual had happened. If a child throws a tantrum in public, his caregiver just has to pick him up and carry him home, talking to him soothingly on the way. It's best not to give in to a child to prevent or stop a tantrum. This is like allowing him to blackmail you.

Some parents manage to get along without ever resorting to physical punishment—except for a rare slap. They say that their own reaction of fear when a child does something dangerous is enough to teach him never to do it again. However, some people think that it's all right for a child to be spanked occasionally—if he endangers his safety or that of others or if he is being "absolutely impossible." This is something about which parents can afford to make up their own minds, though frequent or brutal physical punishment must certainly be avoided.

Parents should not be slaves to a child or let him be disrespectful of their rights. In meeting the needs of others, we must also look out suitably for our own needs. However, most of the time, by far, gentle guidance, along the lines suggested, is sufficient to take care of our needs—and toddlers', too.

- Toddlers want to be grown-up, but often are fearful and unsure.
- They need encouragement, praise, and support, but also reassurance.
- Toddlers have some fears that are realistic and help protect them. Other fears are due to the child's lively imagination.
- Thumb-sucking and similar habits are common ways for children to relieve tension.
- Learning activities should suit the toddler's interests and developmental level.
- Rules must be made to keep toddlers from hurting themselves or others.
- Toddlers need to learn to respect things that belong to others and their own things.

TERMS TO KNOW

hyperactive
negativism
parallel play

1. Children playing next to each other in the sandbox are engaging in _____.
2. Although most toddlers are energetic, some who run around wildly and have trouble sleeping may be _____.
3. A toddler's _____ may prompt him to say ''no'' even to things he really wants.

CHECK YOUR UNDERSTANDING

1. What are two conflicting needs of a toddler?
2. Why do toddlers normally show some babyish, clinging behavior?
3. Describe some dos and don'ts for dealing with a toddler who wakes up frightened at night.
4. List four habits that indicate a toddler may be under stress.
5. If a toddler never seems able to settle down, should parents assume he is hyperactive? Explain.
6. What is the best way for a caregiver to correct a toddler's speech?
7. Why are toddlers often reluctant to share their possessions?
8. Why is a certain amount of sibling rivalry healthy?
9. What is the most basic purpose of setting rules for a toddler?
10. What is the danger of constantly warning and hovering over a toddler?
11. Describe how to handle a toddler's tantrums.

UNIT FOUR

PRESCHOOL
(AGES 3–5)

13

PHYSICAL DEVELOPMENT

Children between the ages of three and five are active and energetic. Their improved coordination helps them master the skills necessary to take care of themselves.

14

COGNITIVE DEVELOPMENT

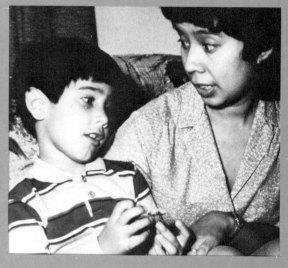

By the end of this period, most children have moved from baby talk to enthusiastic conversations. But language skills are only one aspect of the pre-schooler's growing mental abilities.

15
SOCIAL/EMOTIONAL DEVELOPMENT

The preschooler starts to learn—with care-givers' help—to control aggression and fears. Though the family is still the center of a preschooler's world, playmates become an important part of it as well.

16
INTERACTION

Positive learning experiences and firm, but reasonable, guidance help preschoolers. Now babyish ways are disappearing as the child becomes more inde-pendent, more skillful, and ever more sociable.

$\cdot 13\cdot$
PHYSICAL DEVELOPMENT
OF THE PRESCHOOLER

"I'm hungry!" chanted four-year-old Randy Byers, hopping on one foot.

His cousin Laura, who was visiting for the weekend, looked doubtful. "Aunt Joan, can Randy have a snack?"

"Hold your horses, Randy," Mrs. Byers smiled as she came into the kitchen. "How about half a banana?"

"Okay," said Randy. His mother gave him a banana and a table knife, then watched as he carefully cut the fruit in two.

"I didn't know if you wanted Randy to have snacks between meals," Laura said as Randy sat at the table.

"Well, you were right to ask," said Mrs. Byers. "We try not to give Randy sweets. But if he gets hungry, it's okay to give him fruit, or milk, or a peanut butter sandwich."

"Don't you worry that he won't eat enough at dinner?" Laura asked.

"Oh, I'm more concerned that what he eats all day is healthy, not when he eats it. Of course, we try to keep him on a regular schedule so that he eats his meals with the rest of us."

"I guess that makes sense," Laura said. "Randy's pretty good at meals, really. The girl I baby-sit for just picks at her food. If I try to make her clean her plate, she cries and runs from the table."

"It's not easy to get a preschooler to sit down to a meal," Mrs. Byers admitted. "Sometimes Randy's too busy playing to stop and eat. Quieting him down first with a story usually works. Then we just give him small servings and make sure he eats a little of everything. After all, it's the balance that counts. But believe me, nothing will get him to eat a food that he doesn't like!"

Randy suddenly waved his banana peel. "Hey, I'm done!"

"Good for you!" Mrs. Byers said. "Now can you throw away the peel?"

"Randy sure looks and acts healthy," Laura said as they watched him scamper off. "He must be getting the right things to eat!"

●

Do you think Randy's eating habits are healthy? Why or why not?

●

What could Laura do to make mealtime more pleasant the next time she baby-sits for a preschooler?

The preschooler, even more than the toddler, knows his own mind. He has definite preferences—for food, bedtime, clothing, play activities, and so on.

In the preschool years—ages three, four, and five—motor skills develop rapidly. With greater physical mastery comes a greater feeling of independence and a desire to express it in what may seem to be trivial as well as important ways. The preschooler not only wants to do things—he wants to do them his way. For parents and caregivers, the key word is patience.

Adults should also remember that children are individuals. Individual children may depart from general patterns of physical development and yet be completely normal. This is just as true of preschoolers as of other age groups.

GROWTH AND MOTOR DEVELOPMENT

The child grows steadily in body height and weight during his preschool years. However, like the toddler, he grows at a slower rate compared with the headlong growth of earlier years. His average height at age three is 37 to 38 inches (94 to 96 centimeters). He weighs about 33 pounds (15 kilograms). By the end of his fifth year, he may have grown in height to about 46 inches (115 centimeters). He will weigh an average of about 45 pounds (20 kilograms).

One of the fastest-growing parts of the preschooler's body is his brain. At age three, the brain is about 75 percent of its adult weight. Over the next three years, it grows to around 90 percent of its adult weight.

At the same time, the shape of the preschooler's body is changing noticeably. He is losing fast what is left of his baby fat. His muscles and skeletal system are becoming much more developed. His overall physical coordination shows marked improvement.

By age five, the preschooler's small-and large-muscle development is quite advanced. He can throw well, catch a small ball with arms at his sides, copy a square and a triangle—and fasten all the buttons he can find.

Preschoolers can skip smoothly, imitate dance steps to music, and walk a balance board with confidence. They may be able to tie shoelaces. They may also be able to ride a two-wheeler. Certainly they are likely to show interest in activities requiring skill—whether riding a bicycle, skipping rope, or using a screwdriver.

Among preschoolers there is a very broad range of physical skills, as well as aptitudes. Furthermore, some children use physical skills to express independence more than others. To illustrate, let's look at three preschoolers—Joanna, Andrea, and Jerry—to see how differently they have developed.

Joanna, at three, can run fairly easily. She moves with her legs close together, and with confidence that her feet are going in the same direction as her body. She may still spill some of her food when she eats, but not very much, for she can handle a spoon or fork better. She proudly unbuttons her own coat, the one with the big buttons. She can also put on her own shoes, but cannot lace them.

Joanna cannot yet ride a tricycle, but three-year-old Andrea can. Andrea can also propel a scooter with one foot, and she jumps from the bottom step of the staircase. She runs more easily than Joanna does and is able to start and stop smoothly. On the other hand, Joanna can draw a circle or horizontal line much better than Andrea can. Both girls are normal three-year-olds. The differences in their accomplishments are normal, too. Linking specific abilities to specific ages is always approximate.

Jerry is four, and he behaves physically like the typical four-year-old. He seems to be forever running, trotting, climbing, pushing, or pulling. He was also active at three. At four, however, he moves with more purpose. He has confidence in his growing motor skills, and he enjoys using them to accomplish more complex tasks. For example, his small-muscle devel-

Below is a general guide to the motor development achievements that are most typical of the preschool-age levels.

MOTOR DEVELOPMENT

Age 3

Can run, jump, hop, skip and gallop.

Can march to rhythm and balance on one foot.

Propels a wagon with one foot.

Can ride a tricycle, jump from bottom stair, and walk on tiptoe.

Can push and pull objects, throw and bounce a ball, and catch a ball or beanbag with arms straight.

Can build a tower 8 or 9 blocks high.

Can manipulate puzzles with a few or several pieces.

Cuts out shapes with scissors, folds paper, and uses large crayons and pencils.

Draws things from life, and can draw a straight line.

Can use a spoon and fork with little spilling.

Dresses self except for tying shoes.

Can unbutton buttons.

Age 4

Descends small ladder with feet alternating.

Climbs jungle gyms and other play equipment.

Does stunts on tricycle.

Bounces and catches balls with elbows in front of body.

Shows increased manual skill. Places pegs in a peg board, cuts on line with scissors.

Can make designs and crude letters.

Places blocks horizontally on floor.

Forms crude but occasionally recognizable shapes with clay.

Age 5

Can walk a straight line.

Skips rope.

Plays jacks.

Enjoys large-muscle activity involving the whole body: running, climbing, tumbling, etc.

Catches a small ball with elbows at sides.

Maintains rhythmic beat with rhythm instruments.

Folds paper into double triangles.

Copies drawings of square and triangle.

Can pour from a small pitcher into a glass. Uses knife and fork to cut food.

opment has become refined, so that now he can draw lines and circles that represent human figures. His large-muscle development has also progressed. He has better control over his body when he runs. He can climb up a playground slide as well as go down it and he can perform stunts on his tricycle. He can throw overhand, though not too accurately.

By now a preschooler has probably shown a clear preference for either the right or left hand. A child who insists on using his left hand should be allowed to do so. Although most people are right-handed, there is nothing wrong with being left-handed if that comes naturally to a child. The only problem is that later the child may have a certain amount of difficulty in a right-handed world. Even scissors are generally made for right-handed people. Nevertheless, trying to force a left-handed five-year-old to use his right hand can only lead to frustration.

WELL-BEING AND PHYSICAL PLAY

Physical activity is an important part of the healthy preschooler's overall development. With his body the child explores and learns to master his world and gain confidence in himself.

Again, individual standards of accomplishment are far from absolute. Four-year-old Russell is able to swim and ride a bicycle, while six-year-old Louie can do neither. Louie is a normal, healthy child, but he has not had the

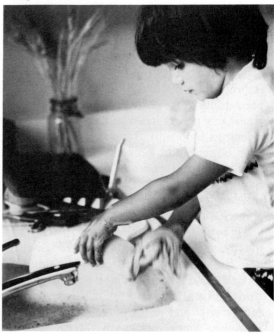

Large-and small-muscle coordination rapidly improves during the preschool years. Children ages 3 to 5 are able to perform everyday tasks for themselves. They exhibit increasing independence from their caregivers.

Left-handed children may face some obstacles in a right-handed world, but they should not be forced to switch.

Many three-year-olds are ready for a tricycle. The main skill the child must learn is to make the trike go by pushing down on the pedals with his feet alternately. In the process, he develops his leg muscles, coordination, and balance.

Balls—large ones for three-year olds, smaller ones for older children—are always in demand. Both girls and boys enjoy ball games, which help develop their **eye-hand coordination** and arm muscles. Blocks, another favorite toy, are excellent for small-muscle development. The three-year-old may do little more than stack his blocks. Or he may use them to build a "yellow-brick road" or a corral for his toy animals. Meanwhile, his eye-hand coordination and finger manipulation are being developed, along with his imagination.

Art materials are excellent for small-muscle control. Moist clay or modeling dough is fun for children and provides good exercise, too. Preschoolers can also paint with finger paints or tempera colors and brushes—when they have learned to confine their artwork to paper!

At age four, as the child moves on to more complex tasks, he may need a greater variety of materials. His block constructions, for example, may require more blocks of various sizes and shapes with columns and curves.

In the playground, four-year-olds tend to climb higher, do stunts, and in general take advantage of their more developed muscles. Swings, roller skates, and scooters are appealing to both four- and five-year-olds.

Most five-year-olds are also ready for jump ropes and bicycles with training wheels. These toys develop large-muscle control and balance.

The five-year-old generally has the patience to do a thing over and over until he gets it right. He can copy a bead pattern and play simple games like dominoes. With his advanced manipulative skills and small-muscle control, he is ready to advance still further. All he needs are the opportunities.

chance to learn these particular skills. However, it is important that Louie be given other opportunities to strengthen his muscles and improve his coordination. If not, his social and personality development could be set back, since the poorly coordinated child may be reluctant to join in group activities and may even be rejected by his playmates. Much of a child's physical progress depends on simply having access to play activities that naturally interest him and that help his physical development.

Three-year-olds are usually attracted to playground equipment such as outdoor climbers. These are excellent for developing large muscles and balance. The best equipment is that which allows for the greatest variety of movement. Not all children like to climb, however. Some prefer to swing or crawl through tunnels or just hang from a low bar.

Preschoolers love to play. They explore on their own and can play alone for longer periods of time. They fantasize often and seem very amused by their own conversation. Cooperative play increases at this time. Children during the preschool years create pretend situations involving their peers, and are also capable of playing simple games jointly. Caregivers need lots of energy and patience during this stage of their child's development.

Preschoolers can eat many of the same foods that adults do. Like toddlers, however, preschoolers tend to be sensitive to strong-tasting foods. They will usually reject the hot, spicy foods that many adults enjoy. Also, the preschooler's jaw is still not fully developed and neither is his stomach. He is not yet ready for tough foods that require thorough chewing.

Preschoolers need about 50 percent more protein per pound of body weight than adults do. A diet overly heavy in carbohydrates like potatoes and noodles does not provide the right nutrients for a child's developing body.

The basic, balanced daily diet for both children and adults continues to include foods from the basic food groups. The exact amounts served are less important than maintaining a daily balance of different kinds of nutrients: proteins, fats, carbohydrates, minerals, and vitamins.

In the preschool years, children continue to find playing, running and almost everything else more interesting than eating. They may have to be reminded or coaxed to stop for lunch or another meal. But if mealtimes are planned according to a daily routine, the preschooler will get used to eating at regular times.

The amount a preschooler eats at each meal can vary from day to day, depending on how active he has been. If he is hungry, he will eat. If not, he won't. Of course, if he doesn't eat much at mealtime, he may get hungry later—often before bedtime. In that case, he may be satisfied with a glass of milk. Few healthy children will miss more than one mealtime, though. Preschoolers *do* get hungry, since they expend so much energy in physical activity.

Choice is important for the typical preschooler. He likes to have a say in things that concern him. Mealtimes are certainly no exception. For example, if someone asks him

Mealtime is more fun when it is shared with others. Children at this age may be fussy eaters and skip meals frequently. They should not be forced to eat, but plenty of wholesome food should be available to them.

whether he wants a piece of fruit, he is likely to take it. If the person commands him to eat it because it is good for him, he is just as likely to refuse. Similarly, it is better to offer him small portions on his plate than to load up his plate with food. That way he has the choice of asking for more and does not feel that he is being ordered to eat a large amount.

Many preschoolers cannot go comfortably from lunch to dinner without some kind of snack. As long as the snack doesn't come too close to a regular mealtime, this is fine. But caregivers should make sure that the snacks they give a child are healthful. "Junk foods" with high fat and carbohydrate content should be avoided. A cup of soup and crackers or a peanut butter sandwich or sunflower seeds can be just as filling, and also provide the child with important nutrients.

ELIMINATION

By age three, most children are in control of their bowel movements—with perhaps an accident now and then. Three-year-olds are usually beginning to exercise bladder control as well. Readiness for bladder control varies widely, however, because children develop at different rates.

If a lack of bowel or bladder control continues into the late preschool years, something may be wrong. Perhaps the child is under some kind of emotional stress, or his body may not be developing properly. A medical checkup is in order.

By age four, most children are dry during the day and go to the toilet without any help—although they often insist on privacy. Most four-year-olds are also dry most nights.

By age five the child usually assumes all responsibility for toilet use. Nevertheless, in the excitement of some activity, he may forget and fail to get to the bathroom in time. Occasionally, too, he may wet the bed. The occasional accident is no cause for concern; but some children suffer from **enuresis**, or inability to control urination. They bedwet most of the time and often have trouble during the day. Eighty percent of enuretics are boys. If the problem persists, for physical or psychological reasons, the child may need professional help.

HYGIENE

The preschooler still needs help in bathing, although by age five he needs and wants less of

Hygienic habits are formed during the preschool years. Children at this age need to learn routines of self-care.

it. Bath time—with rubber duck, ships, and other toys—is generally a fun experience. Many children still resist hair washing, however.

Basically, the parent or caregiver should try to instill in the preschooler simple, fundamental habits of cleanliness. Such habits include washing hands before and after meals and toilet use, and baths after playing outdoors.

Dental hygiene is extremely important. Age three is not too young for a child to have his first dental examination. Most children have all twenty of their primary or baby teeth by that age. By age six, the first permanent teeth—called the six-year molars—are coming in. Many adults think that because baby teeth are going to be replaced anyway, there is no need to be especially careful of them. This is not so. A recent estimate indicates that 10 percent of North American children under the age of five have more than eight cavities. Such neglect can lead to infections. For instance, the **Eustachian tube**—which connects the ears, nose, and throat—can be infected by tooth decay. There may also be problems in the emergence of the permanent teeth if dental hygiene is poor.

If a child acquires the habit of brushing his teeth after meals during his toddler or preschool years, he is likely to keep it. Regular brushing can prevent many dental problems. Studies have shown that preschool children in communities with fluoridated water have approximately half the tooth-decay problems of children in communities where the water is not fluoridated. If the community's water supply is not fluoridated, the child can use a fluoridated toothpaste to help prevent decay.

SLEEP AND REST

Although the preschooler is not growing as fast as in earlier years, his body is changing and he is usually more active. He obviously needs rest to keep pace with his activities. The average is about eleven hours of sleep a night, along with a nap during the day up to age six.

After age six, most children don't nap. Even at ages three and four, many children don't actually sleep when napping, but read or talk to

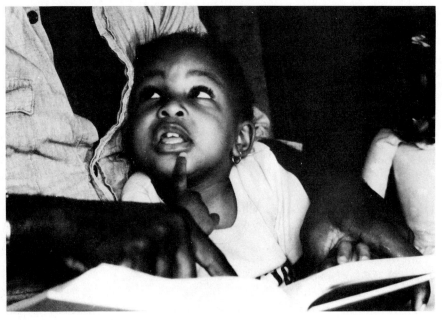

Reading to preschool children is a wonderful way to stimulate their interest in books and also build a good relationship with them. Stories from books allow children to use their imaginations to visualize different characters and various life situations. Listening to stories is a good form of passive play which can replace overdependence on television to amuse children.

As we discussed in the box on page 105, on an Israeli *kibbutz*, or collective farm, children are raised by professional caregivers known as metapelets, rather than by their own parents. Placed in groups according to age, the children play, work, and learn together. In addition, they live in a special center, joining their parents only for supper or, in some kibbutzim, for the night. As the children grow older, the groups remain together. They move on, however, to new sets of caregivers as they advance to higher age levels.

The daily routine is planned to suit each level of development. Very young children are not expected to sit quietly at meals until everyone else has finished. They are free to leave the table as soon as they have eaten. Other activities are just as flexible. The psychologist Bruno Bettelheim, who has studied in detail the kibbutz system of child rearing, describes the program this way: "Demands are at a minimum and what is expected of the child tallies largely with his own limitations."

Dr. Bettelheim and other experts in child development have studied the Israeli system in order to learn how children are affected by collective rearing. A possible effect on physical development was noted when metapelets reported a large incidence of enuresis (bedwetting) among young kibbutz children.

Critics of the system saw this as an expression of tensions created by the fact that the children spent so little time with their parents, lived constantly in a group, and were transferred at regular intervals to a new set of caregivers.

Other observers disagreed. Dr. Bettelheim felt that the kibbutz system was beneficial and did not create unusual tensions in the children. He suggested a far simpler explanation for the prevalence of enuresis. "It took many years for parents and caregivers to realize that if one wishes a child to be toilet-trained, one has to make some effort to teach him....And a collective is not an agent that can effectively toilet-train a child. (Toilet-training in a kibbutz is generally taught by, and learned from, other children as much as from adults. Similarly, it is when the group objects that bedwetting disappears almost immediately, excepting always a few children in whom it is a symptom of specific neurosis just as with us.)"

Whatever the explanation, the problem lessened as caregivers and children began to focus attention on it.

Do you feel that a child is able to respond more easily to peer pressure for toilet-training than he would to such training from a parent or caregiver? Or would he do better with individualized help from an adult?

Read more about child care in a collective system like a kibbutz and report on the significant ways it differs from child care by the immediate family.

themselves. Such a "play nap" is a valuable rest period whether or not the child sleeps. Preschoolers may tire quickly, but they can also recover quickly after only a little rest.

Winding down after an exciting day is easier for the child who has learned to follow a set routine. A regular pattern of activities— bathing, brushing teeth, listening to a story read aloud, putting dolls or toys to bed—quiets the child and prepares him for sleep.

The preschool child's imagination is very active, and many of his fears may show themselves at night. Bedtime is the time for hugs and reassurances in an atmosphere of calm.

Few children—or adults, for that matter—can get the sleep they need if they are under stress at bedtime.

ILLNESS AND ACCIDENTS

The preschool child needs a medical checkup at least once a year, or even twice a year for three- and four-year-olds. During his checkup, the child can be examined to see that his growth and health are normal. By now he should have been inoculated against all the various childhood diseases. At three or four, most children are cooperative enough to be given an eye examination. It is important to find out early whether the child has any visual problems in order to avoid difficulty later when he enters school.

Ear infections are a common complaint of children in the preschool years. The Eustachian tube, connecting ears, nose, and throat, is not fully developed. It allows bacteria to travel easily from the throat to the middle ear.

Preschool children also tend to catch colds easily, and they often suffer from upset stomachs. They generally recover quickly; but if any illness persists, the child should be examined by a doctor.

The signs of illness in a preschool child are not difficult to spot. They range from general listlessness and loss of appetite to the classic runny nose, a symptom of the common cold. Persistent rashes, sore throat, high fever, coughing, and vomiting indicate a more serious illness and the need to consult a doctor.

Accidents may be a more serious problem than illness for some children. According to one study, accidents are the most frequent cause of death among children between ages one and four. Forty percent of those accidents take place in the home.

Because preschoolers are especially active and curious, extra care has to be taken to keep harmful substances out of their way. The preschool child can climb. He can also pull stools and other light furniture to a place where he might scramble up to reach a medicine chest or other possible source of danger to him.

As for the toddler, all medicines should be kept in jars or bottles with childproof tops. Cleansing materials, insecticides, and other chemical products should be stored well out of reach, and the child firmly warned against touching them.

Supervision in outdoor play is a must. Preschoolers, in the heat of activity, may well climb too high, get stuck in a fence, or otherwise put themselves in danger. The classic warning against allowing a child to chase a ball into the path of an oncoming car has been issued over and over again. Yet, year in and year out, this type of accident continues to happen. Small children playing near traffic or driveways must be watched carefully.

Of course, preschoolers are bound to have a lot of minor accidents. Falls—resulting in scraped knees, shins, arms, and elbows—are almost inevitable. Sometimes it seems that every child between three and ten has a perpetual scab from knee to ankle.

Generally, falls are not serious enough to require more than a good washing, perhaps an antiseptic, and a hug of reassurance. Bandage strips are essential equipment when a preschooler is around.

Any serious cuts, burns, or other wounds should of course be examined by a doctor, as should any severe twisting of an arm or leg. The preschooler's bones are growing stronger all the time, but they still contain a lot of soft cartilage tissue. A bad twist can affect later growth.

In general, those who care for preschoolers must exercise common sense to prevent accidents without overprotecting or brooding. It's

Speech Pathologists and Audiologists

"Take a deep breath, Kimmie, and blow up the balloon. Then let all the air out at once." Four-year-old Kimmie followed Molly Zapata's instructions and blew as hard as she could. The balloon slowly grew larger, then collapsed as Kimmie released the air.

"Very good!" said Molly. "Now try the same thing, without the balloon. Watch yourself in the mirror to see just how your mouth looks when you are pretending to blow up the balloon, and when you are pushing out all the air."

Molly is a speech pathologist. Her job is to help Kimmie, who was born with a birth defect, speak more clearly. Kimmie comes twice a week to the learning-disabilities clinic, and she works at home with her parents on the exercises Molly has organized. By the time Kimmie is ready for first grade, she will be speaking reasonably well.

The ability to speak and to hear are closely linked, and quite commonly speech pathologists (those who work with speech and language problems) are also trained as audiologists (those who deal with hearing problems).

Speech pathologists and audiologists first try to find out why children are having language difficulties; they administer series of tests, take family histories, and interpret the findings. Some of the difficulties may be the result of physical defects, injury, or emotional problems or mental retardation. Working closely with doctors, psychologists, and others who know the child's background, the speech pathologist and audiologist work out a treatment program that takes into account the child's individual needs and potential.

Most speech pathologists and audiologists work in public schools, but they may also work in hospitals, child-care institutions, clinics, special speech and hearing centers, or other diagnostic and treatment centers.

This job requires some training beyond college, although a few jobs are open to those with a bachelor's degree. Some special programs lead to a master's degree in speech pathology and audiology. Some states also require teaching certification for work in public schools.

Patience, concentration, and attention to detail are all important for this job. It is important to be able to work well with children and to keep them stimulated and interested through a series of repetitive tasks. Generally, working conditions are good. Salaries are good, too, and the demand for these specialists is growing.

especially important never to underestimate the capacity of a preschool child to get around. He is eager to explore, and his explorations can easily lead him into danger.

Last year, it may have been safe to store the drain cleaner on the shelf above the sink. *This* year, with a preschooler in the house, last year's rules no longer apply.

TIME: Early evening.
QUESTION: Do you know where your children are?
ANSWER: They're watching TV!

Many critics of television feel that this answer is almost as bad as not knowing where your children are at all. Moreover, they think it's an answer that is given far too frequently.

According to Ralph Garry, a professor of educational psychology and a writer for children's TV, it is estimated that one-third of the children three years of age make fairly regular use of television. By school age, it is a rare child who is not a regular TV viewer.

What effect does all this viewing have on children? Surprisingly, hard evidence on this question is in short supply. Nevertheless, if we examine some of what goes on as young children watch TV, we may be able to make some educated guesses about the impact of television on young viewers.

Generally speaking, it is not until the child is six or seven that he can make much sense of a TV story. However, there is some evidence to show that younger children do have enough contact with sound and image to become involved and affected emotionally, even if they can't understand everything. Since young children are not always able to distinguish between what is real and what is fantasy, they believe what they see on TV—whether it's a news program, a commercial, or a drama.

Episodes involving children are likely to have greater impact on the young child than do those involving adults. One of the main points of concern about TV viewing in the preschool years, however, does not involve the programs themselves. It is the amount of time the child spends watching TV—whether well-planned children's programs or unsuitable adult programs. For many experts view with alarm the estimates that most children watch TV between twenty-five and twenty-eight hours a week. Toddlers clock in with a whopping thirty hours, almost a full-time job.

Nearly everyone agrees that excessive viewing has a bad effect on the young child. This is especially true when a caregiver uses TV as an electronic "baby-sitter." In this case the young child may spend several hours a day in front of the TV set, frequently without the company of an adult who could provide interpretation and guidance. Some critics feel that the child's emotional development can be seriously impaired by such unregulated viewing. It may lead the child—especially one who has emotional problems already—to retreat from reality and turn to the fantasy world of TV, rather than face the difficulties and rewards of real-life encounters.

The solution to the problem is not to turn off the TV. Rather it is a positive approach: to provide opportunities for the child to experience various kinds of physical, social, and cognitive activities.

Observe several preschoolers as they watch TV. Do they stop what they're doing? Or do they continue to play with each other or by themselves while viewing?

If you wanted to cut one hour of TV viewing from a four- or five-year-old's day, what activities would you replace it with?

· SUMMARY ·

- The preschooler's motor skills are developing rapidly, and overall coordination is improving.
- Children this age begin to show a preference for the right or left hand.
- Preschoolers may have to be coaxed to stop their activities for meals.
- By age three, most children can control elimination.
- Preschoolers can be taught simple cleanliness habits.
- Nutrition and adequate sleep are important because of all the physical activities of preschoolers.
- Ear infections, colds, and "tummy aches" are common complaints of this age group.
- Preschoolers still need supervision to prevent accidents.

TERMS TO KNOW

enuresis
Eustachian tube
eye-hand coordination

1. The _____ connecting ears, nose, and throat is not fully developed in preschoolers.
2. _____ can be developed by playing ball.
3. Preschoolers who suffer from _____ wet the bed more than just occasionally.

CHECK YOUR UNDERSTANDING

1. What should a parent do with a child who is left-handed?
2. How could poor coordination set back a child's social and personality development?
3. Give some examples of play materials that can help a preschooler's small muscle development.
4. Why is it important to allow a child choices at mealtime? How can this be done while still ensuring good nutrition?
5. What might a lack of bladder or bowel control in late preschool years indicate?
6. What fundamental habits of cleanliness should the caregiver try to instill in the preschooler?
7. Give two reasons why it is important to avoid tooth decay in baby teeth.
8. What is a "play nap"?
9. What are three common types of illnesses in the preschool years?

·14·

COGNITIVE DEVELOPMENT
OF THE PRESCHOOLER

Tom and Joyce Kuttner had just cleared the dinner table when 4½-year-old Amy brought in one of her storybooks. "Can you read to me?"

"I will as soon as we're finished doing the dishes," her mother said. "Why don't you look at the pictures until I'm ready?"

"Amy seems so interested in her books lately," Tom said as Amy went into the living room.

"I hate to discourage her," said Joyce. "Why don't you go on and read to her? I can finish the dishes."

"I've got a better idea," said Tom. He disappeared into the bedroom and came back with a large flat box. In it were some red, blue, and yellow magnets. "My sister gave us these when her kids outgrew them, remember? I think Amy is ready for them now."

As Tom began putting the magnets on the lower part of the refrigerator, Amy came to see what this interesting new game was. "Here, you can finish for me," her father said as he went back to doing the dishes.

"Do you know what those are, Amy?" her mother asked. "Those are all the letters of the alphabet."

"I'm puttin' red ones over here," Amy said, absorbed in her task.

"This was a great idea," Joyce said. "Now we can play with Amy while we work in the kitchen."

"Look!" Amy cried. "This one's 'T.'"

"It sure is!" said her father. "Do you know what sound 'T' makes?"

By the time the dishes were done, Amy had found some other letters she knew: O, C, and S. She set those letters to one side and counted them proudly.

"She'll be learning to read in no time," Tom said.

"Well, she does have twenty-two other letters to go—and a few other things to learn before she's ready!" laughed Joyce.

•

Besides learning the alphabet, what other skills can Amy practice by playing with the magnets?

•

What are some things a child must be able to do before he or she can begin learning to read?

L auren still has two months to go before her fourth birthday. Yet, already, when she wants something, she often figures out how to get it on her own. To reach a box of cookies on the shelf of a kitchen cupboard, Lauren moves a chair over. This takes some effort, but she can do it. Standing on the chair, she is able to reach the cupboard's lower shelf where the cookies are.

Such behavior may upset Lauren's parents. It can also be dangerous. But the behavior is normal for a preschooler, especially at ages four and five. It indicates that the child is developing cognitive abilities as well as motor skills.

Cognition is the act of knowing. Its development begins with the child simply *perceiving* her environment with her senses. Then perception is combined with some *understanding* of how and why things happen. Finally, the child learns to use her understanding to achieve better *control* of her environment—and of herself.

By the time a child is in her preschool years, all three—perception, understanding, and control—are involved in her cognitive development. For example, when she sees a meal being prepared, she can also understand something of how it is being prepared. She can understand causality: "If you do this, then that will be the result." She can understand sequence: "This comes first; that comes next."

Moreover, the preschooler can herself help to prepare a meal. She can stir or mix. She can also do simple things like making a sandwich or instant pudding. Of course, she will take a long time making it—and she will make a mess, too. All the while, though, she is stretching her cognitive abilities and gaining control of her environment.

THE PREOPERATIONAL PERIOD

The cognitive development of the typical preschooler can be seen in her imaginative play.

When she plays with blocks, she no longer plays aimlessly—she has a definite goal in mind, such as building a house. She no longer just scribbles, but tries to draw a picture of something. She pretends and fantasizes: When she pushes her toy truck, she imagines where it might be going.

The preschool child has gone far beyond thinking only in terms of what she can see and hear, taste and feel. That was the period which Jean Piaget calls sensorimotor. The preschooler is already well into the next stage. Piaget calls it the **preoperational period.**

In each phase of cognitive growth, the child develops new mental tools. In the preoperational period, she develops the ability to construct symbols. She is able to see an object not only for what it is, but for what it can represent. Mommy's coat is a coat, yes—but it can also symbolize "going out." For example, Ron, in imaginative play with his doll family, tries to put a piece of cloth around the "mommy" doll. The cloth, he explains, is a coat. Ron's own mommy, it so happens, goes off to work every day—wearing her coat.

Language skills, which involve the use of words as symbols, develop dramatically during the preschool years. At age three, many children are speaking in complete sentences at least some of the time. By age five, most children are using all the parts of speech in complete sentences most of the time.

By the time they are six, all normal children of any culture, speaking any language, have basically mastered speech in that language. Also, during the preschool years—the preoperational period—it is fairly easy for many children to learn two or more languages, especially if more than one language is spoken at home. Older children and adults have much more difficulty learning a second language.

Some children learn to read during their preschool years. Usually they are children to whom parents or caregivers read aloud regularly. After a while, the children begin to take

Preschoolers enjoy "helping out" around the house. During the toddler years they learned what's involved in household work through observation. Now they're ready to test their skills. Children should be given simple chores which really need to be done. In this way they build self-image by taking pride in being truly useful. Caregivers should make sure preschoolers are given tasks which they can accomplish. Overburdening them can lead to frustration and unwillingness to help.

an interest in the meaning of those symbols on the printed page. Not all preschoolers do this, however. Many, including many bright preschoolers, are content for the time being just to have somebody read to them.

Then, too, even if a preschooler can read, there are definite limits to how much she can understand. There are certain kinds of thinking—certain cognitive "operations"— which the child simply isn't ready for in the preoperational period. They will come later, in what Jean Piaget calls the concrete operational period, at around age six or seven.

Piaget has done several experiments with preoperational children which show the cognitive limits of this period. In one experiment, the child is given fifteen wooden beads. Three are blue. The other twelve are white. The child is told, and clearly understands, that all the beads are made of the same material. (In this case, the material is wood. It could as easily be plastic, glass, or some other material.) The child also clearly understands that a few of the beads are blue, but most of them are white.

The child is then asked: "Are there more *wooden* beads, or are there more *white* beads?" A child in the preoperational period will answer that there are more white beads. An older child, in the concrete operational stage, will answer that the question is silly, because *all* the beads are wooden.

The preoperational child—the typical preschooler—can focus only on the beads' color, or on their woodenness. She cannot yet mentally grasp the part-to-whole relationship. By contrast, the older child grasps the relationship quickly: All the beads are wooden. A few of these wooden beads are blue. Most are white.

In another Piaget experiment, a preschooler is given two small balls of clay. They are exactly the same size, a fact that the child clearly understands. She "weighs" them in her hands, examines them, and becomes completely familiar with them.

Then the person conducting the experiment asks the child to take one of the clay balls and change its shape. It is to be rolled into the shape of a long tube, so that it looks like a snake, for example. The other piece of clay remains a ball.

The child is asked whether the amount of clay in both pieces, the ball and the long piece, is the same. A typical preschooler will say no. She will usually say that the long piece contains more clay.

In a variation of this experiment, two short glasses are filled with water to exactly the same level. The two glasses themselves are exactly the same size. The preschooler will readily agree that both contain the same amount of water.

Now the water from one of the glasses is poured into another glass—a tall, narrow one. The water level is, of course, higher in this glass. The preschooler will generally insist that the taller glass contains more water—even though she saw that the amount poured into it was the same as in the shorter glass.

Both these experiments show that a child in the preoperational stage lacks the ability to conserve. **Conservation** is a technical term that, as used here, means the ability to understand that a given amount of anything remains the same (is conserved) even if its shape is changed.

A child in the preoperational stage also finds it difficult to think in terms of **reversibility**. Once she has changed a situation, she cannot think in terms of an operation, or a series of operations, that will change the situation back again.

For example, in both the clay and water experiments, an older child will realize that the amount remains the same. What is more, the older child can prove that the amount remains the same. She reverses the operations. She turns the long piece of clay back into a ball. She pours the water from the tall glass back into the short glass. These reverse operations would never occur to the younger, preoperational child.

In addition, children in their preschool years tend to link events together, in a cause-and-effect relationship, just because the events happen together. Older children may at times do this, too. So may some adults. But preschoolers do it frequently.

One five-year-old, for example, was asked where he thought the rain came from. "That's easy," he answered. "When Granny has the

Preschoolers begin to understand that written symbols represent other things. They often enjoy creating stories while they flip through books and magazines. At this age children may begin to read. Children master reading more rapidly if caregivers read aloud to them often. However, if too much emphasis is placed on books and reading, children may become frustrated and lose interest.

kettle on, the steam comes out and it rains." The two events did happen together once—the steaming kettle inside, the rain outside. Now they are linked (temporarily) as cause and effect in the child's mind.

Most children move out of the preoperational period around the time they enter school. Some children, however, make the move into the next period much sooner than others. The exact age varies from child to child.

What does not vary, according to Piaget, is the sequence. All children pass through a particular period or stage of cognitive growth before moving on to the next one. They may pass through it quickly or slowly—but they must pass through it. And a later period never comes before an earlier one.

A learning experience can help speed up the process—provided the child's mental development has advanced far enough. One five-year-old, for instance, was shown repeatedly—in the case of the water experiment—that if she poured the water from the tall glass back into the short glass, the quantity of water remained the same. After the third time, she "got it." She was ready to move out of the preoperational period, and her learning experience helped her in the case of this

When water from a shorter, fatter glass is poured into a tall, thin glass, children in the preoperational stage do not understand that the amount of water has not changed. If they are asked which glass has more water, they will point to the taller one.

Children's Book Editor

"Once upon a time," the story began, "a fisherman and his wife lived happily in a little cottage by the sea." Barry MacIntyre looked carefully at the illustrations accompanying the well-known story of the fisherman who is given three wishes by a magic flounder. He was trying to decide whether this author's retelling of a familiar tale would be appealing to young children, and whether they would like the softly tinted pictures the artist had drawn. He had already looked at all the published versions of the story, and so he could tell that this one had a special charm, which was enhanced by the illustrations. He decided that at the next editorial meeting he would recommend the book for publication.

Children's book publishing is a big business. Some publishers produce only books for young people; others have special departments for children's, or juvenile, literature. There are two basic distinctions in the field: trade publishing, or books of fiction and nonfiction intended for the general public; and text publishing, or books for school. (Like this book!)

There are, in addition, many other classifications. In trade book publishing, there are picture books for preschoolers, books for children just beginning to read, how-to books, biographies, stories, histories, science books, and fiction for teenagers. In educational publishing, there are books for elementary school children and high school students; science, math, and language books; and workbooks, audiovisual aids, and teachers' materials to accompany the texts.

Barry MacIntyre is an editor specializing in picture books. He works with authors and artists to develop books that appeal to very young children. Working with other staff members, he coordinates all the aspects of book production: design, manufacturing cost estimates, marketing, publicity, and advertising. Children's book publishing is highly competitive, and so the work is often pressured and tense. There are always deadlines to meet. In general, salaries in the publishing industry are not high, although senior staff members are often well paid.

An editor must be creative, well-read, tactful, hard-working, and able to get along well with many different people. A good knowledge of children's literature is helpful, as well as a sense of what kinds of books children like to read or hear. A college education is necessary to get a job as an editorial assistant—usually the first step toward becoming an editor. However, it is not necessary to have taken a particular course of study. There are some summer programs that train college graduates in publishing skills, and there are also valuable college or adult education courses. In general, though, publishing is an industry in which one learns on the job, and entry-level jobs may be quite routine and low-paid.

It takes many months, sometimes even years, to produce a book; but one of the rewards of the field is the satisfaction of looking at the final product and knowing that children will be reading it with enjoyment for years to come.

one operation. But if she were not ready—if her cognitive abilities were not developed enough—no amount of repetition would help.

To use a simple analogy: A tadpole can't hop. It has not developed the necessary physical structure—a pair of hind legs. Similarly, a preschool child can't perform certain mental operations. She has not yet developed the necessary cognitive structure.

SYMBOLIC THINKING

In a sense, children themselves build the next stage of their cognitive development. They use what mental tools they have to take in what knowledge they can and, over time, to develop a new cognitive structure.

The preschooler's most important mental tool is her ability to think symbolically. And one of the ways she sharpens this tool is through imaginative play.

The preschooler can take an ordinary box and turn it into a boat, a plane, a castle, or anything she pleases. A plastic cup may become a telephone receiver, or an old wire lampshade hoop a steering wheel.

Blocks are excellent toys for developing a preschooler's ability to think symbolically.

As the preschooler's imaginative play grows more complex, she is building a foundation for logical thought. After about age four, for instance, she may even be able to divide objects into classes—group them together with other objects they resemble.

Also during the preschool years, children gradually become less egocentric. At age three, their world is still generally centered on themselves. They can role-play imaginatively. For example, a little boy can pretend that he is like his father. But this is imitation. The boy cannot really think of how his father might think or feel. He cannot identify with someone else's point of view.

Nor can the preschooler consider any alternative to her own thought processes. If a child is told she should think about something "this way," rather than "that way," she cannot do it. She can only think one way—her way.

This egocentric thinking changes in part because of the preschooler's developing language skills. Language is one kind of symbolic thinking. It allows the child to represent objects and events with words. But language is not just one-way symbolic thinking. It also allows interaction with other persons.

The typical preschooler definitely does talk a lot. Often she seems to combine nonstop physical activity with nonstop talking. Often, too, she seems to be talking without listening. It's as if she were practicing speech—which in fact she may be doing.

At the same time, she is using speech to interact with other people: parents and other family members, caregivers, other children. She asks questions. She often, though not always, listens to the answers. She discusses feelings, hers and others. She expresses disagreement as well as agreement.

In the process, the preschooler is developing an ability to think about things apart from their relation to herself. She is developing an understanding of other people's existence, their separate reality. And, again, she is laying

Imaginative play grows more complex during the preschool years. Through their play, children try out the various roles they have been exposed to since birth. Roles such as mother, father, and doctor are learned through the child's personal interactions with others. Kings, queens, and soldiers are roles learned from other sources, such as television, stories, and games. Children may pretend to be another person and ask to be called by another name. They may also adopt imaginary playmates. This behavior is normal unless it continues too long.

220

a basis for the distinctions and logical operations that come with the next stage of cognitive growth.

MORAL DEVELOPMENT

As she grows older, a child's sense of right and wrong develops in much the same way that her cognitive abilities develop. According to Piaget, moral development proceeds through three stages. The first stage is what Piaget calls the **morality of constraint**. Most preschoolers are in this stage. They are constrained, or held back from certain actions by adults. Adults make the rules, along with rewards for obeying the rules and punishments for disobedience.

Emphasis, in the child's mind, is on the "size" of a misdeed or the amount of damage done. The "bigger" the misdeed or the "bigger" the amount of damage, the greater the punishment. This is simple "retributive justice"—an eye for an eye, a tooth for a tooth. The person's intentions, whether she acted deliberately or accidentally, are not considered.

Piaget also refers to this kind of morality as "objective," in contrast to a "subjective" morality based on a person's intentions. In experiments with children, Piaget asked them to evaluate two stories. The first story is about a little boy or girl who trips while helping set the table. A tray of cups is accidentally knocked to the floor, and twelve cups break. In the second story, a girl or boy is told not to eat the cookies being saved in the cupboard for guests. The child decides to sneak a cookie anyway, and breaks a cup while climbing up to the cupboard. Most preschoolers think that the child in the first story should receive the greater punishment, because—accidentally or not—that child broke more cups.

Two more stories can be used to demonstrate the same point with respect to lying. In the first story, a child comes home and tells of seeing a pink elephant dancing in the street to a tune played by a monkey with an organ. In the second, a child comes home and tells his mother he got a perfect score on a test at school, when in fact he flunked. Again, younger children tend to consider the lie told by the child in the first story more serious than the one told by the child in the second story. The first lie was "bigger"—a "taller" tale.

LANGUAGE DEVELOPMENT

The development of language skills during the preschool period is in itself a marvelous thing. The average three-year-old child has a vocabulary of about a thousand words. Most of these are names. There are also some verbs (such as "go"), pronouns ("me"), prepositions ("in") and adjectives ("big"). Although she may not use them in her own speech, she can understand simple adjectives dealing with physical space, such as "over," "high," "long," and "tall."

A three-year-old's muscles and coordination are not quite developed enough to handle many of the speech sounds of her language. But within the next two years, she will master all except the most difficult sounds.

She will more than double her vocabulary during this time as well. She will learn grammatical rules—such as beginning a sentence with "I" instead of "me," or "he" instead of "him." She may even learn distinctions such as the differences between "big," "bigger," and "biggest." By the time the child enters first grade, she will usually be speaking as well as her family and the other people around her speak, since she will imitate the grammatical patterns they use.

Preschoolers frequently make errors that arise from their habit of applying language rules too rigidly. For instance, a three-year-old was asked to choose a picture that illustrated the following sentence: "The cat is chased by the dog." The child listened to the sentence, nodded, and then pointed to a picture of a cat

The preschooler is constantly refining her sense of how language rules are applied. She does this, of course, by talking with adults. Her continual "Why?" questions may be a sign of natural curiosity.

Children are clearly helped in perfecting their language skills by adults who have the time to talk and listen. But attempts to correct children's speech errors may not take hold immediately. This can be seen in the following dialogue between a child and his older brother, who is trying to correct the child's speech errors:

CHILD: I see'd some hippos in the zoo.
BROTHER: You *saw* some hippos? Tell me what other animals you *saw*.
CHILD: I see'd some monkeys....
BROTHER: Did you say you *saw* some monkeys?
CHILD: Yes, I see'd monkeys.

Eventually this child will use the correct past tense of "see"—but not until he is ready. Language, as we have seen, is learned by stages, and this child has not yet reached the stage where he can make use of his brother's correction.

TIME AND MEMORY

The preschooler's sense of time is generally egocentric. A period of time is as long or as short as the child feels it to be. She has not yet gained a clear sense of objective time periods apart from her own experience.

Time sense, however, tends to be subjective even for adults. We often hear comments such as: "Yesterday the afternoon dragged; today it just flew." And Albert Einstein, discussing relativity, noted the difference between a minute spent sitting on a hot stove and a minute spent kissing a desirable partner.

Then, too, many cultures do not have the highly developed—some would say "overdeveloped"—sense of time common in Western

As children perfect their language ability they love to ask the question "Why?" Caregivers must have lots of patience and ingenuity to answer a preschooler's questions.

chasing a dog. (There was another picture of a dog chasing a cat, which she could have chosen.) She knew the English word-order rule: subject-verb-object. But, at three, she didn't yet know that the order can be reversed in a sentence using the passive voice.

Blind or partially sighted children may go to a special school for the blind or be in a special class in a public school. However, today there is a trend toward mainstreaming: placing handicapped children in regular classrooms. In these classrooms there is a specially trained teacher available to aid the regular teacher.

An important part of education for the visually handicapped is learning braille, a system of reading and writing for the blind in which embossed or raised dots are arranged in different patterns for letters, numbers, symbols, and certain words. The blind person moves his fingers over these embossed dots in order to read. Children need not wait until they enter school to experience braille. A child can hold her own braille storybook while her parent is reading the same story in print aloud to her. Her hands can be moved over the words by the parent as they are read. Since a sighted child has a multitude of signs and labels to read, a blind child should have braille labels on her possessions and objects in the home.

In the classroom the blind child needs the same prereading preparation that other children have except that extra thought must be given to arrange the learning environment for her. Being made to feel comfortable in the classroom is very important to the sightless child. Getting to know her classmates must be a different process for her because of her lack of vision. Cards with differing textures and objects to sort, such as buttons, beads, and other three-dimensional materials, are excellent for the blind child. Classmates can be very helpful to blind students in their classes by describing what is going on, taking notes for them, and generally accepting them as one of the class.

On the first page of one of the beginning braille readers is a large square of many braille dots. The instructions to the children would be to explore the page with their fingers and describe what they feel there. The following pages present squares, circles, and triangles, growing smaller on each page, until the students are introduced to braille at the end of the book. One of the criticisms of braille reading is that it is slow; therefore programs are being developed to teach students fast braille reading.

industrialized cultures. Nevertheless, a child growing up in a Western culture does learn a sense of time. Even during her third year, she begins to use expressions such as "It's almost time" fairly accurately.

Four-year-olds have a definite sense of past and future. They seldom confuse "tomorrow" with "yesterday." Four-year-olds can also talk about "next Halloween" and "last Halloween," and they can understand time words like "month."

By age five, the child can generally understand and use most ordinary time words. She knows the days of the week, and she knows them in their right order. She knows, too, how old she was on her last birthday—and how old she will be on her next birthday. She likes to mark the dates off on a calendar. She may also be able to use a clock to tell time, but most five-year-olds are not quite ready—though they may pretend they are.

Preschoolers also have a good visual memory for objects or images. If you were to lay several objects on a table, and ask a preschooler to look at the objects and then turn around and call out the names of as many as she can remember, the child would be able to remember quite a few. Activities like this are within the range of preschoolers' cognitive abilities. They are capable of understanding sequences, in which one thing follows another—as long as a sequence is not reversed.

A preschooler will have trouble, though, with any activity that calls for grouping objects—if she has to consider more than one dimension or aspect. This is demonstrated by the experiment with the blue and white wooden beads discussed earlier.

NUMBER, FORM, AND SPACE

Just as most preschoolers can understand sequence, most can count. The three-year-old can generally count at least two objects, and the four-year-old at least three.

The cognitive ability is there, and skills increase with practice. At the end of a child's fifth year, her skills may be considerable. She can probably count to twenty or over. She may even be able to do addition, up to ten, with the help of her fingers. Many children by then can also count by tens to a hundred.

Children pick up very quickly the fact that adults are interested in money. Preschoolers as a result take an interest in money, too. Very early, they can learn to count coins. Between the ages of five and six, they are able to tell the value of certain coins—such as pennies, nickels, and dimes.

These counting skills are useful, both for their own sake and as preparation for working with numbers later. But counting skills and number concepts are not the same thing. A three-year-old may be able to point out and count objects, yet not have a clear idea of number. At three, she may not even understand the difference between *less* and *more*.

Four-year-old Michael understands that difference, but he too doesn't understand number.

Puzzles help children develop their fine motor coordination and also improve their recognition of colors and shapes. Most preschoolers can complete simple puzzles consisting of a few large pieces. By practicing, children learn to do more complex puzzles with pieces which are more irregular in shape and closer in color to those that surround them.

Although he can count to four—his own age—his idea of "fourness" is limited. To Michael, for example, a "lot of blocks" means a *big pile* of blocks—not ten or twenty or thirty. He judges quantity by the size of the whole group together, rather than by "how many."

Michael may be six or seven years old before he begins to think in terms of a certain number of *units* when judging quantity. Until then, his idea of quantity will depend on how big a *bunch* of objects looks to him, not on number.

In recognizing the form of individual objects, Michael is fairly advanced. He recognizes the difference between a circle and an oval, between a triangle and a trapezoid, between a square rectangle and one that is not square. Altogether he can recognize nine different shapes. This is a bit more advanced than usual. The average four-year-old recognizes eight different geometric forms.

Most preschoolers, by the time they are into their fifth year, have a pretty good idea of differences in form. Many have an idea, too, of relative size.

Also, by the fifth year, most preschoolers tend to classify objects by form rather than color. Before the age of four, the opposite is true. Most children focus on color, and they learn to match colors before they learn to match shapes.

In one experiment, a group of four-year-olds was given a set of triangles, some red and some green, mixed with a set of circles, red and green. The children were asked to choose things that were like other things. Well over half these four-year-olds chose to classify the items by color, red or green, rather than by form. In a group of five-year-olds, on the other hand, over 85 percent chose to put the triangles together and the circles together, regardless of color. Older preschoolers are reaching a stage where they focus less on obvious surface characteristics. They focus on other qualities, such as an object's function.

Children's perceptions of form (and of color) naturally affect their ability to deal with their environment. To take a simple example, a three-year-old with a poor perception of form may not be able to ride her tricycle through a doorway without bumping on each try.

Where preschoolers have the most trouble is in relating things to other things. The typical four-year-old, for example, will frequently misjudge her own size in relation to the size of something else. She may also have trouble classifying things, except in the broadest possible way. Everything from pots and pans to matches, and from food to a grownup in an apron, means "kitchen." There are no subcategories in the preschooler's way of thinking.

By the end of the preschool period, though, children are at least beginning to identify common properties of objects. They understand that not only are there dogs, but that some dogs are brown or white or black, that some have pointed ears and others have floppy ears, that some are big and others small—yet all are dogs. As dogs, they are different from cats or horses or cows or birds.

A child cannot be taught to classify things until she is ready—until her mental equipment, her cognitive structure, is well enough developed. But many children in their later preschool years are ready.

A child, for instance, can be shown how to make a game out of sorting her toys. She first picks up all the toys that have red in them, then all those with yellow in them. The next day, she picks up first all the blocks which are round, then all those which are square. Sorting buttons in the sections of an egg carton is another interesting game for many children.

The preschooler's sense of space, like her sense of form, is in the process of developing. She is learning the full meaning of position words like "above," "below," "inside," "outside," "in front of," and "behind." Her progress is helped by suggestions such as "Look behind the door" or "Put it on the table."

A sense of form and color develops during the preschool years. Children at this age may be able to help with household chores by sorting their own clothes and matching their socks.

The child's sense of space develops during her preschool years along with her perception of form, and also her ability to understand relationships. The three-year-old, if asked how to get to the playground, may answer: "Take a bus" or "Walk." The four-year-old may try to say something about the route, such as: "Go past the yellow house."

The five-year-old can follow a well-known route and point out particular landmarks along the way. By the time she is six, she may be naming streets near her home, with a full understanding of where they are located.

By then, too, she is aware of space relation-ships between her home, school, and neighborhood. If she has traveled beyond her neighborhood, she can probably make a mental connection between distant places and her home area.

The child at the end of her preschool years is rapidly becoming a pretty competent person. She will be more advanced in some of her abilities than in others. Yet, in general, she will be ready not only to master her environment, but to expand it.

- In the preoperational period, the preschooler has begun to think symbolically.
- Language skills develop dramatically.
- Preschoolers can classify things in simple, broad categories.
- Conservation and reversibility are not understood by most preschoolers.
- Preschoolers tend to link events together as cause and effect.
- During the preschool years, children gradually become less egocentric.
- The sense of right and wrong at this age is based on the rules, rewards, and punishments given by adults.
- Ideas of time are better understood.
- Most preschoolers develop counting skills and an understanding of shapes, relative size, and spatial relationships.

TERMS TO KNOW

conservation
morality of constraint
preoperational period
reversibility

1. In Piaget's theory, a preschooler is well into the _____ of cognitive development.
2. _____ is the understanding that operations like pouring water from a large container to a smaller one can be done backwards.
3. A preschooler who does not understand _____ will think that a tall, thin glass holds more than a short, wide one.
4. The first stage of moral development is called the _____.

CHECK YOUR UNDERSTANDING

1. Describe three stages in the development of cognition.
2. What mental tool does the preschooler develop in the preoperational period?
3. How does Piaget's experiment with the clay balls show that the preschooler does not understand conservation? Reversibility?
4. Suppose that you show a four-year-old that a tall glass of water holds the same amount as a short glass. After six tries, she still does not believe you. Is it because she is stupid? Explain.
5. How does the development of language skills help the preschooler's thinking become less egocentric?
6. What is meant by "morality of constraint"?
7. By what age is a child usually able to speak as well as her family?
8. How can activities such as picking up toys help a preschooler learn to classify things?

· 15 ·

SOCIAL/EMOTIONAL
DEVELOPMENT
OF THE PRESCHOOLER

"Victor! You haven't even started getting dressed!" said Mrs. Martinez. "Come and put your shirt on. We're almost ready to go."

Three-year-old Victor held up his arms. "You put it on me. I can't do it."

"Of course you can!" said Mrs. Martinez. "You're a big boy. Now hurry up. Grandpa and Grandma are waiting to see your new baby sister."

"I don't want to go!" Victor ran from the room.

Mrs. Martinez found Victor on the sofa, sucking his thumb.

"Now let's talk about this," she said as she sat down and held Victor on her lap. "You've always liked visiting Grandpa and Grandma before. But today it seems you don't want to go. Why not?"

"They just want to see Lisa and not me," Victor said.

"I know they will be very happy to see the new baby. But they love you and want to see you, too."

"I wish we could stay home," Victor pouted. "Not Lisa. Just us."

"I see," said his mother. "You want it to be like before Lisa came, when it was just you and me and Daddy. Is that right?"

"Uh-huh," Victor nodded. "I wish she didn't live here."

"Victor, we love Lisa very much and want her to be part of our family," Mrs. Martinez said. "But it sounds like you feel that we've been too busy taking care of Lisa to spend enough time with you."

"Yes!" Victor said. "I want you to be with just me sometimes."

"Okay," said Mrs. Martinez. "How about if Daddy or I spend some time with you every evening after supper, when Lisa is sleeping. We'll play games or read stories, do just what you want to do. Would that help you feel better?"

"Yeah," Victor said happily. "I love you, Mommy."

"And we both love you very much," Mrs. Martinez smiled.

•

Do you think Victor's mother handled this situation well?
•
Why do you think Victor wanted his mother to put his shirt on for him?

Barbara goes over to a row of chairs she has set up as a make-believe airplane. She plunks herself down in the first chair.

"I'm the pilot," she declares. "I can fly."

"No you can't," Gene argues.

"Yes I can," she insists. "I can do everything."

Barbara seems very sure of her abilities. Gene may be less sure of his. Both children are in the same group of four-year-olds at nursery school. Their teacher says that Barbara "knows who she is," while Gene is still discovering himself. Actually, Barbara, in the roles she plays, is still discovering herself, too.

Self-discovery is part of the emotional and social development of every preschooler. Here is a new person, an individual who has never existed before and whose exact duplicate will never be seen again. Who is he? What is he like? What will he become?

The preschooler himself doesn't think in those terms. He cannot yet consider himself objectively in a detached manner. But he does sense that he is something special. His chief aim in life at this time—though he may not be conscious of it—is to find out just how special he is, and in what ways.

PERSONALITY DEVELOPMENT

An important part of the preschooler's image of himself comes from the changes taking place in his body. He is proud of his physical growth and his rapidly developing motor skills.

"Look how big I am!" he tells the clerk at the supermarket, and then proceeds to use the grocery cart as a jungle gym on wheels. Later he will help unload the groceries. Not long ago he wasn't even able to drink his milk without spilling some.

Mentally, too, he is developing at top speed, though he is less conscious of it. Forever poking into things and asking questions, he is scientist, explorer, and storyteller all at once.

Yet, despite his accomplishments, the preschooler is strongly dependent on his caregivers for his sense of self-worth. If he is treated as a person who is becoming more and more independent, more and more competent, he will see himself that way.

If he is overprotected and babied, he could become timid and passive. Or, if too much is expected of him, and he is criticized or laughed at for not "measuring up," he could easily get an image of himself as a failure.

Because the preschooler does mirror so much of his self-image in the eyes of parents or other caregivers, praise is obviously important to him. This includes praise, when appropriate, for his ability to do things like climb on a stool to reach the light switch. He also feels proud of himself when, for example, he sees his drawing taped up in a place where everybody can admire it. Of course, not everything a child does is admirable, but the disappointment or frustration he feels over a temporary failure or mistake can be soothed by adult reassurance.

The development of personality traits like self-confidence, initiative, and a sense of independence often depends on adult responses. When a preschooler wants to fix his own peanut-butter-and-jelly sandwich, parents or caregivers may either allow him to do so despite his messiness, so that he can learn—or they may be impatient and intolerant of his childish efforts and criticize him for not doing it properly.

However, the child's sense of achievement, when he finally bites into his oozing masterpiece, compensates for the mess. Similarly, when he tries to make his own bed, his trying is more important than whether the bedspread is crooked or the corner of the blanket dragging on the floor.

Most preschoolers, certainly by the time they are five, if not sooner, are ready to take on some real household responsibilities. Picking up toys, emptying wastebaskets, sorting the laundry—such chores can help the preschooler

It takes a lot of practice to learn how to tie shoelaces. Preschoolers feel a real sense of accomplishment when they finally succeed after months of trying.

feel useful and important. He may work slowly, with many interruptions, but he has a sense of himself as a valuable, contributing member of the household.

Such activities also provide opportunities for preschoolers to practice adult roles. To the toddler, pots and pans are for banging. The preschooler is ready to use them as utensils, the way adults do.

Imaginative role-playing, in imitation of adult models, usually begins early in the preschool years. Kathy, for instance, clumps around the house in her mother's shoes, while her cousin Ken "reads" the paper—upside down. Toddlers and young preschoolers also commonly imitate behavior that is not appropriate for their sex—as when Miriam pretends to shave like her father or when Willie imitates his mother putting on lipstick. Such play is normal, and the children will eventually learn to identify more with adults of their own sex.

Preschoolers, it should be noted, model their behavior generally after what they see adults *do*, not what adults *say* to do. When Dorrie is angry, she may slap her favorite doll (or her little sister). And Julio will make up an excuse to get out of doing something he dislikes. Both children are reflecting the way they have seen adults actually behaving—either members of their own family or people on TV. A child may also repeat vulgar words that he has heard an adult use—without actually understanding their meaning.

In the process of identifying with adults preschoolers begin to shape their ideas of **sex-role identity**—what it means to be male or female. Sometimes, in an imaginative role-play situation, who is the "mommy" and who is the "daddy" become a matter of convenience. Lisa and Marianne, with no boys present, take turns being the mommy and the daddy.

More often, though, as children develop during their preschool years, they identify strongly with one sex or the other. They may even show what appear to be romantic feelings for a parent of the opposite sex. A boy may state, for example, that he intends to marry his mother.

Sigmund Freud called this stage of personality development the **oedipal period,** named after King Oedipus of Greek mythology, who unknowingly killed his father and married his mother. Freud saw in the myth a symbol of the child's wish to have the parent of the opposite sex all to himself and to eliminate the "rival" parent. Many psychologists today think that a boy's romantic attachment to his mother is actually his way of trying to identify with his father. Similarly, a little girl forms a special attachment to her father, as a way of identifying with her mother. Of course, in many families only one parent is present. In that case, a relative or family friend may provide a model of the sex of the missing parent.

The extent of oedipal feelings varies from child to child, and most children outgrow them by the age of six or seven. Their world has greatly widened by then, and their involvement with their parents has become less intense.

Socially, of course, sex roles have changed considerably over the past decade or two. In many households, all adult members have jobs outside the home. They may share the housework without regard to sex-role stereotypes.

Pretending is an important part of the preschool years. In their imaginative play, children often imitate those they have observed. Since preschoolers can learn poor habits as well as good ones, adults must be aware of their behavior and speech in front of them. Children can embarrass parents by repeating to outsiders what they have heard at home. Parents are often unaware that children of this age are able to remember and repeat adult conversation.

Children try out different sex-role identities through play. Caregivers must encourage children to develop all their interests and abilities. If girls are allowed only to play with dolls and boys are allowed only to play with tools, this will limit their idea of what women and men can do.

have become less rigid than they used to be. There are male secretaries and nurses as well as female ones—and female executives and doctors as well as male.

Boys and girls are obviously structured differently physically, but it is not known to what extent behavior is influenced by biological factors. Many parents and teachers agree that the average four-year-old boy is likely to be "wilder" in his physical play than is the average four-year-old girl. How much of that is due to social pressure for the boy to act in a way that is considered to be masculine, and how much is due to biological differences, is not easy to determine. There are arguments on both sides. In any case, most children, by their late preschool years, have developed a clear sense of being a girl or a boy—whatever that means to them and those around them.

SOCIAL DEVELOPMENT

The child during the preschool years is doing more than develop a self-image. He is also learning to relate to other people. Not only does he identify privately with adult behavior; he interacts with adults themselves—and with other children—aided by his improving language skills.

Gradually the preschooler becomes less self-centered. He learns that other people don't exist just to serve his interests, and that they have their own needs and rights. He learns—reluctantly, at this age—to take turns. He learns what it is to be fair—and what it is to be unfair. In short, he is becoming socialized. **Socialization** is the process by which a child learns how to function with other people in his society. He learns this through his everyday interaction with others.

Socialization began in infancy, when the baby learned what his family expects of him. During the preschool years, the child becomes further socialized through interaction with his

Sex-role identities are changing rapidly today. Many women are entering the work force in jobs traditionally held by men. Males are learning that taking care of home and family can be enjoyable and are responsibilities that must be shared.

For such people, there is no such thing as "women's work" or "men's work"—there are only jobs to be done.

On television and elsewhere, children today see a wide variety of models with respect to men, women, and work. Although many fields are still dominated by women or men, sex roles

Teacher

"Mr. Ferber, I can't read this sentence. Can you help me with this word?"

"Ms. Moshed, these equations are impossible! I'll never learn chemistry!"

"Mr. Brooks, I just love this new piece by Bach. But the fingering is so hard."

"Mrs. Díaz, could you tie my shoelace?"

All these requests were made by children to their teachers—the first to a fourth-grade teacher in a suburban elementary school; the second to a high school chemistry teacher; the third to a private music teacher; and the last to a nursery school teacher.

Perhaps no career is as closely related to child development as teaching. Whatever the age or interest of their students, teachers have an enormous influence on a child's emotional, social, and intellectual development. Teachers have the opportunity to observe children over a period of time, instruct them in skills, and measure progress. As professionals they can evaluate each child's needs and progress fairly and sensitively; they can also share in and take pride in the joy of achievement.

Teaching is a difficult job, for it demands excellent skills, a strong ability to get along with people, and a sure command of subject matter. As competition for teaching jobs increases, and as teachers are evaluated more closely by school boards and other employers, it will become an even more selective profession.

Preparation for a teaching career can take many routes. A college degree is essential, either in education or in a particular subject area. A teacher who plans to specialize in a particular subject—chemistry or mathematics, for example—will no doubt wish to take advanced courses in those subjects. Each state has different requirements for certification but they generally require some education courses, student teaching experience, and sometimes passing written or oral examinations. Today it is not uncommon to find teachers at elementary and secondary levels with masters' degrees. Doctorates are often required for supervisory jobs such as principals or superintendents.

Teaching in private or public schools is, however, not the only professional course open. Many day-care centers and child-care institutions have teachers on their staffs. A teacher may work only with private students, or may teach courses at museums, recreation centers, or other community agencies. Frequently these are part-time jobs, and offer the teacher time to pursue his or her special interests professionally.

As education has become more specialized, the demand for special teachers has also grown. There are now jobs for bilingual teachers, teachers who teach English as a second language, special-education teachers for the handicapped and mentally retarded, teachers who work with homebound children who are unable to attend school for health or other reasons, remedial reading specialists, and media specialists.

A teacher's responsibilities are great, and the pressures—from parents, school boards, administrators, and the community—can also be immense. It is by no means a job that offers an easy route to security. Yet for those who truly enjoy working with children, it is a highly rewarding profession.

Through play in group settings a child develops a sense of self. He learns that other children differ in appearance, personality, ability, and life style.

peers—other children the same age. While toddlers tend to play beside each other, not with each other, preschoolers actually play together. As they play and argue—over who gets the whole crayons and who gets the broken stubs, for example—they learn how to adjust to each other's needs and personalities.

Also, the preschooler's sense of himself and his own developing personality takes on new dimensions in relation to children his own age. The most obvious comparisons are physical. Some children are bigger than he is, some smaller. Some have different colored hair or different colored skin. Such differences are usually accepted matter-of-factly. Unless cued by adults, a child in the preschool years generally does not feel one physical quality is better or worse than another. Physical differences are interesting to him because they help him define himself.

The same is true of sex differences. At age three, most children—about two-thirds—know whether they are boys or girls. At age four, they are curious about the differences. Undressing and "doctor" games are not uncommon. Questions about where babies come from usually begin at this age. This early interest in sex and sex differences is natural in a child exploring who he is. Again, unless the responses of adults teach him otherwise, he will come to accept sex differences as a matter of fact, without being overconcerned about them.

Physical differences are not the only ones the preschooler notices among his peers. There are also differences in abilities. Dave is the best climber. Rosa can print her own name, while Anita just makes scribbles. But Anita is a fast runner—faster than Dave, though he is much bigger. This is a big part of what a preschooler learns at a day-care center, nursery school, or other play group: what he can do, compared with what others can do.

Different personality traits also show up in group play: "Rosa talks the most." "John says funny things all the time." "Ray is mean." Group leaders soon emerge—and followers find their individual places in the group—while other children prefer to be "loners."

Then, too, as the preschooler makes friends among his peers, he could be introduced to life styles very different from his own. Dave discovers that Luis has different toys from Dave's, eats supper at a different time, and likes foods that Dave has never tasted before. And when Luis talks with his grandmother, he speaks a different language from English.

Millie, who has only one sibling (a bossy older brother), is fascinated by Pat's family, which includes eight siblings (six of whom are sisters). Peter learns that Jack lives with only his mother and sister; Jack's father lives in another state. Anna Marie, on the other hand, lives part of the week with her mother and part of the week with her father in his separate apartment.

Preschoolers frequently come to their parents with questions about the differences they discover at friends' houses, "Susan's daddy has gone away. Will my daddy go away, too?" "Danny doesn't have to eat that. Why do I have to eat that?" "Why can't I stay up and watch TV? Tony's mother lets him stay up."

Four-year-olds, especially, seem to make a point of rebelling against the life style they have grown up with. In fact, they may just be testing the limits, as a way of coping with newly encountered differences in the world of their peers. They are trying to find out what those differences mean in relation to their own life style.

In addition, a four-year-old who engages regularly in group activities with his peers, outside the home, is likely to look more to those peers for attention and praise than to parents or caregivers at home. This will change somewhat around age five, when the child becomes more home-centered again. But at four in particular, a child's self-esteem is strongly influenced by the positive or negative reactions of his peers.

Children who are popular with their group generally show it in their behavior. They tend to be cooperative, enthusiastic, and affectionate. Children who are rejected by their peer group tend to be disruptive, refuse to cooperate, engage in ridicule, and even threaten or attack other children physically. Such behavior usually leads others to reject a child even more. The rejected child often needs the help of adults to bring out the positive aspects of his personality so that he can be accepted by other children and feel better about himself.

Some children are not rejected so much as ignored by the group. They are so shy they simply withdraw into a corner and play alone. They, too, may need adult help. But then, even at this age, there are a few true individualists. They have their own style and go their own way. Eventually they may become leaders of their own little groups.

Actually, most children at age four play well together. "Don't worry, I'm not really a tiger," Jeremy assures Donna, who has become frightened by the snarling creature in the Halloween mask. "It's just a mask." And Kitty is quick to comfort Mario when he falls down and skins his knee.

Social play among four- and five-year-olds is often characterized by **alternate behavior**. One child does something, then waits for a response from another child. Though the group at this age may number as many as six children, each waits his turn. Only one actor, in effect, occupies center stage at any one time.

Role-play situations can become quite imaginative and elaborate. Liz, who at home is rather withdrawn, is a leader in her peer group. In one situation, she is a mommy with a large family. She takes her "babies" (Robin, Manny, and Donna) to the zoo, where "tiger" Jeremy has just escaped from his cage. The tiger is very hungry, but Liz persuades him to

Linda is three and a half years old. She has a friend, "Fishy," who is also three and a half. Fishy is extremely naughty. She writes on the walls with crayons, spills milk at the table, wets the bed at night, and won't pick up her toys. Fishy causes a lot of trouble for Linda and also for Linda's parents. But Fishy is very difficult to correct or get rid of. Fishy is an imaginary child.

Robert is four years old. He has made friends with a grownup named "Chief." Robert and Chief do wonderful things together. They go on fishing trips, paddle in Chief's canoe, and camp out in the woods in a real tent with a real campfire. Robert tells the stories of his adventures to his parents, who listen with a mixture of interest and concern. For Robert has never been fishing or in a canoe or out camping. Chief is imaginary, just like the tent and campfire.

Both Linda and Robert are using their imaginations to cope with problems that are too difficult for them to handle in real life. Linda loves her parents and wants to please them. But their expectations of her are too high. She cannot bear to think that she sometimes lets them down. Answer: an imaginary Fishy who does all the bad things.

Robert craves more attention from his parents, especially from his father, who is a very busy man, regularly bringing work home from the office and often going away on business trips. Robert finds the relationship he wants with his imaginary friend Chief.

Dr. Eric Baum says that imaginary companions, common to young preschoolers, often serve a real purpose. According to Dr. Baum, companions like Fishy and Chief can provide relief from an "all-too-intense" real-life situation.

But imaginary companions are not necessarily a sign that their creators have special needs or anxieties. Often, these magical figures belong to the shining fantasy world of the happy child's play. They take part in the dramas children make up for themselves, share their daily routines, and enrich their daydreams.

What sort of things can we learn about preschool children's needs by listening to them tell about their imaginary companions?

What kinds of problems might occur if a preschooler spent too much time with her imaginary companions? How could imaginary companions interfere with normal development? How could they encourage and enrich it?

settle for some cookies instead of gobbling up Donna. The others decide to join him in his snack, and the game has a brief intermission.

Of course, despite the general atmosphere of cooperation, disputes do arise and tempers do flare. Moreover, children by the end of their fifth year often become more competitive. For instance, they begin to favor prizes in their games. The games themselves change to ones in which there is a clear ranking of winners and losers.

There are many arguments for and against competition at this—or any—age. On the one hand, competition encourages children to do their best. Those who try hard and take risks may find themselves rewarded—as indeed our culture in general tends to reward those who are able to gain a competitive edge.

Some children are able to handle competition at a young age; others are not. Winning should not be overemphasized in games for preschoolers.

On the other hand, for every winner there has to be at least one loser. To make "losers" out of very young children—whose bodies, skills, and personalities are still developing—can hurt them and damage their self-image. More useful for the child's healthy development are cooperative games, in which everyone has a chance to succeed. Everyone can join in a game like Balloon Toss, in which a group of children try to keep a large balloon bouncing in the air. They use only their heads, not their hands. Nobody wins or loses, and the game continues only as long as everybody is interested in playing. A game like this develops both the child's social and physical skills, while giving him a chance to enjoy himself with a minimum of competitive pressure.

One new and important experience for many children in the late preschool years is friendship. Three-year-olds talk a lot about friends. They may even make up imaginary ones. At four and five, however, children tend to pick out one or two of their peers as "best friends."

EMOTIONAL DEVELOPMENT

A child's preschool years are usually nothing if not emotional. He shifts very quickly from laughter to tears, from confidence to fearfulness, from joy to anger—and back again.

Every emotion is intense while it lasts. Moreover, the preschooler has not learned to modify his reactions according to the situation. He cries as hard when his block construction collapses as when his pet rabbit dies.

His range of emotional expression is limited—so that anger, for instance, will be expressed in just one of two ways. Either he will "throw a tantrum" or strike out physically. Only later will he learn to express his anger in words.

It should also be remembered that children express their emotions differently according to individual personality. Steve shows his pleasure with a loud whoop when he opens a birthday present. Liz—whose delight with her present is no less intense—simply smiles and murmurs a quiet thank-you.

Whether or not it is expressed, violence seems to be very much on many children's minds during their preschool years. In one study, children from ages two to five were encouraged to tell stories of their own invention. Some kind of violent action was the main element in all the stories.

Because preschoolers also tend to be "into everything" physically—and tend to subject parents and other adults with a nonstop barrage of questions—the television set is often used by caregivers to keep a child quietly occupied. Certainly it will keep the preschooler quiet in one place for a while. Yet, if a program shows violence, the child is likely to be strongly affected by it. He will remember the violence, especially at bedtime.

The adventurousness of the typical pre-

Every summer you see them at the shore or poolside—toddlers, preschoolers, and older children—standing at the water's edge crying. Daddy or Mommy is valiantly trying to persuade the youngster that the water is fun. "It's fine! Look at Daddy!" Splash. Cries. "I don't want to," wails the child.

Fears come in all sizes and shapes. One of the most common during the years from three to six is fear of the water. Babies usually enjoy splashing about while some grownup holds them safely by the waist. Two or three years later, they refuse to do more than wade in water that only comes to their ankles.

Why this widespread fear of water? Perhaps the most important explanation is that children learn it from adults. Many parents are themselves uncomfortable in the water. They say again and again to the child, "Be careful." "Look out for the waves." "Don't go out so far." The child catches the note of anxiety and begins to feel apprehensive. "Maybe there *is* something to be afraid of," he thinks.

Bluffing does not help. Children are quick to sense when adults are trying to cover up or disguise their true feelings. As Dr. Barry Goldberg, a consultant on the

medical problems of athletes, says: "Young children deal with total body responses, and if the parent pretends no fear of the water and yet walks in stiff and tight as a drum, that discomfort will be conveyed to the child."

If a child is afraid and not sure what he is capable of doing, it may be best for him to learn swimming in a special children's program in the community. Away from his parents' anxiety—and encouraged by the swimming teacher and by the example of other youngsters—the fearful child usually gains confidence and learns to swim.

Having mastered his fear and learned to trust his own abilities, the child develops an increased sense of self-reliance and independence.

Are you yourself afraid of the water? Do you have any other irrational fears, such as fear of the dark? Can you think of influences that might have created these fears in you?

Discuss how parents' reactions can encourage confidence in young children. How can adults handle their own fears so as not to transmit them to children?

---

schooler, according to Erik Erikson, should be encouraged and supported (up to a point). In Erikson's stage theory of personal development, the preschooler goes through two stages. The first of these occurs between the ages of one and four. Erikson calls it the stage of autonomy versus shame and doubt, which we have already discussed in the unit on toddlers.

In this stage, the child is making explorations outside the circle of trust established with his parents as an infant. He is moving toward more **autonomy**. Yet he is doubtful, even fearful of doing so. He needs parental support

and encouragement. His successes, not his failures, need to be emphasized, so that he can develop a sense of self-determination.

The next stage Erikson calls initiative versus guilt. It begins around age four and lasts into the school years. In this stage, the child has emerged as a very active explorer and adventurer. He also begins to learn what he should *not* do. In other words, he needs to achieve a balance between his impulse to boldly investigate new experiences, and his feelings of guilt about behavior that may be disapproved of.

- Preschoolers are proud of their growth and new skills.
- Praise is important. Preschoolers are still strongly dependent on their caregivers for their sense of self-worth.
- Behavior is modeled after what adults do, not what they say to do.
- Ideas about what it means to be a boy or a girl are starting to form.
- Children at this age tend to be attached to the parent of the opposite sex.
- Preschoolers are learning to cooperate with others. They play together, not just next to each other.
- Friendship with peers is a new experience.
- Emotions are intense and may change quickly.

TERMS TO KNOW

alternate behavior   peers
autonomy   sex-role identity
oedipal period   socialization

1. A child who learns to do things on his own and make his own decisions is developing _____.
2. In Freud's theory, a child develops feelings of attachment for the parent of the opposite sex during the _____.
3. Social play among four-year-olds and five-year-olds is often characterized by _____.
4. During the preschool years, the process of _____ continues as the child learns to interact with _____.
5. A preschooler's ideas of _____ are shaped in the process of identifying with adults.

CHECK YOUR UNDERSTANDING

1. Describe how a preschooler's sense of self-worth depends on his caregivers' attitude and expectations.
2. What characterizes the stage that Freud called the oedipal period?
3. By the late preschool years, what point have most children reached in their development of sex-role identity?
4. How does the way preschoolers relate to each other in play differ from their play as toddlers?
5. Contrast the behavior of a preschooler who is accepted by his peers to that of a preschooler who is rejected.
6. What is meant by "alternate behavior"?
7. At what age do children begin to become competitive? What are some positive and negative aspects of competition?
8. List four characteristics of a preschooler's emotions and how they are expressed.
9. What occurs during Erikson's stage of personality development called initiative versus guilt?

· 16 ·

INTERACTION
WITH THE PRESCHOOLER

Alice got back from the five-and-dime store where she worked mornings just in time to meet her five-year-old son, Bruce, coming home from kindergarten.

"Want to know what I did today?" she asked the boy as they went into their apartment. "Sure," said Bruce.

"I worked on a window display for the tropical fish we're selling at the store. I put all the fish tanks out, chose the fish to go in them, and painted the sign telling about the sale."

"Boy," Bruce said, "you're lucky to have all those fish to play with."

"And what did *you* do today?" asked his mother.

"Painted," said Bruce.

"Oh," cried his mother, "let me see it."

"You won't like it," Bruce said defensively.

"How do you know?" his mother asked.

Bruce gave the painting to his mother. "It's the park in wintertime," he said. "Some of the other children said it was no good because I made the snow green."

Alice studied the painting. It had the swirl and freedom that only young children can achieve. "I like it very much," she said. "What did you say to the children who didn't like it?"

"I wanted to show the snow," said Bruce, "but I couldn't make it white, because the paper is white. Anyway, the park is really green under the snow."

"You're right," said Alice. "When you're good, you paint what you know, not only what you see."

"You really like it?" asked Bruce.

"Really," said his mother. "I'm proud of you."

•

Did you know that young children often show remarkable imagination in their paintings? Can you think of why this might be so?

•

Do you think what Alice said to Bruce was helpful to him? If so, in what ways?

reschoolers can be delightful companions. They are able to carry on a conversation easily. They like to "help" their parents and other caregivers (and often are of real assistance). They are openly affectionate, and their curiosity about all that goes on around them helps those who take care of them to see the world freshly.

"Look," says three-year-old Dorie as she shines her shoes with a polishing cloth, "I'm putting the light on my shoes." Five-year-old Sandy announces excitedly that the oil puddle on the garage floor has "trapped a rainbow."

But listening to preschoolers is more than just fun. It offers valuable clues to what they are thinking and feeling. It is one of the most useful tools for figuring out how to interact with them in all kinds of situations. And when a preschooler seems to be having difficulties— as all of them do from time to time — parents and others should make a special effort to hear what the child herself is saying.

During these years children continue to make impressive progress in functioning independently and taking care of their personal needs. By the end of the period, most can manage a fork and spoon with ease, dress themselves completely, use the toilet when they need to, and handle basic hygienic routines such as bathing, hand washing, and toothbrushing.

What was said about helping toddlers move

Preschool children with disabilities learn with the help of trained professionals and special devices.

ahead in these ways applies to helping preschoolers, too. Caregivers need to be patient and tolerant of mistakes and should not expect too much of a child—or too little. They also need to be aware of and respect individual differences.

DIFFERENCES IN "LEARNING STYLE"

Each child not only grows at her own pace, she has her own individual way of acquiring new skills—her personal "learning style." This becomes increasingly apparent during the preschool years. Angela picks up new skills quickly, but tends to rush through them and do a careless job. Her parents have found that she reacts very negatively to criticism or nagging, but does not mind being supervised. So when they think it essential that she do a thorough job—as with toothbrushing, for example— they "keep her company." It is easier for her (and many other children) to stick to a routine task until it is satisfactorily completed if somebody stays with her.

Scott, on the other hand, masters new skills more slowly. He is reluctant to try any new task on his own until he has "gotten the hang of it" from watching and being shown how to do it over a period of time. But once Scott can do something, he takes pride in doing it well. He resents being supervised. He seems to feel that having an adult watch how he is doing is an insult to his ability to manage on his own.

But after Scott has finished a task, he welcomes comments on his performance. If his parents offer a suggestion—that he brush his back teeth a bit more, or wash again behind his ears—he does it with good humor. Corrections given in this way do not upset him. However, he seldom needs them. Scott is very thorough.

Respecting children's individual "learning styles" in such ways as these helps them to experience success as often as possible and keeps corrections or criticism to a minimum. Thus, it adds to their sense of mastery—their confidence in their abilities. This, in turn, encourages them to try out new skills, or develop initiative, which Erik Erikson considers the major psychological task of the preschool years.

EXPECTING ENOUGH, BUT NOT TOO MUCH

Parents and other caregivers need to encourage the preschooler to be as grown-up as she can be but, at the same time, permit her to slip back temporarily into less mature behavior when she needs to. Though growth during this stage tends to be somewhat steadier than during the toddler period, it still has its ups and downs. A child who has been tying her own shoelaces for weeks may suddenly start asking somebody else to tie them for her. Or when you remind her to put her mittens on she holds out her hands for you to do it.

It's best not to make an issue of such matters, as long as they occur only occasionally. Just give the requested help without comment. However, if this begins to happen regularly, then caregivers do have to draw the line, lovingly but definitely.

Vern's baby-sitter went along for several days with the four-year-old boy's assertion that he was "too tired" to pick up his toys before his mother returned home from work. Instead of arguing with him, the baby-sitter did the job herself. Finally she knew the time had come to put her foot down. She told him firmly that he would have to pick up his toys himself or she would be "too tired" to make cookies with him the next day. After some protesting and whining, which the sitter wisely ignored, Vern did the job. After that, he accepted this responsibility fairly willingly.

FAMILIAR ROUTINES ARE REASSURING

Preschoolers are "creatures of habit." This shows especially in their insistence on certain fixed routines at bedtime. It is also evident in many other ways throughout this growth stage.

These children need order in their lives. They are more likely to be cooperative and content if there is a regular time for meals, snacks, outdoor play, napping (or playing quietly on their beds), bathing, and going to bed at night. This does not mean that caregivers must strictly follow the same schedule day in and day out. But it's wise to *have* a schedule and see that the activities occur in the same sequence and at about the same time—at least on weekdays. In many families (perhaps most) the weekend schedule is somewhat different. Still, on these days, too, preschoolers should be able to count on the "different routine" being relatively predictable.

At this age a child may object strongly to any attempt to rearrange her surroundings or change her usual way of doing things. "No, no," Robin protests when her grandmother suggests that she store her shell collection on the top of her clothes chest. "They go here!" she insists, pointing to the floor in front of her toy shelves. Pedro is indignant when his father offers him juice in a "milk glass" instead of a "juice glass."

Parents and others need not become slaves to a child's devotion to familiar routines. Pedro's father has a right to say, "Come on, now. You can drink your juice out of this glass. There's no reason to use another one now that the juice is already poured out." It's important that preschoolers be flexible enough to handle unfamiliar routines, in case an emergency or other special situation comes up. So caregivers should encourage them to be adaptable, as well as provide them with the order they need to feel that the world is a safe, understandable place.

HANDLING SEPARATIONS

By age three most children are able to part comfortably with their parents for several hours at a time. A child who has not yet learned to do this should be encouraged to start. If money for baby-sitters is in short supply, arrangements can be made for her to stay at a playmate's home for a little while, or to go somewhere with relatives or a family friend.

Parents should always inform a child when they are leaving her for a while with someone else—and not try to sneak out in order to avoid a tearful parting. Sneaking out on a child shakes her trust in her parents and increases **separation anxiety.** She may become reluctant to let her parents out of sight for fear that they will be gone for hours—or possibly never come back. Parents must honestly tell the child that they are leaving and explain when they will return, using terms she can understand, such as "before supper" or "after you are asleep tonight." She may protest briefly, but telling her the truth is the only way parents can help her learn to trust them and become able to handle separations comfortably.

When a child is to enter a nursery school or day-care program or be left with a new all-day caregiver, parents should plan to give enough time to helping her get used to the change. It's desirable for a parent to stay with her throughout her first visit to a group program, or her first meeting with a new caregiver. The next day, after the parent has stuck around for a while, the child can be left briefly in the new surroundings, or with the new person. On the third day the parent can leave her sooner and stay away longer, and so on. After a week, the child is usually able to make the separation more smoothly.

IMAGINED HAPPENINGS SEEM REAL

Most children continue to be uncertain about what is real and what is only imaginary, or "pretend," until the end of this growth stage. They still often treat their dreams and fantasies as if they were real, though they gradually become less fearful over these years.

Now that Rebecca is four, if she is awakened by a bad dream, she may look a little sheepish when telling her parents that "a tiger jumped in the window." She *knows* that there are really no tigers in the vicinity other than those in the local zoo. But what she just experienced was terrifyingly real to her. In her parents' presence she agrees that the vision was "just a bad dream." However, to playmates she confides that a tiger often comes in her window at night. None of the children laughs at this idea.

Rebecca's parents have overheard her talking about the tiger with her playmates. They realize that she is not yet fully convinced that dreams are not real. This helps them figure out what is going on when Rebecca comes running into the kitchen for breakfast one morning and asks, "Where's the new car?" Her parents had been talking for several weeks about possibly buying a car, but they haven't done so. Yet Rebecca insists that she saw "our new car" and describes how it looked. "You must have dreamed it," her mother eventually concluded. Since there really was no car, Rebecca was forced to recognize that she must, indeed, have "dreamed it."

DISTINGUISHING BETWEEN FANTASY AND FACT

A child's dreams and fantasies often reflect what she wishes were true. If she tells them to the neighbors as if they were facts—which she is very apt to do at ages three and four, or even five—people who do not understand children this age may mistakenly decide she is a "liar." Parents themselves often worry about a child's "tall tales."

Four-year-old Jake's mother was shocked when the baby-sitter asked her when "the new baby" was due and when the family would be moving to their "big new apartment." Jake's mother was not pregnant and had no plans to move. After setting the baby-sitter straight,

she consulted Jake's doctor about how to handle the boy's "lying." She was advised to talk with her son about the seriousness of misleading people with "make-believe stories," but not to punish him or call him a liar.

Caregivers must help children develop a firm sense of the difference between fantasy and reality, but without scolding them when they confuse the two—and without criticizing them for their vivid imaginations. The approach Jake's mother used should enable a child to outgrow telling tall tales as if they were true by about age six. Whenever a preschooler is not entirely truthful, for any reason, it's best just to say firmly, "You know you only imagined that," or, "You only *wish* that were so," and not brand the child a liar.

A number of children this age invent imaginary companions. In the opinion of many authorities, these help a child learn to handle fears, control aggression, and become more mature in general. At any rate, they are fun—for the child and her caregivers. There is no reason why a caregiver shouldn't go along with Denise's request that a chair be provided for the large imaginary dog who is the little girl's constant companion. However, the adult should make it plain—in words or by his or her manner—that this is all, of course, just "play pretend."

DADDY'S GIRL AND MAMA'S BOY

During these years children often seem to be attached to the parent of the opposite sex in a new way. A girl's attachment to her father may take on a flirtatious nature. A boy's attachment to his mother may show a similar romantic quality.

There is controversy over why this happens—whether it is due to an inborn drive or to the fact that from birth on, in all societies, girls and boys are pointed toward the goal of being

Playing one parent against the other is often attempted by children to get special attention or something they want. A preschooler may seem to flirt with the parent of the opposite sex. Parents must have an agreed-upon philosophy for handling their children's desires. In most cases, decisions by one parent should be supported by the other. However, some flexibility is needed when a parent realizes he or she has made a poor decision.

attractive to members of the opposite sex. Regardless of *why* this happens, it needs to be handled in a way that assures children they are charming, but does not encourage them to trade on their charms or play one parent against the other.

A father should treat his daughter with affection, of course, and make it clear that he admires her as a girl and as a person. But he must not allow her to coax him into siding with her against her mother. When Sophie pulls excitedly on her father's hand and begs him to buy her an ice-cream pop from the truck that is parked near their home, he says with a smile, "You know very well that your mother and I don't permit you to have ice cream so close to lunchtime."

Mothers should be equally careful to present a common front with their husbands in dealing with sons. Children of both sexes must learn that they cannot woo one parent away from the other. Much as they sometimes seem to want to do this, they really love both parents. They need reassurance that they will not lose the love of either.

SINGLE-PARENT FAMILIES

In single-parent families, it is important that the child be friendly with some adults of the sex opposite to that of the parent in the home. These adults might be relatives, friends of the parent who is rearing the child, baby-sitters, or members of the staff of a day-care center or nursery school that the child attends. Such individuals should not be expected to serve as "substitute parents." But they can serve as role models who help the child feel comfortable with members of their sex and learn how to form satisfying relationships with them.

The preschool years do seem to be a time when children are intensely occupied with discovering how to be members in good standing of the sex to which they belong and how to appeal to the opposite one. In this respect, the period resembles adolescence—and it has been labeled a "rehearsal for adolescence."

This does not mean that single parents are less able than those with partners to foster healthy development during these years. It just means that they need to make sure that

The number of children raised in one-parent families is increasing. It is important that these children have contact with adults of both sexes.

their children have contact with adults of both sexes and are not growing up in a single-sex world.

PROMOTING LEARNING

The questions that most preschoolers ask so constantly are one of the most important means by which they learn. These questions should always be answered to the best of a caregiver's ability. "I don't know," may be an honest answer when Kevin asks, "What makes thunder?" But it should be followed up with a suggestion such as: "Next time we go to the library, we can try to find out together."

A child who has not already become acquainted with the local library should certainly do so during these years. Even if parents have a stock of children's books and a basic reference work that explains such matters as "what makes thunder" and why grass is green, the library can open up a whole new world of learning experiences for children.

In some libraries, a child as young as four can have her own library card and will be encouraged to print her first name on it as soon as she is able. She is freer than she would be in any bookstore to look through as many books as she wishes for as long as she wishes before deciding which ones she wants to borrow. She learns that the librarian can direct her parents or other caregivers to books that answer some of her "harder" questions. And all this is free.

Libraries are just one of the community resources that children this age can enjoy. Others are zoos, museums, firehouses, public gardens, and construction sites. The "Y" and similar organizations often offer inexpensive courses for preschoolers in movement skills and the arts.

PLAYMATES

The importance of having friends to play with increases steadily during these years. If a child

Maria Montessori (1870–1952) was an Italian-born educator whose work with preschool children has had a wide influence on education for children of all ages. The special methods and materials she designed for preschoolers are aimed at preparing them for learning in school.

The Montessori classroom is a "prepared environment" in which children are given a wide assortment of learning materials geared to their particular developmental needs. Children work individually or in small groups, and they are free to stay with an activity as long as they like. A specially trained teacher observes the children and provides them with the materials that they are ready to use. The teacher's role is one of gentle guidance rather than "teaching." In effect, it is the children who teach themselves, by being allowed to do what interests them.

Although children enjoy a great deal of freedom in the Montessori classroom, they are expected to observe clearly set limits against destructive or aggressive behavior. They also learn to put materials away when they are finished before going on to another activity.

Traditional nursery schools often emphasize social/emotional growth through imaginative play and fantasy. In the Montessori schools, the emphasis is on cognitive stimulation (language and counting skills), sensory tasks (such as matching and ordering), and motor development (exercise to promote body rhythm and coordination).

Do you think the emphasis on realistic tasks, rather than fantasy play, appeals more to preschoolers? How does it help prepare them for school?

is not in a nursery school or day-care program, parents need to make special efforts to provide her with opportunities to make friends and get together with them regularly. If both parents work and she is being cared for at the home of a relative or neighbor, this subject should be discussed with the person who takes care of her. Ways should be found to see that she spends some time each day with children approximately her own age. This contributes significantly to her social development and also prepares her for entering school.

Preschoolers play *with* each other, not just alongside each other, like toddlers. They are becoming increasingly able to share, wait their turn, and settle their differences without hitting or grabbing and without adult intervention. However, adult supervision is still needed to ensure children's safety and help them resolve disputes when they fail to do so on their own. As children get older, caregivers can gradually provide the needed supervision at a greater distance. They must be on hand in case they are needed, but more and more of the time they just stay in the background.

DIFFERENT KINDS OF PLAY ARE NEEDED

Play is children's "work." Through play they grow in many ways. They develop their bodies, achieving control of the fine muscles of the eyes and hands. This readies them to learn to read and write in school. They explore their environment and become increasingly knowledgeable about it. They try out various adult roles, as when they imitate what they see their parents doing.

Toys, of course, can enrich children's play. They need some toys of their own (though probably not as many as children in our society

248

tend to have). They also need to be encouraged to use their imagination and discover various ways of playing actively and quietly without store-bought toys.

All preschoolers need plenty of active physical play. Games such as hide and seek, tag, hopscotch, and prisoner's base can provide this, and require no equipment, just playmates. Tricycles, skates, and (toward the end of this period) bicycles also encourage active play and help a child develop good balance. Since these items are expensive, parents may want to investigate ways to get them secondhand. Salvation Army stores and thift shops are good sources. School or community bulletin boards often display notices of such toys for sale.

Parents should keep individual differences in mind. Children become able at different ages to skate and bike. Just because Bette learned to ride a bike at five doesn't necessarily mean that her brother Sol is ready to handle a two-wheeler at this age.

Swings, monkey bars, and seesaws—standard equipment in most playgrounds—also provide opportunities for active play and the development of physical coordination. So do balls and jump ropes. Balls promote eye-hand coordination, too, and can be played with in many different ways, alone or with friends. Some anthropologists who have observed children in different cultures around the world say that if they could give a child only two toys, these would be, for both girls and boys, a ball and a doll.

Exploratory play—with such objects as puzzles, beads, blocks, peg boards, buttons, and other toys made up of a number of small

Children grow through play. Toys can enrich play while helping to develop control of the fine muscles. Quiet play helps "unwind" those who have become overexcited.

Children's Theater

Backstage, Marv Bennett applied his white clown makeup and put on his baggy costume and flowerpot hat. His little dog, Snippy, sensing that the show was about to start, yipped excitedly. She was part of the act, too, and loved to perform tricks for the children.

"Five minutes, Marv!" the stage manager called. "Here we go, Snippy," said Marv. And as they pranced on stage, they heard the familiar sound of children laughing. Children love make-believe. They love to create their own plays and act them out; even more, they love to attend theater performances designed especially for them. Good children's theater, however, is difficult to produce, for it takes a perceptive sense of what children laugh at, what is too scary for them, and what their real fantasies are.

Marv Bennett is an actor in a children's theater group. One week he plays a clown in a show about a circus; the next week he plays a fairy-tale prince; and the following week he operates marionettes for a puppet show. The group performs mostly on weekends. Except for rehearsal time when a new show is planned, Marv has the rest of the week free to attend acting classes, perform in television commercials, and audition for parts in plays.

Acting is a demanding and uncertain profession, and few actors can earn a living consistently by acting alone. Children's theater groups are usually not well funded, but the work is often steady. A successful group can operate for years, since there are always new audiences growing up.

Besides acting, there are many other roles to play in children's theater. Theater groups need writers, producers, directors, lighting experts, sound technicians, scenic designers, costumers, fund raisers, publicity organizers, ticket takers, ushers. Anyone who has a real interest in children's theater can find a job to do, regardless of talent. However, many times these are volunteer positions.

Children are not easy audiences. They are in fact often more critical than adults. One of the greatest rewards of children's theater is the sound of sincere laughter or gasps of surprise. When that occurs, everyone knows the show is a success.

pieces—continues to be important during these years. Such play helps the child learn to sort, classify, match, and fit pieces together. It also develops fine-muscle control and eye-hand coordination.

Music, dance, and art appeal to preschoolers. All these activities can be encouraged without spending a lot of money on equipment. Castanets and triangles are musical instruments that children of this age can use to accompany singing and dancing. A wooden spoon and a kitchen pot can serve as a drum. Brown wrapping paper, paper bags cut open and spread out, or even old newspapers can be used for drawing with crayons or for pasting objects on.

All kinds of materials that families usually throw out are potentially useful for arts and crafts projects. Such things as egg cartons, scraps of material, ribbon and gift-wrapping paper, or empty spools give the preschooler a chance to color, cut, paste, and fold.

Dramatic play—or playing "dress-up" or "house" or "make-believe"—is a favorite activity during these years. It allows children to try out many different roles and to work off frustrations, besides permitting them to enjoy and use their imaginations.

When four-year-old Mick says to a playmate, "Now you be the horse and I'll be the driver," he is trying out the role of "leader." He is also working off the frustration that many little children endure at times because they feel so powerless in comparison with their parents (and in Mick's case, an older brother). Mick is likely to find out that leaders have their problems, too. Still, he and his horse may end up "flying," "colonizing space," or who knows what!

Some quiet play—alone or with a parent or favorite caregiver—is also essential. It helps children wind down before going to bed at night and at times when they have become overexcited. Reading to children or telling them a story is one way to provide quiet play. Leaving them to look at picture books or magazines or play with a doll on their own is another. Larry's baby-sitter has found that a sure way to help him calm down is to settle him in a chair with his favorite toy animal and say, "Now you sit there and tell your bear all about what you have been doing today."

HANDLING COMPETITION

During these years children become interested in simple competitive games—board games or card games that require matching pictures or colors, with the outcome decided mainly by luck. Some children are able to play dominoes, checkers, and more difficult board games. Such games can be fun, but preschoolers tend to be poor losers. A caregiver playing with the child is sometimes tempted to let her win, just to avoid a scene. There is no reason to believe this does her any harm, but it certainly doesn't help her learn how to accept losing gracefully.

Sooner or later all children need to become able to manage competition. They should not be frightened by the idea of putting their abilities to the test. Nor should they feel that it is always important, or even possible, to win. They have to develop a realistic awareness of where they stand in comparison with their peers, make the most of their strengths, and live with the disappointments that all of us ex-

perience. It is sensible to start encouraging such learning in the preschool years.

Parents and other caregivers should remind the preschooler not to gloat or boast about winning. They also need to help children accept losing comfortably and graciously. This means patiently and repeatedly pointing out that "It's only a game" and "Nobody wins all the time."

In addition, every child must have opportunities to experience success. This means helping a preschooler find things that she is good at. These might range from the ability to make people laugh, to the ability to turn cartwheels, or skill with numbers, words, music, dancing, or drawing.

Handling competition between **siblings** also involves helping each child identify and cultivate her own individual strengths. Flora is a whiz at puzzles. Since she knows she is very good at at least this one thing, it's easy for her to admire without envy her younger brother's ability to carry a tune, which she still cannot do.

It's essential, too, to avoid comparing siblings with each other. Saying to Dana, "Why can't you remember to shake hands when you're introduced to somebody, the way your brother always does," is no way to help her acquire better manners—or to foster a good relationship between the children.

GUIDANCE AND DISCIPLINE

As children grow, the rules that they are expected to follow must change gradually. Tommy at two is supposed to wait at the curb until his caregiver takes his hand and accompanies him across the street. He is not permitted to use a kitchen knife, turn on a stove burner, or leave his home by himself. But at six he is allowed to cross certain streets on his own, often helps in the kitchen by slicing vegetables and heating up or "turning off" a casserole sitting on the stove, and can leave his

Parents must establish limits for young children. When rules are broken, parents must discipline them firmly but also remain understanding.

ENFORCING THE RULES

During the preschool years children begin to understand the consequences of their actions —and should be expected to accept the consequences. Laurie realizes that her new sweater was chewed up by the family's puppy because she left it lying on the floor in the hall, instead of hanging it in the closet as she had been repeatedly asked to do. Laurie's parents don't punish her for her carelessness. They think that being deprived of her prized sweater is enough to teach her to be more careful. But they don't buy her another sweater right away, either.

Sometimes a child just doesn't seem to learn from experience. Malcolm keeps setting his glass at the very edge of the kitchen table and knocking it over during the course of the meal. Eventually, his father warns him that if he spills his milk this way one more time, he will not be able to watch his favorite television show before supper that day. The next time he spills his milk, his father imposes the punishment. This does the trick. Malcolm starts being more careful.

Depriving a child of a privilege for a day or so is a useful way to help her learn to abide by the rules at this age—and later on. It is generally highly effective and is likely to be viewed as more "fair" by children themselves than physical punishment.

Of course, the punishment should be in keeping with the "crime." It would not be fitting to deprive Malcolm of his favorite television show for a whole week.

A preschooler's own desire to win her parents' approval is probably the single most important factor influencing her to respect the limits they set on her behavior and to learn to discipline herself. This becomes increasingly important as she moves into the larger world, signaled by entry into first grade.

apartment to visit his friend next door whenever he wishes, provided he tells his mother he's going there.

These dramatic changes occur bit by bit. Alert parents will notice when the time has come to allow activities that were once forbidden—at least under certain conditions. They also must be aware of their child's individual capacities. One youngster may become ready to cross streets in the neighborhood by herself at the age of five. Another cannot be trusted to do so until she turns seven. Caregivers should not permit themselves to be pressured into allowing a child to do anything just because she insists that "everybody else does."

Preparing a child for such dangerous undertakings as crossing streets alone, cutting with a sharp knife, or turning on a stove takes place over a period of time. There should be many "practice tries," with the caregiver watching close by, ready to prevent any possible mishap. An important part of the preparation is setting a good example. If the rest of the family always take sensible precautions and seldom have accidents, the children are very likely to be the same way.

- Preschoolers each have their own pace and style of learning.
- Familiar routines give preschoolers a sense of stability and security.
- Preschoolers should be prepared for brief separations from parents.
- Caregivers should help children learn the difference between fantasy and fact, without scolding them when they fail to make the distinction.
- Preschoolers should have opportunities to interact with adults of both sexes.
- A preschooler's many questions are an important part of learning.
- Playing with other children contributes to social development and readiness for school.
- Most preschoolers accept discipline because they want parental approval.

TERMS TO KNOW

exploratory play
separation anxiety
siblings

1. _____ helps the preschooler learn to sort, classify, match, and fit pieces together.
2. Competition with _____ is lessened if children recognize their own individual strengths.
3. Preparing a child for the parents' departure can help reduce _____.

CHECK YOUR UNDERSTANDING

1. Sometimes preschoolers ask for help with something they are capable of doing themselves. How should a caregiver respond?
2. Why is it helpful for a preschooler's daily activities to be kept on a fairly regular schedule?
3. Why should parents inform a child before leaving her with someone else for a while?
4. What are some positive aspects of having an imaginary companion?
5. What is the purpose of making sure that children in single-parent families interact with adults of both sexes?
6. Give three examples of community resources that preschool children may enjoy.
7. What are some ways in which a preschooler grows through play?
8. How should a parent prepare a child for dangerous undertakings?

UNIT FIVE

SCHOOL-AGE
(AGES 6–11)

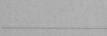

17
PHYSICAL DEVELOPMENT

18
COGNITIVE DEVELOPMENT

Between the ages of six and eleven, children continue to grow and change. Missing teeth, outgrown clothes, and skinned knees are some of the familiar signposts of the school years.

Once in school, the child's intellectual abilities flourish. The mastery of reading opens new horizons. Improved language and reasoning skills are motivated by a natural drive to discover how the world works.

19

SOCIAL/EMOTIONAL DEVELOPMENT

20

INTERACTION

Peer groups become increasingly important in these years. Children who have built up a sense of self-esteem through their family's support and love are able to trust others and form friendships.

For the most part these are happy years for a child. It is a time for exploring talents and interests, sharing experiences with family and friends, and wondering about the maturity that lies just ahead.

· 17 ·

PHYSICAL DEVELOPMENT
OF THE SCHOOL-AGE CHILD

"It's not fair, Dad. I'm ten and Brian's only eight!"

"I'm sorry, Terry," said Mr. Kostas. "I know you feel you should be able to stay up later because you're older. But changing your bedtime from 8:30 to 9:00 just didn't work out. You need that extra sleep to do your best in school."

"Couldn't I just sleep an extra half-hour in the morning?" Terry pleaded. "I'd still catch the bus on time. I get ready real fast."

"Maybe. But our mornings are rushed enough as it is. If you ate breakfast later than everyone else, cleaning up the kitchen would have to wait until the last minute," Mr. Kostas pointed out. "No, I'm afraid you'll have to keep getting up at 7:00, and that means bedtime is 8:30 on school nights."

"Aw, I hate having to start getting ready for bed at 8:00," Terry said.

"Well, if you didn't start your bath by then, you wouldn't make it to bed on time," his father said. "It bothers you a lot, huh?"

"Yeah. I never get to watch my favorite TV show on Thursdays. And I hate taking a bath anyway. It makes me feel like such a baby."

"Then let's try something new," said Mr. Kostas. "Suppose you still had to go to bed at 8:30, but you could read or watch TV until then—and no bath. In the morning you could take a shower."

"That would be great!" said Terry.

"You wouldn't feel bad about having to go to bed at the same time as Brian?"

"Not if I didn't have to take a bath."

"And you'd still have enough time in the morning?"

"Sure. Showers are fast. I'd even help clean up after breakfast."

"Then it's okay with me—as long as you go to bed and get up right on time."

"It's a deal. Thanks, Dad!"

•

Do you think Terry really needs the same amount of sleep as Brian, or was his father being unfair?

•

What are Mr. Kostas' main concerns in this situation? What are Terry's? Was the solution fair to both?

icole knows all the boys in her sixth grade. She has played games and sports with many of them since she was six years old. But this year is different. At eleven, Nicole has suddenly shot up in height. She is now taller than any of the boys. She feels awkward and unsure of herself physically. Her classmate Sharon had a similar growth spurt even earlier. She and Nicole have since become best friends.

These girls' experience is not at all uncommon. The school years, especially ages ten and eleven, are marked by sharp differences in individual rates of physical development. Girls in general develop well ahead of boys. Yet some boys, too, develop early—while some girls develop later than others do. Differences will become even more marked in the adolescent years. Not until the late teens will most individuals catch up with one another.

GROWTH AND MOTOR DEVELOPMENT

During the early school years, up to around the age of ten, a child grows in height and weight at about the same rate she did during her preschool years. She grows at an average yearly rate of about 2 or 3 inches (5.0 to 7.6 centimeters). Her yearly weight increase averages around 4 or 5 pounds (1.8 to 2.3 kilograms).

From age ten on, however, this relatively slow, steady rate of physical growth changes. Growth begins to take place in spurts and stops, with all kinds of individual variations. The new clothes one child wears in the fall may continue to fit through most of the winter. Another child of the same age may completely outgrow her new fall clothes long before winter is over.

Moreover, children who are in the midst of a **growth spurt** may find that parts of the body are likely to grow at different rates. Commonly, the legs, arms, hands, and feet grow

Growth rates differ for girls and boys of the same age during the school-age years. On the average, girls grow more quickly. All children need varied activities which help develop their motor skills and coordination during this period.

School-age children concentrate while playing. They enjoy both team sports and games and activities which can be played alone. Children at this age test newly acquired physical and cognitive skills.

faster. The child may feel—and may in fact look—gangly, awkward, and bony. Girls, on the average, go through this stage about two years before boys do.

Actually, someone going through this stage may not be as awkward as she looks or feels. Motor abilities, coordination, and general body control tend to improve fairly steadily throughout the school years. The older child's "awkwardness" perhaps has more to do with her feelings of self-consciousness than with her actual abilities.

Among younger school-age children, six to eight years old, motor-skill development often means a lot of running around. Their large muscles are more developed at this age than their small muscles—more developed and in constant use. Running, climbing, sliding, playing tag and ball games, the typical six-, seven-, or eight-year old seems to be continually in motion.

From nine to twelve years old, there is more emphasis on small-muscle development. Children around this age generally show a strong interest in model building and handicrafts, activities that help them improve finger **dexterity.** The larger muscles are of course not neglected during this period. Children in this age group tend to concentrate on mastering specific skills, such as playing ball games or skating. They no longer run around just for its own sake, as younger children do.

FOOD AND NUTRITION

In the early school years, appetites tend to be "on" one year and "off" the next. Six is traditionally an "on" year. Not all six-year-olds, of course, live up to their reputation as heavy

The child of six or seven may need help in learning how to print with a pencil or pen. His large muscles are better developed than his small or fine ones, and if he is to begin writing at this age, he needs both instruction and plenty of practice.

Roots, the novel by Alex Haley from which a television movie was made, describes the education of schoolboys during the 1700s in the West African village that Haley's ancestors came from. Here young boys of six or seven were taught to "write with grass-quill pens dipped in the black ink of bitter-orange juice mixed with powdered crust from the bottom of cooking pots." (As in many traditional societies of the past, education of this type was not given to girls.)

Developing this writing skill must have taken patience, time, and effort. Learning how to coordinate fine muscles and write neatly and clearly required concentration and practice. After their lessons, the boys ran off to herd the village's goats into their grazing fields.

Haley's account of life in this West African village shows how a different culture at a different time in the past understood the active nature of the six- or seven-year-old child, and used this energy in a positive way. After working at an activity that involved small- or fine-muscle control, the children relaxed by running and exercising their large muscles. Their education was not limiting and recognized fully the various needs of a growing child.

eaters. And the six-year-old's eye for food often causes her to take in more than her stomach can handle. This is true of many children at all ages. Then the heavy eater of one year can just as easily become a finicky eater the next year.

One thing most six-, seven-, and eight-year-olds share in common is that they don't like to experiment with unfamiliar foods. Given their choice, many would prefer hamburgers as a main course at every meal.

By age nine they are generally more willing to adjust their tastes, and to try new foods (though not always). At eleven and twelve, children's appetites often increase dramatically. Especially if they are in a growth spurt, their capacity for food seems endless. They may argue with their parents at mealtime—over demands that the children clean their plates, or eat less, or eat more of certain foods, for example. But as long as a child is clearly healthy, her food intake is probably best left alone to find its own level.

However, some children do have poor eating habits which can show up in a number of ways. A child, for example, may be either underweight or overweight. Either can be serious.

A child isn't necessarily underweight just because she is "skinny." Some people are naturally thin, always have been, and always will be—no matter how much they eat. The underweight person is the person who weighs less than she naturally should. She is underweight because she is undernourished.

An undernourished child usually gets tired more easily than she should, and is often listless. She tends to have less resistance to disease. Prolonged undernourishment may interfere with both physical and mental development.

The question is: Why isn't the thin child getting the nourishment she needs? It may be that her underweight is a symptom of some illness. A medical examination will be necessary to find out. Another possible cause might be tension and anxiety, which make it difficult for a child to eat. Or perhaps the child is thin because of irregular eating habits, or an inadequate diet. We have already seen that a balanced diet is important to people of all ages.

The opposite problem, overweight, may simply be a matter of too little exercise and too many high-calorie foods, such as rich desserts. A normal amount of strenuous physical activity and not too many snacks between meals are the basic remedies for overweight. A lot of exercise and a good diet are especially important for children who have a natural tendency to put on weight. Some children can eat the same amount of food that their friends eat, yet gain weight while their friends stay thin. In addition, some children overeat out of boredom or because of emotional problems. Obviously, these problems have to be dealt with before the child's weight problem can be solved.

HYGIENE

School-age children seldom need much help in bathing, though six- and seven-year-olds with long hair may need help in shampooing. Children in their early school years usually like taking a bath—once they are in the tub. However, they may be reluctant to get into the tub in the first place! Children often show little concern for personal cleanliness. Taking a bath, washing their hands—these require constant reminders from parents or caregivers.

Appetites of school-age children vary. Sometimes they refuse to eat. At other times they want more than their stomachs can physically handle.

The friendly cartoon lion beams from the television screen. "For a real treat, girls and boys, ask Mom to buy you Choco-Crunchies, my yummy, chocolaty breakfast flakes."

Five minutes later, a puppet moose is singing, "Drink Fruit-Kool, like Maurice the Moose; Fruit-Kool, ten percent real juice." He hugs an enormous jar of the product—ten percent juice, the rest sugar water.

Studies conducted by the Federal Trade Commission (FTC), the American Dental Association (ADA), and other groups show that 70 percent of advertising geared to the children's market is for snacks, candies, and breakfast foods that have a high content of sugar. This is especially true of television commercials.

Several consumer and public-interest groups have been concerned with the number and content of these commercials. The critics maintain that most food advertisements for children encourage bad eating habits that lead to poor nutrition and tooth decay. Opponents of advertising for children's television also stress that half the children under eight years of age have difficulty distinguishing commercials from regular programming. As a result, these children are likely to believe everything they see and hear on TV—fact, fiction, and promotional claims.

Two organizations, Action for Children's Television (ACT) and the Center for Science in the Public Interest (CSPI), have petitioned the Federal Trade Commission (FTC) to ban all television advertising aimed at children under eight. They believe that other sources of funding could be developed. In addition, they want the FTC to prohibit advertising of highly sugared products to all children under twelve years of age. The petition includes a requirement that the advertisers of sugared products for children must contribute money to a fund that would balance their own ads with separate messages about nutrition and dental care.

Network officials, advertisers, and industry trade associations are against government regulation. They claim that eliminating advertisements for a product does not reduce the demand for it. They point to the ban on television cigarette advertising as an example. Instead, they feel that responsibility for regulation should be taken by the industries involved.

Economic factors are also stressed by defenders of TV advertising. Except on public television channels, most children's programs are paid for by the advertisers. Industry officials are doubtful whether alternate funding could be found. If commercials are banned, officials say, special children's programs may have to be eliminated. Moreover, 25 percent of the television industry profit comes from the 7 percent of the programming that is geared to children. These economic factors will play an important part in any debate on the future of television advertising for children.

As children approach adolescence, however, they become more concerned with their bodies and their appearance. By this time, they may prefer showers rather than baths, especially if they are used to taking showers at school after sports activities.

Dental hygiene is important during the school years. Most children get their first permanent teeth at around age six. These are four molars, which come in behind the baby teeth—two molars on each side of the mouth, one top and one bottom.

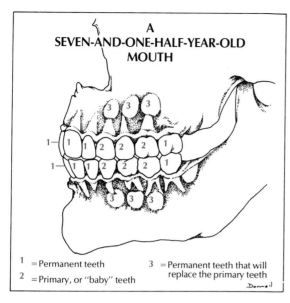

A
SEVEN-AND-ONE-HALF-YEAR-OLD
MOUTH

1 = Permanent teeth
2 = Primary, or "baby" teeth
3 = Permanent teeth that will replace the primary teeth

Young children should visit the dentist every six months. The doctor can spot problems by x-raying the gums and seeing how the adult teeth are developing. Permanent teeth begin to replace baby teeth by age 6.

use, for example. Bowel movements usually occur once a day at around the same time, so the child expects them. Younger children are often reluctant to use unfamiliar toilets away from home, including the ones at school. But that reluctance generally disappears by age eight or nine.

Not only are school-age children capable of attending to their own health-care needs, but they can usually understand why they have to do so. A brief explanation of the reasons for brushing teeth or washing hands before meals will convince most children that these are not chores invented just to take them away from more interesting pastimes. Nevertheless, they often have to be reminded to attend to their health needs, even when they understand why.

SLEEP AND REST

The typical six-year-old is certainly no less energetic than a preschooler and needs about the same amount of sleep—eleven hours a

No baby teeth are lost when the six-year molars come in, but before long the first baby tooth will go—a front tooth. By the time the child is twelve, all her baby teeth will be gone and she will have most of her permanent teeth. She could have some cavities as well.

Tooth decay is an ancient problem. Today, because of fluoridated water and fluoridated toothpastes, it is less of a problem. **Fluoridation** strengthens teeth against decay, but it does not prevent cavities entirely. It is most effective together with good dental hygiene, in particular with regular brushing. And it is important to establish good habits of dental hygiene during the preschool and early school years, when the teeth are still new—if these habits have not already been formed earlier.

Most children, by their early school years, are capable of attending to their bodily needs themselves. Few require any help with toilet

"Don't forget to brush" is a familiar phrase during the school years. Although children this age do need reminders, they are increasingly responsible for their own hygiene.

Recreation Worker

"What's your favorite sport?" Emillio Juarez asked the shy ten-year-old boy who was making his first visit to the Barnham Youth Center.

"Baseball...I guess," Peter replied tentatively. "But I'm not very good at sports. I don't want to play on any team."

"You don't have to play if you don't want to," said Emillio. "But why don't you just come with me and watch? I'm going to be supervising a game with kids about your age. I think you'll see that here the most important thing is to have a good time. We don't expect everyone to be a home-run hitter."

Emillio Juarez is a recreation worker. He specializes in sports, and his job is to create athletic programs that will attract neighborhood children, give them some basic skills, and channel their energies constructively. Other recreation workers at the youth center specialize in arts and crafts, music, dance and theater, and camping. The staff also includes some nonspecialist recreation leaders and a director as well as clerical and maintenance help.

The main goal of recreation work is to stimulate a child's creative abilities, encourage physical fitness, and provide social opportunities in a relaxed but supervised setting. Recreation workers are employed in many different places—including schools, youth centers, parks, hospitals, day-care centers, and child-care institutions.

Most recreation workers have some education beyond high school. Two-year colleges offer an associate degree in recreation work; some four-year colleges offer degrees in recreation or physical education. Those who plan to go on to supervisory jobs should also have some business or administrative training.

Recreation workers may also work part-time, or seasonally, and pursue education or other interests.

Generally, working conditions are pleasant, and the job is particularly attractive to people who like to spend a lot of time outdoors. Salaries are reasonably good and compare favorably with those of other municipal workers (many recreation programs are part of local government).

Recreation workers should have good organizational skills and the ability to get along with children and other staff members. Teaching skills are also important. A lot of energy is required—both physical and mental—to provide stimulating experiences for children. Recreation workers derive much satisfaction from introducing children to new leisure-time activities and watching them develop new lifetime skills.

night—to recoup her energy. At age seven, eleven hours is still pretty much the norm. Then the need decreases. By age twelve, nine hours a night is usually enough. Of course, individuals differ in the amount of sleep they need. There are children—and adults—for whom seven hours sleep a night is sufficient. Other individuals need ten.

As with diet, the test is the child's actual health. If she stays up late to do her homework or watch television with no ill effects, she may be an individual who simply doesn't need the extra sleep. But a continually tired, sluggish, irritable child may need an earlier bedtime.

Usually, young school-age children go willingly to bed at the designated hour. They are tired at the end of an active day, and they go right to sleep after a short bedtime routine. Some like to read or listen to music first, for perhaps half an hour.

From about age ten or eleven, the average child feels she should be allowed more independence. This includes staying up later on holidays and weekends—and sleeping a few hours later in the morning when there is no school.

ILLNESS AND ACCIDENTS

As discussed earlier, many of the once common childhood diseases—mumps and measles, for example—can be dealt with ahead of time, by vaccination. But there is no vaccine as yet for all the various cold viruses. It is highly unusual if a school-age child does not come home with at least one cold during the year.

She may also catch the "flu"—influenza—from one of her classmates, or a sore throat or other minor contagious illness. Some of these may become serious, however, if they are not treated. For example, a sore throat and fever, followed by a rash, indicates scarlet fever. This disease was once a very serious problem. Its after-effects could include permanent blindness. Today, as during the last few decades, scarlet fever is easily controlled with medications. But children with scarlet-fever symptoms must be examined by a doctor before they can be treated. Bed rest, though necessary, is not enough by itself.

Some children have visual or hearing disabilities that show up during their early school years. Frequently a child who is having trouble in school—in reading, for example—has a physical disability which may need treatment in a special program.

Then there are accidents, which are as common among school-age children as among preschoolers. Types of accidents are likely to be different, of course. A school-age child usually

knows better than to taste household poisons, for instance. But she is engaging in a great many activities where an accident is possible—such as running across streets on her way home from school, or riding a bicycle around the neighborhood. Once a child is no longer supervised every minute, it is imperative that she learn to obey rules of safety when playing near traffic. Waiting for the traffic

Yearly visits to the doctor are important during the school-age years. Pediatricians keep medical histories to make sure the children are developing normally. Growth charts are kept which compare each child to others her age.

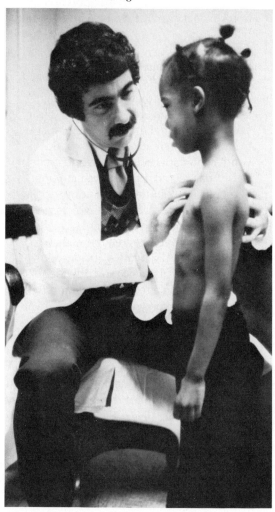

CHILDREN'S ACCIDENTS

Among children five to nine years old, motor vehicles, drowning, fires, and firearms are the main causes of death. Falls, cuts, falling objects, and motor vehicles are the main causes of personal injury.

Highest Incidence of Accidents	Behavior That May Contribute to Accidents
1. Traffic accidents	Is adventurous, active, and daring. Example: Runs after a ball without looking to see if cars are coming.
2. Bicycle accidents	Takes chances while riding a bike, although has fairly good large-muscle control and can ride it easily.
3. Drowning	Takes risks when swimming. Example: May underestimate distance to shore.
4. Burns	Is careless with matches and fire.
5. Firearms	Has keen interest in weapons but little sense of caution about using them.
6. Falls	Attempts whatever peers do; may climb too high on a dare.

Excerpts from YOUR CHILD: STEP BY STEP TOWARD MATURITY by Dorothy Noyes Sproul. Reprinted by permission of Doubleday & Company, Inc.

In many communities accident prevention programs are presented to school-age children by fire fighters and police officers. These safety lectures often stress traffic, bicycle, and water safety because these are the leading causes of death among children in the United States. Safety in the home is also taught to prevent accidents which cause burns or electrical shock.

Physical Therapy Assistant

CLASS REUNION QUESTIONNAIRE:

Tell us briefly what you have been doing since graduation five years ago.

DICK TARIAN REPLIES:

"I am a physical therapy assistant at the Corcoran Children's Hospital. I work with handicapped children, mainly those with cerebral palsy. After graduation I worked for a year as an aide in the hospital, then went back to school for a two-year course to train as a physical therapy assistant. I am now taking a few courses toward getting my license as a physical therapist. I have found a satisfying career and I am looking forward to telling my friends all about it at the reunion."

Physical therapy assistants work with physical therapists, helping people to overcome or live with disabilities caused by birth defects, illness, or injury. Assistants free the therapists from some of the more routine chores, such as getting the equipment ready for the patient or keeping records. However, they also work directly with patients, giving massages, supervising exercises, applying heat, cold, or light to affected limbs, and teaching patients how to use braces, artificial limbs, and other appliances.

Most physical therapy assistants who work with children are employed in hospitals, clinics, or child-care institutions. A two-year college program trains people for the job, and some states have licensing requirements.

Physical therapy assistants who work with children must be strong and healthy, able to work well with their hands, and cheerful and positive in their outlook. Although they use physical means to help the patients, the experience should also be a meaningful emotional contact for the child as well.

Through additional training, assistants can become physical therapists, who get higher salaries. Working conditions are generally pleasant, and salaries are competitive with similar positions in the health-care field. Part of the satisfaction of the job comes from being part of a professional health-care team; perhaps even more satisfying is the sense of achievement when a child takes steps toward health or independence through the therapy.

---

signal and looking both ways before crossing the street is one of the first important rules a child learns—even before she is allowed to cross the street by herself.

Certain kinds of accidents can be prevented with training beforehand. Drowning, for example, is every year one of the leading causes of accidental death. Yet children can be taught water safety as early as age three or four. At age six, most children are ready to learn to swim. Many are ready earlier. Almost every community has courses in swimming given by a "Y," the Red Cross, or some other organization.

A number of communities also have special accident-prevention courses, such as bicycle safety. And everybody—children and adults —can benefit from a course in basic first aid.

· SUMMARY ·

- Growth during the school years takes place in spurts and stops, with many individual variations. Girls generally develop ahead of boys.
- Motor abilities, coordination, and body control improve steadily.
- Younger school-age children don't like to try unfamiliar foods. Older ones are less fussy.
- Underweight or overweight may be a problem needing medical attention.
- Older children become more interested in appearance and cleanliness.
- The permanent teeth start to erupt at about age six.
- The need for sleep usually decreases during these years.
- Vision or hearing problems may show up in school.
- Teaching children safety rules helps prevent accidents.

TERMS TO KNOW

dexterity
fluoridation
growth spurt

1. _____ strengthens teeth against decay.
2. Model building and handicrafts help children improve their _____.
3. The child who is in a _____ often feels awkward.

CHECK YOUR UNDERSTANDING

1. At about what age does a child's slow, steady rate of physical growth change to growth in spurts?
2. What is a physical reason for an older school-age child's feeling of awkwardness? What is a psychological reason?
3. How can a caregiver tell that a child is undernourished rather than just naturally thin?
4. Name some possible causes of undernourishment.
5. What are two possible reasons for overeating?
6. What are the first permanent teeth? When do they come in?
7. What effect does fluoride have on the teeth?
8. What are the symptoms of scarlet fever? Why is it important for a child with these symptoms to be examined by a doctor?

·18·

COGNITIVE DEVELOPMENT
OF THE SCHOOL-AGE CHILD

"All done with your homework?" asked Mrs. Evans as her daughter Molly wandered into the living room.

"Just about," Molly said. She went to the window and poked a finger into the potted ivy on the sill. "This feels kind of dry, Mom. Can I water it for you?"

Molly's stepfather looked up from the book he was reading. "When did you get interested in taking care of plants?"

"Well, it's sort of a project for school," Molly said.

Mrs. Evans suppressed a smile. "The watering can's under the kitchen sink."

"I don't need it," Molly called over her shoulder as she carried the plant into the kitchen. "And don't come in here until I tell you."

"I wonder what she's up to now?" Mr. Evans said. "Last week it was blowing on a piece of paper to see what makes an airplane fly."

"And the other day all she could talk about was how hot and cold air make wind," said Molly's mother.

They were interrupted by a loud rattling and banging from the kitchen. There was silence for a few minutes, then the unmistakable whistle of the teakettle.

"She'd better not be putting boiling water on my plant!" Mrs. Evans said in alarm.

They didn't have long to wonder. "It worked!" Molly yelled. "You can come in now."

Mystified, her mother and stepfather went into the kitchen. The plant was sitting on the counter next to the stove. Above it Molly held a cookie sheet covered with ice cubes. As steam from the teakettle struck the bottom of the cookie sheet, drops of water fell on the plant.

"It's my science homework," Molly said proudly. "I made rain!"

•

Why do you think Molly's teacher assigned this kind of homework?

•

If you were Molly's parent, how would you react to her experiments?

Kevin is watching the cars go by, on a street near where he lives. Kevin is nearly eight years old. Watching with him is his brother, Doug, who has just turned four. But the two brothers do not think about cars the same way. To Doug cars are just wheeled vehicles, different from one another mainly because they come in different colors. Doug has also ridden in a car. He knows how the inside looks, and he knows what a car is for: to go places.

Kevin, however, doesn't see just cars. He sees Fords, Chevrolets, and Volkswagens. He sees little compacts and big gas-guzzlers, station wagons and sports cars. He can tell you certain things all cars have in common and, very generally, some of the ways in which their engines differ.

It is not that Kevin is more intelligent than his younger brother. He isn't. It is not just that Kevin, being older, has had time to learn more about cars. True, he has. But, in addition, Kevin has entered a new stage of cognitive development. He thinks differently from his brother.

Suppose Doug is in a used-car lot. He sees a row of huge, gas-guzzling cars. There are ten of them, standing out from the smaller cars in other rows. Eight are blue, the other two an off-shade of brown. If Doug were asked whether there are more cars in this group or more blue cars, he would probably answer that there are more blue cars. This is, of course, similar to the experiment with blue and white wooden beads that was described in the previous unit.

Doug is still in the **preoperational period** of cognitive development. He isn't yet capable of focusing on more than one aspect of an object at any one time. He sees that all the cars in the group are big. He sees that most are blue. But he can't put both perceptions together to see a relationship: "Most of the cars in this group of big cars are blue."

Kevin not only sees this relationship—he takes it for granted. He would be puzzled if asked the same question Doug was asked. He would wonder why anyone would ask such a silly question.

Kevin is capable of a number of mental operations, including the classification of an object on the basis of several characteristics. He is in the concrete operational period of mental development. This is the stage he will move through all during his early school years. He is progressing toward still another, higher stage—which he will enter at about the same time he enters seventh grade.

CONCRETE OPERATIONS

The term **concrete operations** was coined by Jean Piaget to describe certain kinds of mental operations. These include classifying and numbering, locating things in space under various conditions, and relating things to each other in different ways. Such operations use logical and symbolic thinking. However, they deal mainly with "concrete" situations—with actual experience, rather than with purely abstract ideas or theories.

Take, for example, a familiar type of math problem: Ellen and Ralph are driving to see their grandparents in another town. Ralph drives for 20 minutes at 45 mph. Ellen then takes a turn and drives for 30 minutes at 50 mph. What is the total distance covered?

This is a problem involving concrete operations. To solve it, minutes are converted into fractions of an hour. A basic formula is used: rate × time = distance. The results of Ralph's and Ellen's turns at the wheel are figured separately, and the two are added together.

Most children are doing such problems by the sixth grade. But few children of this age are ready for the kind of theoretical reasoning necessary in, for example, a high school physics or history course. That is the next period of cognitive development.

In the concrete operational period, however,

Special talents are often apparent during the early
school years. Young children show different abilities.
Some are artistic, others musical. Some are interested
in science, others in physical activities. Teachers
try to identify and develop each child's potential.
They vary activities during the school day to keep
every child interested.

Most children have definite ideas about what constitutes "masculine" and "feminine" behavior. In an experiment, sixth-grade children believed that each of the following traits and activities was applicable to either females or to males, but not to both.

running	cold	wild
hitting	brave	passive
crying	neat	sensitive
talking	gentle	worldly
going out	giving up	adventurous
working	acting as a leader	excitable
slow	superior	emotional
soft	polite	kind

Obviously, these words fit traditional stereotypes of what men and women are supposed to be like. It is surprising, however, to discover how many of them are still accepted as true by people of all ages.

How would you yourself categorize the traits in the list? On what basis did you make your choices?

Source: Deanna Kuhn, DEVELOPMENT: BECOMING WHO WE ARE (New York: Harcourt, Brace, Jovanovich, 1975), p. 99

realizes that numbers stand for actual things that can be added to or taken away from a group.

If a child has special artistic or musical talents, these often show up during the early school years. At the same time, almost all children, whatever their talents, like to do artwork and engage in musical activities such as singing and dancing.

Solving problems in art—such as seeing what happens when two colors are mixed, or figuring out how to make a clay horse balance on its legs—can be intriguing for a child in the primary grades. And often a child can express an idea or feeling more effectively through art than in words.

Not all cognitive growth takes place in school, of course. All kinds of games—puzzles, card and board games, checkers and chess, for instance—are more than just fun for school-age children. They are also learning experiences. So are hobbies and sports. Seven-year-old Gail, practicing archery in her back yard, is developing a sense of space as well as exercising her muscles. Ten-year-old Larry learns a lot from building detailed scale models of sailing ships. And Celia, another ten-year-old, can take apart and repair her own ten-speed bike.

The word games, puns, and highly imaginative stories that children love to tell are evidence of their cognitive growth. By the age of eleven, most children are capable of using language in a very sophisticated manner, indeed—and often in a very creative manner as well.

Many eleven-year-olds are capable of some very sophisticated thinking in general. They are, in fact, ready to move out of the concrete operational stage and into the next stage of cognitive development: the period of **formal operations**. As adolescents, they will be capable of deductive reasoning, frequently at a high level. They can consider probabilities and think about what might or might not be under certain conditions. They may even think about their own thinking.

· SUMMARY ·

- Children are now in the period of concrete operations. They can think logically about things that they can see and touch.
- They can understand more complex classifications and arrange objects in order.
- Vocabulary is growing fast, and children enjoy word games and puns.
- Most children are ready to read by second grade, although others do not learn until third or fourth grade.
- Morally, children this age know "inside" what they should or should not do.
- By age twelve, many children are approaching the development of reasoning powers close to the adult level.

TERMS TO KNOW

accomodate
assimilate
conventional morality
internalize
morality of coopera-
tion
postconventional mo-
rality
preconventional mo-
rality
seriation

1. Concern with how one's actions are judged by others is one stage in what Kohlberg calls _____.
2. _____ means putting objects in order.
3. As children _____ new information, their cognitive framework changes to _____ that information.
4. A child who has begun to _____ rules made by adults is on the way toward the stage called _____.
5. _____ involves developing one's own standards of morality.
6. In the first stage of _____, a child is mainly concerned with rewards and punishments.

CHECK YOUR UNDERSTANDING

1. What kinds of mental operations are included in Piaget's concrete operational stage of development?
2. Why might it be said that the more a child of this age learns, the more he becomes capable of learning?
3. Why are some children not ready to learn to read in the first or second grade?
4. What may be the result if a child is pushed to read before he is ready?
5. Explain this statement: In early grade school, a child's sense of language is primarily aural.
6. Describe Piaget's second stage of moral development, the morality of cooperation.
7. According to Kohlberg, in what stage of moral development is a child from age ten to the early teens?

·19·

SOCIAL/EMOTIONAL DEVELOPMENT
OF THE SCHOOL-AGE CHILD

"Mother," Cindy began. The tone of her voice had an edge to it. Mrs. Crow had become used to that edgy tone lately in her eleven-year-old daughter's voice. It usually signaled trouble.

"Yes, Cindy?"

"Mother, why do you always wear that same old sweatshirt every Saturday?"

The question took Mrs. Crow by surprise. She thought a few seconds. "It's comfortable," she finally replied, "and I'm used to it. Why should I dress up to do housework?"

"My friends see you when they come over. When *you* have company, you don't want *your* friends to see your children in rags."

"Oh, come on. When did your friends ever come over when I was wearing this?"

"Well, they could. They could anytime."

"Cindy, why're you trying to pick a fight?"

"I just care about the way my mother looks. And I think you could care a little about the way you look, too!"

Mrs. Crow tried not to be too upset as she watched her daughter stride out of the room. This was supposed to be typical eleven-year-old behavior. Yet she was a little hurt, and missed the gentle, confiding Cindy of just a year ago. But she knew that mood changes were part of being eleven, too. When she went in later to say good night, Cindy was feeling remorseful.

"I'm sorry, Mom, for what I said about your clothes. I don't know why I picked on that. It was just—I don't know what it was."

"Don't worry about it. We all get in a mood sometimes and look for something to take it out on."

"You know something, Mom—I love you!"

•

What are some of the other ways in which Mrs. Crow might have reacted to her daughter's criticism?

•

What is the lesson for parents in the way this situation was handled?

Isabel passes a note to Molly in math class: "Don't forget. Club meeting after school." Molly slides the scrap of paper into her textbook. She opens the book as if checking a problem and gives the note a quick glance. Then she nods slightly to her friend. Isabel settles back with a smile. Behind her, Jean, who has seen the whole transaction, frowns. It is clear that the two girls are planning something for their new club—which Jean has not been asked to join. All three girls are nine years old, an age when belonging—or not belonging—to a group begins to be very important, for both boys and girls.

In the past, when they were younger, they were part of a loose cluster of children, girls and boys who played together most of the time. New members could easily join their group. Usually everyone would agree if a parent of one of the children suggested: "Tommy is new here, and he's probably feeling kind of lonely. Couldn't you ask him to play, too?" But now they are more choosy about who may join their play.

In the future, when they are eleven and twelve, Isabel, Molly, and Jean will probably join groups organized like formal clubs. Members of such a group may be interested in the same subject, such as stamp collecting or skating. Meetings will be held at a set time every week. Rules will be carefully written out. Children of the opposite sex will not be allowed to join, even if they should want to, which is unlikely. Adults may never be involved, except to provide food and transportation as needed.

But for the present, the nine-year-olds are not concerned about forming their group around any single activity. What's important is the sense of belonging, of feeling "on the inside" while somebody else is "on the outside."

INTERACTION WITH PEERS

After she enters school, a child's developing sense of self is obviously going to be strongly influenced by her relationships with other children. More and more time is being spent away from her family, whether in class or playing with her friends. And, as we have just seen, most children begin to see themselves as members of a group of chosen friends—in addition to being members of the first or second grade or the general school population.

At age seven, friendships may still form as they did in earlier years, more because of convenience than by real choice. Groups still develop when children happen to live nearby or are brought together by their parents. But by eight, most friendship groups form on the basis of deliberate selection. Children choose other children as friends because they like them.

Of all the children in the second grade, Billy likes Lisa, Ted, and Maryanne the best. They feel the same about him and each other. Gradually, as they play together, these four begin to think of themselves as a group.

There are individual rivalries. Billy and Maryanne compete to see who is the fastest runner. Ted sometimes complains that Lisa is too bossy. But, by and large, they all count on one another for approval and encouragement. The group may be short-lived. Friendships constantly change at this age. For now, however, this is a four-way mutual-admiration society.

At ages nine and ten, groups become more structured. The loose combinations of friends characteristic of ages seven and eight give way to clubs, complete with secret code words and special signals.

By the time children are eleven and twelve, their clubs may have acquired written by-laws and officers (generally including all the regular members). Many children of this age also join organizations such as the 4-H Clubs and the Future Homemakers of America, the Wilderness Society, and the Boy Scouts or Girl Scouts. Membership in a formal organization of peers gives a child independent status, while at the same time satisfying her need for social interaction.

If children have poor self-concepts, can anything be done to help them feel better about themselves? A recent experiment with thirty boys and girls, all of whom were judged to have poor self-concepts, attempted to find out. The children, ranging from kindergarteners to fourth-graders, were given special attention and encouragement to see if some change could be brought about in the way they felt about themselves.

As soon as a child did something appropriate or successful, teachers, aides, and student assistants asked the child to tell them something good about herself. Then they gave the child a hug or a pat on the back, or said they were proud of her. They did this eight times a day for every child. If there were any children who were unable to say anything positive about themselves, the adults would say something and ask the children to repeat it.

There were other children with low self-concepts who were not reinforced in this way. They were the control group, and they did not receive any kind of special treatment.

After forty days, a test given to the children showed that those in the first group were noticeably more confident. Their self-concepts had clearly improved. The children in the control group had not changed.

Some psychologists question these results and wonder if the test administered to measure self-concept was a good test. Perhaps the results of this test were not valid, and the improvement in self-concept was not a real or lasting improvement.

In any case, more research and study are needed in this area. But at the very least, this report shows how simple it is to influence emotional growth in the classroom. Praise and appreciation have a strong positive effect on the child, and their daily use by sincere teachers should be encouraged.

What can be done to help a child who has a low self-concept because of a physical condition, such as being overweight or having poor coordination?

How might a child's relationship with her peers contribute to her low self-concept? How could this relationship be improved?

Many children also go away to some type of camp during the summers. Ten-year-old Raul goes to a camp in a semi-wilderness setting, far from home and school. He is learning social skills among his peers as well as how to be more independent in looking after himself. Raul and the other campers take part in after-dark songfests around the campfire, hiking trips, camp shows, and competitions between cabin groups. They have learned to make their bunk beds in less than a minute's time. When Raul returns home, he will bring with him a new sureness in dealing with his peers and a stronger sense of his own self-worth.

Not every child's group experiences are so positive, however. At any age, groups can be cruel—both to their own members and to those who do not belong. School-age children don't mince words with each other. "Cry-baby, cry-baby!" they jeer, or: "You're just stupid, that's all!"

Jeers and insults are one weapon. Exile from the group is another. For no apparent reason, a group may refuse to have anything to do with a particular child. Group members in this way

Children with physical disabilities are often excluded from groups of their peers. They must develop strategies for communicating or playing with others while learning to cope emotionally with their physical problems.

gain a sense of superiority, a sense of themselves as "insiders." The child who is excluded, of course, may be thoroughly miserable. However, the exclusion may be only temporary. At this stage, personal relationships still change quickly.

The child who has no contact with any group—whether because of shyness, unpopularity, or some other reason—may need extra help from adults during the early school years. Being a loner is not easy even for the child with a natural taste for solitude, and especially when everyone else is so involved with group activities. Adults usually cannot do anything about that situation, but they can encourage the child to develop her own special interests and help to give her a sense of self-worth.

A different kind of problem arises when the group has a negative influence on a child's personality development. Debby, for example, who is usually a warm, sensitive person, joins the rest of her clique in giggling openly at a new student's "weird" clothes. And Joey tries shoplifting when the other members of his gang dare him to do it.

Unfortunately, in cases like these, adult intervention in the form of "Don't do it!" is often useless, and the children may even feel challenged to persist. Sometimes, however, children can be put in contact with a different, less destructive group.

One aspect of children's group behavior, being closely observed today by psychologists and other professionals, is the tendency of children to separate themselves by sex. Traditionally, from about age nine on, boys tend to associate mainly with boys and girls with girls.

The extent to which this tendency has been influenced by social stereotypes about male and female roles is difficult to determine. Certainly children today are less rigid about the kind of behavior expected of someone because of her or his sex. The old labels of "sissy" and "tomboy" are becoming pointless as more and more children feel free to engage (or not to engage) in any kind of activity, without regard to old sex-role stereotypes.

Nevertheless, the tendency of children to group themselves by sex after age nine is still obvious. Children of the same sex sit together during school activities unless a teacher assigns the seating. And after school, they go off generally in groups of the same sex.

There are other factors in personality development at this age besides belonging to a group, important as that is. Doing well in school, for example, is also important for developing both social skills and a clearer sense of self. Psychoanalyst Erik Erikson stressed this aspect of child development when he described the early school years as a period of **industry** versus **inferiority**. For the most part, children in this period *are* industrious. They are also enthusiastic and curious.

They delight in mastering new skills. They are proud of being moved to a more advanced reading group or of finishing a tricky math

Some school-age children never feel they are part of a group. Caregivers should encourage them to pursue activities which interest them.

Children often ostracize from their group those who differ from them in appearance, personality, interests, or cultural background. Most children find groups to join or develop close friendships with one or two friends. Those who are constantly rejected by others may suffer emotionally. Caregivers need to assess the needs of each child. Some can develop normally without peer support. Others may need professional counseling to resolve personal problems.

Children may lack interest at school if they are doing poorly. But each child has need for a feeling of accomplishment and success. Caregivers must help children "discover" their own talents and abilities.

problem before anyone else. Their sense of accomplishment enhances their images of themselves as capable, independent individuals.

On the other hand, a feeling of failure at school produces a sense of inferiority. If Hal always does poorly on spelling tests or never seems to get the math homework right, he may become anxious and insecure. The other children seem to learn everything so easily, while he has trouble just keeping up.

Such a child clearly needs extra help immediately, before he falls too far behind. In addition, children can overcome feelings of inferiority by discovering and developing the things they are good at doing. These can range from sports and art activities to helping to teach younger children in an afternoon play group. A child like Hal needs to develop the same delight in industry and pride of accomplishment that his classmates are feeling.

FAMILY RELATIONSHIPS

The front door bangs, announcing that ten-year-old Cathy is home from school. A jacket sails through the air in the general direction of the closet, misses its mark, and lands on the floor. Cathy hops over it and heads for the kitchen.

"Hi, Mom, what's for supper?"

"Tuna casserole. How was school?"

"Okay. Need any help?"

"Not just now, thanks."

Cathy turns toward the living room where the television set is waiting.

"No more news?" her mother asks. "Didn't you do anything special today?"

"Not really." The television set snaps on and a loud voice begins discussing floor wax. A moment later, Cathy reappears in the kitchen doorway. "Oh, by the way, Mom," she says casually, "we did have a math test today."

"A math test?" Her mother's tone is neutral. She is not sure whether to expect a report of success or of failure. "How did you make out?"

"Well, somehow or other, I didn't make a single mistake!" her daughter informs her, pride breaking through at last. "My score was the best in the whole class!"

Through all the changes taking place during the school years, one element remains constant: a child's need for a close relationship with her family. Cathy—leisurely as she may be about the process—will not enjoy her success to the fullest until she has shared it with her mother. Gary's disappointment at not getting the lead in the school play will not be completely relieved until he has poured out his feelings at home.

To be sure, the nature of children's relationships with their families changes during the school years. It can't help changing as a child develops other relationships with friends and with adults outside the home, such as teachers and coaches. But the family unit is no less important.

In many countries, older siblings are responsible for their younger brothers and sisters. A common sight in Latin America, especially in rural areas, is a six- or eight-year-old carrying a two-year-old sibling on her hip. If she is not carrying the child, then she is watching him or her in a hammock, swinging it to and fro. It is her responsibility to keep an eye on the younger child.

In North America, on the other hand, both the six- or eight-year-old and the two-year-old would be cared for by an adult: either a parent, a baby-sitter, or another caregiver. It is a rare situation for the older sibling to be in complete charge of the younger one all the time, although in many large families, older children do play a role in child care.

Growing up in these two cultures is a different experience for the children involved. In Latin America, responsibility toward others is given at an early age, and children are expected to take care of their younger siblings much of the time. This is their job. In North America, childhood is usually not interrupted by important responsibilities, and most children are not given the care of their siblings.

There are, of course, exceptions. If all the adults in a family have jobs outside of the home, and there is no extra money to pay a baby-sitter, then older children may be needed to help out with child care and other chores. But in general, North Americans feel that children should have time to play and learn, and that taking care of younger siblings should not be their concern. In addition, adults also feel that children may not have sufficient maturity to be given sole charge of a younger child.

But if North American children have the advantage of more freedom, they do not have the satisfaction that comes from helping their families in a very important way. The Latin American child may find her little brother or sister a nuisance, but all the same, she is proud to be in charge.

These different approaches to child rearing also affect the rate at which children develop socially and emotionally. In Latin America, children often become part of the adult world, at least in a limited way, while they are still very young. In North America, they remain in the special world of childhood for many years.

The term "family unit," however, has come to take on more than one meaning. In most industrialized countries throughout the middle decades of this century, most children have been raised in a **nuclear family,** consisting of father, mother, and children.

But in recent years, a number of variations have developed. More and more common today is the **single-parent family,** in which only the mother or the father lives with the children, because of divorce, separation, or death. When two adults, each with children from a previous marriage, remarry, they become a **blended family.** Another type of family is the **cooperative family,** in which several parents and their children join forces to share a single home. The **extended family,** in which several generations live together, is becoming increasingly rare in Western society.

Family size and structure can affect the kind and amount of attention that children receive. In a nuclear family, for instance, there are

No matter what type of family children belong to, they need love and security. Nuclear families consisting of a father, mother, and two children make up only sixteen percent of families in the United States today. Increasing numbers of children are being raised in single-parent and cooperative family homes. However, the number of extended families has declined in recent years.

The world a child grows up in can influence his or her behavior in a variety of ways. North American children, especially those raised in urban areas, are usually more competitive and less cooperative than children in many other countries.

Soviet children, according to psychologist Urie Bronfenbrenner, are brought up in a society where individual competitiveness is not encouraged. At school, they divide into "teams" which compete against one another for the highest grades, the best attendance record, the neatest appearance. If one child is persistently late to school or falls behind in his homework, the standing of his entire group is affected. As a result, his teammates will hold a meeting to criticize or offer extra help. The teacher is present as an adviser, but it is the pressure of the peer-group members that influences the child most strongly.

In the same way, if a child wins special distinction, the whole group shares in the honor. In the Soviet system, individual achievement is encouraged only as it benefits the larger group—or the State.

Group cooperation is strengthened by providing children with the chance to share in adult activities. If a blizzard strikes, children help to clear not only the school paths but also nearby public sidewalks as well. Soviet schoolchildren know that they give much-needed help to their communities, and they are proud of being able to contribute.

In North America, on the other hand, children are encouraged to be independent, to win and achieve on their own. They receive prizes, good grades, or extra allowances for doing so. Children also learn to focus on their special interests and abilities. One of the goals of education in North America is to help children discover their individual capabilities and develop them to the fullest.

Sometimes, this individualistic approach leads to excessive competition. Schools are beginning to set up situations in which children are encouraged to work together on a common project, such as planting a school vegetable garden or building a model city. Here cooperative behavior is fostered.

Another new approach for North American schools is to enlist the children's help in community activities such as collecting scrap or reclaiming a neglected park.

Bronfenbrenner believes that both the Soviet and the North American system have good and bad points. Each culture could learn from a study of the other culture's schools. In addition, his research shows how strongly a society can affect the values its children eventually adopt.

fewer adults for the child to turn to. Emotional responses may become intensified. The child who depends for love and support primarily on her parents may be deeply disturbed if one of them falls sick, goes away, or simply becomes angry with her. In such a small world, any change can seem threatening. If the child lives with only one parent, she may feel even more insecure.

In a larger family, the presence of other adults offers a kind of security to the child. If one grownup is not available, there is sure to be someone else nearby. In addition, there are a variety of adults who can serve as role models.

A disadvantage in the larger family is that the individual child does not have as much chance to develop a one-to-one relationship

Institutional Child-Care Worker

CLAUDIA MICHAELS: I'm here at Montvale Home for Children to get some information for a story I'm writing for the *Montvale News*.

DAN SUZUKI: I'm a child-care worker, and I've been here for four years. I live and work with a group of eight-year-old boys. As you know, all our children are emotionally disturbed, and some have physical handicaps as well. Our goal is to help them learn to take care of themselves and to live comfortably with others. Eventually some of them will be able to go home with their families.

CLAUDIA: What is your own background?

DAN: I was graduated from college with a degree in sociology but not very much idea of what I wanted to do. I spent one summer working at a camp for emotionally disturbed children and decided that I wanted to make that my career.

CLAUDIA: What are the greatest satisfactions and the greatest problems of your job?

DAN: That's easy. The answer to both is the same: the children. It's very difficult to work with such troubled children, but there is nothing in the world quite like seeing one of them show definite signs of progress.

Hundreds of thousands of children, mostly aged six to eighteen, live in child-care institutions. Some of them are emotionally disturbed, others are physically handicapped or mentally retarded. Many have a combination of problems. Some children live in institutions because their families are unable to care for them and there are no suitable foster homes available.

Institutional child-care workers are responsible for the growth and development of these children. They must give the children the special care and guidance they need, understanding their limitations and difficulties but also their potential. The workers, who usually live with the children in cottages, are in some ways substitute parents. They are aided in their job by many specialists—doctors, nurses, psychologists, physical therapists, speech therapists, teachers, and others. Because each child has unique needs, a special program must be developed to promote his or her physical, intellectual, and emotional development.

Child-care institutions are operated by many public and private agencies. The working conditions vary; some institutions are very modern and have excellent facilities; others are quite dismal indeed. The attitudes of the staff also vary considerably, depending on the leadership of the institution. Salaries are generally low, although not at all institutions.

An institutional child-care worker must have special qualities of dedication and patience. Progress for these children is often measured in very small steps, and a person who is easily frustrated or who cannot tolerate setbacks will not be happy in this job. The most successful workers are people who are tolerant, patient, determined, and persistent. At the same time they must be warm and loving. The rewards of the job cannot be measured in terms of money or prestige, for these are few, but by the knowledge that they are helping special children achieve the most out of life.

CAREERS

In 1799 in southern France, a boy was found running through the forest half naked. When he was captured by hunters, he was exhibited in a cage like an animal in a zoo. Somehow, the "wild child" managed to escape, but French authorities recaptured him and sent him to be examined by scientists. Their report was that the boy had such limited intelligence that he should be classified on the lowest level of mental retardation, which in those days was labeled as "idiot."

One expert disagreed. Jean Itard, a French doctor, believed that the boy's wild, animal-like behavior was the result of being isolated from other human beings. Victor, as Dr. Itard named him, was about eleven years old when he was first captured. He had been living alone in the woods for over six years. It seemed probable that the boy's development had been handicapped by his solitary existence.

Dr. Itard took Victor to live with him in his own home and began a systematic training program to "humanize and civilize" the wild child. He discovered that Victor could hear well, but only paid attention to sounds associated with food. The boy took little notice of human conversation, but became highly alert at the sound of a nut cracking or an apple falling from a tree. His eyes were keen, but he seemed unable to focus on anything for more than a few seconds.

Victor lived with Itard for more than five years. The doctor taught him to wear clothes, focus his eyes, sleep in a bed, and eat with a knife and fork. But although Victor even learned how to read, write, and speak a few simple words, he never learned to communicate very well. He had almost no social relationships. He seemed to feel affection for Dr. Itard and for the housekeeper who took care of him, but other people remained unimportant to him for the rest of his life. Eventually, he was sent to an institution for the retarded and mentally disturbed, where he died at age forty. He never became a fully normal human being.

Victor's story seems to illustrate the importance of interpersonal relationships. It shows, too, how cognitive and emotional development may be severely crippled when such relationships are lacking or inadequate.

This photo is from *L'Enfant Savage*, a 1970 movie about the wild child and Dr. Itard.

From CHILDREN: BEHAVIOR AND DEVELOPMENT, Third Edition, by Boyd R. McCandless and Robert J. Trotter. Copyright © 1977 by Holt, Rinehart and Winston. Copyright © 1967 and 1961 by Holt, Rinehart and Winston, Inc. Reprinted by permission of Holt, Rinehart and Winston.

294

with her parents or caregivers. In a nuclear family, on the other hand, the relationship may be very close and rewarding, not having to be shared with a number of other relatives.

The child in a home where both parents work faces a special situation. Much of the time, she must look to adults other than her parents for part of the attention and affection she needs. She may resent this, or she may develop a sense of pride in her own self-reliance.

Another factor affecting the child's personality is **birth order**—the child's position within the family in relation to her **siblings**. An older child, for example, may have less self-confidence than her younger brothers and sisters. At the same time, she may be especially conscientious and anxious to succeed.

Some psychologists believe that such characteristics result from the fact that when the first child is born, her parents are new to parenthood. They do not feel as capable and self-assured as they will later, when their other children are born. Parents may tend to worry more about their first baby, overprotect her, and not let her try enough things on her own. The result is less self-confidence as she grows older. At the same time, she may have a need to keep proving herself to her parents. This carries over into school. First-born children tend to be high achievers.

The youngest child in the family, by contrast, tends not to be so highly motivated to succeed, but is more self-confident. The road was paved for this child by her older siblings and was somewhat easier for her. She assumes cheerfully, on the basis of past experience, that she can do whatever she sets out to do.

A middle child may feel she has no status in the family, being neither the oldest nor the youngest. Yet, she may also be able to share something of both worlds—joining in activities with older siblings and still helping with the baby. It is important for the middle child to discover special interests and abilities that establish her as an independent person in her own mind.

An only child's personality, to the extent that it is shaped by her social environment, is influenced by parents, other adults, and peers. At one time, it was thought that an only child had special problems and that she was likely to be either spoiled and conceited or shy and timid. Recent studies have shown, however, that such assumptions don't hold, so long as the child has positive social experiences with adults and peers.

EMOTIONAL DEVELOPMENT

Children's emotional growth in general tends to follow a pattern in which periods of stability alternate with periods of instability. This is the normal pattern also during the school years. Yet, to most parents and caregivers, the periods of instability will probably seem less marked during these years.

Especially by ages nine or ten, the typical school-age child gives the general impression of being in control of her emotions. She may still get angry, particularly if she feels someone is being unfair. But her anger is less likely to become physical than was the case in earlier years.

As noted earlier, this is the period which Erikson characterizes as industry versus inferiority. Both socially and intellectually, the school years are devoted mainly to achievement and mastery of skills—and the child's feelings are involved with this process. The sense of achievement she gains is important. Its opposite, a sense of inferiority, could have a harmful effect on her long-range emotional development.

· SUMMARY ·

- Belonging to a group is important to a school-age child.
- Groups gradually become more structured during these years.
- Membership in a club or other social organization gives the child a sense of belonging as well as independence.
- Children tend to divide into groups of boys and groups of girls for work and play.
- Success or failure in schoolwork influences the child's sense of self.
- Family relationships continue to be important during the school years.
- Family size and structure, as well as birth order, can influence the child's personality.
- Emotional growth follows a pattern of stability alternating with instability.

TERMS TO KNOW

birth order
blended family
cooperative family
extended family

industry
inferiority
nuclear family
single-parent family

1. In a(n) _____, more than one generation lives together.
2. A child develops a feeling of _____ when he is unable to master certain skills.
3. A(n) _____ may result from divorce, separation, or death.
4. Several families sharing a home form a(n) _____.
5. A child's position within the family, or _____, can affect her personality.
6. A(n) _____ consists of a mother, father, and children.
7. The marriage of two adults who have children from previous marriages forms a(n) _____.
8. _____ is Erikson's term for the mastery of skills marked by a sense of achievement.

CHECK YOUR UNDERSTANDING

1. How do group friendships change from age seven to ages nine and ten?
2. What are the benefits of membership in a formal organization of peers?
3. What are two ways in which school-age children can be cruel to their peers?
4. What can adults do for a child who, because of shyness or unpopularity, is not part of the group?
5. At what age do children tend to group themselves by sex?
6. Why is doing well in school important to a child's personality development?
7. What conflict did Erikson use to describe the early school years?
8. What are five kinds of families in our society today?
9. How have opinions about an only child's social development changed?
10. Describe the emotional development of a typical nine- or ten-year-old.

·20·

INTERACTION
WITH THE SCHOOL-AGE CHILD

Mr. Lewis stood at the door of his ten-year-old son's room, staring in disbelief at the clutter of his playthings, books, comics, sports equipment, and stray socks.

"Rob, your room looks as if a hurricane hit it!" he exclaimed.

Rob looked around as if noticing the mess for the first time. "Yeah—Hurricane Rob!" he said, grinning.

"This is no joke, young man," his father said. "You're old enough to start taking better care of your things. For starters, you can put your baseball bat and mitt in the closet where they belong."

"Aw, Dad, what's the use of putting it all away if I'm only going to take it out again tomorrow?" While Mr. Lewis pondered the logic of this, Rob added, "Anyway, it's my room. Why can't I keep it the way I want?"

"You can—up to a point. But you've got to have some consideration for the rest of us," Mr. Lewis said firmly. "I'll tell you what. I won't ask you to clean up more than once a week—and when company comes. But you must promise to make your bed every day, and empty that thing"—he pointed to an overflowing trash can—"at least once a day."

"Well . . . okay," said Rob. "I'll try. As long as you promise not to nag me more than once a week!"

"I'll try, too," said Mr. Lewis with a smile.

•

Do you think Mr. Lewis was right to compromise with Rob? Or should he have laid down the law?

•

Do you think Rob's father should have offered him some money to clean his room every week? Why or why not?

tarting "real" school is a turning point in the lives of most children. It is accompanied by dramatic changes in the pattern of the child's days and in his feelings about himself, his parents, and his peers. Entering junior high school is another such turning point. But the years between these two milestones seem to go by in a relatively smooth fashion. Progress is steady and more or less predictable.

Of course, a fifth-grader needs to be treated differently from a second-grader. Yet they share important characteristics with each other and with elementary school children in general. Natalie's mother says, "These are the years when it's easiest to *reason* with children." Other parents have noted that "You know where you stand with your child and can usually figure out why he does what he does," or that "They're on their own a great deal of the time, but they don't often rebel seriously against authority."

For such reasons many caregivers find the school years an especially easy and rewarding growth stage. It is a comparatively peaceful time between the more demanding early years and the dramatic changes of adolescence.

A major task of parents during these years is to help their children maintain an adequate sense of their own worth and capabilities. This may seem surprising, in view of how much importance girls and boys this age attach to the opinion of their **peers** and to what occurs in school.

Still, despite the importance to children of "making it" in the world of their agemates and (in most cases) in school, they continue to be strongly influenced by their parents. They want their parents to think well of them. Also, supportive parents can make it easier for them to weather the temporary troubles and setbacks they encounter away from home.

IMPROVING A CHILD'S SELF-IMAGE

Erwin was no good at sports. He was always the last to be chosen when his classmates

Peers play an important part in the development of school-age children. Most children seek acceptance from others their age. They may begin to adopt similar attitudes and habits.

Day-Care Workers

Althea Walker, director of the North Side Day-Care Center, was interviewing Paula Santini for a job as an aide. "What have you been doing since your high school graduation last year, Paula?"

"I've been an office clerk and a supermarket checker. But I decided that what I really want to do is work with children."

"There's lots of routine and dirty work here, I'm afraid," Althea said. "But you also have a great deal of contact with the children. And it's never boring. After we're finished talking, I'd like you to spend some time with Jack Barton, an aide. I want you to get some idea of how the team works here before you make up your mind about the job."

Teamwork is indeed an important part of any day-care center. The staff is responsible for the physical care, educational development, and personal growth of the children who stay at the center while their parents are working. Some of these children are infants and toddlers, but most are in the three-to-five age group.

Usually each day-care worker is responsible for the care of about six to twelve children. There are assistants and aides to help. The workers organize suitable games and activities; they observe and guide the children's social behavior; they supervise mealtimes and perhaps help in food preparation; and they provide special attention when necessary. Day-care workers consult with other staff members, outside specialists, and parents to share information about each child's progress and problems.

As an aide, Paula would be starting at the lowest job level at the center. Others had started as aides and worked up to higher positions. The teachers at the center had college degrees, and the director had just received a master's degree in elementary education.

In addition to education appropriate to the level of responsibility, day-care workers should have certain personal qualifications: good mental and physical health; a warm, open personality; a tolerance for stress; flexibility; a willingness to cooperate; dependability; and a strong sense of responsibility. Of course, a genuine interest in children is essential.

At present, day-care workers are not highly paid. Salaries vary considerably in different areas of the country and from one center to another. Generally, larger centers, which have better funding, offer better salaries. Day-care centers will undoubtedly increase in the future. In addition to public and private centers, there are centers run by companies for their employees' children.

Working conditions vary considerably. Day-care centers are open long hours to accommodate the needs of parents; workers may have to work irregular hours. They must be willing to adjust their personal lives to fit the demands of the job.

Some centers are in new buildings with good facilities; others have very poor facilities. A center may be poorly heated or need repairs. Most day-care workers, however, feel that the success of their work depends more on staff attitudes than the physical setting.

Working in a day-care center can be tiring, frustrating, and demanding. However, for those who are committed to promoting the development of young children, and who take pleasure in watching children flourish in a group setting, it can offer substantial personal gratification.

divided themselves into teams for games. Sometimes he was teased about his poor performance. Usually the teasing was good-natured, since Erwin was not really disliked. But it hurt. By the time he was nine, this was seriously damaging his image of himself.

His parents spent a lot of time trying to help him improve his skills. As a result of their tactful teaching, he learned to swim and ride a bike well. This boosted his self-esteem. So did their attitude toward him. They made it plain that they were concerned about his athletic ability only because he was. They didn't think every boy needed to be a whiz at sports. They considered themselves fortunate to have a child like Erwin who, as his father said, "is healthy, fun to be with, and doing well in school." Gradually Erwin began to worry less about what he couldn't do and gain more satisfaction from what he was good at. His self-image improved. He became a respected member of a group of fourth-graders whose interests were not primarily athletic.

Erwin's parents did not try to force their beliefs on him. But they did make these beliefs clear. At the same time, they showed their desire to help him get along with his peers in his own way.

This is the best approach to dealing with children from the early school years on. They usually just become annoyed if parents or other caregivers criticize their friends or the values of the peer group. However, as in Erwin's case, parents can play an extremely important role in helping a child come into his own, as long as they do not make their child feel that they are trying to run his life.

FINDING OUT WHAT'S WRONG

Parents can usually tell when a child's self-image is slipping. But they may not immediately know why. Mrs. Li was aware that her seven-year-old daughter, Melinda, had seemed unusually touchy and reserved for several weeks. There had been no changes at home that might explain this. So Mrs. Li arranged to take time off from work for a conference with her child's teacher.

The mother learned that Melinda's former best friend in school had recently been pairing up with another child. Melinda, instead of trying to make other friends, had withdrawn into herself. The teacher felt that there were several children who would like to be friends with Melinda if only she would make an effort. The teacher gave Melinda's mother some names. Mrs. Li then managed, with Melinda's assistance, to invite three children for a Saturday afternoon trip to Chinatown. The outing was a success. This did not immediately heal Melinda's hurt over being rejected earlier. But she did gain new friends and was happier at home and school.

EACH CHILD IS SPECIAL

Though parents cannot "buy" success for a child in the world of his peers, they can help him find his own way of fitting in. This requires being sensitive to individual differences, as well as to what a child is experiencing at the moment.

Benjy's parents welcome his friendship with Phil, another fifth-grader who shares his pleasure in reading and chess. They know that life can be difficult for an academically gifted child like Benjy and are delighted that he is beginning to seek the company of others like himself, rather than striving to be accepted by the "in" group of youngsters with whom he has little in common.

Delina's parents recognize that she is unlikely to become the star athlete that she currently dreams of being. However, she does have a talent for gymnastics. They arrange for her to take a class in this at the local "Y." As a result, she becomes good enough to gain the

School-age children seek parental reassurance. They want approval of their actions and resent criticism. Many school-age children do not communicate openly. Parents must be able to sense when children are willing to discuss their problems with them. Caregivers need to develop the ability to listen without showing disapproval.

recognition among her sixth-grade classmates that she so much wants.

SECURELY ON THEIR OWN

As we have seen, school-age children need little or no help with tending to such personal needs as dressing and grooming themselves, using the toilet, bathing, and maintaining good dental hygiene. Seeing that they get the sleep they need may require somewhat more parental supervision, especially during the early part of this period. However, firm insistence that they go to bed at the agreed-upon time is usually all that is needed. Of course, the bedtime hour should be changed appropriately as the child grows older.

The child is no longer likely to wake up frightened in the middle of the night. Or if he does, he can handle his fears by himself, without help from his parents.

Increasingly, children are able to cope on their own with all their fears. An occasional sympathetic comment from parents—to the effect that everybody is afraid sometimes—is usually enough to reassure them that their fears are normal and manageable.

During these years the child also becomes increasingly able to travel around the community on his own. He needs to be permitted as much independence of this sort as he can safely handle. This contributes importantly to his growing sense of competence. It also affects his standing with his peers. The second-grader who is still being escorted to and from school and everywhere else by a grownup may be looked down on—and possibly teased—by his classmates as "babyish."

Nevertheless, parents cannot afford to allow a child any more freedom than they are sure he is ready to handle safely. Children differ greatly in this respect. By the time they enter school, they should have learned that their caregivers do not give in to the argument that "everybody else does it." However, parents do sometimes need to find out if this is true. If it is, it's wise to ask themselves *why* their child can not be allowed to do this or that. Are the parents being too protective? Have they failed to train their youngster to handle a particular challenge?

Victor's mother learned at a parent-teacher conference that her son was the only child in his second-grade class who was never allowed to go to and from school on his own, though he lived only four blocks away. His teacher thought this lowered his standing in the other children's eyes and discouraged him from becoming more mature in many areas. She pointed out that the neighborhood was considered a safe one.

The boy's mother protested at first that he was a dreamer who could not be relied on always to wait for a green light and to check for cars. However, she soon had second thoughts. She realized that she sometimes "crossed on the red" with Victor when she was in a hurry and there was no traffic in sight. And she had never practiced standing at the curb with her son and having him tell her when it was safe to cross.

After a week of exposure to specific training doing this and consistent parental example, Victor showed he was clearly capable of getting to and from school by himself. Taking this step was followed by a noticeable advance in his general maturity.

CHORES

Traditionally, the practice of assigning children certain chores has been viewed as a way to help them develop a sense of responsibility. By the age of six a child is capable of providing a good deal of real assistance around the home. He can empty wastebaskets and take out trash and garbage (provided the load is not too heavy for him to carry). He can set and clear the table, and often can be trusted to help wash

302

dishes and put them away. Some cleaning jobs and tasks associated with maintaining a yard or garden are within his capabilities. He can be expected to make his own bed, pick up his toys and other belongings, and put his soiled clothes in a laundry hamper.

Many parents say that just when a child becomes able to be of real assistance, he begins to resent being asked to do so. Trish at three begged to be allowed to use the vacuum cleaner. At seven she finds the activity anything but appealing.

Interestingly, the reluctance to do chores is more likely to be typical of children growing up in industrialized Western nations than those in less advanced societies. Probably this is partly because children in so-called "primitive" cultures are routinely expected to take on certain tasks at certain ages. Unlike their agemates in an industrialized society, they are subject to traditions hundreds of years old that set forth precisely what their roles will be throughout their lives.

In part, too, children in the Western world resent being assigned chores because they do not feel that their help is really needed. In their view, the home (or yard) looks clean and neat enough the way it is, there is no reason to make a bed that will be "unmade" the same evening, and soiled clothes are not harmed by lying on the floor until somebody decides to do a wash.

Caregivers should give children responsibilities in the home and understand that children may lack the skills to carry them out perfectly.

CHILDREN NEED TO FEEL USEFUL

When a child's help is obviously needed—as it often is, for example, in **single-parent families** or if both parents are employed—children tend to be more agreeable about performing regularly assigned chores. Also, they are generally happy to be of assistance in a true emergency. Nine-year-old Danny willingly fetches water from a neighbor's house when the electric pump that supplies water in his own home breaks down. Seven-year-old Gina is pleased to accompany her mother to the basement of their apartment building and shine the flashlight on the family's meter box while her mother replaces a blown fuse.

If chores are to help a child develop a sense of responsibility, and not be a continuing source of parent-child conflict, they must be thoughtfully assigned. The child should feel that he is making a definite—and needed—contribution to the family's welfare. He should be able to take pride in the results of his labor, and his parents should express appreciation for his efforts.

When ten-year-old Ward began complaining steadily about helping to wash and put away the dishes, his parents asked if there was another chore that he would do without so much fussing. He said he would prefer to clean the bathroom regularly—by himself. They gave him this responsibility. He handled it well and was clearly pleased about the good job he did.

ALLOWANCES

An important part of teaching a child to be responsible is helping him learn to manage money. This is best done by giving him a regular weekly **allowance.** At the beginning of the school years his allowance can be limited to the amount of "pocket money" that his parents would normally give him over a week's time—the total sum that he usually gets to spend on treats such as ice cream or inexpensive toys.

By handing him an agreed-upon sum of money once a week, parents not only help him learn to budget his resources and plan ahead, but also lessen the amount of whining they are subjected to every time they pass an ice-cream vendor or toy store with him. Besides, it is more dignified than giving a child a little change at a time, under pressure. Children shouldn't have to beg for their pocket money.

A child needs to be free to spend his allowance as he wants to, including "wasting" it occasionally, if that is his choice. Otherwise, the money is not really his and the allowance does not serve as a teaching tool. Children have to be permitted to learn from their mistakes—without an "I told you so" from their caregivers.

Toward the middle school ages, a child's allowance can be increased to cover some of his regular expenses, such as certain school supplies and transportation fares. This gives a youngster a larger sum of money to budget and also helps him learn to shop thriftily. A third-grader who pays for his own pencils and school notebook paper quickly learns to look around for the best buys.

Most authorities believe that it is not wise to make a child's allowance dependent on good behavior or the satisfactory performance of chores. He benefits from knowing that his money comes to him with no strings attached. It is his because of his membership in the family, not as a reward for obedience.

If parents believe that it is worthwhile to deprive a child of money when he fails to do assigned chores, then they can offer him a specific sum for doing these chores reliably—over and above the amount of his basic allowance. They should make it clear that he receives this additional sum only if he does the work. Natasha's parents, for example, give their nine-year-old daughter a basic weekly allowance

Children's Librarian

"Tell me a story."

"Where can I find a book on ants?"

"What basketball team did Bill Russell play for?"

These are just a few of the hundreds of requests that Anna Jensen receives every day. Anna is the children's librarian at a large public library, and her patrons range from toddlers and their parents looking for picture books to teenagers writing school reports. Anna tries to help each one find the right book or the information. At the same time she shows library users how to use the library resources on their own.

A children's librarian is a specialist; she or he must have both a good knowledge of child development and advanced training in library procedures. Working with the children who come to the library is only part of the job. The librarian must also be able to evaluate and select books, order them, catalogue them, and keep track of their circulation. Most libraries also have collections of records, tape recordings, filmstrips, and other audiovisual aids. The children's librarian must be familiar with these resources as well.

Children's librarians must also arrange programs such as story hours, reading contests, films, displays, and demonstrations. These events require good organizational and publicity skills as well as strict attention to detail. In all the librarian's work, a sense of what children want to know and what appeals to them must be uppermost.

To become a children's librarian, a college degree is essential, and a master's degree in library science is required for some jobs. This advanced work usually takes one year at a graduate school; some programs also involve working at a library while taking courses in library management. Additional courses in child psychology, children's literature, and sociology are also helpful. Of course, some library jobs—clerks, assistants, and others—are open to those with a high school diploma.

Children's librarians can work in many different settings: in small libraries (where they may have other responsibilities as well); in large libraries (where they may have a large staff); in schools; in child-care institutions; in inner-city libraries; or in rural areas (where they reach the children with "bookmobiles").

Considering the amount of education required, children's librarians do not receive high salaries. However, the working conditions are usually quite good. Libraries are usually clean, attractive, and well lighted. Some work on weekends is required, but this is usually compensated for with time off on other days. For those who love both books and children, no job could be more satisfying.

of several dollars. Out of this she pays for her school lunches, paper, pencils, and ball-point pens, and transportation if she takes a bus to a friend's house. There is not much left over for personal treats. But, in addition, Natasha receives another dollar a week if she sets the table for breakfast and the evening meal. She rarely fails to earn that extra dollar.

PROMOTING LEARNING

Mastering formal learning in school is one of children's major tasks during these years. This comes easily to some of them, less easily to others. Parents can be most helpful by supporting the child's efforts to learn, while accepting the fact that he learns at his own pace and has his own individual learning style. Praising

Children perform better in school when caregivers take an interest in their work. However, caregivers should not push children beyond their abilities or do their schoolwork for them.

him when he does succeed and avoiding destructive criticism, pressure, and comparison with other children are essential.

Some children (especially boys) may not start to read until third grade. This can worry both parents and child. David's mother was a third-grade teacher. She had taught many able children who entered her class unable to read. Yet this did little to decrease her concern about having a nonreading eight-year-old of her own.

Fortunately, however, she kept her concern from David. She read him stories regularly before his bedtime, let him keep score when they played card games together—he was good at arithmetic—admired his art work, and encouraged his interest in building model airplanes. She would read the directions for assembling the models when he could not figure out what to do just by looking at the illustrations. One day as they were examining the directions for a new model together, he began to read them aloud, haltingly at first, then with growing assurance.

The importance of helping a child maintain a positive image of his capabilities was stressed earlier. David's mother did this. Also, she saw to it that he was exposed to intellectually challenging activities that could aid formal learning.

PARENTS' ROLE IN SCHOOLWORK

By the middle of this period most children will be having some homework to do—spelling words to memorize, a short reading assignment, a few arithmetic problems, or some written work. From the start, parents need to help their children take their homework (like school) seriously and provide them with a place where they can do it comfortably.

There is nothing wrong with permitting a child to do his homework stretched out on the floor or his bed (provided the area is well lighted) or listening to music. The important thing is how well he does the work. Some children can do very good work while watching a baseball game or movie on television. Individual differences in how a child prefers to learn and work should be respected, within reason.

Nevertheless, there are times when every child needs a cleared table to work on in a quiet, well-lighted spot—and know that he will not be interrupted. If possible, parents should provide each child with such a space all his own. He can put his books and materials there when he returns from school, and do any work there that requires sitting at a table.

Schools often encourage parents to "check" a child's homework after he has completed it, but warn against "doing the work for him." The distinction is not always easy for parents to make.

When Sybil shows her father a story about "My Summer" which she has written as a school assignment, he points out spelling and grammatical errors. Then he suggests a way to rearrange the sentences to increase suspense in the story. The final product gets a mark of "Excellent!" and is read aloud in class. Sybil tells her father this news proudly. He congratulates her, but decides that next time he will just check spelling and grammar.

PARENTS AS MODELS FOR LEARNING

Still, sometimes it makes sense for parents to become deeply involved in a child's homework, even if this leads to his getting a higher grade on it than he might otherwise receive. Providing substantial help can be essential to arousing his interest and making sure that he learns. Teachers can tell what a child is able to do on his own. If his parents are giving him too much assistance, his teacher will know and will inform them of this when she has her next conference with them.

Children's attitudes toward learning are very likely to reflect their parents' views. If parents value success in school, their youngsters usually will, too. A parent need not be a scholar to instill a love of learning in his child. Sam's parents run a neighborhood grocery store. Both of them had to drop out of school and go to work before graduating from high school. Yet, from the time Sam was a toddler he has been exposed to books, good music, and educational television shows. He has picked up his parents' deep interest in learning and their feeling that a good education gives a person crucial advantages in life.

Louella's mother also left school before graduating from high school. She is a moderately successful night club singer. When Louella was three, her mother took time off from her career to get a high school equivalency diploma. She is not against her daughter going into the entertainment field if she wants to, which Louella currently does. But Louella knows how much her mother wishes that she herself had secured a college degree

—"so you have something to fall back on in the hard times." At present Louella is a very good student and plans to go to college.

Of course, parents sometimes put too much stress on the importance of succeeding in school. A child is unable to live up to his parents' high expectations for him and feels worthless. Or he rebels and stops trying. A year ago Arthur's teacher warned his parents that the ten-year-old boy seemed tense and dissatisfied with his academic progress, though he was a solid B student. The teacher thought that Arthur was under too much pressure to make better grades. She suggested that his parents ease up on him academically and encourage his interest in mechanics and drawing.

PLAY REMAINS IMPORTANT

All children need time off every day from the demands of formal learning—time to relax, play with their friends, do nothing, dream. For some youngsters, the time spent away from school is, for reasons that nobody entirely understands, the only time when they actually learn. A skilled teacher of a special class for twelve-year-old "nonlearners" was surprised to find out that one of his students had a job in a bowling alley keeping score for tournaments—a task requiring mathematical skill of a high order.

For those children who do learn in school, play is still an important way to expand their knowledge of the world, as well as just have fun. Group activities occupy much of school children's free time. Team sports become increasingly popular, especially with boys. So do hobbies and a variety of **extracurricular** activities, such as scouting.

Girls and boys continue to need plenty of active play, as well as time for quieter pursuits. Children who are not drawn to team sports (or are not good at them) can be helped to enjoy

Learning to play and work cooperatively toward goals is an important part of development during the school-age years. Group activities should be available in which children can participate no matter what their skills.

activities such as bicycling, skating, gymnastics, jogging, or dance.

Board games, such as checkers, and numerous card games are favorites with children this age. Though some are mostly a matter of luck, others require considerable skill and contribute importantly to cognitive growth. Alma is a fifth-grader who for the time being is more interested in her social life than in schoolwork. But she spends a lot of time playing chess and backgammon with her friends—and is quite good at both games. Alma is obviously being stimulated mentally, even though she is not working hard in school at the moment.

Toy models, as we have seen, also foster cognitive development. So do jigsaw puzzles and many hobbies, ranging from stamp and coin collecting to sewing and cooking. A sixth-grade boy who has always enjoyed helping his parents cook thinks that this activity aroused his interest in science—he says that following a recipe for custard is like doing a chemistry experiment. Cooking also taught him a great deal about geography, since his parents prepare dishes from a variety of cultures around the world.

TEACHING SOCIAL BEHAVIOR

School children know the importance of sharing and waiting their turn. Most of the time they are able to do this. Usually they can also settle their differences verbally, without resorting to physical force. However, most of them need help at times with recognizing how their behavior affects other children—or adults.

Louise is inclined to be bossy. Her parents are trying to help her become more aware of her bossiness and understand that other children don't like it. Timmy annoys his classmates by bragging about his successes and being a bad loser. When he fails at something, he makes excuses instead of accepting the defeat gracefully. Abby's table manners are so bad that the parents of her friends object to the seven-year-old girl's being invited over for a meal in their homes. Even the children themselves find Abby's eating habits offensive.

It is up to parents to help their children "see themselves as others see them." This needs to be done tactfully, of course, so as not to harm a

"Take Me Out To The Ball Game..."

Many activities and games that children engage in today are timeless ones. In European cities during medieval times, children played with tops, horseshoes, and marbles just as they do today.

They tried their luck on stilts and enjoyed swimming, ice skating (with wooden blades), and early forms of football and tennis. In medieval days, a ball game was played in which players wore a covering on the hand in order to hit a ball over a net. The basic game was much the same as the tennis we know today.

Children played with dolls of baked clay or wood, and people of all ages played chess, checkers, and dice.

While scientific technology has influenced the production of modern games and toys, and new products are put on the market every year, the traditional favorites are not forgotten. Children still play marbles, spin tops, and throw horseshoes. Stilt-walking is not as popular as it used to be, but modern children practice balancing in other ways: with skate-boards, balance beams, and bicycles.

Some of the old games have acquired a new look. Today's young tennis players have a variety of rackets to choose from: large and small, wooden frames and metal frames, endorsed by one tennis star or another.

Dolls come in all shapes, sizes, and professions, and in both sexes. In earlier days, most dolls were either mama-dolls or baby-dolls, but today's dolls may be cowboys or cowgirls, astronauts, nurses, or television characters. And although in the past doll play was mostly done by girls, today both boys and girls play with dolls, as well as with puppets and stuffed animals.

Checkers, chess, and other board games have also kept their popularity. Children still enjoy planning moves in advance and learning strategies that will defeat their opponents.

Above all, in every period, the magic of make-believe has been a central ingredient in children's play. Medieval children pretended to be queens and kings; modern children pretend to be space explorers. But the fascination of leaving the everyday world for some imaginary realm is still the same.

Many toys and games played in the past are still favorites today. The setting or the equipment may change, but the need to have fun is the same.

OF INTEREST

child's self-image. However, unless it is done, youngsters such as Louise, Timmy, and Abby will be seriously handicapped in getting along with their peers and with adults.

GUIDANCE AND DISCIPLINE

During the school years, rules obviously need to be changed frequently, as a child grows and becomes increasingly competent. A twelve-year-old is permitted a great deal more freedom than a child of six or ten. Parents must constantly strike a balance between letting their youngster be as independent as he is able to be and protecting him adequately.

Typically, a healthy, happy school child seems to be almost continually "pulling at the bit"—pressing his parents to grant him more independence. At the same time, however, children tend to abide by the limitations set on their behavior with surprisingly good grace. Deep down they seem to know that such limitations are a sign of parental love. Also, at times they are grateful to have a parental prohibition to use as an excuse for not undertaking activities that they recognize are not in their best interests.

BEING CLEAR ABOUT THE RULES

To gain children's cooperation during these years, parents have to be sure that all rules are clearly stated. School-age children are quick to detect and make the most of loopholes. Telling Willard that he has to be home "before dark" can lead to a lot of useless arguing. It is far better to set a specific hour when he is expected to be in the house. Even if Willard, at seven, does not have a watch and is not yet able to tell time, he is mature enough to find out what time it is from a friend, a friend's parent, a local storekeeper, or a passing police officer.

Sometimes parents fail to state rules clearly because they are unsure in their own minds what they really want. Liza's parents have told her repeatedly that she is never to go home with a schoolmate whose parents they have not met. Yet Liza's mother is eager for her daughter to be a social success. She makes exceptions to this rule if the schoolmate in question has prominent parents or lives in a fashionable area. Liza, at eleven, has figured this out. She does not always tell her mother the truth about where she is going or whom she is with.

Mark has been warned by his father against fighting. However, he senses that his father really admires the boys in Mark's second-grade class who have a reputation for toughness. Mark is confused by this. Sometimes he tries to do as his father tells him to. At other times he breaks all the rules in an effort to be the boy he senses his father secretly wants him to be.

STANDING FIRM

Children who know that their parents always enforce the rules firmly are less likely to try to talk their caregivers into making an exception "just this one time," or to go behind their backs. When they do break a rule, they are not seriously resentful of the scolding or deprivation of privileges that inevitably follows. They are aware that they "had it coming."

Parental consistency and firmness of this sort not only encourages good behavior, but also contributes to their feelings that the world is an orderly place in which they will generally encounter fair treatment. This adds to their optimism about their future.

· SUMMARY ·

- School children are easy to reason with, are on their own much of the time, and do not usually rebel against authority.
- Caregivers should help each child value his or her own worth and capabilities.
- Assigning chores helps children develop a sense of responsibility.
- Managing a weekly allowance teaches a child to budget and plan ahead.
- Children's attitudes toward learning often reflect their parents' views.
- Play is still important for learning, socialization, and fun.
- Parents can help children realize how their behavior affects others.
- Guidance and discipline should strike a balance between letting children be independent and protecting them.
- Rules for school children should be clearly stated and firmly enforced.

TERMS TO KNOW

allowance
extracurricular
peers
single-parent families

1. _____ activities, or those outside of the regular classroom, are popular with this age group.
2. Children in _____ may be more willing to do chores because they feel their help is really needed.
3. A child's _____ lets him handle his own pocket money.
4. School-age children attach a great deal of importance to the opinions of their _____.

CHECK YOUR UNDERSTANDING

1. Why do parents continue to be an important influence on the school-age child despite the increasing importance of peers?
2. What are two reasons for allowing the school-age child to get from place to place as independently as possible?
3. How does the child benefit by being assigned household chores?
4. Explain what is necessary for chores to be a positive force in the child's development rather than a source of parent-child conflict.
5. What does a child learn from being given an allowance for regular expenses and pocket money?
6. How can parents promote learning in the school-age child?
7. How can parents' overly high expectations negatively affect learning?
8. Why is it important that rules for the school-age child be clearly stated?
9. Why should parents be consistent in enforcing rules?

· UNIT SIX ·

ADOLESCENT
(AGES 12 & UP)

21

PHYSICAL DEVELOPMENT

22

COGNITIVE DEVELOPMENT

Some of the most dramatic physical changes since the first year occur in adolescence. It is a time of self-discovery as girls become women and boys become men.

Adolescence brings new skills in logic and abstract reasoning. The ability to weigh possibilities and develop moral principles helps teens make responsible choices.

23
SOCIAL/EMOTIONAL DEVELOPMENT

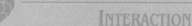

24
INTERACTION

Seeking an identity and a place in society, adolescents may seem self-preoccupied. They conform to peer pressure in many ways, yet strive for individuality.

The adolescent stands—sometimes tentatively, sometimes confidently—on the brink of maturity. With the support of family, friends, and others, teens learn to meet new challenges.

·21·

PHYSICAL DEVELOPMENT
OF THE ADOLESCENT

"Want to look in here, Debbie?" asked Mrs. McNeil as she and her daughter walked by a clothing store.

Debbie shook her head. "I really don't need any clothes, Mom."

"I just thought you might be wanting something a little special," said Mrs. McNeil. "Isn't your freshman class dance coming up soon?"

"Yeah, but I won't be going."

"What makes you say that? Don't you want to go?"

"Sure I do. But who'd want to go with me?"

"Sounds like you're pretty worried about this," Mrs. McNeil said. "But I don't see any reason you should be. You seem to have made a lot of friends in your classes and in the science club. Why don't you think anyone would want to go to the dance with you?"

"Oh, Mom. Isn't it obvious? I'm six inches taller than any of the boys in my class. I feel like some kind of freak!"

"Well, it's true you've had a growth spurt lately," Mrs. McNeil said. "But that doesn't make you a freak. It's just a normal part of growing up. It'll take the boys a few years to catch up, that's all."

"And what am I supposed to do in the meantime?" Debbie asked. "No boy I know would want to be seen at the dance with me!"

"In the first place," her mother said firmly, "you're really quite attractive—especially when you're relaxed and feeling confident about yourself. And in the second place, I'd bet those boys are more worried about their own height than they are about yours. A lot of them would probably really like to ask someone, but they're embarrassed about being short—just as you're embarrassed about being tall."

"Do you really think so?" asked Debbie.

"I'm sure of it. So if there's someone in particular you'd like to go to the dance with, why don't you ask him yourself? You might be pleasantly surprised!"

•

Do you think Mrs. McNeil is right when she says that many of the boys in Debbie's class feel embarrassed about their height?

•

How can feeling self-confident affect the impression you make on others?

The stage of development called **adolescence** can be defined simply as the stage between childhood and adulthood. In fact, the word "adolescent" means "becoming an adult."

In the physical sense, adolescence means that the body becomes capable of reproduction. A boy becomes a man in that his body can produce **sperm,** which can fertilize an **ovum** to produce a new life. A girl becomes a woman in that her body can produce ova capable of **fertilization** by male sperm. In other words, she is physically able to become pregnant.

Social and emotional maturity do not come automatically with sexual maturity in our society. Teenagers are normally expected to delay marriage and parenthood until they have completed their schooling and become emotionally mature and economically responsible. Because of their physical maturity, some teenagers may endure this period of delay with impatience and discomfort. Others may be glad that they don't have to take on the responsibilities of adulthood too soon.

In societies other than ours, there may be no separate period of adolescence as we know it. In many tribal societies, for instance, when young people are physically developed, they marry and take on adult roles immediately—except perhaps for a brief ceremony to mark their passage from childhood to adulthood.

PUBERTY

When girls and boys have developed to the point where they can reproduce, they are said to have reached **puberty.** The average girl reaches puberty one to two years earlier than the average boy. Of course, as in all stages of human development, some people develop earlier and some later than the average. Late or early development is within the range of the normal. However, teenagers especially tend to be worried about their own development, since

In traditional Cheyenne society, the onset of puberty was an important occasion for a girl—and for her family. The girl was now entering the stage when she would be ready to bear children, adding to the tribe's numerical strength and therefore its power. When a girl had her first menstrual period, practically the first thing she did was to tell her mother —who, in turn, told her father. The girl's father proclaimed the event from his lodge door and, if he had wealth, gave away a horse to celebrate the occasion.

The girl herself was administered to by older women of the tribe. First she unbraided her hair and bathed. Then the women painted her entire body red. She donned a loose robe, and a coal from the community's main fire was placed in front of her. Grass, juniper needles, and white sage were sprinkled on the coal to make a kind of incense. The girl stood over the coal and held her robe so that the fragrant smoke passed around her body.

Afterward, the girl went with her grandmother to stay for four days in a small lodge. There she would be instructed in the things she needed to know in order to take on the role of an adult woman.

they are sensitive to what others think of them and feel uneasy about being "different" from the rest of their **peers.**

Puberty for girls is marked by a biological event called **menstruation.** As we saw in the unit on prenatal development, each month a woman's body releases an ovum, and each month the lining of the **uterus** builds up a rich supply of blood vessels that will nourish a fetus if conception takes place. If conception does not occur, the uterus sheds its lining of blood. The blood comes out of the **vagina** over a period of several days. This is menstruation. After the menstrual period is over, the uterus once again acquires a fresh lining to prepare for possible conception.

A girl's first period—the beginning of menstruation—is called the **menarche.** Some girls take the menarche in stride, especially if they have been talked to beforehand about what to expect. Other girls who have not been prepared may be frightened or puzzled. It is important for a girl approaching puberty to understand that menstrual bleeding is a natural process, not at all related to the kind of bleeding that comes from a cut or wound. The menarche is simply a sign that the girl is now, physically at least, a woman.

Puberty in a boy is indicated by the ability to ejaculate, or eject, semen from the penis. A boy's first **ejaculation,** like a girl's menarche, signals the physical ability to produce children. The first ejaculation may occur while the boy is sleeping. This is called a nocturnal emission.

Puberty in both boys and girls is accompanied by other physical changes as well, as we shall see in the next section.

OTHER BODY CHANGES AND GROWTH

Most of the dramatic physical changes associated with adolescence take place around the

The biological change from girl to woman occurs at puberty. Societies have different rites of passage to mark this developmental stage. These Masai girls are adorned for a puberty festival.

"Self-concept" means the way we see ourselves or the way we think others see us. Among other things, our physical appearance generally affects our self-concept—and more so during adolescence than at any other time. This is why differences in individual growth rates are felt to be so important, even though they will eventually become less noticeable and then disappear altogether by age nineteen or twenty.

Suppose two boys who are best friends at age eleven mature at greatly different rates. One boy, by age fourteen, already has had his growth spurt and is shaving. He also shows interest in girls—and they are interested in him, too, since he is one of the few boys in their class whose physical maturation has matched that of most of the girls. In sports, his size and strength is admired by his peers.

The second boy matures much later than his friend. Not until his junior year of high school does he "shoot up" to over six feet, an awkward height for him at this point. But later, when he fills out, this late maturer will be taller and bigger than his early-maturing friend. But will he have the same confident self-concept his friend developed at age fourteen?

Studies have been done charting personality differences among adults who were early and late maturers as adolescents. The results tend to be what one might predict. Early maturers are generally confident and socially at ease with themselves. Late maturers, by contrast, are less sure of themselves, but they are often high achievers.

What other general personality differences would you predict between early- and late-maturing adolescents? Are such differences inevitable?

What other factors besides physical appearance could affect a teenager's self-concept?

---

time of puberty. This is the time of the familiar adolescent growth spurt. Legs and arms grow longer, hands and feet bigger. Then the body trunk grows larger in breadth, followed by an increase in trunk length, making the adolescent taller.

A girl develops breasts, and her pelvis and hips widen. A boy's **penis** and **testes** grow larger and his shoulders broaden. Both girls and boys tend to develop fat deposits under the skin near the time of puberty. In girls this is much more noticeable, especially around the hips. This fat is like a protective cushioning of the internal reproductive organs.

Internally, the heart nearly doubles in weight during the adolescent years. Lung capacity increases rapidly, as does stomach capacity. A normal adolescent appetite is huge during this growth spurt. Not only is stomach capacity greater, but more nourishment is obviously needed to support the rapid body growth taking place in general.

Along with general body growth, there are such changes as the growth of hair in the pubic region near the sexual organs and also under the arms. Hair later grows on the legs of both boys and girls, and boys begin to see signs of a mustache and beard. Some girls, too, have a light growth of hair on the upper lip.

Both girls' and boys' voices become lower, boys' voices much lower. This is because the larynx, or voice box, enlarges. Some boys (and some girls, too) have a little trouble at first controlling their deeper voices. Their voices may "break"—deep one moment, high-pitched the next.

All of these activities are triggered by glands, in particular the pituitary gland located at the base of the brain. One of the functions of this gland is to regulate growth. It does that by sending chemical substances called **hormones** into the blood stream. These act as chemical "messengers."

A hormone called the gonadotropic hormone is sent out by the pituitary gland before puberty. It sets the whole process in motion. Other glands are stimulated. More hormones are sent through the bloodstream. These include sex hormones like **estrogen,** which stimulates the growth of female sex characteristics, and **androgen,** which promotes male characteristics.

Hormone-producing glands are sometimes called ductless glands. They send substances directly into the bloodstream, rather than

An adolescent's physical growth rate often determines whether or not he will be on the football team in high school.

through a duct or tube. But there are glands that do operate through ducts. Among them are the sweat glands and the sebaceous glands in the deep part of the skin.

These glands are also stimulated during

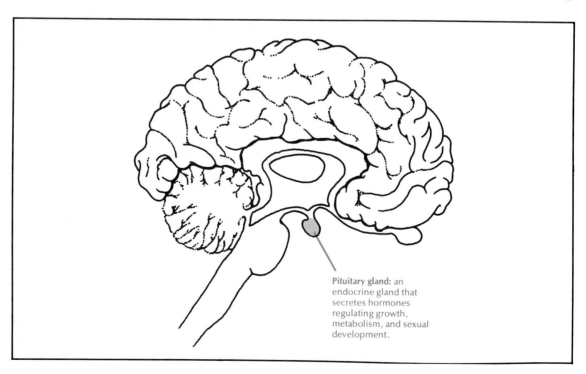

Pituitary gland: an endocrine gland that secretes hormones regulating growth, metabolism, and sexual development.

A lot of teenagers are having babies, and a lot are having them early. That observation is backed up by statistics which show that every year more than a half-million teenage girls get pregnant and carry their babies to term.

Close to a third of these teenage mothers are very young teens, fourteen or younger. One reason is that the menarche, or the first menstrual period, has on the average been occurring earlier and earlier over the years in both Europe and North America. No one is quite sure why. Improved nutrition is one possible cause. But, whatever the causes, girls today menstruate an average of four and a half years earlier than they did two centuries ago. In the play *Romeo and Juliet*, written by William Shakespeare in the sixteenth-century, Juliet was fourteen years old when she fell in love with Romeo. But although she was old enough to fall in love, she was probably not physically developed enough to be a mother. A twentieth-century "Juliet," on the other hand, would more than likely be physically mature at fourteen.

Yet, though today's young teenage girls may be able to conceive a baby, they could have trouble delivering. Often a young girl's pelvis, even a year after her menarche, is still not sufficiently developed to enable her to bear a child. A sizable percentage of babies born to teenagers are delivered by means of a Caesarean operation. The percentage of birth defects is also higher among children born to teenage mothers.

In addition to physical problems connected with teenage pregnancy, there are emotional problems. Incidents of child abuse, for instance, occur much more frequently in families where the parents are teenagers. This is a tragedy, because usually the reason is simply that the teenagers aren't yet emotionally ready for parenthood. Given a few more years, they probably would not be abusing parents.

---

adolescence. The result can be heavy perspiration and pimples. These conditions are natural, if miserable, facts of life for many adolescents. Both conditions, however, are temporary.

Overall, early adolescence is clearly an awkward time—made socially more awkward by individual differences in the rate of physical change.

Puberty itself is a climactic event in a whole period of change, frequently labeled the pubescent period. This period, during which the major growth spurts and sex-related changes occur, lasts perhaps two to three years. But for some individuals it is longer, for others shorter.

The ages during which the pubescent period occurs also differ—and they can differ considerably. On the average, **pubescence** takes place between ages ten and thirteen for girls and between ages twelve and fifteen for boys. But a great many individual variations have been put together to get those averages.

Socially, of course, it is not the "average" which is most noticeable, but the variations. In a typical group of fourteen-year-olds, there will be girls who have not had their first period or even shown signs of a growth spurt. Some may be nearly out of high school before anything happens.

The same is true of the boys. Some fourteen-year-old boys have developed early and already look like high school seniors.

Others may actually be high school seniors before they are at the same stage of development. Eventually, everybody catches up. The person who is left out of high school basketball because he or she is too small could well become a star athlete in college.

Although adolescence has a definite starting point—puberty—its end point is less certain. Some persons are still growing—in height, for example—after age twenty-one. Others have about completed their growth, in every respect, by age eighteen or younger.

"FUEL" FOR GROWING BODIES

The need for food during adolescence is tremendous. An average thirteen-year-old girl may need as much as 2,400 calories a day—whereas at twenty-six the average woman only needs 2,100 calories or less. The average sixteen-year-old boy may need 3,000 calories a day, compared with 2,700 a day for the average man. Physically active adolescents and adults need even higher calorie intakes.

The reason adolescents need to eat more is obvious enough: Their bodies are growing. Teenagers at the peak of their growth spurt might gain twenty pounds in one year without becoming at all overweight (depending, of course, on individual body build).

Nutrition is important to both males and females at all stages of development. But during adolescence girls may need extra iron, since the body loses iron during menstruation. Lack of iron can cause a disease called **anemia,** which is common among teenage girls.

Some teenagers may tend to overeat. Great as the adolescent need for food may be, it can be exceeded, especially by a person who doesn't get much physical exercise.

Some teenagers—usually girls abnormally concerned about being overweight—go to the opposite extreme and undereat. This can go so far as to become a serious health problem.

Friends who may have been the same size during the school years can develop very differently during adolescence. Growth occurs unevenly and can continue past the age of twenty-one.

There are teens, for example, who literally starve themselves to death or at least to the point of serious illness. The medical term for such self-starvation is **anorexia,** and it is more common than many people realize. It is, in large part, a psychological problem. Even though their friends tell them they look like walking skeletons, persons suffering from anorexia think they look fine.

But this is an extreme problem. Most people know well enough when they aren't eating enough or when they are eating too much. Especially during adolescence, if their eating habits are harmful, their bodies are going to let them know, in one way or another—even if through just a general lack of energy.

HYGIENE AND HEALTH CARE

Generally, people are concerned about the impression they make on others. That concern often begins in adolescence. Partly it is a matter of style, such as dress style or hair style. Partly it is a matter of basic personal hygiene—for example, more frequent showers or baths on account of the increased perspiration that comes with adolescence.

Some problems of personal appearance, such as **acne,** have to be lived with until they disappear. Acne, a pimply inflammation of the skin of the face, and sometimes the back and chest, is related to the hormones being secreted during adolescence. There is little that can be done about acne, except to wash thoroughly—although some cases can be successfully treated by a doctor. Pimples should not be squeezed. The infection can spread and even cause permanent scarring.

Dental care continues to be important in the adolescent years. During this time the second and third set of molars erupt. (The first came around age six.)

Adolescents require the right kinds of food for good growth and normal development. Snacks should be nutritious and not consist of "empty calories" which provide few nutrients.

School Lunch Program Worker

LUNCH MENU
Tomato-rice soup and crackers
Grilled cheese sandwiches
Carrot sticks
Milk
Choice of apple, pear, or banana

Sonia Tanner assembled the lunch trays quickly and efficiently. "Just five minutes until the bell rings," she called to her co-workers. "And I know that this is a favorite lunch, so there'll be lots of impatient kids here very soon." And sure enough, when the bell rang, the lines formed quickly. Chatting eagerly, the students moved rapidly through the cafeteria to the lunch tables to enjoy their meal with their friends.

Lunchtime is an important break in the school day, for both social and nutritional reasons. For many children, it is their only well-planned meal of the day.

School lunch program workers—dietitians and cafeteria workers—must work together to make the meals attractive, well-balanced, and satisfying to the children.

Generally, the director of the program is a home economics teacher or a qualified dietitian. This job requires a good knowledge of foods and nutrition, costs, and the ability to organize a kitchen efficiently. Health and safety standards must also be strictly observed. It is important, too, to be able to adjust menus to children's tastes.

Although salaries are not high for cafeteria workers, the job offers pleasant working conditions. Many cafeteria workers are mothers who want to work part-time. This job offers them the opportunity to work only when their children are in school, and to share their vacations.

For all the changes taking place, adolescence is usually a stage of good physical health and vitality. However, it is possible to push a normally healthy body beyond its level of endurance.

Overfatigue is common among adolescents. The strain of schoolwork, late hours, social and emotional stress—all of these contribute. The answer, of course, is more sleep. Teenagers must schedule themselves so they are able to get the sleep they need.

ACCIDENTS AND ILLNESS

Since adolescents take part in a wider variety of activities than children do, the kinds of accidents they might have are different. Teenagers are more prone to sports and driving accidents, for example. Boys are somewhat more likely to have injuries due to fights. This is simply because boys tend to fight more than girls, since physical fighting is generally considered inappropriate behavior for girls in our culture.

Teenagers are no longer as susceptible to many of the contagious diseases common in childhood. Stomach upsets continue to be fairly common for both sexes, slightly more common among girls.

Some adolescent girls experience discomfort when they first start to menstruate. They may

Putting in late hours to finish schoolwork is a common cause of overfatigue among teenagers.

Active teenagers are susceptible to sports injuries and other types of accidents. Staying in shape, warming up before exercise, and avoiding overexertion can help prevent injuries.

have painful cramps in the pelvic area. Painful menstruation is called **dysmenorrhea.** It can often be relieved with aspirin or a heating pad or hot-water bottle. If the menstrual flow is heavy, it often helps to lie down with the lower part of the body raised, as on a pillow. Very severe dysmenorrhea may require a visit to the doctor.

Orthodontist

"Before" and "After"—Dr. Abingdon showed the two photographs to Gabriele, who had been his patient for two years. "How do you like the way you look now?"

Gabriele beamed when she saw the recent photograph, taken the day after her braces were removed. And she looked at the old photograph with disbelief. "Did I really look like that?" she exclaimed.

"You sure did," Dr. Abingdon said, "but remember that we weren't just trying to make you pretty with all that work. We wanted to keep your teeth and gums healthy for a long time."

More and more children (and adults, too) are undergoing orthodontia, the process of straightening teeth or adjusting poor bite or other problems through the use of wires, braces, or other appliances. As Dr. Abingdon pointed out, it is not just a cosmetic process, but an important preventive dental health measure.

Orthodontists must spend several years as students before they can practice this dental speciality. Most students have at least a bachelor's degree when they enter dental school. After four years of dental school, they earn either a D.D.S. (Doctor of Dental Surgery) degree or a D.D.M. (Doctor of Dental Medicine) degree. Orthodontists need from two to four years of additional training.

The work is not easy; it requires a great deal of patience, physical stamina (the dentist often stands up all day), and tact. It is important for an orthodontist to be able to motivate young patients to follow the prescribed routines carefully for long periods of time, and so a good knowledge of child development is essential.

Despite the hard work and the demands of the profession, it is growing. For one reason, orthodontists earn very good incomes, either from private patients or as staff members of health-care institutions. Another attraction is the high prestige of the profession and the chance it offers to make dramatic changes in an individual's appearance and personality. Orthodontists frequently see shy and withdrawn children blossom as a result of their work; this is surely a fitting reward for their years of study.

Many women do experience some discomfort during menstruation. Or they may feel depressed or nervous a few days before the period begins. This is called premenstrual tension. It can be accompanied by a "bloated" feeling due to the retention of excess water in the body's cells. This is only temporary, however. Normally a girl need not restrict her activities while menstruating. In fact, exercise can even relieve cramps because it promotes circulation throughout the body.

Sometimes at the beginning, menstruation is irregular. After the first period, there may be none for several months. Absence of menstruation is called **amenorrhea.** In most cases the body will regulate itself in time and there is no need for medical treatment. But if an adolescent is very worried about amenorrhea, she should consult a doctor. It may be that the amenorrhea is caused by an inadequate diet or some other easily corrected problem.

If a girl who has reached puberty needs to see a doctor, she may either see her pediatrician or a **gynecologist,** a doctor who specializes in women's health problems. However, most teenage girls who do not have major problems need not go for regular gynecological checkups until later—usually at the time of marriage or in the early twenties.

Adolescents sometimes face problems they can't seem to handle on their own. There are many community groups who can recommend the right professionals who are specially trained to help teenagers.

TOBACCO, ALCOHOL, AND DRUG USE

Adolescence is a beginning stage for many of the patterns of adult life. Habits begun in the teen years frequently persist for years afterward—and some of these habits are plainly harmful to the health.

One such habit is smoking. Smoking is directly related to cancer—not only lung cancer, but cancer of the mouth and throat. It is directly related as well to the lung disease emphysema and to heart disease. Actually, the nicotine in tobacco is a powerful drug. It has been shown to be physically addictive for most smokers.

Any drug taken into the body in large amounts over a long period of time can be physically dangerous. This is as true of tobacco and marijuana smoke as of alcohol or of cocaine or heroin.

In some cases, the dangers are obvious and the effects immediate. A heroin overdose kills quickly. If barbiturates or sleeping pills are taken along with alcohol, the user goes into a coma. Without quick medical help, convulsions and death may follow shortly. The same thing might happen with PCP, known by the slang term "angel dust."

Not all the physical dangers of drug abuse are that obvious or that dramatic. In most cases, they take time to develop—as in the case of alcoholism, a long-term disease.

Yet many teenagers do drink a lot of alcohol. And many are starting early. There are numerous alcoholics today, still in their teens, who experience blackouts and already show signs of liver damage. These are symptoms of advanced alcoholism appearing in teenagers.

With the prevalence, in general, of various kinds of drug abuse today, a drug emergency of some kind is always a possibility. For this reason, many communities have local drug hotline numbers and other sources of help to refer to in an emergency.

· SUMMARY ·

- At puberty, the body becomes capable of reproduction. In girls, this is marked by the onset of menstruation; in boys, by the ability to ejaculate.
- Other physical changes accompany puberty. They are triggered by hormones.
- Girls usually reach puberty before boys.
- Teenagers need to eat a variety of nutritious foods because of their rapid physical growth.
- Adolescents are susceptible to different types of accidents and illnesses than children.
- Teenagers may damage their health by experimenting with tobacco, alcohol, and drugs.

TERMS TO KNOW

adolescence
amenorrhea
androgen
anemia
anorexia
dysmenorrhea

ejaculation
estrogen
gynecologist
hormones
menarche
puberty

1. The onset of _____ is marked by a girl's first menstruation, called _____, and by a boy's first _____.
2. Some teenagers undereat to the point of serious illness, or _____.
3. A(n) _____ specializes in women's health problems, such as _____ (absence of menstruation) and _____ (painful menstruation).
4. _____ is the stage between childhood and adulthood.
5. Chemical substances called _____ include _____, which promotes female characteristics, and _____, which promotes male characteristics.
6. _____, caused by lack of iron, is common among teenage girls.

CHECK YOUR UNDERSTANDING

1. What does adolescence mean in the physical sense?
2. What marks puberty for a girl? For a boy?
3. How does the pituitary gland regulate growth?
4. At about what age does pubescence take place for girls and boys?
5. Why do adolescents need more calories per day than adults?
6. Why do adolescent girls need extra iron? What may result from a lack of iron?
7. What can be done about acne?
8. What factors contribute to overfatigue among adolescents?
9. What kinds of accidents are teenagers more likely to have than are children?
10. What are the harmful effects of smoking?

· 22 ·
COGNITIVE DEVELOPMENT
OF THE ADOLESCENT

Phil had just told his father he didn't want to go to college—that he wanted instead to become an apprentice boat-builder in a little town on the coast of Maine.

"Why?" was Phil's father's first reaction. "You're intelligent. You get top grades. It's true we're not rich, but somehow I think we can manage your tuition. With your grades you might even get a scholarship . . . So why?"

"I like working with my hands, Dad. I always have. You know that. And last summer in Maine I fell in love with boats. Building wooden boats by hand the way they used to—well, I just know that's what I want to do."

"I agree it's important to choose a career you enjoy. But let me ask you this: Are you giving yourself enough scope? Think about it a minute. People get interested in all kinds of things, hobbies or whatever. But this is full-time, Phil. And you've got a really good mind. A good mind needs scope, range to operate. Is building boats in a small town in Maine going to give you what you need?"

"I don't think you understand, Dad. There's a lot of intelligence needed to be a good boat-builder, or to be a good craftsman of any kind. And it's a business, too, you know. There are people willing to pay money for hand-crafted boats built to order. No, I don't agree. I think there's a lot of scope for whatever mental abilities I've got."

"Well, you've obviously thought it through. It's not what I would choose for you, but then I'm not you. Can we talk it over some more? I still don't feel good about it, but you've got my support—whatever you decide."

•

What are the merits of the case Phil made for his course of action? What are the merits of his father's case?

•

With which point of view do you agree and why?

Sixteen-year-old Leroy Jackson works after school at his aunt and uncle's service station. He pumps gas and helps service the cars. Leroy, however, looks beyond the cars he helps service. In his mind's eye, he sees different kinds of cars—cars which are powered by electricity and simpler to service and repair. He imagines how these cars will look and what new kinds of service stations they will need.

Leroy also thinks about his personal future. He asks himself different versions of certain basic questions: Who am I? What does all this mean? What's going to happen? What do I want to happen?

From the standpoint of Jean Piaget's stages of cognitive development, Leroy is in the final stage. This is the stage of **formal operations.**

By formal operations, Piaget means reasoning characterized by theoretical or abstract thought.

Leroy, when he was younger, thought at the level of **concrete operations.** He was helping out at the service station at age ten. He was perfectly capable then of dealing mentally with concrete problems. He knew how, for instance, to run a car through the necessary tests to detect an engine problem. He was mentally at home in the real world of here and now.

But as an adolescent, he thinks beyond that. He thinks not only in terms of realities, but in terms of possibilities as well.

HIGH-LEVEL THINKING PROCESSES

Adolescents and adults think most of the time at the level of concrete operations. Their think-

Adolescents often think about who they are and where they're going in life. They are capable of abstract or theoretical thought during this stage. They can think of possibilities as well as realities. Piaget calls this the stage of formal operations.

ing is logical, but it is applied to what they can see and work with right away.

The brakes on Phil's bicycle don't work, so he tries to figure out what is wrong with them, how he can fix them, and how else he can travel if they can't be fixed. He is dealing with things that are happening now. In his mind Phil is carrying out concrete operations, thinking about a real situation that presents itself at the moment: "What is wrong with my bike?" "What can I do about it?" "How do I get to school?" In daily life, most people answer such questions—"What?" "Where?" "When?" and "How?"—through the process of concrete operations.

Most adolescents and adults are capable of thinking at an even higher level, the level of formal operations. They can think, as Leroy did, about the future. They can go beyond the actual and think of possibilities. They can consider several ideas and concepts at once to reason about relationships between things; this way they arrive at a new awareness about issues, people, and objects in their lives. Piaget calls this **propositional thinking.**

When Phil's brakes stop working he considers fixing them immediately, but then reasons to himself: "If I don't get to school on time, I will miss my chemistry class and be unprepared for the exam next week; so I'll take the bus to school now and fix the bike later." Propositional thought enables Phil to weigh the possibilities of the situation and come to a logical conclusion. Through his actions he gives himself a better chance of doing well in his chemistry course.

Propositional thought can begin at about age eleven or twelve and develop until about age fifteen, when it becomes like an adult's. But not everyone's thought develops that far. According to Piaget, people can move to the next highest stage only if they are mature enough and have the intelligence to do so.

At the higher levels of propositional thought, a person makes logical connections

Gaining practical experience in an area which interests them is one way teens can assess their talents realistically. They may help out at home, or take part-time jobs after school, on weekends, or during the summer vacation.

between the propositions themselves. For example, because Joan never has to study hard for exams, she thinks she is very smart. (This is the first proposition Joan makes.) One day she takes an exam and fails. Joan is very upset about this and thinks to herself: "I failed an exam; I'm getting stupid." (This is Joan's second proposition.) Joan's two propositions are inconsistent with each other. After she calms down, Joan reasons to herself: "People don't get stupid all of a sudden. There is something about this subject that is giving me trouble. I'll have to talk to my teacher to see if I can figure out what went wrong and what to do about it." Joan sees that her two propositions don't agree

High school can be very competitive. Good work environments help students concentrate on their studies. Work areas should be in a quiet place away from distraction. A desk or table, a comfortable chair, and good lighting are all essential. Sometimes students cannot find a good work place at home. Most libraries have quiet rooms which are good for studying.

and goes on from there to construct a new idea to deal with the problem of her failure.

Someone who has reached the level of formal operations is obviously able to grasp more complex ideas. A high school student is able, for example, to understand some of the problems of international relations—in which different social and political systems interact in multiple ways.

In the use of language, abstract words and concepts become understandable at the formal operational stage. Terms like "justice" or "morality" or "value judgments" can be discussed fully with real understanding. So can feelings. What is guilt, for example? What is love? How are your feelings different from mine? These kinds of abstract questions have meaning at this stage.

New creative possibilities open up. At the level of concrete operations, someone may be able to write a science fiction story—but very likely the emphasis will be limited to unusual futuristic machines. At the formal operational level, a science fiction writer is truly able to think in terms of entire imaginary worlds and to project ideas across time and space. In every sense, it is a level of new and limitless possibilities.

HIGH-LEVEL MORAL THINKING

At Piaget's highest stage, the stage of formal operations, the way people think about moral issues has developed to its fullest. (Not everyone attains this level, but those who do have had to grow through Piaget's stages in a step-by-step process.)

At the highest level, behavior is more than simply "good" or "bad," as it is at the concrete operations stage. Rules and laws are questioned before being accepted. The adolescent at the formal operations stage insists upon fairness and thinks it is all right to break an unjust rule. When a person judges someone who has broken the rules, he or she considers that person's age, past behavior, and what the person meant to do.

Suppose Tom finds out that his co-worker Mark lied about his age in order to get his job. At the concrete operational stage, Tom might decide without hesitation that since lying is wrong, Mark should be punished. But at the stage of formal operations, Tom weighs many factors before coming to a decision. He believes that in getting a job to help support his family, Mark thought he was doing the right thing. Tom also knows that lying is unusual behavior for Mark. On the other hand, Tom still feels that lying is wrong. Whether or not Tom decides to keep Mark's secret, his weighing of the situation is characteristic of the formal operations level.

Like Piaget, Lawrence Kohlberg believes that moral concepts develop in step-by-step stages that are the same for all people. According to Kohlberg, older children are at a higher level than younger children, but not everybody achieves a high enough level of moral reasoning to get to the final stage.

Kohlberg charts three major stages of moral development. At the lowest, the preconventional stage, the young child (or adolescent or adult who has not developed further) acts morally because he wants to be rewarded or because he wants to avoid punishment. At the middle stage, the conventional, the older child (or adult who has not progressed beyond this stage) tries to do what his friends, his family, and people in high positions expect of him. He wants an orderly world and does not want to break the rules of his society. He identifies with people in his life (teachers and political or religious leaders, for example). At the postconventional stage, the highest level, the individual acts morally because it is demanded by

The number of runaways aged ten to seventeen has reached epidemic proportions—hundreds of thousands leave home each year according to a study done a few years ago. Such studies report that most runaways leave home because of family problems. Not being allowed enough freedom by parents and intolerable home situations are given as reasons for leaving by young people. Personal problems—loneliness, depression, low self-esteem, being in trouble with the police, dislike of school, and pregnancy—account for the next largest group of runaways. A smaller proportion are not running away from anything, but toward what they think will be independence, adventure, and new friendships.

For most young people, running away is a sudden decision, and often follows a fight with their parents. Half of them leave with no money, and only the clothes they have on. Most of the runaways stay with a friend or relative in their own town. A very small proportion stay in runaway shelters, set up to protect and aid runaways. The young people usually stay within 100 miles of their home. Among runaways aged sixteen and over, 28 percent went over 100 miles and 11 percent of that 28 percent went over 1,000 miles. Half of those who leave home go alone; the others usually go with a friend of the same sex.

One-fourth of all runaways described the experience as good; 20 percent felt it was bad. Some of the long-term runaways get jobs to support themselves, while a lesser proportion resort to crime to get money. Forty percent of the young people returned home on their own, most of them before the end of the first week.

Runaways often have not had good experiences with their family and school. They need to be made to feel that they are valued members of their family. To do this, their parents must learn not to reject them, but to discipline them with caring, to make them a part of decision making, to involve them in household duties, and to spend time with them. At school they must be helped to become more successful socially and in their school work; they must not be labeled as "trouble makers" or "stupid kids." Teachers and counselors must find ways to help them feel good about themselves. Runaways are often members of delinquent peer groups where they learn the runaway behavior. The school can discourage these delinquent peer groups by not grouping failing or problem students together in classes. This intervention in the environment of the runaway would need to be accomplished through counseling: the focus would be on the parents and their parenting style, and on the school and its treatment of the students. The student would also receive individual counseling, but the environment at home and school must be changed because the counseling alone cannot correct the problem.

Other resources provide more immediate help for runaways. *The National Runaway Switchboard* is a hotline that young people anywhere in the United States (except Hawaii and Alaska) can call for help. The toll free number is *800-621-4000*. This service is available 24 hours a day; it is free, and parents will not be contacted unless the young people want them to be. Runaways may either send a message to their parents or talk to them free of charge. The volunteers will tell these young people where shelters or housing are available at no cost to them, or help them with any problems they have. Another hotline is in Texas, with similar services, and that toll free number is *800-231-6946*.

There are many reasons for cheating. In today's society it appears that one of the most frequent occurrences comes about through peer pressure.

Under what circumstances will students be most likely to cheat? This was a question two psychologists tried to answer in an experiment with 111 college-prep high school students. The experimenters first asked the students to make as many English words as possible in eight minutes from the letters in the word "generation." The students were told this was a creativity test. After their papers were collected, the students were asked to return the next day.

When the students returned, they were assigned (unknown to them) to one of three groups. Students in a "success" group were told, individually, that they had done very well on the creativity test and had constructed an above-average number of words. Students in a "failure" group were told that they had done poorly. The third group was a control group. Students in this group were given no special information.

The students got back their papers unmarked. (The experimenters, of course, had counted the number of words on each paper.) In addition, they were given copies of a list containing all possible words that could be constructed from the word "generation." The students were told to circle on the list those words that they had constructed the day before. They were to hand back this list with words circled. They could keep their original papers.

In the control group, 43 percent cheated and circled more words on the list than in fact they had actually constructed on the original test. In the "failure" group, 61 percent cheated. Most surprising, more than half—56 percent—of the "success" group also cheated. Obviously, all these students had a fairly high level of what the two psychologists called "achievement anxiety."

What other conclusions might be drawn from this experiment?

What does the nature of the experiment—involving as it does some deception of student subjects—suggest about the moral level of the experimenters? How might the experimenters justify the deception?

his own high standards. (Very few adults ever reach this stage.) At this stage one is concerned about the welfare of other human beings. This is also called the "principled stage."

Kohlberg interviewed children and adults to find out which stage of moral reasoning they were in. He presented them with a number of moral puzzles and asked them what they would do. A well-known one is the "Heinz story": Heinz's wife is dying and can be cured only if she has a drug that has been invented by a druggist in his town. The druggist charges $2,000 for the drug, much more than it cost him to make. Heinz does not have the money, but manages to raise a large portion of it. Still, the druggist refuses to sell Heinz the drug for less than $2,000. Finally, desperate to save his wife's life, Heinz steals the drug from the drugstore.

Kohlberg asked students at various ages: "Should Heinz have done that? Why or why not?" Kohlberg was interested in the reasons behind the students' answers rather than the answers themselves.

Students at the preconventional stage were afraid Heinz would be caught and punished for stealing. Students at the conventional stage worried about what the druggist and towns-

Museum Worker

Dear Mr. Chu:

We want to thank you very much for the wonderful tour you gave our class when we visited the museum last week. We especially enjoyed seeing the dinosaurs and the volcano exhibit. We learned a lot and we had a good time, too.

Jackie Mazara
Class Secretary

Mr. Friedman's Third Grade
Hillmont School

Gregory Chu smiled as he read the letter. "I remember that group," he said to a co-worker who was looking on. "They sure were lively. I don't think I ever had to answer so many questions at one time."

There are many types of museums—natural history, art, science, historical, local history, planetariums, toy museums, building restorations, and so on. Their purpose is not only to provide entertainment for the public but primarily to educate. Almost every museum plans special programs and displays for children, who are encouraged to attend either on their own, with adults, or as part of class trips or other groups.

Sometimes curators—people who are in charge of obtaining and preserving special collections in the museum—plan and carry out the children's programs. Other times they only plan the program and then teach tour guides to work directly with the children who come as visitors. Some programs are planned so that children can also touch exhibits and operate phones or films that describe the exhibits. Museum workers have to understand both the material they are presenting and the needs of the children. They must try to capture the visitor's attention quickly and to keep the child interested throughout the tour or program.

Curators or others with technical expertise must have a college degree and advanced training in a particular field. Many technical museum jobs call for skilled craftspersons, such as display artists, cataloguers, researchers, and taxidermists. However, tour guides usually need only a high school education; they are trained to handle groups and to answer questions. Sincerity, friendliness, a good memory, and an ability to get along with people are important for any museum job that involves public contact. It is especially important for those who work with children to be able to respond quickly and firmly to questions and to control a group. A real interest in the subject matter of the museum is vital, as is a skill in communicating one's own enthusiasm to others.

Museum salaries are not particularly high, especially at lower-level positions, but they improve with education and experience. Generally museums are interesting places to work and have a stimulating atmosphere. Working with children at a museum offers both a chance to learn and a chance to teach. This is an attractive combination to many people.

Teenagers think about and compare moral values. Peers may exert tremendous pressure to behave as others do. It takes courage to hold on to one's own beliefs.

people would think of Heinz. Students at the postconventional stage did not care about punishment or what people thought of Heinz but were concerned that by stealing, Heinz went against his own moral principles.

Some psychologists see a relationship between Kohlberg's stages of moral reasoning and Piaget's stages of cognitive development. Kohlberg's postconventional stage, they say, is the equivalent of Piaget's stage of formal operations.

Other psychologists have discovered that as children grow older, their moral thinking changes. J. F. Morris found that teenagers from thirteen to fifteen years old cared less about themselves and more about others than did younger children. He also found that when making moral judgments, these adolescents were less concerned about what people in authority thought.

A final point: Because people *reason* at a high moral level, this does not necessarily mean they always *behave* at that level. In certain situations, a person may fail to act according to his own moral principles. For example, a teenager may believe that shoplifting is wrong, but he might be tempted to do it anyway because he wants to be accepted by a group of peers who insist that he "prove himself" in this way. In the face of such pressure, it may take considerable courage for him to stick to his own beliefs.

· SUMMARY ·

- In the period of formal operations, reasoning is characterized by theoretical or abstract thought.
- Adolescents can solve problems mentally, without having to work with concrete objects.
- They can compare realities with possible alternatives.
- They can organize information into logical propositions and then develop logical connections between them.
- Language development shows the understanding of abstract words and concepts.
- Teenagers are beginning to think about and compare individual moral values.

TERMS TO KNOW

concrete operations
formal operations
propositional thinking

1. _____ involves considering several ideas at once to reason about the relationships between things.
2. In Piaget's theory, the final stage of cognitive development is the stage of _____.
3. A child who thinks only in terms of things that can be seen and felt is in the stage of _____.

CHECK YOUR UNDERSTANDING

1. What is meant by formal operations?
2. Does the concrete operational level of thinking end at adolescence? Explain.
3. Describe propositional thinking.
4. List Kohlberg's three major stages of moral development.
5. According to Kohlberg, why does the young child act morally?
6. Which of Kohlberg's stages of moral development is also known as the "principled stage"? How can it be described?
7. In interviews conducted by Kohlberg, how did students in the preconventional, conventional, and postconventional stages react to the Heinz dilemma?
8. Explain: A person may reason at a high moral level but not always behave at that level.

· 23 ·

SOCIAL/EMOTIONAL
DEVELOPMENT
OF THE ADOLESCENT

"I'm not a little kid anymore!" Leona protested. "I'll be seventeen in two months, and in one year I'll be graduating from high school. I think I'm old enough to stay out a little late with my friends."

"Leona, I'm not saying you can't go out with your friends on the weekends," her mother said. "I just don't want you staying out later than midnight. That's late enough."

"But the movie wasn't over until 11:30, and then we just had a pizza. What's wrong with that?"

"Nothing—if you'd told me ahead of time where you were going and when you'd be back. I had no idea where you were last night, none whatever."

"In other words, you don't trust me."

"Leona, don't get me wrong. I trust your judgment—I really do. I know you wouldn't intentionally do anything wrong or dangerous. But a lot of things could happen to you in spite of that. What if you were in an accident? Or what if you and your friends ended up in a bad part of town late at night? If anything happens, I'm responsible for you—legally—until you're eighteen."

"But nothing did happen."

"That's not the point. Look, you're my daughter and I love you. I worry when you're out late and I don't know where you are."

Leona started to protest, then paused. "You're right. I guess I should tell you where I'm going to be."

"That would be reasonable," her mother agreed. "And do you think you could arrange your plans ahead of time so that you're home by twelve? I'd be willing to let you stay out later once in a while—as long as I know where you are and when to expect you."

"I'll try," said Leona. "And Mom—thanks for worrying about me."

•

Have you ever been in a situation like Leona's? How did you feel?

•

Do you think the solution reached by Leona and her mother is fair? Is this likely to be the last such incident?

337

In many ways, adolescence is like a second "toddlerhood." Both the adolescent and the toddler are on the brink of a new independence. Like the toddler, adolescents naturally resent adult interference with their wish to exercise their autonomy. The toddler, emerging from babyhood into true childhood, is in the process of discovering her individual identity and is eager to reach out to the larger world beyond the home. At the same time, the toddler is often beset by doubts and insecurities. Similarly, the adolescent, emerging from childhood into adulthood, is discovering her identity as a grownup. She also is about to take her place in a larger world than that of home and school. And for the adolescent, too, there are times of confusion, doubt, and emotional upheaval.

Both a fourteen-year-old and a two-year-old might be called **egocentric.** For a time, being self-preoccupied goes hand in hand with growing self-awareness. Of course, the toddler does not have the developed self-awareness that the teenager has. Still, teenagers, like small children, may become so self-preoccupied that they create, in effect, their own personal reality to go along with the ordinary reality of everyday life.

Part of the teenager's personal reality is what psychologist David Elkind calls the **imaginary audience.** In other words, she judges herself as if from the point of view of other people who she imagines are observing her. They can be a highly critical audience, always pointing out her physical defects and personality faults. She is a lot harder on herself—through what she imagines other people are thinking about her—than other people actually are.

Terri is, of course, unique as a person—as everyone is. But she feels that she is totally different from others. She feels she has emotional experiences unlike those of anyone else. She feels sometimes that she can do things no one else can. Elkind has a term for this conviction of having special problems or special powers. He calls it a **personal fable.**

There are many people—not only teenagers—who play to imaginary audiences of one kind or another and create personal fables. Constructing fantasy realities is not harmful—as long as a person keeps in touch with actual reality. But suppose someone assumed as part of her personal fable, for example, that a drug overdose could never happen to her. In this case, the fable could clearly lead to dangerous consequences.

Toddlers and teens are alike in that both are egocentric. They dwell on their own needs until they pass into another stage of development. Confusion, doubt, and emotional upheaval decrease as self-awareness grows.

Adolescence, though it begins with a physical event—puberty—is more of a socially defined state than it is physical. In nearly every society, certain events during adolescence are considered, formally or informally, to mark the passage from childhood to social maturity.

In a number of societies, these events are formal initiation ceremonies (termed by anthropologists rites of passage), after which the adolescent is officially a young adult. In Mexican villages, for example, the young person will be addressed differently after puberty—*joven* or *señorita* rather than *niño* or *niña*.

Initiation ceremonies themselves vary widely. In ancient Rome a boy donned the *toga virilis*, or "toga of manhood," on March 17 during the Liberalia—a public festival honoring the deities Liber and Libera. In tribal societies of modern times, such as those of Pacific Melanesian groups or Australian aborigines, puberty rites were often elaborate and sometimes painful.

Today, in our own society, the passage to adulthood tends to be observed more informally. Nevertheless, certain events stand out as social signposts on the way: the Jewish bar or bas mitzvah, the Christian confirmation, getting one's first driver's license, reaching voting age (at eighteen or twenty-one), graduation or commencement ceremonies. It is significant that in recent years some state governments in the United States have lowered the age at which a person can be held responsible for a crime. This means that convicted persons between the ages of 13 and 15 can be given the same punishment as adults, whereas previously "youthful offenders" received lighter sentences.

Usually, as adolescents reach their middle or late teens—if not before—they emerge from their self-centered world. By this time they have generally formed close relationships with other adolescents, traded intimate thoughts and feelings, and made comparisons. In the process, they come to realize the ways in which they really are unique as well as the ways in which they are the same.

SEEKING IDENTITY

The chief overall need of the adolescent—in line with Erik Erikson's theory of personality development—is to come to terms with herself and establish a sense of identity.

In the meantime she may feel terribly uncertain, in the middle of what Erikson calls an **identity crisis.** He uses the analogy of an aerialist: "Like a trapeze artist, the young person in the middle of vigorous motion must let go of his safe hold on childhood and reach out for a firm grasp on adulthood, depending for a breathless interval on a relatedness between the past and the future, and on the reliability of those he must let go of, and those who will receive him."

The "breathless interval," however, can last for years. It is a time of delay during which adolescents experiment with various roles in which they can recognize themselves and feel recognized. In different ways, they are looking to answer the basic question "Who am I?"

At first there is role confusion, when an adolescent doesn't know which of many possible roles really reflects who she is. Erikson considers this natural and healthy. There is no need for young people to commit themselves too soon, without having tested alternatives.

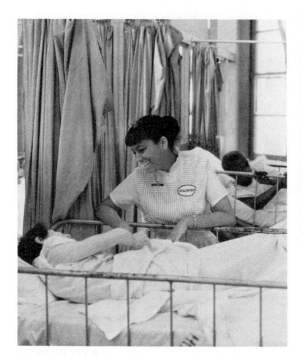

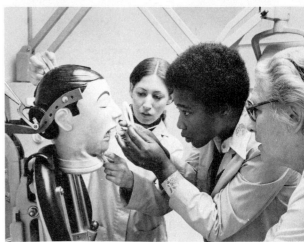

Career goals determine the types of education and experience needed by teens. Adolescents have different interests and abilities. Some are academically oriented. Others have technical skills or are creative in the arts. There are special programs to meet most needs. Volunteer groups are one way teens can get a feeling for professions which require further academic training. Special programs leading to certification in a variety of occupations are another.

Neither do adolescents have to accept passively the roles in which adults may try to cast them. They have to define for themselves who they are.

CAREER AND SEX ROLES

An important part of the search for identity is the search for an occupational role. Finding a suitable career and becoming economically independent are an important measure of adulthood in our society.

Here, the question "Who am I?" takes the form: "What do I want to be in the world of work?" Some persons answer these questions to their satisfaction as early as the ninth grade. These may change, however, just as college students often change their major more than once before they graduate. Probably few people pursue the occupational goal they set for themselves when they were first asked, at age five, "What do you want to be when you grow up?"

Among the many factors that go into the choice of a career, the influence (or pressure) of parents and other adults is clearly important.

Teens who are planning to attend college have many decisions to make. Choosing the right college for their needs is difficult. They must consider their career goals, the type of college or university they want, and their ability to gain admission and finance their education. Good career counseling and information about schools are needed in order to make the best selection.

Economic circumstances and educational opportunities also make a difference, in some cases a big difference.

But the major factors are, or should be, a person's own aptitudes, personality, and aspirations. It may take a while to find a good "fit" between these factors and a particular occupation. Indeed, many people today change careers two or three times during the course of their work lives.

Another important part of the adolescent identity search concerns sex roles—what it means to be a man or a woman. Children learn and come to accept their biological gender identity quite early. In addition, they see around them in today's society a variety of models with regard to sex-role identity.

Then, by adolescence, they are ready to carve out their own individual styles of being women or men. During this testing period, they may try a number of alternatives. In the world of work, for instance, a girl might get a summer job in a restaurant or on a repair crew. A boy might get a job at a day-care center or a factory.

The loss of a loved one or the inability to cope with what an adolescent may consider a "hostile" environment are just two of the many reasons why a teenager may consider committing suicide. There are periods in their lives when, thinking the world is against them, they consider ending their lives because they feel there is no one to turn to…no one to understand their desperation.

Unfortunately, suicide is a major cause of death among adolescents. Thousands of persons in their teens take their own lives every year, and for persons in their early twenties the suicide rate more than doubles. For both teenagers and 20-year-olds, the rate is going up.

One cause of suicide is severe depression. This illness can affect even small children. It is, however, a curable disease.

Another reason some adolescents might contemplate or attempt suicide is that, perhaps more than any other age group, adolescents are under enormous stress—particularly if we extend the definition of adolescence to include the older student in graduate school. Medical-school students have an especially high suicide rate.

Nearly everyone thinks about suicide at one time or another in her or his life. People contemplating suicide often talk about it a lot before making any actual attempt. They may unconsciously hope that someone will stop them. A person talking about suicide should be listened to seriously, not laughed at. Many communities now have suicide prevention centers where counseling is available. Convincing someone to call one of these centers, or going to the center along with that person, could save a life.

What kinds of problems might cause an adolescent to consider suicide?

Suppose a close friend of yours told you that he or she wanted to die. What would you say or do to help your friend?

RELATIONSHIPS WITH PARENTS

Part of adolescents' identity search involves becoming independent of parents—and, ideally, the parents should help them achieve this goal. Surprisingly, a great many parents come close to this ideal—"surprisingly" because so much attention has been given in recent years to parent-adolescent conflicts. In fact, research shows that adolescents tend to get along better with their parents than many people think they do.

Some conflict is inevitable—and it can be heated at times. Both parents and teenagers get impatient with each other. But the frequency of these instances has been overplayed. On the other hand, Mark Twain's remark about the way adolescents view their parents is still worth quoting today: "When I was fourteen my father knew nothing, but when I was twenty-one I was amazed at how much the old man had learned in those seven years."

THE ADOLESCENT PEER GROUP

The importance of the peer group during adolescence has been studied and debated often and at length. That the peer group (usually in the form of a small group of friends) does become more important in adolescence is obvious enough. As teenagers move away from reliance on their parents, they quite naturally turn more to a group of their own peers.

There is also a clear tendency to conform—

at least on the surface—to the styles, behavior, expressed opinions, and general attitudes of a peer group. But studies have shown that peer-group conformity, on the average, peaks at around ages thirteen to fifteen. Although it continues to be strong through high school, it is on a downward grade. By age twenty-one, it has decreased considerably.

That an adolescent peer group sets standards of style and behavior is probably less important, in the long run, than that it provides a social testing ground. Any peer group is a mini-society. As a person moves through her adolescence, she can try out different social roles in her various peer groups.

Moreover, as a mini-society, an adolescent peer group has its leaders and followers, its power struggles and checks and balances—in addition, of course, to emotional supports. In the peer group, an adolescent can test herself and begin to develop an identity—a sense of herself that feels right to her, yet gives her an accepted place in society.

When does adolescence in the social sense end? The social definition of adulthood varies depending on the culture. In a modern industrial society like ours, the transition period between childhood and adulthood is a long one. At the least, adolescence extends until after high school graduation.

But there are considerable individual differences within the society. For the high school graduate who soon gets a good job and possibly starts thinking about marriage, adolescence is clearly over. For someone going on to college, and then graduate school, full economic independence may not come until after age twenty-five. However, few people think of themselves as adolescents at twenty-five, even if they are still students. They may not be able to say just when they left adolescence behind—but by that age, they know that they have.

Adolescence is filled with self-doubt and indecision. Emotional support is especially important during this stage. It can come from good relationships with parents or peer groups.

· SUMMARY ·

- Adolescents are moving toward adulthood and want to make their own decisions.
- Sometimes teenagers are confused and have doubts about themselves. They swing back and forth emotionally.
- They tend to be preoccupied with their own thoughts and emotions. They may create an imaginary audience or personal fables.
- An adolescent's chief overall need is to establish a sense of identity.
- An important part of the search for adult identity is planning a career.
- Though they may have conflicts with their families, adolescents tend to get along better with their parents than many people think.
- Teenagers often want to conform to the styles, behavior, and opinions of their peers, in addition to wanting to express their individuality.

TERMS TO KNOW

egocentric
identity crisis
imaginary audience
personal fable

1. An adolescent who is trying to come to terms with herself but frequently feels terribly uncertain is experiencing what Erikson calls a(n) _____.

2. Elkind describes a(n) _____ as the feeling adolescents frequently have of being totally different from others.

3. Both adolescents and toddlers can be called _____.

4. An adolescent may feel as if a(n) _____ is watching and judging her.

CHECK YOUR UNDERSTANDING

1. Why is adolescence like a second toddlerhood?
2. How can an imaginary audience affect an adolescent's self-image?
3. Describe the types of beliefs that may make up a personal fable.
4. According to Erikson, what is the chief overall need of the adolescent?
5. What is role confusion? How is it viewed by Erikson?
6. What factors go into the choice of a career?
7. Explain how the adolescent peer group provides a social testing ground.

·24·

INTERACTION
WITH THE ADOLESCENT

"Wait just a minute," Mr. Cobb exclaimed. "Who says you can sell that trumpet? We paid good money for it!"

"I say so," retorted his daughter Nancy. "It was a present, so I can do what I want with it. It's none of your business!" The bedroom door slammed, and the blast of a stereo began inside.

"I guess I didn't handle that too well," Mr. Cobb said to his wife. "But why can't she see that she's making a mistake?"

"You don't think she should be allowed to sell it, then?"

"Certainly not! She wants the money for that jacket we refused to buy her. That crazy-looking thing is just a fad. Playing the trumpet is something she could enjoy all her life!"

"You're right about that," Mrs. Cobb agreed. "But Nancy has a point, too. It *is* her decision to make. Besides, I doubt she'd be willing to sell the trumpet if she really enjoyed playing it."

"Still . . . " Mr. Cobb sighed in frustration. "I keep thinking about when I quit the piano. Now I'd give anything to be able to play well."

Mrs. Cobb smiled. "So who's the one with musical ambitions—you or Nancy?"

At dinner that night, Mr. Cobb cleared his throat. "Nancy, I'm sorry I gave you trouble about the trumpet. You can sell it if you want to. And you can use the money for the jacket."

"Really?" said Nancy, somewhat suspiciously.

"Really. But whatever your decision is, you'll have to take responsibility for it. If you change your mind and want to play in the band again, you'll have to buy an instrument with your own money."

Nancy grinned sheepishly. "Actually, I'm not so sure I want to give up on the trumpet just yet. Maybe I could get the money for the jacket some other way."

"It's up to you," said Mrs. Cobb.

"Thanks," Nancy said. "And Dad—I'm sorry I yelled at you."

•

What was Mr. Cobb's basic motive in wanting Nancy to keep the trumpet?

•

Why does Mr. Cobb feel the decision should be Nancy's? Do you agree?

Interaction has a special meaning for adolescents, for their contacts reach far beyond friends and family. All the world may have an impact on a teenager's life. Society's values, noble and not, bombard the teenager through radio, television, and magazines. Celebrities—from rock stars to evangelists—have their effect. There are also teachers, employers, neighbors, community leaders, parents, and peers. The adult who emerges from the teenage years will be a product of many forms of interaction with people from his home, his town, his school, his society, and beyond. What will determine the adolescent's response to all these influences?

To begin with, an adolescent's relationship with his parents or principal caregivers has the greatest influence on his behavior. Even as he rebels, the very type of rebellion a teenager may choose is based on behavior and values within his family.

A family that practices open communication may find a fourteen-year-old turning sullen and secretive. A family that values self-control may suddenly have a rough and rowdy fifteen-year-old to deal with. With understanding and a minimum of pressure, these families will be able to ride out such temporary rebellions.

After the family, it is the peer group that influences much of an adolescent's life. From clothing style to eating habits, from favorite music to special vocabulary—what's okay with his friends is usually okay with a teenager.

Interaction with peers may take many forms. Subtle pressure may be applied to do whatever the group does, right or wrong. Yet at the same time the group may provide warmth, a sense of belonging, and reassurance that the teenager is not alone with his problems, doubts, and needs.

As for the rest of the people in an adolescent's life—those who are neither friends nor family—their impact may depend on the circumstances of each interaction. For example, a teenager in search of a goal may be inspired by a police officer's heroism to work toward that career himself. Or a bad experience, such as being unfairly harassed by a patrol officer, may begin a lifelong suspicion of all authority. An individual teacher, employer, religious leader, or neighbor may have a short- or long-term influence on the adolescent's goals and behavior.

Finally, despite all this interaction with others, adolescence may still be a very lonely time. Loving parents, close friends, neighbors, and heroes can do no more than *help* the teenager to meet his needs. Establishing independence, building self-esteem, and carving out an identity are goals the individual must pursue on his own.

MAINTAINING BALANCE

"Balance" is the word to remember throughout the adolescent period. It is the key to fulfilling the young person's need to explore the adult world, to build a unique identity, and to gain independence. For parents and other caregivers, balance is needed between the desire to share and the respect for privacy; between giving advice and showing acceptance. It's difficult for parents to stand by and watch their teenagers repeat mistakes that caused the parents pain when they were young. However, they must realize that advice often seems an invasion of privacy. It may even keep young people from an important lesson that can only be learned firsthand. Of course, adults cannot always stand by and watch. When children of any age are involved in activities that endanger their health or that are against the law, adults must draw the line.

Conflicts and confrontations are best handled in families in which relationships are

Mood swings are a part of adolescence. Teens need privacy and space to work out conflicting emotions. Communication during this period is often difficult. Parents need to show patience and understanding.

based on trust and respect. Even as he rebels, a teenager may realize that advice is not meant to keep him from living his own life, but is evidence of love and concern. This helps the adolescent to develop similar good intent and responsibility.

Of course, teenagers are not always wrong and adults are not always right. In a family power struggle, the adults in charge may push too hard to be obeyed, ignoring the rights of the adolescent. At their worst, these confrontations can result in the breakup of a family. Many adolescents leave home and never go back. Balancing judgment with understanding can help families avoid this tragedy.

UNDERSTANDING MOODINESS

Young people's feelings change dramatically from day to day—or even from one hour to the next. Adults never feel sure about what response will meet their simplest questions. Many families give up communication entirely.

Why do teenagers respond so unpredictably? Most adolescents do not deliberately behave so as to keep others guessing. In fact, adolescents themselves are surprised by their own mood swings. They do not know how they will react because they are not sure of who or what they are. Are they bright, talented, ambitious, and attractive? Or are they dull, awkward, angry, and doubtful? Yes—and no. Family and others who deal with teenagers can reach them best by being consistent, no matter how inconsistent the adolescent may seem.

Knowing that people can be counted on to accept their jumbled feelings helps teenagers to open up and be more reassured. Of course, parents and other caregivers cannot approve of all behavior, even if the feelings behind the behavior are accepted. This may cause the friction that some parents feel is the last straw. But others claim it is the "salt in the soup"—making life with teenagers interesting, even though it is unsettling.

BUILDING SELF-ESTEEM

An important psychological need for adolescents, as well as younger children, is for self-esteem. There are many ways that a positive view of oneself may develop. Some factors already mentioned include consistent acceptance of adolescents' feelings and demonstration of love and concern. But there's more. Parents and other caregivers can begin by developing nonjudgmental attitudes toward a teenager's behavior. This means considering the reasons behind what he does. It means putting oneself in the adolescent's place and not labeling him as good or bad on the basis of a few actions.

It also helps for adults to realize that not all teenagers follow the same pattern of development. Individual behavior varies just as physical development does. Some fifteen-year-olds are ready to take on many adult roles and responsibilities, while others have barely worked out the problems of childhood. Each adolescent deserves individual consideration. A young person can be made to feel unworthy and unsure when pushed into situations for which he is not psychologically ready. Or he may feel frustrated and held back when prevented from taking on challenges for which he *is* ready.

How does a parent or caregiver know what to do? Helping adolescents to build self-esteem often means acting on instinct and taking risks. Young people must be given the chance to prove themselves and earn a place in the adult world. What happens if the adolescent fails? Ideally, there should be an adult there to listen and back him up. Most important, the adolescent should not be made to feel like a failure, through insults, harsh criticism, and "I told you so's." And when the adolescent succeeds, praise should be given without reservation, to let him know there are things that he can do well.

Sometimes, families who want to give an adolescent much love and support must take it in stride when he goes outside the family for help with problems. The family closeness that caregivers try so hard to foster may seem suffocating to young people. At times they find it easier to communicate with neighbors, friends, or teachers.

ACCEPTING RESPONSIBILITY

Self-image is closely tied to another psychological need—the need for responsibility. What exactly is responsibility? According to one teenager, "It means that whatever goes wrong—I'm responsible!" This is a common feeling among adolescents. But there's a more positive side to responsibility. In part, it means seeing the relationship between what we do and say now, and the results that will follow in the future. It also means acknowledging those results and carrying out related obligations.

Responsibility is attached to every meaningful area of life: to earning a living, to schoolwork, to friendships, to community and family. For example, having responsibility

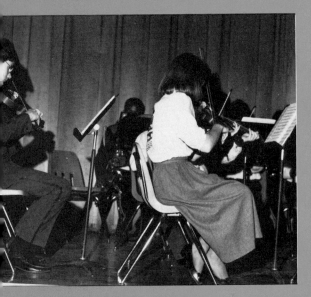

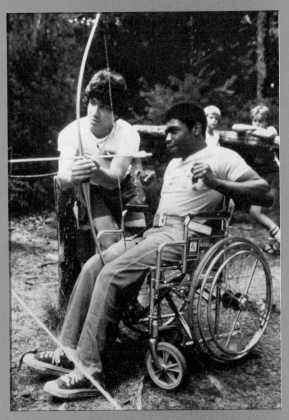

Teenagers need positive interaction with others. Working with peers on projects requiring intelligence, skill, or talent helps build self-image. Teens want to accept responsibility for their actions. They should initiate their own projects and receive adult advice when it is sought or really needed. Adults should avoid taking charge.

Some adolescents accept responsibility easier than others. Handling obligations on their own helps teens learn to be rewarded by—or suffer the consequences of—their own behavior.

means showing up for basketball practice even if the team usually loses. It means walking the dog every day even if there are more interesting things to do. And what can be gained by being responsible? In some cases, as with the basketball team, there may be the thrill of winning a game. But more often, satisfaction lies simply in the knowledge that one is dependable. This knowledge can add to a feeling of self-esteem and becomes a sign of maturity.

Responsibility, like many other psychological needs, comes naturally to some teenagers and comes hard to others. What makes the difference? It may depend on how much practice the adolescent has. Learning by living is the best way to develop responsibility. The teenage years are the crucial time for this lesson to take place. Having a job, doing volunteer work in the community, dating, driving, and baby-sitting all offer opportunities to practice responsibility. In each case a young person takes on an obligation and must carry it through over time. While adults may be available for guidance, it is important for adolescents to feel that the weight of their actions and decisions rests only on them.

BECOMING INDEPENDENT

As they gain in responsibility, adolescents are preparing for the independence of adulthood. While parents and caregivers still want to protect and guide the adolescent, he needs to try life on his own. Conflict seems inevitable. Parents and caregivers may find that looking back to their own struggle for independence helps most in understanding what the adolescent is going through. Young people who do not learn to act independently can never have a full life as adults.

And yet full independence cannot be won overnight, since a teenager's safety and future may be at stake. Again, practice—with adults providing opportunities for the adolescent to gain independence gradually, and balance between freedom and control—will foster independence and self-confidence.

DEALING WITH ANGER

No matter how hard adolescents and their parents may try to avoid it, anger and conflict are sure to arise sometimes. How can families keep anger from doing permanent damage to their relationships? First, everyone must realize that anger is an honest and natural emotion. Trying to suppress anger makes adolescents and adults feel guilty and uncomfortable. When family members can talk openly about what bothers them, anger burns itself out. Kept inside, it smolders and grows into a more painful and lasting resentment.

All parents get angry with their children. It is evidence that they care, that their children's behavior affects them deeply. When anger is expressed in a nonviolent way, it lets the adolescent know where he stands.

When the adolescent feels anger, his lack of maturity and experience may make it more

All teenagers need to learn independence to prepare for adulthood. Teens with disabilities may find this harder than others, but they can succeed with patience and persistence.

difficult for him to deal with it. However, if he has been shown throughout childhood that his anger is valid, the strong and sudden anger of the teenage years will be less unmanageable for him.

FINDING AN IDENTITY

Independence, acceptance, self-esteem, responsibility—all the psychological needs add up to one thing: a sense of identity. In trying to find out who he really is, the adolescent suffers self-doubt and uncertainty. He feels that he is made up of opposites: love and hate, idealism and cynicism, generosity and self-centeredness. His adult personality is emerging, and in the meantime he must experiment and explore.

In order to cover up self-doubt, the adolescent will often pretend feelings he does not have. He rejects ideas and values of the people around him in his search for his own values and identity. When older people tell a teenager,

"I know just how you feel," the young person often becomes annoyed. It disturbs him to think that emotions he finds so new and difficult are so easily understood by others.

Identity cannot be supplied for an adolescent. He must work it out himself from his past and present, his dreams and abilities. People who interact with adolescents can help by providing a consistent, reassuring atmosphere in which a teenager may experiment, within reason. They can express tolerance—if not approval—of rebellion. And when they disagree, they can say so, without making the teenager feel totally rejected.

IN SCHOOL

"School's a drag. Nothing I learn there has anything to do with real life."

"What a great teacher! Now I know what that book is really about."

"I'm just killing time in school. I can't wait to get out and earn some money."

The search for identity is an important part of adolescence. It is characterized by turbulent emotions. Some teens are more caught up in the process than others. Parents tend to "brush off" teen emotions about identity because they understand that these types of conflicts are usually resolved with age. Teens do not have this perspective and they require understanding and reassurance.

"That movie on child abuse really made me think. Maybe I could do something to help."

These comments seem to have come from four very different students. But they didn't. They were made by the same student at four different times. How can one person have such mixed-up feelings about school and learning? It's not unusual for the adolescent. He is capable of thinking great thoughts and understanding great books. He is also idealistic, ready to learn and to do whatever is necessary to change the world. But he can also be bored, "out of it," and altogether unreachable. What makes the difference?

Often it is the way the adolescent interacts with an individual teacher. A creative teacher can make any subject exciting. This teacher's style helps students make the connection between the subject and their everyday needs and problems. Ideally, each student's needs are considered and he is given some control over what he will learn and how he will learn.

But the teacher is not wholly responsible for the adolescent's success in school. Classmates may affect his learning as well. A student who is unable to keep up with classmates may feel lost and frustrated and just stop trying. Or a student who is able to learn at a greater pace than others becomes bored, but may not admit it for fear of drawing attention to himself. In either situation an understanding teacher or counselor can often help.

Of course, an adolescent learns best when his family values education and supports his efforts to learn.

AT HOME

Throughout childhood most learning takes place at home, through interaction with caregivers and siblings. As the child reaches adolescence, learning takes place in many other places as well. But the values taught in the home still determine the way the teenager will be affected by other learning experiences. A positive attitude toward education must be constantly reaffirmed. Parents can help

An adolescent's rapport with a teacher affects his attitudes toward school. Creative teachers consider all their students' needs and are able to make school enjoyable and worthwhile. Sometimes students may have difficulty interacting with a particular teacher because of poor communication or a clash of personalities. The student and teacher need to discuss the problem. Help may be needed from parents or other school personnel.

The atmosphere at home affects a student's performance in school. Good family relationships make studying easier and learning more enjoyable.

teenagers study by providing space and time, without distractions, for students to do their work.

Adolescents are not too old to learn by example. It is hard for them to accept demands that they study and read while the rest of the family spends the evening in front of the television set. When the whole household takes time to read, it is much more likely that the teen will buckle down as well.

Caregivers can also aid learning by showing an interest in what goes on in the adolescent's world. Communicating with teenagers is tricky, and questions such as "What did you learn in school today?" seldom start off a fruitful discussion. However, by sharing feelings and experiences from their own school days, adults can encourage young people to do the same.

Besides reinforcing the learning that takes place in school, family members have many skills to share. These may include building furniture, running a home, fixing a car, caring for children, and more. All people learn best by helping with the interesting aspects of a job as well as the drudgery, in ways that are within their abilities. More than practical skills can be taught in the home. The very atmosphere of the home and the attitudes of those living there continually teach the adolescent how to listen, to share, to help, to protect others, and to respect himself.

THE WORKING TEENAGER

Along with school and home, work is a great teacher for the millions of teenagers who have

Camp Counselor

Name ————————————————

Address ————————————————

Date of Birth ————————————————

Education ————————————————

Previous Experience ——————————

What can you offer the campers at Camp Seneca?

————————————————————

Marian Woolf filled out the first questions with no trouble. But when she came to the last question, she paused. "Why *would* they want to hire me instead of someone else?" After some reflection, she decided to describe her work as an assistant basketball coach after school last year, her camping skills acquired during a trip two summers ago, and her guitar playing. "I can teach all these things to the campers," she thought.

Summer camps offer good possibilities for summer employment for students and others such as teachers who have the summer off from their jobs. Generally counselors must be eighteen years or older, although some camps hire junior counselors who are sixteen. Summer camps can be day camps or sleep-away camps. Children may attend for the whole summer, for a month, or perhaps even for a week or two. Some camps are privately owned; others are run by public agencies.

There are special camps for children with emotional or physical problems.

Counselors are usually responsible for a particular group of children; at a sleep-away camp, the group lives together in a cabin or tent. The counselor must make sure that the children understand the safety and health rules of the camp, and that they keep the cabin tidy. Counselors also try to encourage the children to participate in all the activities, and take care of problems such as minor scratches, homesickness, jealousies, and personality conflicts.

Some counselors are also instructors in a special skill—swimming, arts and crafts, drama, music, camping, and the like. Depending on the camp, they may also be required to lead overnight hiking trips or other strenuous activities.

Camp counselors generally receive small salaries, in addition to room and board. The amount of free time varies, and should be determined before the job is accepted.

Most camp counselors find that the experience is a good one; they have many opportunities to participate in athletic and other activities along with the children; the rest of the staff is usually congenial; and above all, they gain invaluable experience for careers in teaching, counseling, or psychology. Counselors can also advance in the camping field, becoming head counselors and eventually camp directors.

By working hard at making camp fun for the children, most camp counselors find that they are having fun themselves.

jobs. Besides learning a skill, the adolescent may learn about responsibility, safety, and honesty. Or in a poor work experience, the young person may learn about exploitation or inequality. A teenager may learn more about himself: that he tries to do too many things at once, that he works well with his hands, or that he needs better training to find a really satisfying job.

Many good role models may be found in work situations. Through interaction with employers or co-workers, adolescents can establish lifelong career goals. For some young people, work relationships may supply some of the emotional support and attention that is lacking at home. Working with people of different types may help the adolescent learn to respect people of other ages and cultures. And when work experiences are coordinated with school through **cooperative programs,** adolescents may begin to learn a trade that will satisfy them for years.

AT PLAY

Play is not just for little children; it's a tool for people of all ages. Each stage in a child's development has its appropriate toys and games. For the adolescent, "toys" may be computers and chess boards that help build mental skills, or racquets and frisbees that help discharge energy and build physical fitness.

Interacting with other young people in team sports is part of the ongoing process of **socialization.** The adolescent learns to cooperate, to work toward group goals, to handle competition, and to develop strategies. In fact, many adults with successful business careers claim that their experience in team sports contributed directly to their management skills.

Sports such as tennis or running also develop important character traits such as independence and endurance. Winning helps teach the player to take success in stride, and

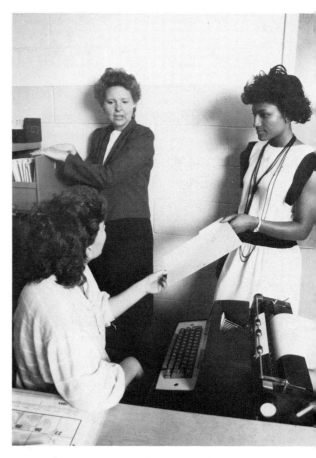

Teenagers learn new skills and meet different types of people at work. Interacting with employers and co-workers teaches them what is needed to succeed in the work force.

losing teaches him to look ahead to the next challenge.

Through play, adolescents may find a comfortable way to interact with others. They may gain insight into the special problems and abilities of different age groups and find a new way to communicate at a time when action is more comfortable than words.

GUIDANCE AND DISCIPLINE

Guidance and discipline present a special challenge during adolescence. Parents may find it hard to give up authoritarian roles. But as they suddenly stand eye to eye with their children, they must recognize that a new style of discipline is needed. The purpose of discipline during these years is not to affirm the power of the parent, teacher, or other adult. It is to help guide the adolescent safely through the dangerous years of experimentation, toward independence.

There is no single right way to discipline all adolescents. For each young person, each caregiver, and each situation, there are workable methods to be found by trial and error.

WHY GUIDANCE IS NEEDED

Most parents do not want to watch or control their teenagers all the time. Young people are expected to test the limits of their freedom. Sensitive adults remember the problems of following rules in their own youth and would probably like to spare the next generation some of that pain and conflict. However, adolescence is not the time for caregivers to let go completely. A balance is needed between freedom and concern. The adolescent needs to know that rules and limits are meant to protect him and to preserve peace in the family and community.

Many caregivers find it difficult to allow adolescents to make their own decisions because the results of those decisions can be so serious. Alcohol, drugs, and sex are among the areas in which the teenager may have to make decisions. Making the wrong choice in any one of these areas can harm a teenager for life. And yet if adolescents are not given the space to make choices, they may never be able to live independent adult lives.

HOW RULES ARE SET

Rules and limits exist in every family and most other groups in society. In some homes, restrictions are set without regard for the adolescent's feelings. A better approach is to set limits that allow an adolescent to preserve self-respect. Family values are the basis for

Adolescents continue to learn through play. Team sports teach cooperation toward common goals. Players must develop strategies for overcoming any obstacles. Competition helps prepare teenagers for work experiences they will encounter as adults. Winning helps adolescents deal emotionally with success. Losing prepares them for coping with future disappointments.

these rules, and following them helps build character.

Setting successful limits depends on the ability of the rule-maker to distinguish *feelings* from *behavior*. A teenager's thoughts and feelings are his own business and cannot be controlled by others. A caregiver cannot govern whom a teenager will love, what clothing styles he will admire, what goals he will aspire to, or what wishes he has for the future. But rules can and should be made to control activities such as the time a teenager must come home, when he may use the car, what household chores he does, and how he should behave toward others.

Exactly what rules will be set depends on the values, goals, and operating style of a family or group. Some questions a parent or other rule-maker may use to evaluate rules are:

Will this rule allow the teenager to maintain self-respect?
Will this rule help the teenager to become independent?
Would I make the same rule for a child of the opposite sex?
Is this rule based on a real danger or an exaggerated fear?
Have I provided a model for the adolescent in following this rule?
What will I do if this rule is broken?

WHEN RULES ARE BROKEN

Adolescents may not break every rule, but they are sure to break some and to bend others. What happens next depends on the situation and the people involved. It is important that responses to the adolescent's behavior are related to the seriousness of the action, and that abuse of any kind never be used.

It is understandable for caregivers to feel anger and disappointment when a teenager goes too far, and these emotions should be expressed. More important than the specific reaction to any one wrong act is consistency of response to all unacceptable behavior. It may sometimes be the easier way out for caregivers to look the other way when rules are broken, rather than to cause an angry confrontation. But this can harm the adolescent who needs guidelines and limits to show him that he is cared for and to help him learn to take responsibility for his actions as an adult.

Adults may find, however, that a tolerant approach is sufficient discipline in many situations. Expressing disapproval of a teenager's clothing style, music, or speech without demanding a change in behavior can give the adolescent space to rebel in relatively harmless ways. It also provides him an opportunity to change his behavior voluntarily, without feeling that he has been forced into it.

But what happens when adolescent rebellion moves beyond safe territory? What about acts that harm him his health, disrupt the family, or break the law? For caregivers in this painful situation, open confrontation is usually the best response, followed by help and emotional support. Situations this serious are often beyond the abilities of a family to cope with. Families in crisis can then get help from special groups and professionals in their community.

THE REWARD

It's no wonder that children and their families look forward to the adolescent years with mixed excitement and dread. Despite popular opinion, these years are not always filled with pain and problems. Adolescents and those around them get on well for the most part. The style of interaction that a family develops during the adolescent years will determine family relationships for the adults later on. And the challenges of living with teenagers can bring out the creative best in everyone around them.

- Adolescents must be given a chance to prove themselves, even though they may make mistakes or fail occasionally.
- Parents must balance their desire to help with the adolescent's need for privacy, independence, and acceptance.
- Understanding is needed to cope with the unpredictable moods of a teen.
- Accepting responsibility comes naturally to some adolescents and is difficult for others.
- Anger should be accepted as an honest and natural emotion.
- Consistency and reassurance can help adolescents deal with self-doubt.
- The family's attitude toward learning can contribute to success in school.
- Both work and play help adolescents prepare for adulthood.
- Guidance and discipline present special challenges during adolescence.

TERMS TO KNOW

cooperative programs
interaction
socialization

1. Students are given a chance to learn a trade through _____ between employers and schools.
2. Team sports can teach cooperation and other aspects of _____.
3. _____ is meaningful activity between two or more people.

CHECK YOUR UNDERSTANDING

1. Why should parents sometimes resist giving advice to adolescents?
2. How can parents help an adolescent develop a positive self-image?
3. How can responsibility bring satisfaction to an adolescent?
4. Why is conflict between parents and adolescents inevitable?
5. How can families keep anger from doing permanent damage to their relationships?
6. Describe how the family can help motivate an adolescent to succeed in school.
7. Besides learning a skill, what can the adolescent learn on the job?
8. What is the purpose of discipline during the adolescent years?
9. Describe how limits for an adolescent should be set.
10. How should caregivers react if an adolescent's behavior is harming his health, disrupting the family, or breaking the law?

· APPENDIX ·

Safety Checklist   361

First Aid   364

Safety Checklist

Caregivers cannot and should not hover over children or give constant warnings. They must, however, take steps to make the child's environment as safe as possible. Following the guidelines given here will not eliminate every chance of an accident, but it will go a long way toward helping children explore their world and their abilities in safety.

INFANTS

- Never leave an infant alone in the house, apartment, or car, even for a few minutes.
- Don't turn your back on a baby who is on a table, bed, or chair.
- Be sure the bars of a baby's crib are spaced no wider than 3½" (89 mm) apart so that the baby's head can't become caught between them.
- Watch out for cords or strings that could get wrapped around the baby's neck. (Check the baby's clothing, crib toys, nearby curtain cords, etc.)
- Keep plastic bags, small objects that could be swallowed (pins, buttons, coins, etc.), and sharp objects (scissors, razors, knives) away from the infant.
- Select a baby's toys with care. (See "Choosing Toys," page 362.)
- Never leave an infant close to a hot stove or radiator.
- Check bath temperature with a thermometer or your elbow to avoid scalding the baby.

- Do not allow pets and toddlers to play with a baby unless an adult is on hand.
- Use an approved infant carrier when traveling by car. Follow the manufacturer's instructions for use.

CRAWLING INFANTS

- Continue to follow the guidelines given above.
- Remove heavy, sharp, breakable, and valuable objects from the baby's new "territory."
- Cover electrical outlets with safety caps.
- Anchor lamps or other furniture that could be tipped over by a crawling baby. Make sure there are no dangling electrical cords or tablecloths for the baby to pull on.
- Keep all medicines, cleaning products, cosmetics, garden supplies, paints, cigarette butts, and other poisonous substances out of the baby's sight and reach.
- Keep windows closed or barred. Block off stairs with a gate until the baby is old enough to climb up and down safely.
- Make sure houseplants are not poisonous.

TODDLERS

- Continue to "childproof" the home by keeping heavy, breakable, sharp, poisonous, and otherwise dangerous objects out of a toddler's sight and reach. (See the suggestions under "Crawling Infants.")

- Remember that a toddler develops new abilities rapidly. Items that are beyond his or her reach one day may become dangerous playthings the next. Always think one step ahead.
- A high, locked cabinet is the best place to keep poisonous substances such as medicines and cleaning products.
- Keep toddlers away from matches and lighters.
- Never leave a toddler alone in the kitchen, especially when food is being prepared. Keep pot handles turned toward the back of the stove. Be sure knives, hot liquids, and other dangers are out of reach. Teach toddlers not to play with the stove.
- Check toys for safety. (See "Choosing Toys.")
- Don't let a toddler play with small objects that could cause choking. Avoid giving a toddler nuts, raisins, popcorn, hot dogs, or hard candy.
- Keep stairways, sidewalks, and other paths clear of toys and other objects that may cause falls. Be sure loose carpets are tacked down. Throw rugs should have a nonskid backing.
- Never leave a toddler alone at bath time, even for a few moments. Place a nonskid material on the floor of the tub.
- Teach toddlers not to run into a street or driveway.

Avoid toys with these dangers:
• Sharp edges, wires, prongs, or pins
• Parts that may come loose and be swallowed (until the child is age 3 or older)
• Glass, mirrors, or other breakable material
• Heavy toys that could injure a child if dropped
• Lead paint or other toxic material
• Highly flammable items

- Make sure toddlers are far out of the way when lawnmowers and other machinery are in operation.
- Supervise toddlers when they are playing on outdoor gym equipment such as swings, slides, and monkey bars.
- Use approved safety equipment when carrying a toddler in a car or on a bicycle or motorcycle.

PRESCHOOLERS

- Continue to keep dangerous substances and objects, such as poisons and firearms, well out of reach—preferably locked up and out of sight.
- Help the child learn about safety. Make children aware of indoor and outdoor hazards through gentle but repeated reminders.
- Supervise outdoor play, especially near traffic, bodies of water, and other hazards.
- Begin teaching safety rules for the supervised use of knives and other tools.
- Set a good example. Don't expect a child to learn how to cross a street safely if you jaywalk or ignore traffic signals.

SCHOOL-AGE CHILDREN

- Continue to watch for hazards in the home. Enforce basic rules for safety—no clutter left on stairs, no running in the house, and so on.
- As the child gains greater independence away from home, be sure rules about talking to strangers, exploring new or isolated areas, etc., are clearly understood.
- Make sure the child understands and obeys traffic rules for walking and riding a bike.
- Teach the child swimming and water safety if possible.

First Aid

CUTS AND SCRAPES

- For minor cuts and scrapes, wash the wound with soap and water. Blot dry and cover with a clean, dry bandage.
- If there is severe bleeding, cover the wound with a thick pad of cloth. Press firmly to stop the bleeding. Keep the person lying down and warm. Get medical help.

SLIVERS AND SPLINTERS

- Wash the area with soap and water. Remove the object with tweezers. Wash again. If the sliver or splinter is large or deep, get medical help.

BRUISES AND SPRAINS

- Apply a cold cloth or ice bag. Elevate the injured area if possible. Rest the injured part.

FRACTURES

- If you think a bone is broken, do not move the person. Get medical help.

BITES AND STINGS

- For insect bites, scrape out the stinger, if present, with your fingernail. Apply a cold cloth to the area. Get medical help if there is a reaction such as hives, rash, weakness, nausea, or vomiting.
- For animal bites, wash the wound with clean water and soap. Blot dry and apply a clean, dry bandage. Consult a physician. If possible, have the animal caught and observed for rabies.
- For snake bites, treat the same as a cut. If the snake is poisonous, keep the victim lying still and get to a doctor or hospital at once.

BURNS AND SCALDS

- Cool heat burns and scalds with cold water. Cover with a dry, clean bandage. Do not clean a burn or break blisters. If the burn is large or serious, get medical help.
- For chemical burns, wash the burned area thoroughly with water. Consult a physician.

ELECTRIC SHOCK

- Stop the current if possible. If not, pull the victim away from the source of the shock. *Do not use your bare hands.* Use a dry rope, wooden broom handle, or loop of dry cloth.
- Start mouth-to-mouth breathing if needed. Call for help immediately.

EYE INJURIES

- To remove a foreign object from the eye, use a moist cotton swab. If the object is not removed after a few tries, get medical help.
- If chemicals get in the eyes, flush with plain water. Get medical help.

Mouth-to-mouth breathing for infants and small children

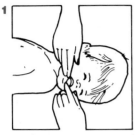

1 Clear victim's throat of water, mucus, food, etc.

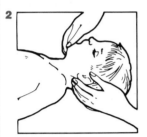

2 Tilt head back to open air passage.

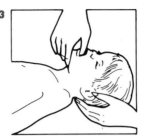

3 Hold jaw in jutting-out position, keeping lips slightly open with thumb.

4 Keep child in position so that his tongue will not fall back.

5 Open your mouth wide, seal your lips around the child's mouth and nose. (For older child, if you cannot cover both, mouth-to-mouth is preferable but pinch the nose with your fingers.)

Blow into mouth and nose until you see chest lift. Then remove your mouth and let the child breathe out. As soon as you hear the breath come out, repeat the process.

Repeat 20 times a minute, or every three seconds. NOTE: For infants, blow only small cheek puffs of air—not deep breaths.

Continue until the child resumes normal breathing or until aid arrives.

NOSEBLEEDS

- Have the person lean forward. Apply steady pressure to the outside of the nostril for five full minutes. If the bleeding does not stop in five or ten minutes, consult a physician.

FAINTING

- If the person feels faint, have him or her lie down or sit with the head between the knees.

- If the person becomes unconscious, loosen clothing around the neck. Elevate the feet and keep the person warm. Get medical help if the person does not revive in a few minutes.

CONVULSIONS

- Turn the person's head to one side. Do not try to hold the person down or put anything in the mouth. If the convulsion does not stop soon, get medical help.

HEAD INJURIES

- Treat cuts or bruises and have the person rest. Check for signs such as persistent headache, dizziness, vomiting, speech difficulty, or unconsciousness. If any of these develop, get medical help.

POISONING

- For swallowed poisons, call for medical help. If the container is available, use the antidote recommended on the label. If none is given, call a hospital emergency room or your local poison control center. Tell them the kind of poison taken.
- For poisonous fumes or smoke inhalation, get the person to a well-ventilated area. Use mouth-to-mouth breathing if needed. Get medical help.
- For poisons on the skin, see "Burns and Scalds."
- For poisons in the eye, see "Eye Injuries."

CHOKING

- If the person can cough, speak, or breathe, don't do anything. Be ready to take action if needed.

- If the person *cannot* cough, speak, or breathe, have someone call for medical help or the police or fire department. Then follow one of the steps below.
- If the person is standing or sitting, stand behind him or her. Place your fists just below the rib cage. Press the fists into the person's abdomen with a quick upward thrust.
- If the victim is lying down, place the heel of your hand slightly above the person's navel and below the rib cage. Place your other hand on top of the first and press with a quick upward thrust.
- For an infant, hold the baby facing away from you on your lap. Place the first two fingers of each hand on the baby's abdomen just below the ribs. Push in with a quick upward thrust.
- Continue these measures until the object is cleared from the windpipe, or until medical help arrives.

THE BASIC FOOD GROUPS

THE BASIC FOOD GROUPS

Food Group	Foods Included	Nutrients Provided
Milk-Cheese Group	Milk, buttermilk, cheese, yogurt, cottage cheese, ice cream	Calcium Phosphorus Protein Riboflavin Vitamin A Vitamin D
Fruit-Vegetable Group	Citrus fruits, greens, potatoes, tomatoes, apples, bananas, berries, squash—all fruits and vegetables	Vitamin A Vitamin C Calcium Phosphorus Iron B vitamins Fiber
Meat-Poultry-Fish-Beans Group	All cuts of meat, poultry, fish, shellfish, eggs, dried beans or peas, nuts, peanut butter	Protein Iron B vitamins
Bread-Cereal Group	Whole-grain or enriched breads, cereals, rice, noodles, pasta, cornmeal, and other grain products	Carbohydrates Iron B vitamins

FOOD NEEDS OF CHILDREN

Food Group	Recommended Number of Servings	Average Serving Size
Milk-Cheese	*Ages 1 to 9:* 2 to 3 servings	1 cup (250 milliliters) milk, buttermilk, or yogurt
	Ages 9 to 12: 3 or more servings	2 slices American or Swiss cheese
Fruit-Vegetable	4 servings	About 1 tablespoon (15 milliliters) of food for each year of the child's age
Meat-Poultry-Fish-Beans	2 servings	About 1 tablespoon (15 milliliters) of food for each year of the child's age
Bread-Cereal	4 servings	1 slice of bread

FOOD NEEDS OF ADOLESCENTS AND ADULTS

Food Group	Recommended Number of Servings					Sample Serving Sizes
	Adolescent	Adult	Pregnant Woman	Nursing Mother		
Milk-Cheese	4 or more	2 or more	4 or more	4 or more		1 cup (250 milliliters) milk, buttermilk, or yogurt 2 slices American or Swiss cheese
Fruit-Vegetable	4	4	4	4		1 medium apple or banana 1 cup (250 milliliters) berries or raw leafy vegetables ½ cup (125 milliliters) cooked fruits or vegetables, or juice
Meat-Poultry-Fish-Beans	2	2	3 or more	3 or more		2 to 3 ounces (55 to 85 grams) cooked lean meat, poultry, or fish 2 medium eggs 1 cup (250 milliliters) cooked dried peas or beans 4 tablespoons (60 milliliters) peanut butter
Bread-Cereal	4	4	4	4		1 slice bread 1 roll, biscuit, muffin, bagel, or pancake 1 cup (250 milliliters) ready-to-eat cereal ½ to ¾ cup (125 to 175 milliliters) cooked cereal, rice, or pasta

GLOSSARY

A

accommodate To adapt, as when a child adapts his or her existing ideas to fit new ideas that have been learned.

adolescence The stage of development between childhood and adulthood when the human body becomes capable of reproduction.

adolescent As used in this text, a young person from age twelve through adulthood, primarily one in the early teens.

afterbirth See **placenta.**

alternate behavior Social play among preschoolers when one child does something, then waits for a response from another child.

amniocentesis Withdrawal of amniotic fluid by a needle from a pregnant woman's uterus to test the health of the fetus and detect potential genetic problems.

amniotic fluid The watery sustance in which the embryo or fetus floats during pregnancy.

amniotic sac The membrane containing the fluid in which the fetus floats during pregnancy; when it breaks, it is a sign that labor will begin.

androgen A hormone which promotes the growth of male sex characteristics.

anorexia Self-starvation; a psychological problem sometimes found among teenage girls, resulting in a refusal to eat and a dangerous loss of weight.

assimilate To incorporate new information.

attachment The strong emotional feeling between child and parent or some other person. Attachment to parents is an important part of a baby's process of establishing relationships with other people.

aural Related to hearing. Before they learn to read, children learn language aurally rather than visually.

autism An illness of children who do not develop normal emotional or social relationships.

autonomy Independence. Moving from dependence to autonomy plays an important role in a child's social development, according to Erikson's theory.

B

Babinski reflex The fanning of a baby's toes upward and outward when the outside sole of the foot is touched.

basic trust Erikson's term for child's learning to feel good about himself and his world through his parents' loving care.

Bayley Scales One of three most widely used tests to determine infant intelligence; covers the ages from birth to three.

birth canal See **vagina.**

birth order A child's position within the family in relation to older or younger brothers and sisters.

blended family A family in which one or possibly both parents have been married before and have children from that marriage living with them. There may be more children born to that new couple.

bonding The process of forming attachments with other human beings. Bonding between mother and child usually takes place in the first few hours after birth.

C

Caesarean section A surgical method of removing a baby from the uterus through the abdominal wall.

Cattell Infant Intelligence Scale An adaptation of standard adult intelligence tests for infants; tests perception and motor skills.

causality The concept of cause and effect, which babies gradually learn as they realize that some things they do produce certain results.

central nervous system The brain and spinal cord; the complex network that carries messages between brain and nerves throughout the body.

cervix The entranceway between the vagina and the uterus. The cervix dilates, or widens, during labor in order for the baby to pass through.

chromosomes Microscopic, threadlike bodies in the nucleus of the cell, carrying hereditary characteristics.

clique A group of people who band together, excluding others.

cognition The mental processes involved in knowing, thinking, and learning.

cognitive Relating to knowing, awareness, and perception; intellectual.

cognitive development Gradual, orderly growth of a child's knowledge and logical thought.

colic A cause of continued, intense crying in infants. Fairly common in early months of life, it may be due to stomach pains.

conception The union of egg and sperm, resulting in pregnancy. Also called fertilization.

concrete operational stage In Piaget's theory, the cognitive stage from about age seven to age eleven, when a child can solve problems having to do with concrete things that can be seen and touched. Major achievements include the ability to conserve, reversibility, and seriation.

conditioned learning A kind of learning in which babies associate certain behavioral responses with particular sounds, sights, or smells.

conserve To understand that a given amount of a substance remains the same even if the shape is changed.

conventional morality The middle level in Kohlberg's theory in which the individual's actions conform to what society labels "good" or "bad."

cooperative family Several parents and their children sharing a single home. Communal.

D

diarrhea Irregular bowel movement that is loose or runny.

differentiated A term describing a baby's crying after the first month of life. The sound of crying differs depending on whether the baby is hungry, uncomfortable, or angry.

directed groping A learning activity in which the infant discovers, by trial and error, that objects can behave in different ways, depending on what is done to them.

Down's syndrome A genetic defect characterized by mental retardation and/or other abnormalities; mongolism.

E

egocentric Self-centered; believing the self to be the center of all things. Children gradually become less egocentric as they begin to understand others' points of view.

ejaculation In males, the release of semen from the penis.

embryo The unborn child at the stage of development from the time the fertilized egg is attached to the uterus until the end of the second month after conception.

emotional development The gradual, orderly growth of a person's feelings and personality from birth onward.

enuresis The inability to control urination, especially bed-wetting at night.

estrogen A hormone which stimulates growth of female sex characteristics.

exploratory play Play in which the child "discovers" how things work, by examination, experimentation, etc.

extended family A large family group that may consist of grandparents, parents, children, and other adult relatives.

F

Fallopian tubes The passageways connecting the ovaries to the uterus in a woman's body.

fertilization The union of male and female reproductive cells (sperm and ovum) to form a cell (zygote) that will develop into a new human being. Also called conception.

fetus The unborn child during the period of development from the ninth week after conception until birth.

fine motor skills Actions that use the small muscles of the body, such as those of the hands and fingers.

fontanel The "soft spot" on top of a baby's head.

forceps An instrument resembling tongs, occasionally used to help deliver a baby.

formal operations In Piaget's theory, the period of cognitive development beginning at adolescence, characterized by logical reasoning and abstract thought.

formula A milk or milklike food used in bottlefeeding infants.

G

general anesthetic A substance used in surgery and sometimes in childbirth to make a person unconscious and do away with pain.

genes Microscopic parts of a chromosome that are believed to be the smallest unit of heredity.

genetic defects Abnormalities or illnesses passed on to infants through the genes.

grasp reflex The response of a baby's fingers or toes to curl in, or "grasp" something, when the palm or sole of the foot is touched.

gross motor skills Actions that use the large muscles of the body, such as those of the arms and legs.

growth spurt A rapid period of growth, usually followed by a slower phase; common in adolescence.

gynecologist A physician specializing in the female reproductive system.

H

heredity The transmission of genetic physical or mental characteristics from parents to their children.

hormones Chemical substances, formed by the body, which enter the bloodstream and influence the activities of some organs or cells.

hyperactivity A behavior disorder in which children cannot control their physical activity.

I

imitative learning Learning by watching or listening to other people and doing what they do.

immunization Treatment by injection or orally to prevent certain diseases.

industry Erikson's term for the mastery of skills marked by a sense of achievement, one of the goals of the school-age child.

infant As used in this text, a baby from birth to age one.

inferiority Erikson's term for the feeling of failure or inadequacy when a child is unable to master certain skills or do well in school.

initiative Erikson's term for the child's efforts to explore, learn, and seek mastery over new skills.

interaction Meaningful activity between two or more individuals.

internalize To make the values or rules of family and society part of one's own inner beliefs. Internalizing moral values is an important stage of moral development in the child.

J

jargon In language development, the wordlike sounds that are used by infants but are usually meaningless to others.

L

labor The natural process by which a baby leaves the mother's body when she or he is ready to be born.

local anesthetic A substance that numbs only a part of a person's body during an operation or childbirth.

locomotion The ability to move from place to place.

M

malnutrition Lack of proper food for the body's needs; poor nourishment.

manipulation The use of hands and fingers to hold and move objects.

manipulative skill An action that involves handling objects; important in a child's physical development.

maternity leave Time off from a job for a woman to give birth and spend time with her baby before returning to work.

maturation The process of reaching full development.

menarche The beginning of menstruation; a girl's first menstrual period.

menstruation   In females, the release of blood from the uterine lining through the vagina over a period of days, usually occurring every 28 days.

mental retardation   The general inability to achieve normal cognitive development.

miscarriage   The loss of the incompletely formed fetus from the mother's body, usually before the fifth month of pregnancy.

morality of constraint   The first stage of moral development, according to Piaget, when a child's sense of right and wrong is based on rules, reward, and punishment.

morality of cooperation   The stage of moral development, according to Piaget, when the understanding of right or wrong has been internalized so that children can make their own moral judgments.

Moro reflex   A self-protective action of the newborn in which the arms move as if there is a fear of falling.

motor skills   Actions involving muscle movement.

N

neonatal   Of or relating to the newborn.

neonatal intensive care units   Special hospital departments that treat newborn babies, primarily those with breathing problems.

neonatology   A specialized area of medicine that treats the health problems of newborns.

nocturnal emission   An ejaculation during sleep, often occurring among boys during puberty.

nonverbally   Without words; a baby's way of communicating before he or she is able to talk.

nuclear family   A family group consisting of both parents and their children.

O

object permanence   The concept that an object continues to exist even after it is removed from view, learned during infancy.

objective   Describing a kind of morality in which judgments of an action are made regardless of a person's intentions, whether deliberate or accidental.

observational learning   Learning behavior and emotions from watching others.

obstetrician   A doctor who cares for a woman during pregnancy and childbirth.

obstetrics   The branch of medicine and surgery concerned with caring for and treating women before, during, and after childbirth.

Oedipal period   A stage of personality development, in Freud's theory, in which a child develops feelings of attachment for the parent of the opposite sex.

operant conditioning   A kind of learning in which certain behavior is reinforced by rewards.

operational stages   A child's periods of readiness for certain kinds of thinking.

ovaries   The organs that produce eggs in a woman's body.

ovulation   The process by which an ovum or egg is released from one of the ovaries in a woman's body, usually occurring once a month.

ovum   A female sex cell; egg. (Plural: ova.)

P

parallel play   The play of young preschoolers in which children play beside each other, but without interaction or cooperation.

passive play   Activities in which children observe or listen rather than actively participate.

paternity leave   Time away from work granted to a father so that he can help care for his baby. At leave's end, he returns to his job, which has been held for him.

pediatrician   A doctor who specializes in the medical care of babies and children.

peers   Persons of the same age or level of ability.

penis   The male sexual organ.

perception   The ability to use the senses to receive information.

physical development   The gradual, orderly growth of the body in well-established patterns.

placenta   The organ by which the unborn child is attached to the uterus. It enables nourishment to pass into the baby's body and waste material to pass out. When it is released from a woman's body at the end of labor, it is called the afterbirth.

postconventional morality The highest level of moral development, in Kohlberg's theory, in which the individual develops her or his own personal standards of morality and sticks by them.

post partum depression Emotional strain, or the "blues," often experienced by women soon after childbirth.

preconventional morality The first level in Kohlberg's theory, in which the individual's actions are based on avoiding punishment or gaining reward.

premature Before the proper time. Premature infants are fully formed babies weighing under 5½ pounds (2.5 kilograms) at birth.

prenatal Before birth.

preoperational period A stage of cognitive development in Piaget's theory, from ages two to six or seven. The child develops the ability to construct symbols, as in imaginative play and the use of language.

preschooler As used in this text, a child from age three through age five.

propositional thinking Perceiving data, organizing it into logical propositions, and then developing logical connections.

puberty The beginning of sexual maturity in adolescence, marked by menstruation in girls and ejaculation in boys.

Q

quickening The movement of the unborn child in the uterus.

R

reflexes Automatic reactions of the body to certain kinds of stimulation; involuntary actions.

reinforcement The encouragement of certain kinds of learning or behavior, in the form of rewards or approval.

reversibility The understanding that thought sequences or operations, like pouring water from one container to another of a different size can be reversed or done backwards.

Rh incompatibility A harmful reaction between mother and fetus when the parents have opposite Rh blood factors and the baby inherits the father's Rh type.

rooting A baby's way of searching for something to suck on; related to the sucking reflex.

S

school-age As used in this text, the ages six through eleven.

sensorimotor period In Piaget's theory, the phase of cognitive growth from birth to about two years, when the child learns largely by means of bodily movements and the senses.

seriation The arrangement of objects in order according to size, weight, number, or date.

sex-role identity The sense of what it means to be male or female.

sibling Sister or brother.

sibling rivalry Competition for parental attention between brothers and sisters.

SIDS Sudden Infant Death Syndrome, or crib death, when apparently healthy babies die of unknown causes while sleeping.

single-parent family A family unit which contains only one parent.

sleep apnea Periods during which babies stop breathing for a few seconds during sleep.

social development The gradual, orderly growth of a child's sense of self and attachments to other people.

socialization The process by which a child learns how to get along as a member of society.

spatial relationships The relationships of objects in space; a concept that children learn when they discover the relative differences between people, places, and objects, such as the word "above" and "below," or when they learn to fit an object into a bigger one.

sperm A male sex cell; also called spermatozoon. (Plural: sperm or spermatozoa.)

sphincters The muscles which provide controlled restraint of waste from the body.

startle reflex The arching of a baby's back and flinging of the arms and legs in response to a loud noise or a bright light.

stools Bowel movements.

surrogate Substitute.

swaddling The practice of wrapping an infant snugly in long bands of cloth; practiced in some cultures today to calm babies who are fretful.

symbolic representation Classification of objects; Piaget believes this learning is an important stage in the toddler's cognitive development.

T

testes The male reproductive glands.

toddler As used in this text, a child aged one through two.

U

umbilical cord The cord connecting the embryo or fetus to the placenta, allowing fresh nourishment from the uterus to reach the unborn baby, and carrying waste from the fetus to the placenta.

undifferentiated Not in defined patterns; descriptive of a newborn's crying in the first months of life.

uterus The organ in a woman's body that holds and nourishes the developing baby until birth; the womb.

V

vagina The passage leading from the uterus in a woman's body to the external opening; the birth canal.

W

wean To accustom a child to feeding from a bottle instead of the breast, or to drinking from a cup instead of from the breast or bottle.

Y

zygote The fertilized cell formed by the union of sperm and ovum, capable of creating new cells by repeated divisions.

REFERENCES

Ainsworth, Mary. "Patterns of Attachment Behavior Shown by the Infant in Interaction with his Mother." *The Merrill-Palmer Quarterly of Behavior and Development,* vol. 10. 1964.

Ambron, Suann Robinson. *Child Development.* 3rd ed. New York: Holt, Rinehart & Winston, 1981.

Ames, Louise Bates, and Joan Ames Chase. *Don't Push Your Preschooler.* New York: Harper & Row, 1981.

Belz, Tom. "How Babies Learn to Love." *America's Health,* spring 1979, pp. 18–19.

Bettelheim, Bruno. *The Children of the Dream: Communal Child-Rearing and American Education.* New York: MacMillan, 1969.

Braun, J., and D. Linder. *Psychology Today.* 4th ed. New York: Random House, 1979.

Brazelton, T. Berry. *Toddlers and Parents: A Declaration of Independence.* New York: Dell Publishing, 1976.

Brearley, Molly (ed.). *The Teaching of Young Children.* New York: Schocken Books, 1970.

Brennan, Tim; David Huizinga; and Delbert S. Elliott. *The Social Psychology of Runaways.* Lexington, Mass.: Lexington Books, 1978.

Briggs, Dorothy Corkville. *Your Child's Self-Esteem.* Garden City, N.Y.: Doubleday, 1970.

Brisbane, Holly. *The Developing Child.* 3rd ed. Peoria, Ill.: Bennett & McKnight, 1985.

Brockman, Lois M. "The Development of Children's Rights." *Canadian Home Economics,* January 1979.

Bruner, Michael Cole, and Barbara Lloyd (eds.). *The Developing Child* Series. Cambridge, Mass.: Harvard University Press, 1977.

Caplan, Frank. *The First Twelve Months of Life: Your Baby's Growth Month by Month.* New York: Bantam Books, 1978.

Caplan, Frank, and Theresa Caplan. *The Second Twelve Months of Life: A Kaleidoscope of Growth.* New York: Putnam, 1979.

Charles, C.M. *Teacher's Petit Piaget.* Belmont, Calif.: Fearon Publishers, 1974.

Cherry, Sheldon H. *Understanding Pregnancy and Childbirth.* Indianapolis: Bobbs-Merrill, 1983.

Children's Bureau, U.S. Department of Health, Education and Welfare. *Prenatal Care.* New York: Child Care Publishers, 1970.

Clarke-Stewart, K. Alison, and Joseph Glick (eds.). "Developing the Mind of the Child." *The Development of Social Understanding (Studies in Social and Cognitive Development),* vol. 1. New York: Halsted Press, 1978.

"Computer Sleuth Tracks Down Baby Disease." *New Scientist,* June 28, 1979. p. 1070.

Draper, Mary Wanda, and Henry E. Draper. *Caring for Children.* Peoria, Ill.: Bennett & McKnight, 1979.

Erikson, Erik. *Childhood and Society.* New York: W.W. Norton, 1964.

Fein, Greta G. *Child Development.* Englewood Cliffs, N.J.: Prentice-Hall, 1978.

Foss, B. M. *Determinants of Infant Behavior.* vol. 1. London: Methuen & Co., 1961.

Fraiberg, Selma H. *The Magic Years.* New York: Scribner, 1968.

Garfield, Sydney. *Teeth, Teeth, Teeth.* New York: Simon & Schuster, 1969.

Garrison, Karl; Albert Kingston; and Harold Bernard. *The Psychology of Childhood.* New York: Scribner, 1967.

Garrison, K. C., and K. C. Garrison, Jr. *Psychology of Adolescence.* 7th ed. Englewood Cliffs, N.J.: Prentice-Hall, 1975.

Gersh, Marvin J. *How to Raise Children at Home in Your Spare Time.* New York: Stein & Day, 1983.

Gesell, Arnold; Frances Ilg; Louise Ames; and Glenna Bullis. *The Child from Five to Ten.* New York: Harper & Row, 1946.

Gies, Joseph, and Frances Gies. *Life in a Medieval City.* New York: Harper & Row, 1981.

Ginott, Haim G. *Between Parent and Teenager.* New York: Avon Books, 1973.

Golubchick, Leonard; Barry Persky; and The American Federation of Teachers. *Early Childhood Education.* Wayne, N.J.: Avery Publishing Group, 1977.

Gordon, Sol, and Mina Wollin. *Parenting: A Guide for Young People.* New York: Oxford Book Co., 1975.

Grinder, R. E. *Studies in Adolescence.* 3rd ed. New York: MacMillan, 1975.

Haley, Alex. *Roots.* Garden City, N.Y.: Doubleday, 1976.

Hall, Edward T. *The Hidden Dimension.* New York: Doubleday and Company, 1966.

Hartup, Willard (ed.). *The Young Child.* National Association for Education of Young Children, 1972.

Hassid, Patricia. *Textbook for Childbirth Educators.* 2nd ed. Philadelphia: Lippincott, 1983.

Hawkes, Glenn, and Damaris Pease. *Behavior and Development from 5 to 12.* New York: Harper & Bros., 1962.

Helfer, Ray E., and Henry C. Kempe. *The Battered Child.* 3rd ed. Chicago: University of Chicago Press, 1982.

Hurlock, Elizabeth. *Child Development.* 6th ed. New York: McGraw-Hill, 1978.

"Impact of Television on Children, The." *Insights into Consumer Issues.* 1979.

Jersild, Arthur; Charles Telford; and James Sawrey. *Child Psychology.* Englewood Cliffs, N.J.: Prentice-Hall, 1975.

Johnson, Ronald C., and Gene R. Medinnus. *Child Psychology: Behavior and Development.* New York: John Wiley & Sons, 1977.

Jones, Molly Mason. *Guiding Your Child from Two to Five.* New York: Harcourt, Brace and World, 1967.

Kagan, Jerome. *The Growth of the Child: Reflections on Human Development.* New York: W. W. Norton, 1978.

Kawin, Ethel. *Early and Middle Childhood.* New York: Macmillan, 1963.

Klaus, Marshall H., M.D.; Treville Leger; and Mary Anne Trause, Ph.D. *Maternal Attachment and Mothering Disorders: A Round Table.* Sausalito, Calif., October 18–19, 1974. Johnson & Johnson Baby Products.

Kuhn, Deanna. *Development: Becoming Who We Are.* New York: Harcourt Brace Jovanovich, 1975.

Kuhn, Deanna et al. "The Development of Formal Operations and Logical and Moral Judgment." *Genetic Psychology Monographs,* 95L (February 1977), pp. 97–188.

Leboyer, Frederick. *Birth Without Violence.* New York: Alfred A. Knopf, 1975.

Lolly, Dr. J. Ronald, and Dr. Ira J. Gordon. *Learning Games for Infants and Toddlers.* Syracuse, N.Y.: New Reader Press, 1977.

Lowenfeld, Berthold. *Blind Children Learn to Read.* Springfield, Ill.: Charles C. Thomas, 1974.

McCandless, Boyd R., and Robert Trotter. *Children: Behavior and Development.* New York: Holt, Rinehart & Winston, 1977.

Mead, Margaret, and Martha Wolfenstein (eds.). *Childhood in Contemporary Cultures.* Chicago: University of Chicago Press, 1963.

Mee, Charles L. Jr. *Daily Life in Renaissance Italy.* New York: American Heritage, 1975.

Minuchin, Patricia P. *The Middle Years of Childhood.* Monterey, Calif.: Wadsworth Publishing Co., 1977.

Mischel, Walter. *Introduction to Personality.* 3rd ed. New York: Holt, Rinehart & Winston, 1981.

Moss, Stephen J. *Your Child's Teeth.* Boston: Houghton Mifflin, 1977.

Mussen, P.H. (ed.). *Carmichael's Manual of Psychology,* vol. 1, 3rd ed. New York: John Wiley & Sons, 1970.

Mussen, Paul, and John Conger. *Child Development and Personality.* 5th ed. New York: Harper & Bros., 1979.

Muuss, Rolf E. *Theories of Adolescence.* 4th ed. New York: Random House, 1982.

Neill, A. S. *Summerhill.* New York: Wallaby Books, 1977.

"New Technology for the Handicapped." *American Education,* 1978.

Newman, Barbara, and Philip Newman. *Infancy and Childhood.* New York: John Wiley & Sons, 1978.

"Overweight Children." *Newsletter of Parenting,* vol. 1, no. 3 (September 1978), Highlights for Children.

Papalia, Diane E., and Sally Wendkos Olds. *A Child's World: Infancy Through Adolescence.* 3rd ed. New York: McGraw-Hill, 1982.

Piaget, Jean. *The Moral Judgment of the Child.* Glencoe, Ill.: Free Press, 1948.

Piaget, Jean, and B. Inhelder. *The Psychology of the Child.* New York: Basic Books, 1969.

Piers, Maria W. *Growing Up with Children.* Chicago: Quadrangle Books, 1966.

Pines, Maya. "Good Samaritans at Age Two?" *Psychology Today,* June 1979.

Princeton Center for Infancy. *The Parenting Advisor.* Frank Caplan, General Editor. Garden City, N.Y.: Anchor Press/Doubleday, 1977.

Pritchard, Jack A., and Paul C. MacDonald. *Williams Obstetrics.* 16th ed. New York: Appleton-Century-Crofts, 1980.

Pulasksi, Mary Ann Spencer. *Understanding Piaget: An Introduction to Children's Cognitive Development.* New York: Harper & Row, 1980.

Safire, William. "On Language." *New York Times Magazine,* May 27, 1979.

Salk, Lee. *What Every Child Would Like His Parents to Know.* New York: Warner Books, 1972.

Salk, Lee, and Rita Kramer. *How to Raise a Human Being.* New York: Random House, 1969.

Scanzoni, Letha, and John Scanzoni. *Men, Women and Change: A Sociology of Marriage and Family.* 2nd ed. New York: McGraw-Hill, 1981.

Schell, R. E., and E. Hall. *Developmental Psychology Today.* 4th ed. New York: Random House, 1983.

Selman, R. L. "Toward a Structural Analysis of Developing Interpersonal Relations Concepts." Anne D. Pick (ed.), *Minnesota Symposium on Child Psychology,* vol. 10. Minneapolis: University of Minnesota, 1976.

Shelton, Jev, and John P. Hill. "Effects on Cheating of Achievement Anxiety and Knowledge of Peer Performance." *Developmental Psychology,* vol. 1. 1969.

Skinner, B. F. "My Experience with the Baby-Tender." *Psychology Today,* March 1979. pp. 29–40.

Skinner, B. F. *The Shaping of a Behaviorist.* New York: Alfred A. Knopf, 1979.

Sluckin, W. (ed.). *Early Learning and Early Experience.* Middlesex, England: Penguin Books, 1971.

"Small Talk: How Children Learn Language." *Current Lifestudies,* September 1978. pp. 21–23.

Smart, Mollie S., and Russell C. Smart. *Children: Development and Relationships.* 4th ed. New York: Macmillan, 1982.

Spock, Benjamin, *Baby and Child Care.* New York: Pocket Books, 1981.

Sproul, Dorothy Noyes. *Your Child: Step by Step Toward Maturity.* Garden City, N.Y.: Doubleday, 1963.

Stone, L. Joseph, and Joseph Church. *Childhood & Adolescence.* 5th ed. New York: Random House, 1984.

"Television: Turn-On or Turn-Off?" *Current Lifestyles,* December, 1978.

Thornburg, Hershel (ed.). *Preadolescent Development.* Tucson: University of Arizona Press, 1974.

Travers, John. *The Growing Child.* 2nd ed. Glenview, Ill.: Scott Foresman, 1982.

Trien, Susan Flamholtz. "Pain Relief for Childbirth: An Update." "Expecting." *Parents,* spring, 1978.

Vander Zanden, James W. *Human Development.* New York: Alfred A. Knopf, 1978.

Watson, Robert I., and Henry Lindgren. *Psychology of the Child and the Adolescent.* 4th ed. New York: Macmillan, 1979.

Westlake, Helen Gum. *Children: A Study in Individual Behavior.* Lexington, Mass.: Ginn & Co., 1973.

Whiting, Beatrice B., and John M. Whiting. *Children of Six Cultures: A Psycho-Cultural Analysis.* Cambridge, Mass.: Harvard University Press, 1975.

Zimbardo, Philip. *Psychology and Life.* 10th ed. Glenview, Ill.: Scott Foresman, 1979.

INDEX

D

Fontanels (or soft spots, in baby's skull), 49
Food and feeding:
 basic food groups (chart), 367
 during adolescence, 320-321, 368
 baby's, 64-67, 99, 114, 116
 early school years, 258-260, 367
 preschoolers, 204-205, 367
 toddler stage, 140-141, 367
 See also Diet
Forceps, delivery by, 47-48
Forebrain, 91
Form, concept of, 224-226
Foster child, 8-9
4-H Clubs, 284
Fraiberg, Selma, 116
Fraternal twins, 168
Freud, Sigmund, 102-103
Friendships, 238, 284
Frustration cry, 109
Furniture, baby's room, 10
Future Homemakers of America, 284

G

Games, 202, 309; *See also* kinds of games
General anesthetic, 44
Genes, 19-21
Genetic defects, 28-29
Gerbner, Dr. George, 274
German measles (or rubella), 26, 75, 148
Gesell Developmental Schedules, 93
Gifted children, 279
Girl Scouts of America, 284
Glands, hormone-producing, 318-319
Goldberg, Dr. Barry, 239
Golub, Howard L., 86
Gonadotropic hormone, 318
Gonorrhea, 49
Good-night kisses, 146
Gorer, Geoffrey, 69
Group cooperation, 292
Grandparents, preparing for new baby's arrival, 39
Grasp reflex, 58
Greeting, lifting arms in, 106
Gross motor skills, 60
Group behavior, tendency to separate by sex, 287
Growth:
 adolescence, 316-321
 newborn's, 59-60
 preschoolers, 199-201

school years, 257-258
 toddler's, 131-132
Guidance:
 during adolescence, 357
 baby's first year, 125-126
 preschoolers, 251-252
 school-age, 310
 toddler stage, 191-193
Gynecologists, 325

H

Hair growth, teenager, 317
Hall, Edward T., 271
Head banging, 117
Health care and hygiene:
 in adolescence, 321-322
 preschoolers, 205-206
 school-age children, 260-262
 toddler stage, 145, 148
Heart disease, 29
"Helping out," 214
Hemophilia, 29
Heroin, 26, 325
Hide and seek (game), 249
High-risk pregnancies, 28-30
Hindbrain, 91
Hoffman, Martin, 171
Homemade baby foods, 66-67
Hopscotch (game), 249
Hormones, 38, 318
Household items, as safety hazards, 169
Household responsibilities, 229-230
Hygiene, *see* Health care and hygiene

I

Identical twins, 168
Identity:
 acquiring of, 167-168
 seeking and finding (adolescent years), 339-340, 352
 sex-role, 231-233
Illness:
 during adolescence, 322-325
 baby's, 74-77
 preschoolers, 208-209
 school-age child, 264-266
 See also Health care and hygiene
Imaginary audience, 338
Imaginary companions, 237

guidance and discipline, 310
improving self-image, 298-300
parents' role, 306-307
play, 307-308
promoting learning, 305-306
rules, 310
social behavior, 308-310
useful feeling, 304
toddler stage, 177-195
bedtime, making easier, 183
conflicting needs, 178
cooperative play, 188-190
drawing the line, 193
fears, calming, 182
guidance and discipline, 191-193
independence, 178-180
language development, 188
making learning fun, 186-188
playmates, 191
play opportunities, 185
reassurance, 180-181
rules and rule enforcement, 193-195
sibling rivalry, 190-191
stress, 183-185
Iron, lack of, 320
Itard, Dr. Jean, 294

J

Jargon, 158
Junk foods, 30, 205

K

Kaplan, Eleanor, 89
Kaplan, George, 89
Kibbutz babies (Israel), 105, 207
Kiddie gates, 169
Kohlberg, Lawrence, 276-278, 331, 335
Kurtachi people, 35

L

Labor:
meaning of, 42
signs of, 42
stages of, 42-44, 46-47
See also Childbirth
Lamaze, Dr. Fernand, 45
Lamaze method of childbirth, 45-47
Language behavior, 93

Language development:
preschoolers, 221-222
symbolic thinking, 219-221
school age, 270-273
of the toddler, 159, 162
guiding, 188
Language difficulties, professional help for, 209
Larynx (or voice box), 317-318
Layette, 10-11
Lead paint, danger from, 10
Learning style:
differences in, 243
school-age, 305-306
Leboyer, Dr. Frederick, 49
Left-handedness, 201
Libraries, 247, 305, 330
Lipsett, Dr. Louis P., 55
Live measles vaccine, 75
Local anesthetic, 44
Locomotion, 60
Love, 33, 38, 59, 113, 114, 126, 182, 352
Low-birth-weight babies, treatment of, 80
Lullabies, 70, 90
Lung cancer, 325

M

Mad or angry cry, 109
Magic Years, The (Fraiberg), 116
Malnutrition, 60
"Mama" (sound), 87, 88
Mama's boy, 245-246
Manipulation, development of, 60-62
Marijuana, 325
Masculine, children's concept of, 281
Maternity clothing, 23
Maternity leave, 7
Mead, Margaret, 108
Medieval children, 309
Memory:
preschoolers, 222-224
use of, 86
Menarche (or first menstrual period), 316, 319
Menstrual period, 22-23
Menstruation, 315, 324
Mental retardation, in infants, 80
Menu (for the pregnant woman), 25
Midbrain, 91
Middle Ages, 69, 309
Midwifery, 12, 13
Milk, 139; *See also* Bottle feeding; Breast feeding

ILLUSTRATIONS